Julie Myerson was born in Nottingham in 1960, read English at Bristol University and worked for the National Theatre and Walker Books before becoming a full-time writer. She has published five acclaimed novels: *Sleepwalking*, *The Touch*, *Me and the Fat Man*, *Laura Blundy* and, most recently, *Something Might Happen*. She lives with her partner Jonathan; their three children have all grown up in the house in Clapham. For more information visit www.homethestory.com

For automatic updates on Julie Myerson visit harperperennial.co.uk and register for AuthorTracker.

From the reviews of *Home*:

'Fascinating … pure magic … Festive, curious, full of other lives and voices and quiet existences raised to the exuberant point of historical pageantry … You can feel the warmth, like a fire in the hearth, of the love of family and place, and the sense of what it means to feel at home. A wonderful book'   PHILIP HENSHER, *Spectator*

'The history of this one mid-Victorian terrace house turns out to consist of a series of dramas, including abandoned children, bigamy, birth and death, breach of promise, and marriage … Ordinary people lead far more extraordinary lives than is usually supposed … Julie Myerson has thought up a worthwhile and original project, carried it out effectively and described it enthusiastically. *Home* may well become the instruction book for a popular new hobby'
Literary Review

'Part memoir, part historical fiction, part sleuth-like detective story; it works on every level. The people she unearths are as vivid as characters in a novel, and it makes you think about your own home in a way you never did before'

ESTHER FR   *ear*

D1322041

'Myerson uncovers some fascinating stories [which] add up to a rich domestic history of the twentieth century ... Compelling'

Mail on Sunday

'The discovery of the house takes on the tension and excitement of a detective novel ... the characters and their stories are more compelling that anything Myerson could have imagined ... What is particularly appealing about Myerson is the way she becomes so involved with the people she writes about ... A genuinely moving testament to all the people who lived at 34 Lillieshall Road'

The Tablet

'A heartfelt and humane endeavour that attempts to salvage ordinary London lives from forgetfulness' *Time Out*

'Myerson draws us into the magic of the minutiae of family life in all its messily interesting normality ... She has the simple gift of finding the enthralling elements in the most everyday phenomena ... Her background in fiction lends her an unerring ear for the dramatic depths in the stories she uncovers ... [She] has created a record, a genuine slice of life that catalogues the rise and fall of these personal stories' *Sunday Business Post*

HOME

The Story of Everyone Who Ever Lived
in Our House

JULIE MYERSON

HARPER PERENNIAL
London, New York, Toronto and Sydney

Harper Perennial
An imprint of HarperCollins*Publishers*
77–85 Fulham Palace Road
Hammersmith
London W6 8JB

www.harperperennial.co.uk

This edition published by Harper Perennial 2005
2

First published by Flamingo 2004

PS™ is a trademark of HarperCollins*Publishers* Ltd

Julie Myerson asserts the moral right to
be identified as the author of this work

A catalogue record for this book
is available from the British Library

ISBN 0 00 714823 2

Set in Minion

Printed and bound in Great Britain by
Clays Ltd, St Ives plc

For
Elsie Hayward 1883
and
Jamie Jess Pidgeon 1984

CONTENTS

HOME

Chapter One

CALLING OUT THEIR NAMES

The Myersons
Since 1988

Last autumn I came home from the local archives library where I'd been trying to research a novel set in the nineteenth century.

'You'll never believe what I found out today,' I told my daughter Chloë, 'about this house and the people who lived here before us. I found out that in 1881 there was a writer and journalist living here called Henry Hayward – '

Chloë stopped on her way up the stairs and paused, hand on banister – a banister sticky with the marks of three children who don't often wash their hands.

'A writer? Just like you, you mean? Was he famous?'

'I don't know but listen, this is the good bit – he had a wife called Charlotte and three kids who were just exactly the same ages as you three are now.'

Chloë's eyes widened. 'Hey, cool! What were the kids' names?'

I told her: Frank, Arthur, and Florence.

'And Florence was my age?'

'I think so, yes.'

'Hmm . . . good names.'

Chloë swung round and sat on the stairs.

'I wonder,' she said, 'how long since anyone shouted those names out in this house.'

'You mean the way we shout for you to come downstairs?'

She nodded. 'Yes, except we never do.'

I laughed.

'A long time,' I said. 'Years and years. A hundred years at least, I suppose. It's a funny idea, isn't it?'

I watched her think about this. It was dusk on a chilly October evening. We carried on upstairs and stopped together on the landing. I had a pile of ironing in my arms. Chloë had blue ink scrawls all over hers.

'I wish you wouldn't write on your arms in biro,' I said.

She ignored me and stepped over her cat Zach who was sleeping in his regular, hazardous position, draped right across the middle stair of the next flight up.

'Shall we say them now?' she whispered.

'Say what?'

'Their names. Shall we say them out loud because of how it's been a hundred years and all that?' She put her fingers on the fat white soft-ness of Zach's stomach. He opened one eye and closed it again. 'Florence!' she called shyly. 'Arthur! Frank!'

'Henry Hayward!' I said more forcefully, and Zach jumped up and spilled himself off downstairs.

Chloë laughed. 'You don't need to say Hayward, Mummy. He knows what his own surname is.'

'Charlotte!' I called.

Our voices sounded strange, mostly because we didn't know what we were doing or why we were doing it. Chloë looked at me and almost giggled but then checked herself. Her face went solemn and she listened. I listened as well. The house listened. Someone else seemed to listen too, but I still don't know who it was. Maybe it wasn't anyone. Maybe it was just the sense of the strong, clean lines of the present bending for a moment, going shaky and blurred. Whatever it was, for a few uneasy seconds I felt surrounded – not by people perhaps, so much as by moments, lost moments. Forgotten days and nights, lost hours, old minutes that had ticked away and would not come again.

Chloë shuddered, but it was a shudder of excitement.

'Hmm. I liked that,' she told me in her precise, Chloëish way. 'Do you think they heard?'

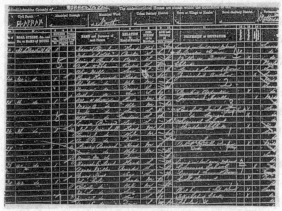

'Do you know what a census is?'

Later, putting the clothes away in his drawers, I found her older brother Jake, playing Super Mario Tennis.

'I found out something good about our house today,' I told him.

He rolled his eyes to show he'd heard, but kept them on the screen. Two grubby thumbs continued to work the control.

I touched his head then bent to kiss his hair. It smelled of boy – a heady combination of old jumpers and school dinners.

'Do you want to know what it is?' I said.

Still holding the control, he turned round. On the screen two blue men froze their less-than-friendly poses.

'Do you know what a census is?' I asked him.

He sighed and his eyes flicked back to the screen. 'We did them at school. I know everything there is to know about them.'

'Well, today I looked up our house on the 1881 census and guess who lived here?'

He put down the control and waited. 'Who?'

'A writer called Henry Hayward and his wife and three children – who in 1881 were exactly the same ages as you three are now!'

He shrugged. 'Great.'

'A family just like us,' I told him. 'Don't you think that's extraordinary?'

He seemed to think about this. 'No.'

'Come on, you've got to admit it's a bit funny – '

'How do you know they were like us?'

'I don't. But they sound like us.'

He sighed. 'What were the kids called?'

'Arthur and Florence and Frank.'

'It's sad,' he said then. I asked him why. 'I don't know,' he said. 'Would any of them have slept in my room?' He looked worried. He didn't want anyone in his space – he hadn't been keen when we did a house swap with New Yorkers two summers ago. A Victorian child pushing its spectral way in would be the last straw.

'I don't know. Yes, I expect so – they must have done.'

He picked up his control again. 'Look, Mummy, I don't mean this in a nasty way, but if you find anything else out, could you please not tell me?'

And then this happened. Two months later, on Boxing Day, in the odd, no man's land that stretches from Christmas to New Year, we suddenly found ourselves with nothing to do. No one had invited us anywhere, we'd made no plans, we had no work to finish.

I found myself pacing up and down our hall in the fading light after lunch, a cardigan tossed over my shoulders and realizing something fatal, if only because I knew that now I would never be able to unrealize it.

'It's the wrong colour,' I told Jonathan finally, 'the hall and stairwell.

Right to the top. I don't know how I could have ever thought dark turquoise. All this time, I knew there was something. It's just – well, I'm sorry but my heart always sinks when I walk in the door and now I know why.'

He was reading on the sofa. Or trying to. I snapped the uplighter on and he narrowed his eyes at me. He reminded me that he'd already painted the whole hall and stairwell twice ('because you decided the lilac was a mistake too') and asked me what day my period was due.

I threw myself down in an armchair. The whole room felt dark, oppressive. We'd painted it a chic, pale grey more than a dozen years ago, back when I was pregnant with Chloë. It was the winter that Thatcher went. I remember the joy of varnishing the bare boards on my hands and knees one winter's day, the baby a fluid weight beneath me, while listening to the news on Radio 4. Every minute seemed to bring a fresh excitement.

Back then the dove grey walls had seemed grown-up, calming. Now they just looked drab. I thought I wouldn't mind changing the colour of this room too. But I knew better than to say so.

'OK,' I told Jonathan, 'you're right. Forget it. The hall's fine.'

He shut his book, calmly noting the page number. 'I didn't mean it like that.'

'Three weeks. My period's due in three weeks – OK?'

'Three weeks?' He looked suspicious.

'I am definitely not pre-menstrual.'

'What colour would you want it?' he said.

'I don't know.' I looked at him. 'Pink?'

Raphael looked up from where he was sitting on the floor sticking football stickers in a shiny album. 'I'm not living in a gay house.'

'Blue's fine, Mummy,' said Chloë. 'Relax. It's just your hormones.'

'The only way it would be worth doing,' said Jonathan, who always warms to my plans in the end, 'would be if we did it properly this time. That means stripping every single scrap of wallpaper off and then replastering and making good. No short cuts. Get a nice clean finish.'

I smiled. Because he likes his nice clean finishes. I'm not saying he's wrong; it's just that I will always sacrifice a nice clean finish for something more rapid and exciting – the instant, vivid gratification of a pot of paint slapped on a wall.

He saw my smile. 'It would mean a lot of work,' he warned. 'You couldn't rush it. We're talking serious effort. Weeks of work.'

I smiled again.

'The finish has always bothered me, actually,' he said.

'OK.' I went and got a scraper from the cellar.

'What are you doing?'

'Starting.'

'Now?'

'Of course now. Why not now?'

'You are a crazy woman. I don't know why I live with you. You need the steamer anyway.'

He sighed and got up off the sofa. 'I'll get it. And the dust sheets.'

And that's how we ended up undressing the very old lady that is our house. One dark, aimless Boxing Day, we started stripping her down to her most private, underneath self.

It was three o'clock, almost dark. It felt strangely moving and intimate, scraping the layers off – history unpeeling itself. There was a smell of dissolving paper, of oldness – the hiss of the steamer in the silence, the sight of naked walls. Even patches of mauveish, higgledy Victorian brick in some places where the plaster fell away in large, crumbling, worrying chunks.

'Oh gross,' breathed Chloë. 'What's all that hair?'

'Horsehair,' Jonathan said. 'They used it to bind the plaster together.'

The odour was odd and sour. The kids fought over who did the scraping but, at thirteen, Jake was the only one who really had the strength to get much off. The light was fading so fast that Jonathan set up an Anglepoise so we could see what we were doing. A circle of white

8

illumination in the misty gloom. It felt magnificent and formal, more like an archaeological operation than DIY.

And the layers of paper curled and rolled off and dropped onto the floor – and, quite perfectly preserved, half a dozen different patterns were revealed: imitation wood grain (the sixties?), brown zigzags (the fifties?) – then a bold Art Deco style in cobalt and scarlet (the twenties?). Under that, large Morris-style chocolate ferns and flowers, and beneath that a solid layer of thick custard-coloured paint, then a fuzzy snatch of long-ago roses, then another more satiny paper with tiny gold and mauve squares. Each layer – imperfectly glued, faded, merged – revealed another.

'the layers of paper curled and rolled off'

'What smells so horrible?' said Jake, wrinkling his nose.

'The glue, I think,' Jonathan said. 'Probably made from bones.'

'Wicked!' said Raphael and then, frowning, 'But would vegetarians have used it?'

'Weren't really any vegetarians then.'

'Just think,' I said, as another William Morris-style lily showed us its black, almost funereally rimmed edges, 'how long since anyone saw these patterns. I wonder when each one was covered up.'

'Which one was the Haywards' wallpaper?' asked Chloë.

'I imagine that's something we'll never know.'

But even a little information is seductive. Once you know names, you start to see things. It's impossible not to – impossible to resist. I know

9

almost nothing real of Henry Hayward but my imagination has already begun to whisper. And I admit it, I've begun to listen.

He's tall, whiskery, gingery-haired (Hayward is definitely a gingery name). And maybe a bit of a punter, inclined to slope off to the races at Epsom or Goodwood, though he never loses too much – he has it in check. His wife Charlotte is much shorter, plumper and more self-effacing – a terrible worrier, especially about what other people say. Sometimes she thinks she only sees herself through other people's eyes. Take away that critical, slightly warped perspective and she's really not quite sure who she is – not that she'd ever think of expressing such a flighty idea to anyone.

Her ample figure is clad in brownish velveteen, the pile worn slightly thin around the bosom. She has a plain face, strong teeth (which she's always been glad about), big thighs that always seem even bigger when she catches sight of them in the glass in the wardrobe door. She's not well educated, doesn't read much, and is always intellectually in thrall to her (she supposes) much cleverer and more artistically tuned husband. She tells herself this doesn't matter, that she wouldn't have it any other way, but some days it depresses her. Some days she can't see a way forward, not even through this marriage. She calls these days her Glooms, though even to give them a name is overstating it, allowing herself a luxury she can only perceive as uselessly self-indulgent. She's a happily married woman, for goodness' sake. She worships at St John the Evangelist on Clapham Road. She believes in being content with your lot, especially if you can't change it. She was quietly overjoyed when they managed to afford to rent this new, red-brick Clapham house in such a swiftly expanding neighbourhood.

Here she is now, carefully locking our front door with a hefty black key and stowing it in her skirts. Then moving solidly down our brown and cream tiled front path. Brushing past the very young laurel (now grown to a dreary spotted monster that blunts my seca-teurs every year). That's her shadowy, tentative presence over there –

hesitating in the space now occupied by our wheelie bin and green Lambeth recycling boxes.

The totter's coming. She thinks she'll let him have the old broken fireguard from the small room upstairs that they don't need any more now that Frank's left home. She pulls out her key and turns back, wondering whether to leave it till another day when Henry can lift it. But then Henry may stop her giving it away and she's nigh on sick of all the bits and pieces they seem to store.

She waits, undecided – frozen on our path in a moment on a May morning in 1892. I have a photo of Jake aged two on that exact same piece of ground – blond and dimpled and dungareed – it now too seems to come from another time. Where did that small child go?

'blonde and dimpled and dungareed'

But these are just a writer's irresistible imaginings, not facts. What do I know? The totter may not have come that morning at all, and anyway the fireguard may still have been in use. And it might all have been quite the other way round. Charlotte might have been a quite different woman – shrill, sharp-tongued, wealthier by birth than her husband who, she never ceases to remind him, may be an author but is hardly a successful one.

He's yet to earn more than a few shillings from it. It's pathetic, at his age – all very well to dub himself 'author and journalist' when the census man calls round, but when's he going to get more than the odd article published in the *South London Press*? If it wasn't for the money left her by her mother, they'd still be living out in the falling-down cottage in Deptford and would never have afforded somewhere so swanky and clean and new.

This summer, we've lived at 34 Lillieshall Road for exactly fifteen years. It's a narrow, three-storey, slightly subsiding, dirty red-brick, mid-Victorian Clapham terrace with a mature, spreading hydrangea in front of the bay window and a glossy scented jasmine that climbs up past the front door to the first-floor window.

The bedroom windowsills each sport a wooden window box, made by Jonathan and painted hyacinth blue by me and filled with whatever flower I can keep alive each season. The paintwork around the windows is white and peeling. The bricks need cleaning but it would cost a fortune so, like everything else, we put it off. There used to be a lawn in front but now there are seaside pebbles, bought by the bagful from a place behind Clapham North tube station. It's a stylish, romantic look but would be much better if we'd killed the weeds first. As it is, the dock and groundsel and nettles spring hopefully up between the pebbles. Shingle beach meets urban waste ground.

I am perfectly, unquestioningly, at home in this house. After a childhood spent moving house almost every year, I had told myself roots didn't matter, that being with the people you loved was all there was. I think I even believed it. I used to brag about my lack of domestic continuity, my aloof and nomadic style. Until I met Jonathan. He lived in a terraced cottage with two cats, a full fridge, and honeysuckle round the door. He was only six months older than me yet somehow had managed to achieve this state of grown-upness, of stability and domestic warmth. I fell in love with the life as much as the man.

We decided to have a baby. And a joint mortgage.

Big things and small things have happened to me in this house. I became a mother here – once, twice, three times – and, later, a writer. Standing holding the phone in the far corner of the bedroom, I listened to my mother tell me that my father had sealed himself in his garage and killed himself. I was leaning against a wall that no longer exists because we made a door through into the bathroom. Downstairs in the hall, I had my final terrible argument with my younger sister and watched her walk away down the front garden path. I sat and trembled afterwards on the bottom step of the stairs.

Upstairs, at the top of the house, I wrote a novel in the spare bedroom. I wrote another two in the tiny room on the first-floor landing. I walked fretful babies up and down the bathroom in the dead of night and, pregnant and exhausted, I once lay down on the kitchen floor in front of two baffled toddlers and wept. A squirrel terrified us when it became trapped in the chimney in Jonathan's study. It scratched and snuffled and panicked all day. A funny and beautiful friend ate pasta at our kitchen table and told me straight out that she was dying. I watched a terrified man jump from the top floor of the refugee centre opposite when it was on fire one scary summer night. Another time, another summer, a burglar came into our bedroom as we slept and rummaged through my handbag.

All of this in our house. Real drama, yes, but no more or less than has happened to most people in most houses.

I loved 34 Lillieshall Road from the start but I was never someone who thought she'd stay anywhere long. And then one day it dawned on me that I had been here ten years and might actually be here another ten. Might even grow old here. I was surprised that the thought didn't frighten me. In fact far from it – it was oddly comforting. It tempted me. All those years you rush around, waiting for your life to happen. And then you realize it's just a question of taking a breath and daring to stand still long enough. Let your life come floating down, let it settle around you.

* * *

'I'm going to write a detective story,' I tell Raphael as he kicks a dog-chewed foam football around our kitchen, closely followed by Betty, the dog who chewed it. 'About our house.'

He looks worried. Why do my kids always look worried when I try to tell them about what's in my head?

'And we're the detectives, right?'

'That's right. We're going to find out everything we possibly can about every single person who ever lived here!'

Even as I say it, it sounds unlikely and Raph looks suitably incredulous.

'Even the children? Even the dogs?'

'If we can – even the dogs. Cats too – if there were any.'

He likes this. But then his face falls. 'But – what if we can't find it all out?'

This has occurred to me too. Mostly in the middle of the night when this house seems to be one great big, ferocious, empty space full of secrets. 'Then I'll write about that too.'

'Huh! Great,' says Jake with his own unique kind of deflating candour, 'a book about nothing. Fascinating.'

'It'll be my job to try and make the gaps and blanks fascinating,' I tell him – hoping I believe that myself.

Where Do You Get Your Ideas From? It's one of the great reliable questions that every writer gets asked. A huge, baggy question that we tend, privately, to smile at. Which isn't fair, because actually it's a perfectly reasonable thing to ask.

But, deep down, it scares us. It's impossible to answer because we really don't know where our ideas come from. And most of us wish we did, because then we could make sure we never ran out. But the truth is they come from anywhere and everywhere and nowhere and sometimes they don't come at all. We laugh about the question because it reminds us of just how tenuous and slippery a good idea is.

Until now. Because I know where my idea for this book came from.

It came from all the things you've just read. It came from a fusty South London archive and a helpful librarian who showed me how to use the microfiche. It came from a happy coincidence, a man called Henry, whose wife may or may not have been self-effacing, who may or may not have given a fireguard away to a totter, but who once must absolutely certainly have walked up and down our front path and stood where our dustbin is now.

It came from my kids and their scary sharpness, their sometimes shattering curiosity, their likeable ability to cut through the fancy adult rubbish to the gleaming urgent flesh of fact beneath.

'my kids and their scary sharpness'

And it came from a bit of over-hasty DIY on a dark Boxing Day afternoon and a house where we've spent such a significant part of our lives, but which is never quite the right colour. And the fact that, in the end, we all of us have one compelling thing in common. We inhabit spaces and we know we aren't the first to do so and we know we won't be the last either.

I began to wonder how it would feel to find out about the ones who came before – to turn them from the vaguest idea back into substance.

I wondered whether it might be possible to persuade our house to give up its secrets, to allow me to know the people, to hear the stories, to resurrect these ordinary lives – some of them long forgotten.

'It's not really our house at all, is it, Mummy?' asked Chloë soon after I'd started on my project. 'It's like we're just the top layer. And one day there'll be another layer right on top of us, squashing us down.'

I smiled. 'Do you mind that?'

She gave me a sharp look and went back to cutting pictures of shoes out of magazines.

'I'll have to think about it,' she said.

Chapter Two

THE BOY IN THE TOTTENHAM
HOTSPUR ROOM

The Pidgeons
1981–1987

We bought this house from a man called John Pidgeon.

Just walk through the hall and into the kitchen and immediately you'll spot a couple of crucial things about John Pidgeon. The first is that he likes to do his own carpentry – all the kitchen cupboards are hand-made by him, with fat, optimistic little bluebirds carved in each corner. And the second is that he had a habit of not quite finishing the task in hand – none of the cupboards have handles.

Right from the start, we viewed this trait of his with a kind of frustrated affection. 'Pidgeonesque' became the word we used for anything where the idea was good but the execution lacking. Or maybe it was just that we identified with it so closely ourselves. After a year we decided to paint the white cupboards bright blue. It took us about six months to get around to the second coat. Maybe this syndrome was infectious.

When I first saw the house, in May 1988, Jonathan and I had just found out we were having a baby. We weren't married but the baby was planned – though it wasn't expected so quickly. Where was all the 'trying' you were supposed to do? At twenty-seven, we were young and romantic enough to feel we might have quite enjoyed the suspense.

Still, now that it had happened, we decided we had to move. It wasn't just a question of space but also of a new start, a home that belonged to both of us. I didn't mind about the lack of a wedding – or at least back then I didn't think I did – but I wanted pots and pans, paint swatches, the paraphernalia of a life chosen together.

We looked at houses around Clapham but none of them were quite right. The only one I'd been drawn to wasn't all that suitable – it was just, as Jonathan astutely pointed out, that the exhausted woman who showed us round had a dribbling newborn baby on her shoulder. Tiny towelling babygros dripped on a rail over the bath, the whole place smelled of Wet Wipes. I wanted it. Meanwhile details of a house in Lillieshall Road arrived in the post one Saturday morning. It was firmly out of our price range.

'It looks absolutely gorgeous,' I told Jonathan, 'and look at that garden.' The photo showed a smooth green lawn going on forever, punctuated with the pink, red, and yellow blobs of roses.

He agreed. 'It's a lovely road too. Beautiful houses. But look at the price. There's no point even thinking about it.'

I agreed with him. He threw the details in the bin.

An hour later, I retrieved them.

We rang the estate agent. He said the house had been on the market for a year. The owner had moved to the country. It had been standing empty all that time.

'If no one wants it,' I pointed out to Jonathan, 'maybe we can get the price down?'

He laughed.

'I'm just going to look,' I told him, 'just on my own. Just in case.'

'In case of what?'

'Just to put my mind at rest, OK?'

Number 34 Lillieshall Road. Even the street name sounded like flowers. Lilies and shawls. Armfuls of scented lilies and, yes, baby shawls. We'd been to Mothercare and bought several satisfying cellophaned packs of white cellular baby blankets. Just to have in the cupboard. They looked impossibly small. They looked like they were made for a doll's cot. I couldn't believe we'd ever use them.

Lilies and shawls. Flowers and babies.

It was a hot afternoon in May. The young man from the estate agents – sweating in his shirt and suit – unlocked the door and said he'd leave me to wander round on my own. A fatal thing to let me do. Like leaving a pair of Victorian lovers unchaperoned. Maybe he knew it. Maybe he knew how hard my heart was pumping. Don't ever go house-hunting when you're pregnant. As bad as doing the weekly food shop just before lunch. Too hungry, you'll buy too much.

I was hungry.

I fell in love immediately, as expectant, first-time mothers do with houses that are beautiful, empty (unloved!) and streaming with sudden late afternoon sunshine after rain. I paced those rooms, the dusty air lit with magic, and knew that it was mine already. It was waiting for me to fill it with children. I could have had my babies right there and then, on the wide, dusty floor of the bedroom.

In fact, I could already hear the furious laughter of toddlers echoing round the terracotta-tiled kitchen. I could see the small wellington boots lined up in the hall, the school blazers hanging – torn and stained – from the pegs by the stairs. I could even, if I strained hard enough, hear the dull thud of teenage music from an upper room, the slam of an adolescent bedroom door. The house wasn't empty at all. It was full of my life, my future.

'Like it?' asked the young man who stubbed out a cigarette as I re-emerged into the sitting room.

'It's just perfect!' I said. Then I worried. Was I supposed to sound cooler?

But how could I? It was quite simply the most perfect house I'd ever walked into.

The rooms were large, light, the walls rag-rolled. Apricot and gold in the sitting room, lavender and hyacinth in the first-floor bedroom. In fact it was a house full of decorative surprises. The loo on the first-floor landing was papered in black and white striped felt, exactly like a zebra, with a silken tassel (a tail!) to flush the loo itself. The top (second-floor) bedroom was described in the details as having 'wallpaper with matching hand-painted blinds'. What it neglected to add was that the wallpaper was Tottenham Hotspur wallpaper – blue and white shields repeated so many times that it sent you dizzy – and the blinds had 'The Spurs! The Spurs!' hand-stencilled on them.

'I know,' said the estate agent with an apologetic laugh. 'We weren't sure whether or not to come clean about that. I mean, it could be off-putting – unless you're a fan?'

'My husband's a cricket man,' I told him, 'but we've got a baby on the way.'

'Oh, well then. You never know.'

He left me alone again and I went and stood in the garden, which was eighty feet long and clearly cherished. The magnolia had just finished flowering – huge waxy teardrop petals flushed with pink and still damp from the recent shower. Grass springy and damp underfoot – scent of lilac, honeysuckle, and the strange deliciousness of parched soil after rain. A blackbird called down the lawn.

I had to live here. The baby in me wouldn't be born till the following January, but I'd recently felt it move for the first time – a fluttery zigzag I could just feel if I lay on my stomach and shut my eyes. Now I knew for certain that this child would live here in this house. It would be his or her house – the place where he or she cried and laughed and took his or her first steps. I went back and told Jonathan.

He put his head in his hands and then he said what he always says in these situations: 'We'll just have to find the money somehow then.'

We only met John Pidgeon once, at the house, to talk through fixtures and fittings. He was living out in Kent and should, we reckoned, have been relieved – grateful even – finally to be done with his bridging loan. But if he was, he didn't show us. He played it so very cool. Years later, all I remembered about him was that he had brown hair and a beard, was a little older than us, and was in rock music journalism. Also – as he told us then – that his wife was an interior designer. This explained the rag-rolling.

We stood with him on the lawn and talked about the big white marble fireplaces in the sitting room. They'd been stolen while the house was standing empty but Val across the road had seen the burglars in action and they'd been caught red-handed. So the fireplaces had been returned and reinstalled, but badly. You could see all the joins between the marble slabs and the mantel of the one at the front wasn't quite straight.

John Pidgeon agreed to sell us the huge mirror that was screwed to the bathroom wall (I really wanted the house exactly as I'd seen it that first afternoon) and then he announced that he wanted to dig up some plants. The yellow rose, for instance – it had been planted for a child who died. And the magnolia, too, was of sentimental value.

'He can't take the magnolia!' I told Jonathan, horrified.

I'd dreamed about that magnolia several times by now – vague, happily disorganized dreams in which our nameless, faceless baby also featured. The magnolia, with its generous green arms lifted to the sky, was already a part of my life. Trees are owned by places, not by people. They belong to the ground. That magnolia wasn't going anywhere.

I did feel for him about the dead child, but a meaner part of me wondered whether he was actually telling the truth. But then could a person make that kind of thing up? The fact that this thought crossed my mind shows that I might have been going to be a mother, but I really knew nothing yet of the ferocity of birth and death, of everything that parenthood makes you stand to lose. If I had, would I have begged him to take the rose away? 'Have it – please, I understand.' I'd like to think so.

All of this is on my mind as I write to John Pidgeon at the forwarding address he left with us in 1988. The letter comes back a week later, scuffed and creased and marked 'Not known at this address'.

Meanwhile, I go to the Minet Archives Library in Knatchbull Road – the same library where I first glimpsed Henry and Charlotte on the juddering microfiche – and ask the librarian whether there's any way of finding out the names of people who lived in our house. She has thick black hair and a frowny face and is drinking coffee from a mug with a picture of the Teletubbies on it.

'I suppose you could look in Kelly's,' she says.

Kelly's?

She leads me over to a shelf of volumes and tells me I can just look up our address, year by year, and the names should all be there. It's a kind of phone book from before there were phones; the first half is more like the Yellow Pages, listing shops and tradesmen, and then there's a long list of 'householders', street by street, house by house. It's that easy.

'It'll only be the adults,' she says, 'but it should give you a list of names, if that's what you're looking for.'

I go through the volumes – experiencing a small jolt each time I see 34 Lillieshall Road printed on the page. I'm surprised at how just an address can feel like a part of you. In a way, it's hard to believe that those words existed before we lived here. More than a hundred years of letters plopping through the letter box with that precise number and those words on. Crowds of different people who'd write '34 Lillieshall Road' each time they had to fill in a form or begin a letter.

How many people?

An hour later, I have a crowd of names in my notebook.

After Henry and Charlotte Hayward, there's Elizabeth and then Lucy Spawton, Isabella Bloomfield Hinkley and Walter Hinkley. Then Charles Edwin Hinkley, Walter Stephen Hinkley. Beatrice Haig, Phyllis

Askew, Vera Palmer, Annie and Theodore Blaine, Amy and John Costello, Joan Russell, Olive Russell, Rita Wraight, Mavis Jones-Wohl, Dorothy and Wilfred Bartolo. By 1960, Gloria Duncan, Aston and Melda McNish, Louisa and Stanley Heron, Clarence Hibbert, Salome Bennet, Vincent Dias, Gerald Sherrif, Thomas H. Kyle, Veronica and Doreen Ricketts, then the Pidgeons, then –

I gaze at my notebook, almost dizzy with the sheer number of names, the sound and shape and idea of them. What is it? Didn't I expect to find so many? Had I even thought about it? I suppose, when your house is a hundred and thirty years old, it's not so unlikely that all these people will have lived there. But so many different names, sometimes all at once – presumably the house was sometimes rented out as rooms. It's a shock. Or maybe it's the names themselves, each one bulging with a mass of possibility, each one suggesting a life, an attitude, a type, a race, a class.

Most of us live in our homes knowing we're not the only ones to have done so. But we rarely confront those shadows in any significant way. Why should we? This is us and that was them. Their clutter, their smells, their noises, and their way of doing things is long gone. We've painted, plastered, demolished and constructed or converted – a loft, a bigger kitchen, a new power shower in the bathroom.

Our moments have blotted out theirs. Maybe this is a necessary element of domestic living – maybe it's the only way we can co-exist comfortably with each other's past lives, each other's ghosts. If Lucy Spawton or Melda McNish – a wonderfully sharp-tongued tartan name! – or Salome Bennet ever stood in our kitchen and sobbed or kissed or opened a fatal telegram, then it's all gone now. If it wasn't, the sense of claustrophobia would overwhelm us. We'd be stifled by years of emotional history every time we passed through a doorway or climbed the stairs.

When Jacob was about four years old, he asked me why people had to die. 'Why, Mummy? Why does it have to happen?'

I thought quickly and came up with what I decided was a brilliant (and true) answer – for a four-year-old anyway.

'Because, darling, if people didn't die, then the world would fill right up and there'd be no room to move or have fun or anything.'

He frowned. 'We'd have to stand on top of each other?'

'Exactly. It would be very uncomfortable and everyone would get very grumpy and it would be awful.'

It's 4.30 – closing time at the Minet Library. As the librarian slides the bolts on the big wooden door and turns the sign to 'Closed', I go and sit in my car outside and leaf through my notebook again and look at all those pencilled names (no biros allowed near the archives). Louisa Heron, Salome Bennet, Thomas Kyle, Gloria Duncan, Isabella Bloomfield Hinkley . . .

It's beginning to rain. I don't know why I feel oddly deflated when actually I've just found out so much. This, then, is it – the beginning of the trail. I should feel inspired and excited, but in fact I just feel sad.

I flick on the radio and it's a repeat of a programme I heard earlier in the week, about a Hungarian who fell in love before the war and lost her sweetheart; then, through a series of coincidences, she met up with him again more than fifty years later and married him. A year later he was dead of cancer.

We moved into 34 Lillieshall Road on 4 July 1988. It was a hot day and still early enough in my pregnancy for me to be feeling constantly sick.

The only other thing I remember is that some good friends of ours happened to have moved into a house on a parallel road on the exact same day. In the evening Jim and Ruth came round and we shared an Indian takeaway among the cardboard boxes and packing cases. The turmeric in the sauce stained our best grey melamine coffee table bright yellow.

We tried everything, but nothing would remove the bright yellow cloud. And then one day, almost a year later, it just disappeared all by itself.

'That's all you remember?' Jonathan says. 'About moving in here?'

'It was a big thing,' I tell him, 'one of those things you can just never explain.'

Dinner at Nick and Beth's in Wandsworth. They are a bit older than us and, I half-suddenly remember, old friends of 'Bubbles' (real name Susan) who happens to be John Pidgeon's ex-wife.

In the seventies, Beth lived in Macaulay Court, the 1930s art deco block at the far end of Lillieshall Road, where it turns sharply left and becomes Macaulay Road. And Bubbles lived at 61 Lillieshall Road with John and wore gold platform boots – or at least that's what Beth once told me. And eventually John left her to live in our house, on the other side of the road and just a few doors down.

Now as Beth and I walk up their garden steps to inspect her echinacea and phlox before dinner, I decide I ought to question her about John Pidgeon. Bubbles must know where he is. So could Beth give me Bubbles' phone number so I can ask – as delicately as possible of course?

'Oh, Bubbles and him, they really really don't get on,' Beth says. 'But he works at BBC Radio now, I think – he's big, head of something – just send an e-mail to the BBC, you'll get him.'

Next day, in the kitchen, Jonathan – chopping onions – asks me what I did today.

I tell him I sent an e-mail off to John Pidgeon at the BBC.

'That's all? But did you at least start chasing the deeds? You need to know which of those millions of people actually owned the house.'

I tell him the truth – that I'm a bit stuck on that. Because the other day I called the Bank of Scotland, our mortgage company, and all they would give me was a fax number for the deeds department.

'You mean you can't phone them?'

'No, they said there wasn't a number for them – only a fax number. So I faxed them, explaining.'

'But that's ludicrous – will they fax you back?'

'I think they said they'd phone or e-mail.'

'How soon?'

'They didn't say.'

> **From:** John Pidgeon
> **To:** Julie Myerson
> **Sent:** Friday, March 10, 2003 2:51 PM
> **Subject:** 34 Lillieshall Road
>
> Julie
>
> yes it's me and yes we'd be happy to talk about the house. As for who we bought it off, the name Ricketts does ring the vaguest of bells but it was a long time ago. I saw the house towards the end of 1979 – I was already living in Lillieshall Road (at 61) but parting from my first wife – and moved in in April 1980. I bought it via the ABC estate agency. The interior doors were covered with hardboard and painted orange. There was a purple carpet in the front room. I fell in love with Julia (my wife) there. We were very fond of 34 . . .
>
> Best
> John

I ask him where he lives and if it would be possible to come and see him. He says they live in 'deepest Kent – between Canterbury and Hythe' and that his wife Julia has 'quite a stash of 34 Lillieshall Road photos' and that I can come and visit them this Saturday if I like. I tell him that would be great and we fix a time.

I bound downstairs and tell Jonathan I finally have a date to talk to someone from the house. 'One down . . . and about forty-five to go.'

'The Pidgeons are the easy ones,' he says, as if I needed reminding.

* * *

I leave it a couple of days and then I decide Enough is Enough. I am going to phone the Bank of Scotland to chase the deeds. My faxes have all gone unanswered.

The man starts to ask me for my name and mortgage account number and I interrupt politely to explain that it's not an enquiry about the mortgage.

'What then?' he asks me in a slightly ruder voice. I explain that I'm a writer, actually; that mine is an unusual request; that I just want to look at the deeds of my house for research purposes. I faxed them four days ago and I've heard nothing. Can't I just be put through to the department. Please?

'No one,' he says very frostily, 'can actually speak to the deeds department.'

'But why?'

'They don't deal directly with people.'

'But – why?'

'It's just the way they work.'

'So they're only reachable by fax?'

'That's right.'

I sigh. 'But what if they don't ever fax back?'

'I'm sorry, madam, that's not for me to say.'

'But you work for the Bank of Scotland!'

'I'm not in the deeds department.'

I try to work this one out. 'But – so there's no way of chasing them other than by sending another fax?'

'I'm afraid not.'

I try another tack. 'Do you think it's likely they got it?'

'I really couldn't say. If you sent it through then I dare say they have it.'

'So – how long do you think I should wait to hear?'

He takes a breath. 'They won't have prioritized it, madam,' he says at last.

Eventually and grudgingly he gives me the name of the deeds manager. I say I'll send yet another fax to him, a personal one.

'That might be an idea,' he says.

I put down the phone. A tabby cat lands with a thump on the desk, walks her muddy rainpaws all over my Post-it notes.

I'm driving to Kent to see John and Julia Pidgeon. I'm nervous. Ridiculously so. It's just the idea of seeing John again, of meeting the mysterious Julia – of asking them a whole lot of personal questions about their lives in this house that I'd never dreamed I'd have to ask.

How will they react? Won't they mind? Is it any of my business anyway? All I can think of is the beautiful garden we didn't maintain, the fireplaces we eventually ripped out, and the sentimental rose I didn't let him take.

'Bear in mind it's far worse for them,' Jonathan tells me before I leave. 'The one thing you can usually rely on when you sell your house is that you'll never have to see the person who bought it ever again.'

He's right, of course. You stand on a lawn somewhere between exchange and completion and have a brief altercation about a bathroom mirror (I think we handed over £50 cash), a magnolia tree, a rose bush – but at least you think there's nothing to lose. You'll never see each other ever again. And when the new owner discovers that painted-over damp or the collapsing ceiling, you'll be long gone.

John had said 'deepest Kent', and that's just what this is: soft, sweet, English butter-wrapper countryside, rolling fields, sudden canopies of trees that turn the light an underwater green as the car dips beneath. Even though John sent me meticulous directions, I still manage to drive right past the house and all the way up to the end of the lane where it peters out into a rough track. And then nothing, no space to move forward. I have to back out and turn around in a clearing, branches and brambles scratching against the roof of the car. I rumble all the

28

way back down the track and eventually find the house, a long low cottage set back from the road. Quiet and tranquil and utterly rural. As different as it could be from Lillieshall Road.

As I crunch across the gravel, a nervy, noticeably beautiful woman with reddish hair and a plum-coloured shirt comes striding out. Julia is slim, wide-mouthed, bright-eyed – younger than I'd expected. She holds out a hand. I tell her it's so good finally to meet the person whose walls and curtains we lived with for so many years.

She laughs quickly. 'Ha! The sponging, yes!'

And we always thought it was rag-rolling.

She calls to John, who's doing something in the hedge. He steps down the bank, some kind of pruner in his hand and holds out the other one. He is just exactly as I remember him – solid, gruff, bearded, and slightly on edge. But then so am I.

We go in the kitchen – a little farmhousey kitchen whose long low window is filled up with a view of smooth country lawn. Julia makes coffee and John clears stuff off the table, spreads a load of photos out, and straightaway starts to tell me how he was in the process of buying the house – in 1980 – when he met Julia.

'My wife and I lived at No. 61, but we'd decided the marriage wasn't going anywhere. And she went to stay in her parents' place in Kensington – a mews, I think they still have it. Anyway I think the sign went up at No. 34 on the Saturday morning – and I went straight round to the estate agent and the house was hideous, dreadful decor and all that, but I remember still thinking it was under-priced. I bought it immediately. For – guess how much?'

I shake my head and bite my lip. I can't guess.

'£32,000.'

He smiles and straightaway so does Julia. They both know we paid £217,500 for it just eight years later.

Julia pours coffee, pushes the sugar and milk across the table.

I ask him if he can remember who the seller was, but he can't. He vaguely thinks that when he was first shown round the house there was a large black woman living there.

'Was she called Kyle maybe? Or Ricketts?'

'I don't know. The name Ricketts rings a bell, like I said in the e-mail.'

Suddenly Julia takes a bottle from the fridge, pours herself a glass of water, and stands and tips her head back and drinks it all in one. We both watch her.

'It was hideous,' John says again as if he realizes this spectacle has been distracting. 'The house.'

'But you could see its potential?' Julia prompts.

John tells me exactly what it was like. 'The front door was orange and hardboarded over with a rectangular panel of fluted glass – '

'I thought it was bobbly?' Julia says, pouring more water.

'Or bobbly. Bobbly or fluted anyway – down the middle. All the internal doors were hardboarded over too and the banisters. I pulled the hardboard off and there were no – what do you call them? – actual banisters, the verticals.'

I'm surprised. 'None?'

'I had to put them in – the ones you have there aren't the originals, far from it. I got them from a squat on Clapham Park Road. They were pulling this squat down – I knew some people there – and so I whipped out the banisters.'

I laugh. Because it's surprising and funny, the idea that the banisters in our house – which we've painted and repainted reverently and have always assumed were original – actually came from a Brixton squat.

'They were pulling it down anyway. So you didn't actually do anything wrong,' Julia interjects quickly.

John ignores this. 'They don't match at all,' he points out. 'Some of them are completely different. Haven't you noticed?'

I tell him I haven't but then I am famous in our family for not noticing that sort of thing (and besides I always make an excuse when it comes to tedious banister painting), but I know that Jonathan, who misses nothing, will have noticed.

John tells me that there was an outdoor loo which they later turned into a pantry.

'But it never felt right,' Julia adds quickly. 'We never quite liked the idea of it, did we? You know, a loo being a pantry.' She wrinkles her nose.

'There was also a bath right under the kitchen window,' John says. 'That was the only bathroom, you know.'

'What?' I ask. 'You mean a horrid sixties one?'

'No, no, not at all. A really nice cast-iron one. I had it outside the back door for ages and then eventually a rag-and-bone man came by and I said he could take it away. But I got something in return. Come and see.'

He takes me through into the low-beamed sitting room. Julia follows close behind. There on the wall are two brass candelabra-style light fittings, with flowers and bows. 'I asked for those – they were on his cart – so he gave them to me in exchange.'

Julia says it was funny but in those days you still had this man with a cart and a bell – 'a real rag-and-bone man' – and as she says it, a dim memory slides back into view.

'I remember him too!' I say. 'He still used to come when we first moved in.' I realize he was one of those things you took for granted and then didn't notice when he'd gone. The area comes up in price, times change, people too . . . the man with the cart goes.

I ask John how the house was arranged. Was it split up like flats for instance?

'Oh no, not at all. No actual partitioning. But there were certainly different people living separately in different rooms.' The little room at the back on the first landing (this is now my study but it's also been a baby's nursery and Raph's room) was the kitchen. He says that in the (real downstairs) kitchen, the brick fireplace was plastered over with a nasty gas fire in it.

'We pulled it all off and discovered this glorious original brick chimney breast behind.'

I apologize and tell them that in fact we finally got rid of it – 'There was no light, we couldn't see each other when we were cooking.'

John doesn't react to this but says there used to be a door to the left of the fireplace – so those were originally two separate rooms. And the slab of York stone in the hearth came from Lassco Reclamation Yard. And we thought this was original as well. When we extended the kitchen out over the yard, we put the slab of stone in the garden, beneath the swing seat to stop feet scuffing the grass.

Julia asks if we kept the floor in the kitchen.

I hesitate. 'The terracotta tiles? No, I'm afraid not. It wasn't that we didn't like them – in fact, we did, we loved them – but when we extended the kitchen they had to go.'

Julia gives John a private look and sighs.

'I'm sorry,' I say, putting down my pen.

'Oh,' she says, 'but they were so special.'

He smiles uneasily. 'They took a while to find.'

'I'm sorry,' I say again and I mean it. I realize I don't especially want to mess with their memories. If the house was such a special and happy place for them, if they invested so much care in its decoration, do they really want to hear how we trashed so much of it?

But Julia's face brightens. 'Don't be silly! We have practically the same here,' she says, and I look at the floor and it's true, they do. The earthy warmth of terracotta with little blue and white china pat-terned tiles at the corners, just like the ones that used to be in our kitchen. John asks me if I remember the zebra print wallpaper in the upstairs loo?

'With the tassel tail you pulled to flush it?'

We all laugh. I tell them that for years we used to send guests upstairs to check out two things: the zebra loo and the Tottenham Hotspur Room.

'Ah,' says John and his face relaxes into a smile, 'that was Leon.'

He shows me a photo of Leon in bed in the corner of Jake's room. There's the famous wallpaper with its blue and white Tottenham Hotspur logo repeated over and over. Leon is about Raph's age – maybe nine or ten – and he has a Tottenham Hotspur duvet and a television and most of the rest of the room is taken up with a snooker table. Jake would be so jealous.

We kept the wallpaper for the first few months and then, that first Christmas in the house, with the baby due in late January, I began my maternity leave. The first thing I did was paint that room. It took me a week: Radio 4, the cool white light of mid-winter, and the sudden luxury of waking in the morning with no office to go to.

The Sanderson colour I chose was called Bisque – a pale, almost beigey, antique doll pink. It took a maddening number of coats to cover the Tottenham Hotspur shields. I wore a brown striped woollen dress and an old green apron and I stood awkwardly halfway up the ladder, holding on tight, an unborn pair of feet sporadically pounding me in the ribs. My body felt full and absurd, as if this baby should already be out.

By the time the last coat was dry, the baby's head was engaged. The cellular blankets had come out of their cellophane and were waiting – neatly and satisfyingly stacked – in the small room on the first landing, where there was also a tiny Moses basket, a medium-sized changing table and a pine Mothercare cot which looked large enough to take a Great Dane.

John shows me another photo of Leon, in our garden this time. Our garden before he made it beautiful – a flat, barren, and barely recognizable expanse of scrubby lawn with a concrete path down the left-hand side. Leon is scowling at the camera and wearing a different football strip.

'That was before he switched allegiance,' John explains. 'That room was almost a Chelsea room.'

I ask him how he and Julia met and he says it was in the Bowyer Arms on Clapham Manor Street. I tell him this is now the Bread and Roses, a Workers Beer Company pub – Jonathan goes there for Labour Party meetings in the upstairs room.

'She was living in Iveley Road and trying to set up her own painted textiles business. But she came to help work on the house, with the decorating and so on, and when I moved in I had a kind of house-warming party and I invited her.'

'And you went for my tight jeans!' she says.

'That's when it started,' he agrees soberly.

Julia tells me that she helped him take all the horrible old lino and rubbish out of the two top rooms that were going to be Leon and Lucy's rooms.

'And you chucked the stuff out of the second-floor window down into the yard below, and then you had a huge bonfire on the lawn, and there was this moment when you put your arm around me and we both looked back at the house and that was when you declared your love for me!'

John frowns. 'I thought it was when you were varnishing floor-boards in the house.'

'OK, but I remember it was the first time for something big, I know it was, the first snog or something.'

'But we were already going out together by then, so it couldn't possibly have been the first snog – '

'Oh well, but you said something like you were glad to have me there or something.' Julia turns to me and throws her hands up. 'There you are, you see, Julie. Something significant happened to us on that lawn and we can't even agree on what it was!'

I laugh and tell her it's exactly what I'm trying to explore. The experiences people had when they were standing in certain parts of the house or garden. And also how they remember or feel about it now – or maybe even how they don't. Because it's true – more and more I'm realizing that entire moments dissolve and fall off the edge of memory. Sometimes you're too late to pull them back, however much you'd like to. Or worse, perhaps, you reach out and pull them back in the nick of time, only to find that no one else remembers. You're alone with the shreds of that moment that once mattered so much to you.

Think of Julia on the lawn that day – the same lawn where I stood under the magnolia less than a decade later and found myself falling under the spell of the house.

Autumn – a smoky, sharp day, trees bending, a little chilly when the wind gusts, smoke billowing sideways into the gardens of 36 and 38. Is she wearing her jeans, an old, third-best pair perhaps, maybe a plaid shirt or a denim one, some kind of a waistcoat over it all? Are her cheeks smeared with dust and smoke, eye-liner smudged, eyes shining with the physical effort of it all? And does she know that John was watching earlier as she bent to gather up the mouldering underlay and chuck it out through the sash window and into the yard below? Rubber and old lino and dust falling through the air – decades of feet treading those boards, now worn to jetsam. Does she love him already? Does she know he loves her? And does he put his arm around her and turn with her to look back up at the wide, unblinking eyes of the house – the upstairs windows where so many other faces have appeared and disappeared over the years?

John and Julia tie the knot on a bright, freezing day in February 1984 at Brixton Registry office.

Ian MacLaglan, who toured with the Stones in 1978, comes over with his wife and they all get wrecked together the night before and then have a champagne breakfast before heading down to the Town Hall in Brixton. They queue for almost an hour to get married, but they're so plastered and happy they can barely remember any of it. Afterwards they take over the Tim Bobbin, the pub at the end of Lillieshall Road, and the day after that they go to some wine bar in Abbeville Road for lunch. By the time they stagger back across the frozen Common to Lillieshall Road it's almost dark, so they just fall into bed and stay there until about the same time next day.

Their bed. John designed and made it – just a simple, low, wooden plinth and above it small white carved wooden cupboards with mirrors in them and a shelf running between them, all of it backed by a panel of white cotton that Julia has lovingly painted with pale blue and pink and yellow stripes. Ice cream colours. She's also done a matching flounce on the central ceiling light, and the walls are sponged lavender and blue. It's a bit of a woman's space, but John doesn't mind that. In fact it gives him a little burst of pleasure – the way she's already put her mark on the house in this fatally feminine way.

'I love it,' he tells her. 'Everything you do, I love. I love you.'

'I want a baby,' she says, one morning in March.

'OK,' he goes and he's surprised to find he means it.

They do the house up gradually, as and when the money allows. A songwriting deal with Virgin pays for the carpets – deep hyacinth in the bedroom and a sensible grey pattern for the landings and stairs. Cream for the sitting room – the sort of nubbly carpet that will go with the apricot walls. The house feels completely different with carpet – it makes the place look new and smell clean. That lino was vile.

Once, in a flush moment, they toy briefly with putting a sauna on the roof terrace – until they realize what it would cost. Thank God, they both agree a year later, that they didn't.

Meanwhile they dig the garden over. At first John cuts the path down the left-hand side – just a straight path that will lead him and his barrow down to the compost heap, but he feels it doesn't look right. So he scraps that and starts again, deciding finally on a plump figure-of-eight, with the lawn snaking in and out to create half-moon-shaped beds that he plants with shrubs, roses, hydrangeas, California poppies, lilies, and large saucer-shaped daisies.

When he first cuts the lawn to that shape, it looks too bald and forced. But he knows that once the plants have expanded, it will be fine. At first Leon helps him, lifting the discarded clumps of turf into a bucket. But soon the boy forgets what he's supposed to be doing and ends up kicking a ball around instead.

John's work is going well. He has quite a few projects on the boil. He does some songwriting for Island Music – lyrics and stuff – and he produces a huge documentary series for Capital Radio on the music of the seventies. Meanwhile he writes a book about the pop group Slade and it becomes a bit of a cult book – people write to him from all over the world trying to get hold of a copy. He starts up a rock magazine called *Let It Rock* with his friends Simon Frith, the rock music journalist, and Charlie Gillett, who lives down the road.

In between all of this they get on with the house – their project, their thing. If Julia chooses the colours and paints an atmosphere, then John's forte is foraging for stuff and getting it cheap, or sometimes even for nothing. He frequently finds things on skips. He has an eye for pieces he can transform, and he really gets off on the idea that the house is made up of so many items discarded by other people but which still have life left in them, if only you can see it.

The stained-glass doors on the kitchen cupboards, for instance, are found in an antique shop on the Wandsworth Road – he happens to be passing and he knows they're right and he persuades the man to part with them for about half of what he was originally asking.

Meanwhile, best of all, he's still wondering what to do about the hideous orange front door with its crinkly glass panel, when Number 36 – where Frances and Chris Calman live – is broken into, the whole door bashed in with a sledgehammer. He can't believe his luck when he sees a brand new door being delivered.

He asks Chris if he wants the old one and Chris, baffled, replies that they were on the verge of ringing the council to get it taken away. So John rips out the untouched middle panel of the Calmans' discarded door and uses it to replace the glass in his own door. It fits perfectly – these doors are standard. A lick of white gloss and it looks just fine – a proper Victorian front door, born from the scraps of two neighbouring front doors, the joins indiscernible. Just like the banisters.

Julia remarks that the place is fast turning into a Frankenstein's monster of a house. John laughs. You could say the same of Lillieshall Road itself, which begins with eight tiny two-up-two-down cottages, some of them paint-peeling and short-life squatted since the fifties, others with their new pointing and Laura Ashley curtains in the windows.

After the cottages come the slightly larger, two-storey houses, two on each side of the road, then come the three storeys, like Number 34. On the even-numbered side there are five of these, only two on the opposite side.

And then as you walk further up the street, the even bigger houses begin – ending with Number 61 where Bubbles still lives with Leon and Lucy, who trot more or less happily back and forwards across the road. These have steps up to the front door and grand basement kitchens, big pine tables visible as you pass by on the pavement.

Quite a contrast to the tiny cottages with their buddleia-cracked walls and side entrances straight into the main living room. For many years the pop band the Thompson Twins reside in one of these but the landlord of the Tim Bobbin doesn't like squatters and bans them from the pub. When their music career suddenly and dramatically takes off, they carry on squatting. But one evening they pull up at the Tim Bobbin in a limo. Out comes the landlord, furious-eyed, hands on hips, and says, 'I don't care what fucking car you fucking well drive, I don't want no fucking squatters in here.'

* * *

Meanwhile Julia discovers she's pregnant. They work out that it must have happened almost immediately after the wedding in February which is weird because they've been very laid back about contraception all this time, so why suddenly now? A honeymoon baby! Except they didn't really have a honeymoon, Julia reminds him. Well, OK, a love baby anyway.

Julia feels fine and looks great, a little pale and tired in the mornings but otherwise the pregnancy suits her, she's so happy and excited. But long before she's reached full term, she wakes one night, clearly in labour. They rush her to St Thomas's Hospital and the baby – an impossible shred of a thing – is born in the early hours of the next morning. A boy. They both hold him, stroke the fragile curve of his small head, the doll hands, fingers tight-curled – feel the barely-there weight of him in their hands.

For a day and a half, they actually think he might live. They sit and hug and kiss and convince each other that this really is a possibility. He looks quite perfect after all – the shape of his face, the stretch of his small limbs. And premature babies can survive, can't they? The hospital walls are covered in the photographic evidence: shiny polaroids of the ones who made it – little scraps with huge eyes and cotton hats on their bald heads, who grew up to be loud, bouncy toddlers in dungarees. But the doctors know better than to get their hopes up. They talk quietly, kindly. There's a noticeable sense of calm around the baby. No one's rushing. They're just waiting. He dies in their arms at lunchtime on the second day.

The nurses bring a cup of tea, touch them on the shoulder, say very little except 'Sorry' – then leave them to hold onto him a little while longer. When the moment comes to let go, they just do it, they find they can do it – they help each other.

There's a funeral at Streatham Crematorium. A wavy blue August day. Mr Whippy vans tinkling in the streets. Just John, Julia, Leon, Lucy, and this tiny tiny coffin. It feels odd and wrong and terrible. It's far too soon after the wedding to be gathering again, around something barely bigger than a shoe box.

They ask politely if they can have the ashes and the man says he's sorry but, frankly, there won't be any: they just get blown up the chimney. He apologizes for his bluntness, but John and Julia agree later that there's something reassuring about this. The idea that what's left of their baby boy is just flying up and away into the sky. They can live with that. It's OK.

People are good. A few days before the funeral, Ronnie Lane, bass player from the Small Faces and an old friend of John's, sits there in the kitchen at Lillieshall Road with his scuffed DMs on a chair and rolls a joint and says something that John will always hold onto.

'The thing is, mate,' he says, 'when you see a poor dead baby bird lying on the street, it's kind of reassuring to look up because there are always more eggs up there in the nest.'

The idea stays in John's head. He wonders about it – wonders why he can handle the idea, why it at least doesn't make him feel any worse. It's not that it unwrites the death – how the hell can you ever do that? – but it's that thing of looking up.

Yes, he likes that. If you don't believe in God or an afterlife, and he certainly doesn't, then isn't that all you can do, look up? Once you've held your own small child in your arms and felt his tiny volume of blood stop, then isn't that all that's left? You can still raise your head. You can still look up.

He asks Ron if they can say that at the funeral, the bit about the baby bird, and Ron nods and yawns, leans back, shuts his eyes, and says, 'Of course, mate, of course.' Years later, John reminds him of it – of that great and touching thing he said and how very comforting they found it, especially at the funeral – and Ron looks blank. Did he really say that? But he's not well himself by then. A few years later he too is dead, of multiple sclerosis. He's had it for ages.

Meanwhile Frances Calman, next door at Number 36, is a great help too. She's a consultant radiologist, married to a GP and mother of Tom and Barney, two small, loud boys – a warm, strong, upbeat woman.

'What you've got to bear in mind,' she tells them in her down-to-earth voice, 'is you get all these stories about how a miracle 2 lb baby survives . . . but you hardly ever get any stories eighteen years later saying "Miracle baby gets three A levels and goes to Oxford".'

The baby would never have got to university. The baby blew away in the wind. They call the baby who blew away Jamie. Jamie Jess.

John and Julia support each other, dig the garden, plant a yellow climbing rose in his memory. By next summer it will be halfway up the metal arch, a cluster of tight-curled lemony sunshine buds. John will feed it with manure, spray it for blackfly. And half a decade after that, it will be a full-blown mature rose and another young pregnant woman, who has just fallen in love with the house, will stand in the garden and breathe in its scent and take its existence entirely for granted in a way that only the still childless can.

Meanwhile the magnolia that they planted blossoms for the first time – white waxy blooms poised like birds on the edge of flight. A year later, their daughter Collette is born, followed a couple of years after that by their son Barney.

'Here they are.' John shows me a colour snap of a small girl and boy running at the bottom of our garden. 'And this one's Collette' – a red-haired child in a sticky-out dress stands on the terrace outside my study and squints into the sun. I recognize her as the lanky auburn girl in jeans who skulked in the kitchen when I first arrived today in Kent.

John tells me that at first he used that room – the small room at the top of the first flight of stairs – as a bathroom because it already had plumbing. And he used the larger room next to the master bedroom as a study. But then he found he hated working in the larger room – he could never settle in it for some reason – so he switched and worked in that smaller room and converted the big one into a bathroom.

I tell him that little room has been my study on and off for ages and I too like its smallness, its view over the garden, the evening sunshine that floods in. Sometimes I take a cushion and a glass of wine and camp down on the terrace outside to read. Especially in the evenings when the house is empty of kids, dog, man. If you get down low enough, all you can see is the sky, the tops of the trees, the birds going to bed.

I ask John about his older daughter Lucy. I realize I know which Leon's room was but not hers.

'Was she in the other room at the top?' I ask him. 'The one next to Leon's? Because that's our daughter Chloë's room now.'

'Yes,' he says, and starts telling me why he eventually left the area – that he just felt it changing. That Lucy and Leon used to be able to walk to school – the primary school on Wix's Lane – or else go up to the Common with their bikes without worrying. But the gap between the rich and the poor seemed to be growing and he was uncomfortable with it.

'There were more BMWs in the street,' he says, 'and house prices were becoming unreal.'

He gathers all the photos off the table and tells me Julia says it's fine for me to borrow them.

'You're sure?'

'It's fine. There's lots of the house and garden in there.'

'Is Jonathan a photographer?' he asks me as he walks me out to my car.

I tell him no, he's a lot of other things though: writer and director, even a local Labour Councillor now.

He looks puzzled. 'Oh. Only I could have sworn I saw him taking pictures at a party a little while after you bought the house. And I was feeling so guilty about the price you paid that I avoided him.'

I laugh.

'We didn't think we paid too much,' I say.

'Oh, didn't you? Oh good.'

We say a warm goodbye and I drive off down the lane in the Saturday March sunshine, brambles snapping at my windscreen.

Now I want to hear Leon's story. And Lucy's.

Back home in the little room that was once John Pidgeon's study and is now mine, I open my notebooks.

So many names, so many families to discover and unearth. Some of these people must surely still be alive – Ricketts and Kyle and Sherrif from the late seventies, perhaps? And the Reynolds and McNishes and Duncans from the sixties? Maybe even the Bartolos and Costellos and Blaines from the fifties. And I realize that my list includes only adults – how many children are lurking under those grown-up-only lists?

And then as I go further back, I'm definitely not going to be looking for ex-residents but descendants: children and grandchildren of the Askews and Hinkleys and Spawtons and Haywards. Maybe I'm tired but the task suddenly seems impossibly daunting. Where do you start? With one name or several? With a year or a whole decade?

More for something to do than anything else, I've typed the names into a chart, so I can see who was here with whom, who was here for longest, whose stay coincided with whose. But staring at all the names, repeated and re-listed, almost feels worse. A tidal wave of names and dates, about to knock me right over.

I must simplify this somehow.

Right, Lucy Spawton lived in the house from 1895 to 1944; no one has ever lived here longer. So if I can just find her children or, if they're gone, her grandchildren, they should be able to tell me all about her. Shouldn't they?

The Family Records Centre in Islington is a daunting place – a big, modern, purpose-built building with lots of wide, automatic glass doors and wheelchair ramps, nylon staticky carpets and metal ware-house shelving.

It's full of the retired and the semi-retired – the Bettys and the Kenneths and the Rosemarys, the ex-teachers and the ex-accountants from Surrey and Pinner, who bowl up here with massive energy and enthusiasm, to investigate their ancestors and research their family trees. They're here for the day, they bring sandwiches, they have ring-binder files.

Relishing the sudden novelty of so much free time, they've come to find out where they came from, what the dead who gave them life were called. They want names, dates, places. The notes they make are metic-ulously legible – geography essay handwriting, purposeful and clear.

'I've gone back as far as 1764,' a man in a bottle-green sweatshirt with a picture of a golf club on the front tells a grey-haired woman as they wait for the lift. 'My wife's gone back further on her side.'

You might expect it to be a quiet or reflective place, but it's not. It's frenzied, hectic. There's the constant sound of volumes being pulled off the shelves for a start – opened, flicked through, snapped shut, banged back. Handbags are shifted cagily along the carpet, books and biros gath-ered up, but coats and shopping bags must be deposited in the lockers downstairs. You need free hands in this place, if you mean business.

I decide to look in the registers of death certificates for Lucy Spawton, starting with the year when her name leaves Kelly's Directory, when she's no longer resident at our house. I'm going to assume – rightly, wrongly? – that she died in 1944.

I pull out a heavy black register – black for Death – and slam it down on the sloping counter. There are four registers for each year, each labelled MAR, JUNE, SEPT and DEC, and inside long lists of hand-typed names. The paper is greasy and brown with a million thumbings. Flick to the right page, then down the list: SPAVINS, SPAWFIELD, SPAWSON, and then SPAWTON. But no Lucy in March 1944. Hoist the volume – metal-cornered and about as big as a church bible – back into the shelf and take out the next. No SPAWTON, LUCY. Hoist it back, slam the next down.

And there she is. SPAWTON, LUCY. She was seventy-seven years old when she died and her death was registered in July 1944.

I know what to do next. I've seen other people doing it. I reach for the purple form, 'Application for DEATH Certificate – For use in the PUBLIC SEARCH ROOM only'. I write Lucy's details into the form, write my own name and address, and sign it. Then I queue at the cash counter, wait for the airport-announcement ding-dong to call me to the next window, pay seven pounds, and then the man behind the glass says, 'It'll be posted out to you on Friday.'

This is fun.

Flushed with success, I go straight over to the red birth registers, find the reference to Lucy's birth (easy once you have her age at death) and order her birth certificate as well.

I'm on my way.

The Pidgeon photographic archives – the thirty-odd photos that Julia let me borrow – move and fascinate me far more than I ever thought they could or should.

I sit at the kitchen table and shuffle them, unsure of what exactly I'm looking for, and unable to understand why they touch me so deeply. They're just ordinary snaps, the sort you'd find in any normal family album. Some are good, some indifferent, some sharp, some fuzzy, some taken on ordinary days, some on birthdays. The subjects seem sometimes to be willing, sometimes not, sometimes – in the best ones – oblivious.

But this is the recent past. There's nothing especially noticeable or exotic about the 1980s. If I can find photos of Henry and Charlotte Hayward – the 1880s – now that will be exciting.

So why, then? Why do these pictures shake me up? Is it just that they show me something I know about, but would never normally get to see: another family living and talking and having birthdays and Christmases and babies in a home that is, quite recognizably, ours? Our house. Julia's sponge-effect walls survived enough years to appear again and again in our own family albums, yet here they are – somehow preposterously! – in theirs.

There are whole pieces of the past that lie just around the last corner, closer perhaps than we'd like to think. We may choose to forget this, but the house doesn't. The house has seen it, done it, felt it all before.

So there's Julia, grinning widely and pushing a pushchair up the front path just as I've done, another baby in a sling (just like I used to have) – our familiar green-yellow privet hedge lit by the sun, the old wooden white gate (which eventually fell apart, never to be replaced). And here she is again, photographed from above, sitting cross-legged and tender-faced, on the lawn with a child in her arms. The garden is new-laid and freshly dug around her – strangely clean and young, yet recognizably our garden.

'here she is again . . . cross-legged and tender faced'

Here's Collette, about five years old, standing squinting in the garden, red hair lit by sunlight. And Leon – also red-haired – kicking a football, scowling at the camera. Maybe he resents that he has to stop for even one second for the shot. He wants to keep on moving, he doesn't want the camera to freeze his life for the sake of posterity, to curtail the urgent swing of his foot. Here he is again, looking happier – winter. He's just built a snowman. This time he doesn't mind being photo-graphed. He knows the snowman will melt and the photo will be his only lasting proof.

And here's Leon yet again, sitting in the kitchen – our kitchen! – patting a dog, a birthday cake on the table. How many birthday cakes of ours have we had in that kitchen? Just counting our own three children, I make it thirty-seven! So how many birthday cakes has the house seen in that kitchen? Hundreds? How many lit candles? Thousands, maybe?

'What's the matter? What are you thinking?' Jonathan asks me, finding me almost in tears over the Pidgeons' photos.

'he knows the snowman will melt'

'That we're just the latest layer,' I tell him, 'that we'll go and there'll be others.'

'Mmm . . . so?'

'It's just kind of shocking to realize it, that's all.'

He smiles and touches my shoulder. 'You've only just realized it?'

I shuffle the photos. 'Only just seen photographic proof, I suppose.'

'But they're really nice photos.'

'I know, I love them. They seem like a nice family. Nicer than I used to imagine actually.'

'So . . . that's a good thing.'

'It's good but – it's so sad. It seems like nothing, no time at all – but these babies, these kids are all grown up, just as ours will be any minute. It all goes so fast. I can't bear it.'

'Funny girl,' he says. 'If you hadn't seen the photos, then you'd never have given it any thought.'

'you'd never in a zillion years let me have wallpaper like that'

I show the children the one of Leon in his bed in the Tottenham Hotspur Room. The duvet matches the wallpaper.

'How come he had that wallpaper?' Raphael immediately asks. 'You'd never in a zillion years let me have wallpaper like that.'

'You don't support Spurs,' Chloë points out with acid speed.

'No – shut up, Chloë – I mean Liverpool wallpaper. And anyway I'm thinking of changing teams. Daddy says I ought to support a London club and Alex supports Tottenham.'

'I painted that wallpaper over when I was pregnant with Jake,' I tell them wistfully.

'I wish you hadn't,' says Raph, 'I might have supported Spurs right from the start if you hadn't.'

Jake looks at the photo and shrugs.

'Guess how old he is now.' I say.

'Dunno. My age?'

'He's thirty.'

Raphael takes a breath. 'Thirty years old! A whole man! But that photo doesn't look like the olden days.'

'It's not, it's about twenty years ago.'

'Were you alive then?'

'Come on, Raph, you know I was. Twenty years ago isn't that long. I was at university.'

'It's funny,' says Chloë, 'to think that you were at university when that boy was sleeping in Jake's room.'

'Except it wasn't Jake's room then,' I remind her, 'it was That Boy's room.'

'Hmm. I don't like him,' Raph says.

'You don't know anything about him.'

'I do! He supports Spurs.'

'Yes, OK, you do know that about him. But he may not support them any more.'

'Maybe now he's switched to Liverpool,' Jake suggests.

'Or maybe he's gone off football altogether.'

Chloë laughs, a cackle designed to get at Raph.

'You don't go off it,' Raph says firmly. 'Not if you love it when you are a child.'

In an attempt to switch this gruesomely one-track conversation, I show the kids the other photos but they're less impressed. It's the wallpaper that gets to them. The hard physical evidence of another child getting to inflict his taste, his interests, on the walls of the house that, as far as they're concerned, is theirs and always has been and always will be.

But it won't. Everything changes, everything goes. The fireplaces are gone, the walls are repainted, the cake eaten, the snow melted, the babies grown. Theirs and ours. And others after us.

From: Leon Pidgeon
To: Julie Myerson
Sent: Monday, March 27, 2003 11:53 AM
Subject: 34 Lillieshall Road

Hi Julie
I am the son of John Pidgeon, who you interviewed last weekend about living at 34 Lillieshall Road. He mentioned to me that you may be interested in getting in touch with me.
If this is the case then you can email me back at this address.

Leon

My first conscious memory of being alive and somewhere. Sitting in bright warm light. Under me is softness, above is warmth, dazzling warmth.

My bottom is on the ground but my arms are moving. In my hands is something light and easy, something very interesting to me – there are colours in it, maybe the curves and dots of a smile. I lift it up higher, higher, then let it come jerking down. When it moves, the rest of me moves. I am so alert to that thing in my hands and I am squeaky, I am exhilarated. I am a baby on a sunlit patch of carpet, holding a toy.

'Olive Oyl!' my Mum said recently when I mentioned this memory. 'You had an Olive Oyl doll at Gresham Gardens. A bendy rubber thing. But we left that house when you were a year old, darling. You can't possibly remember anything about being there.'

But I can.

In my family, I am the funny one – the one who remembers things she can't possibly remember, has sudden thoughts that go nowhere, asks too many questions, worries unnecessarily. Funny old Julie – the jumpy, difficult, strange one.

'you can't possibly remember anything about being there'

After Gresham Gardens, we move to another house just around the corner – The Chalet, 2 Middlebeck Avenue, Mapperley Plains, Nottingham. Now I am two years old and I have short fair hair with a red gingham ribbon tied in a bow but I am not sweet, I am sitting crossly on the little landing halfway up the stairs – behind me a window, with black metal and white paintwork – new and clean and glossy.

My tights are black and they itch me. I spend most of the time on my knees, though sometimes I come downstairs on my bottom as it feels safer. Don't want to fall. I am an anxious child.

The hall down below me has black and white lino tiles, which Mummy polishes with a strange whirring machine called a Goblin that has an actual goblin on the front. I like to sit and run my fingers over the little red creature, enjoying its raised-up feel, the hard plastic still buzzy and warm from being used.

I follow Mummy around as she does the housework. She says I am like a little dog. When my baby sister Mandy's awake, she's screaming or feeding and Mummy's busy, but when she goes down for a rest Mummy and I are pals in those afternoons of furniture polish and doll's clothes and prickly roses and the wet exciting smell of the paddling pool on the concrete patio, filled by a dark green hose on a hot day.

I have ideas. Sometimes these ideas make me tremble with excitement. I am four now and I sit in my place on the landing and make a Big Girl Box for Mandy who's getting bigger, even though she can't talk or do anything yet. In the shoebox, there will be: a crayon (not a wax one, which is only for babies), a rubber to rub things out, some paper, and one of Mummy's old pinkish lipsticks with its sugary, big-lady smell.

I rub a bit of it on Mandy and she laughs and I see that her nappy has got so fat that wet is coming down her leg. I show her how to scribble all over the paper like a grown-up. She won't so I try to make her but in the end she gets tired and crawls away and I shout at her to come back right now! – but she won't. It's tempting to hit her but I know that if I do she'll scream and then I'll have a smack bottom.

'she can't talk or do anything yet'

The dress I am wearing has no front or back fastenings and every time Mummy pulls it on or off me, I almost suffocate. If you can't breathe, then you die. Every morning our goldfish, Tish and Tosh, throw themselves out of the bowl and Daddy nearly steps on them when he goes down to make the tea. But he always puts them back in and they gasp back to life and swim off. Until one day he puts them back in and they just float. 'Too late,' he says. 'Sorry Tish, sorry Tosh, you've had it this time.' He sounds sad but you can tell from his face that he thinks it's funny.

Another day – by now I have two sisters – we are sitting in our wicker chairs in the playroom watching *Robin Hood* on TV and smoke snakes silently in through the door behind us. I begin to scream.

'The house is burning down!'

Mandy stamps and wails. Only Debbie dares run and find Mummy, who is chatting on the phone. She puts the fire out quickly – a whoosh under the cold tap. It's not much of a fire – just a thing she was melting down in a pan for Daddy, something to do with his work.

Mummy takes us upstairs where you can't smell the smoke and we have warm Ribena on the edge of our beds. I don't dare watch *Robin Hood* on television again for about ten years, in case it gives me the house-burning-down feeling.

Our bedroom is a safe place. On summer nights when I am in bed and it's still light, I like the sound of Daddy wheeling our tricycles in from the lawn, the slump of water as the paddling pool empties. Sometimes I kneel up at the window and watch. Something about the way he holds the cigarette between his lips, as he bends and uses both hands to tip the water onto the grass, makes me feel loved.

Next door are the Smiths. Luke is two and Jack is the same age as me, five. He's my best friend. We have our polio boosters together, a sugar lump on our tongues – same taste, same moment.

Luke is always lying on the bed having his nappy changed and he is ill. So in fact is Jack, even though they don't look poorly. We are not to mention it, Mummy says, and I don't, though Jack has already told me and we've laughed about it secretly.

Then one morning Luke is in his Mummy's arms waving to us from the bathroom window and the next day he's died. I decide I'll never wave to anyone again, in case I stop breathing.

Mummy is crying. I don't cry but I walk very slowly and quietly on tiptoes to show that I know something bad has happened. We hold hands and go round in a circle and sing 'All Things Bright and Beautiful'. Each little flower that opens, each little bird that sings. I ask Mummy where Luke is right now this minute and she says it's all right, he's in Heaven.

Jack and I are in the sandpit. He says it's for the best that Luke is gone.

'Is he in Heaven?' I ask, testing him.

He shrugs, lets the sand run through his fingers into a blue cup. 'At peace,' he says.

I laugh and so does he and then we wriggle around together in the sand and then he takes me inside and shows me a glass door in their house and says, 'Lean against it,' and I do but the glass isn't there and I fall through and bang my head and cry.

Dear Resident of 2 Middlebeck Drive

Please forgive this letter coming totally out of the blue but I'm a writer writing a biography of our Victorian house in Clapham, South London. I'm trying to find out as much as I can about every single person who has lived in this house from the day it was built in 1872, through to the present.

Because the book is about the idea of home and how we feel about the people who have inhabited our spaces before us, I'm really keen to go back and revisit my own childhood homes. I lived in your house in Nottingham as a baby, until I was five years old. I wondered whether you'd mind if I called in for a quick look around?

You can reach me by writing to this address – or else phone me on the above number and I will of course phone you straight back . . .

* * *

After more than two hours at the Family Records Centre, I can find nothing – no birth or marriage date or anything – for Charles Edwin Hinkley. Kelly's Directory tells me that there was Isabella Hinkley, Walter Hinkley, and Charles Hinkley. I've decided to look for a son but I remind myself that was always just a hunch. Maybe Charles is a father and I should have started with the older books. It's just so hard to know how far back to go. Hinkley is a fairly unusual name (Thank You, God) but the truth is I'm getting nowhere.

I give up, bored with Charles Edwin, and decide to try Isabella Bloomfield Hinkley. It's an imposing, rather glamorously Victorian name – a name that would fit inside a cameo brooch. She leaves the Kelly's Directory list in 1948, so, assuming she died in that year, I check deaths for 1948. And find her almost immediately, in the July to September volume: HINKLEY Isabella B 90 Hackney.

I flush with excitement and satisfaction. I've got her! But can it really be this simple – can this be her? Well, surely it's got to be – even if for some strange reason she did die in Hackney.

The truly unsettling thing is, if she lived to be ninety, then I must revise my whole picture of her. It means she was much older than I imagined – quite a late-middle-aged lady when she came to our house in 1918, just as the First World War ended.

I cross over to the other side of the room and check the births for 1859 – birth records for the 1850s are on satisfyingly thick, yellowed paper, curly handwritten. And there, in January to March 1859, I find her: Isabella Bloomfield, born and registered in the district of Billericay. This time, I feel a surge of real delight. That is definitely my Isabella.

Stunned and suddenly exhausted, I go to the room downstairs and sit and eat an apple, though an espresso is what I really crave. A white-haired woman, her hair zig-zagged with kirby grips, fidgets at a locker. She can't get the key in – 'I can't get the key in, Brian' – and various elderly men walk slowly up and down the room with loose change, ordered by their wives to fetch a bag of Quavers.

Isabella. Oh, Isabella. When I started my research this morning I had a firm picture of you lodged in my head. You were a slightly haughty, youthful, black-haired woman, a woman in your prime. Now in the space of an hour or so, I've uncovered an entirely different Isabella. A very old lady, living in Clapham, dying in Hackney. And an Essex baby.

An Essex baby with whom I have nothing at all in common – except that she grew up to inhabit the very same rooms, gaze out of the very same windows, in the very same house, year in year out.

From: John Pidgeon
To: Julie Myerson
Sent: Wednesday, April 7, 2003 9:17AM
Subject: 34 Lillieshall Road

Dear Julie
Leon is a lovely person. Ask him if he remembers playing snooker after school listening to Prince's 'Raspberry Beret'. I do. And the ceiling falling down.

Best
John P

I go up to Leon's old room. Jake's bed is unmade and there are used cereal bowls and half-full glasses of water all around it. On the floor are old discarded boxer shorts, school books with their covers half torn off, the silver discs of CDs, Warhammer magazines, cat fluff. School clothes are falling out of the open drawers. Kitty, Jake's cat, black and somehow angry, lies in one of the other open drawers among the socks, one open eye gazing at me. And the green eye of the Playstation glares at me from the opposite corner.

I pick as much as I can up off the floor and ask Aga, our Polish cleaner, to hoover the room thoroughly.

* * *

I'm in Nottingham, driving towards The Chalet, where I lived from the age of one to five. Whoever lives here now hasn't replied to my letter but we decide to call in anyway, hoping they'll be sympathetic.

We turn off Mapperley Plains – all of it unfamiliar – and drive slowly down the steep slope of Middlebeck Drive. This junction is where I first learned to tell left from right, in the back of Mum's pale blue Mini. Whenever I think of left or right now, this road is what I see in my head.

Middlebeck Avenue is exactly as I remember it – though it can't be quite because one or two of the houses look brand new. Dark purplish brick, clipped hedges, dwarf conifers, hanging baskets spilling with pink and scarlet Bizzie Lizzies. The kind of cul-de-sac where men wash their cars on Sundays, local radio on, soapy water spilling in the gutter. I recognize the house immediately, only it doesn't seem to be called The Chalet any more. Just plain 2 Middlebeck Avenue.

'You think anyone in this day and age would actually want to live in a place called The Chalet?' Jonathan says.

'No, but what I mean is, I think I wrote to the wrong person. I've got this awful feeling I wrote to 2 Middlebeck Drive, not Avenue.'

We ring the chiming bell and a tall, quite elderly and rather gentle-looking man opens the door and gazes at us, baffled.

Before I can begin apologizing for disturbing him and telling him who I am, I realize what I'm looking at. Just over his shoulder is the small first landing where I made my Big Girl Box. The same white banisters with their curly metalwork. I smile politely and explain that I am a writer (but inside I feel four – the itch of the tights on my legs, the sweet smell of Mum's old lipstick).

No, he says, he hasn't had any letter. I pretend to be mildly surprised.

He looks at me carefully, his lip trembles. He says he would love to show me round but his wife is very ill at the moment. He grips the doorframe and shakes his head. 'I'm grappling with so many problems right now, you see.'

I tell him I'm so sorry and that we'll of course leave him in peace. But he keeps us there, somehow unwilling to close the door. Scratches his head, tells me he's been here twelve years but he always thought that before that it had been owned by the same people – right from since it was built in 1959.

'Mac someone – the editor of the *Guardian*, do you know him?'

'The *Guardian*?'

'The *Nottingham Guardian* – I'm sure he was – oh my goodness, what was his name?'

I tell him my parents were called Pike.

'Ah. Yes, that rings a bell, yes.' He says he thinks he has heard of them. 'Pike. Yes. They must have been the first people then?'

I tell him I think we arrived in 1960 or '61. He's warming up now.

'The Smiths,' he says, gesturing at the house next door.

'Brenda? And John? You knew them?'

He nods. 'Oh yes, they're still there.'

'But – after all this time! – I can't believe it.'

'Oh yes, nearly forty years it must be.'

'And Luke?' I ask him suddenly. 'Their son? He was my age. Do you know how Jack is?'

I last saw Jack in 1971 when we were eleven. We decided to start an ornithology club. 'I like birds,' he said, quickly adding, 'the feathered kind.' I felt shy and couldn't look him in the eye. I had just started to notice boys and I saw now that he was quite good-looking in his slim blond way. We made badges out of cardboard with safety-pins stuck on, we had a meeting. Then we forgot to write to each other and that was that.

The man's face falls.

'Oh . . . both of their sons died,' he says. 'One died as a baby, the other was about sixteen, I think. Cystic fibrosis, wasn't it? I think they adopted a child – another boy – after that.'

The sky is getting greyer, heavy with morning rain. He apologizes again for not being able to show us round – another time perhaps?

I say I'd love to call again – maybe I'll write to him. He says that would be good. He gives me his phone number too. I look very hard at those stairs and that little landing once more before he shuts the door. As we leave I show Jonathan the space at the side of the house, where in my day there was a white painted door with a black metal keyhole.

'Jack and I used to look through that keyhole and see things. There was a huge lake, with people in bright coloured boats, canoeing. We'd watch them for hours.'

'But – they weren't there?'

'How can they have been? I must have made them up.'

'But you'd watch them?'

'All the time. Jack saw them too.'

As we walk back to the car, I wonder what I'd see, if I could look through that keyhole now. Dustbins? A dull narrow yard with a black drainpipe, or a huge shimmering lake? Or just the long-ago shadows of two small kids – a blond-haired boy and a brown-haired girl, running barefoot on a smooth green lawn?

Leon is expected at six. At five-fifty I'm still trying to finish a piece of work. Chloë is standing in my doorway in knickers and T-shirt, furious because I won't let her have her ears pierced.

'Just one hole, I'm begging you, Mummy – right high up, here. Look.'

'Please can we talk about this later? I'm still working and Leon Pidgeon's about to arrive. And can you put some trousers on?'

'Here! Look, I said! You haven't even looked – '

She clutches her upper ear lobe and rolls her eyes dramatically skywards.

'I Am Working,' I tell her, eyes firmly on my screen.

'I just don't see what's wrong with one little hole – one little hole in one ear, do you hear me? Oh God, I'm never allowed to do anything.' Her voice crumbles into a wail.

I give in and look up from my screen.

'I haven't said No. I've said you're only twelve and we'll discuss it later. And you're not making your case any stronger by bloody well crying.'

She tosses her long blonde hair and narrows her eyes. She looks like Jonathan when she does that.

'I'm a baby, apparently. Too babyish to get my ears pierced. Babies are allowed to cry.'

I push my door gently shut. 'Go away,' I tell her as softly as I can.

As if an explosive twelve-year-old wasn't enough, outside in the street someone seems to be letting off fireworks. Every time there is a bang, the dog (a tough, no-nonsense Border Collie who is not allowed upstairs) rushes upstairs and trembles on the landing. With each subsequent bang, she dashes one flight higher, till she finally emerges, flat-eared and with nowhere else to go, in Jonathan's study in the loft extension.

Jake walks her downstairs again, dragging her by the collar.

'When I leave home,' Chloë shouts, 'I'm getting holes everywhere – anywhere it's possible to have a hole, I'm getting one, OK?'

'Be my guest!' I shout back.

'And I'm going to draw all over my legs in biro now!'

She storms up to her room and slams the door three times and then once more.

Leon is tall and slim, with soft eyes, and a tentative yet open face. Someone you would notice in the street because he looks kind. Just like his Dad said, in fact: a lovely person.

'Come in,' I say but he doesn't. He just stands there on the doorstep and stares, speechless, and it takes me a moment to realize why.

'Is this really weird for you?' I ask him. 'I mean, even standing here? It must be.'

He tells me even walking down the street gave him the strangest feeling. 'I almost didn't recognize the house,' he says. He stares around him, at our Dulux Sexy Pink walls.

'Completely, totally weird,' he says. I like him immediately.

I get him a beer and we sit shyly in the sitting room, him still staring around, me wondering how to make him more comfortable. I wish I'd thought to light the fire, put music on before he came. To do it now seems forced.

We talk about the area – the house at 61 he used to live at with his Mum, the way he came and went between the two, the way he played football in the bit of driveway in front of the garages at the end of the road (where local boys still do), the fact that he didn't know that many kids in the area, but he knew a few.

Room by room, beer still in hand, I show him round the whole house. He's amazed by the kitchen, the way we've extended it over the yard. The size of it. I remember the pictures of him sitting in their old kitchen, near the cellar door with a dog. Layers of time and space. I realize that it's just as weird to think of his ten-year-old self in here as it is to imagine Isabella Hinkley or Henry Hayward in the same space.

The grown-up Leon smiles when he sees the cellar door – a thick wooden door without a proper handle. 'I remember that. You have to shove it really hard to open it, yeah?'

We go upstairs. He stares around my tiny study and peers out at the terrace and swears it's got smaller. In our bedroom – his Dad and Julia's room – he says he remembers the louvred wardrobe doors. 'I can't believe it. I never thought I'd see those wardrobe doors again – what I mean is, it's so weird that I remember them.'

The kids are all in Jake's room – Leon's old room. The boys are doing Playstation. Chloë is sitting on the floor with a Scrabble set, throwing the letters at the bed as if they're darts. She scowls at me, multiple body piercings clearly still dominating her thoughts.

But they all gaze at Leon with real interest and he looks back at them.

'Hi,' says Raph.

'Hi,' says Leon.

Leon looks at the boy in his room and Raph looks back at the boy in his and it's as if two childhoods momentarily collide. The kids can't decide how to react – is he a grown man or a little boy?

Chloë is the first to find something to say. 'Is it the same?'

Leon looks around, from windows to door, to mantelpiece. 'Kind of. It's smaller.'

'You're bigger.'

Leon considers this as if he's only just thought of it. 'It may be that, yes.'

I tell him how we used to bring friends up to see the amazing Tottenham Hotspur wallpaper.

'How come you were allowed to have that?' asks Raph straightaway.

Leon laughs. 'What, the wallpaper?'

'Yeah.'

'I don't know. I just was. My Dad . . . and then I grew out of it I suppose, as I hit fifteen. It would have become embarrassing if we hadn't moved.'

The kids keep on playing, glancing shyly at Leon. I get him to tell me exactly how the room was, where all his stuff was. He says he had the quarter-size snooker table right in the middle, the table on the wall that you could let down and had a train track running on it – the chest of drawers just at the end of his bed.

'If I had a friend to stay, they slept over there,' He points to the window corner. 'There was a Madonna poster over my bed just here.'

Jake registers this with a faint flicker of amusement.

'Jake likes Madonna,' says Raph.

'No, I don't.'

'He doesn't,' agrees Chloë, 'he likes Britney.'

'No, he doesn't,' says Raph, 'he likes Warhammer.'

'Because he's a nerd,' says Chloë.

I tell them That's Enough.

Leon smiles. I find his openness and enthusiasm very touching – the way he makes no attempt to be above any of this. In the room, he's just another kid who remembers exactly how it felt to live and sleep and play in here.

I don't especially want to drag him out of his old room but neither do I want him to feel he has to stand there any longer. I show him Jonathan's study – the loft we converted – and though he glances at the view, you can see he has no interest in being in this meaningless bit of post-Pidgeon space.

We go down and finish our drinks and then I put some pizzas in the oven for the kids and he doesn't seem to want to go so I give him another beer. He looks through the photos that John gave me – bends his head and really studies them. He seems absorbed, amazed.

'Just totally weird to look at these pictures while actually sitting here in the house,' he says, shaking his head.

The kids eat their pizza and show off. They all talk at once, throwing questions at him. It's finally dawned on them, I think, that he really did live here.

'What school did you go to?'

'Wix's Lane Primary.'

'Not Macaulay?'

'Macaulay was for the posh kids.'

'Did you used to play on the Common?'

'All the time, yes.'

'What's your sister called?'

'Lucy.'

'By the way, do you still support Tottenham Hotspur?' Raph asks through a mouthful of Roasted Vegetable Pizza.

'Kind of,' says Leon, and Raph nods sagely.

'I may switch from Liverpool,' says Raph.

'Just like that?' says Chloë, laughing at him.

'I'm just thinking about it,' Raph tells her hotly.

Leon finishes his beer and gets up to go. I ask him if he'll come again with his girlfriend perhaps? Or maybe when his Dad comes over? He says he'd love to. 'It was really good,' he says, 'seeing all this. It really meant something.'

As he leaves, I notice Chloë watching him intently.

'Wasn't he lovely?' I say as we load the dishwasher.

'You never asked him about the ceiling falling in.'

Leon Pidgeon's my first – the first person to come back to this house – and he's been relatively easy to find. But I wonder who else I'm going to be able to discover and lure back.

A Costello or a Blaine or a Spawton descendant perhaps? Will I ever track down Vincent Dias or Veronica Ricketts, whoever they are? And if I do, then will they even want to come back? People are unpredictable about that kind of thing. Some do and some don't want to go back and, especially now I've tried it myself, it's something I can understand. The past can be an unexploded bomb best left untouched.

I've been lucky with Leon – he seems to have only good memories of the house; and anyway, if you're only thirty, then childhood is perhaps still close enough not to be too much of a leap. But are the others going to have the same interest in going back into their adult pasts? I suppose it will all depend on what those pasts were like.

There are two Pidgeon photos I return to again and again.

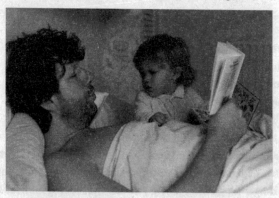

'hair all slept-on, reading a story to an absorbed toddler'

John, unshaven and sleepy, sitting by the old brick kitchen fireplace and cradling a very small newborn baby against his shoulder. And John again, lying back in bed this time, hair all slept-on, reading a story to an absorbed toddler in a yellow babygro.

We have photos of Jonathan doing exactly the same things. Shattered and unshaven, holding a day-old Jacob in a chair next to the same fireplace. The sleepy-ecstatic time after the birth of a baby. And lying back in bed in the same lilac and blue bedroom – a small baby sprawled on his chest.

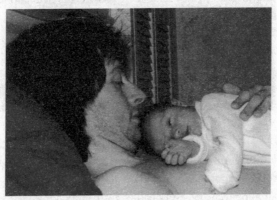

'the sleepy-ecstatic time after the birth of a baby'

Different men, different babies, different lives perhaps but eerily identical experiences played out again and again against the same back-drop. And only the house knows.

You think your life is the first – of course you do, you have to – but it's not, it's all been done before. We all go through the same motions, in the same way, in the same spaces.

You walk a baby up and down the room in the middle of the night, knees caving in with exhaustion as you desperately try to soothe it back to sleep. Someone else has done the same, felt the same, in the same room, years back. You light the candles on a pink and white birthday cake and kiss your child's sweet musty-blond head and dim the lights. It's happened before in this same room – a dozen or fifty or seventy years ago. Happy Birthday to You. And you, and you, and you.

'someone else has done the same, felt the same'

Every little gesture or whispered word, every burst of laughter or ragged sob, every tooth lost, every promise kept or broken, every sulky, door-slamming teenager, every baby's burp, every name tape sewn on, every brief, shuddery orgasm, every broken heart – life just repeats itself over and over. Past, present, and future colliding in a single house.

Lucy Spawton's birth and death certificates arrive in the post. Her parents were Elizabeth Spawton and Thomas Harlock Spawton and it says that he was a master draper and that Lucy was born in 1867.

It seems like a huge step forward, to suddenly have this information right here in front of me on the kitchen table, but I'm still not sure how to use it. How is it going to get me any nearer to finding her grandchildren or great-grandchildren who, let's face it, may not even be called Spawton any more?

The trouble is, I'm not like all those people at the Family Records Centre, launching their massed attacks on posterity. They're ploughing steadily backwards through time, trying to find out who their eighteenth or even seventeenth-century ancestors were. But it's descendants I want, not ancestors. I just have this single name, marooned in the 1880s, and I need to move forwards, not backwards.

'She was a drapery buyer,' I tell Jonathan. 'Look, isn't that amazing? It gives her profession on the death certificate.'

'Oh, but look at this.' He snatches it up and looks more closely. 'This isn't good news, is it?'

'What?'

'That she died a spinster.'

I hadn't even seen that. I'd been so absorbed in her profession, her age at death and her illness that I hadn't noticed that small word on the death certificate that changes everything. Lucy Spawton – who lived here in this house for so very long and who has to be so very important in my story – never married and, presumably, never had kids.

'Well, that's it then,' I sigh. 'I just don't know where I go from here. How am I ever going to find a single person who even knew her?'

I'm silent for a long moment as I stare at that horrid little word, handwritten in black ink. Spinster.

'Don't panic,' says Jonathan. 'You always give up too early. How about a will? If she didn't marry and she could afford to own this house.'

'We don't know for certain that she actually owned it.'

'OK, but she clearly had the means to live here. And she was a working woman. So she must have left either the house or her money to someone.'

'And you really think it's possible to find it? After all this time?'

'Definitely. Or, at least, all wills are in the public domain. Once they've been through probate, I know that.'

I look at Jonathan with interest. His father was a barrister and he himself is a JP so he tends to know about legal things. Actually, it's nothing to do with any of that. He just tends to know things.

'That's brilliant,' I tell him, 'because if I really can find her will, then it will tell me who her closest descendants are and that's what I most need to know. As long as they're alive, of course.'

'And if they're not,' says Jonathan, warming to his own scheme, 'then all you have to do is find their wills . . .'

'And so on! You know, I think we've cracked it. Why did we never think of this before?'

'Well, I just did actually.'

March 1980, a sunny Saturday morning.

John has just picked a grumpy Leon up from his mother's to take him to football practice, and he can't believe it when, heading off down the road, he sees a 'For Sale' sign going up at Number 34. Well, about to go up anyway. He stops the car – 'We're gonna be late, Dad,' moans Leon, but he ignores him.

He gets out and looks up at the house, dirty windows even dirtier in the shrill spring sunshine. It's not in a good state. The brick is drab and stained, the paintwork's peeling and the front door's hideous, with some kind of bobbly glass in the centre. Is it flats?

'Da-ad!'

'Just hang on a minute, boy, I'm coming.'

Squinting through the letter box, he can only see a dingy brown hallway, monstrous dark carpet with a swirly pattern, an orange door, nasty with hardboard panels over it. No signs of partitioning, though. He goes over to the bay window, overgrown with nettles and weeds, and peers into the front room. Ugly purple carpet in there, some kind of zigzag embossed wallpaper, a couple of threadbare armchairs, dark brown three-piece suite, a rubber plant that looks almost dead. Original fireplaces, though – pale marble, ruined by gas fires. And a pair of huge double doors dividing the room from the next. He bets they're the original pine underneath.

The guy hasn't even got the For Sale sign up yet. He's hammering in the post.

'Who's it on the market with?' asks John.

'ABC.'

'Where are they?'

'Acre Lane. Just past the traffic lights on the left.'

'You're not going to buy that house, Dad?' Leon is frowning and chewing his fingers.

'Don't know, I might. Take your hands out of your mouth.'

'It's awful. I hate it.'

'You haven't even seen it. You've no idea. And anyway, wouldn't you like us all to live in the same road? It means you and Luce could come round any time, whenever you felt like it.'

'What about Mum?'

'I don't think Mum's going to want to come round.'

'Would I have my own room?'

'You know the Spurs wallpaper we saw? You could have a whole room done in that if you wanted.'

'Seriously?'

As soon as he's dropped Leon off, John goes round to ABC.

He hadn't actually thought about another house in Lillieshall Road, but then again he doesn't imagine that Bubbles will necessarily stay around here anyway. And if she does, well, it really would be good for the kids. And he's always loved this bit of Clapham. Why should he be the one to move away? The house needs stuff doing to it, but he can already see its potential. In fact the idea of having to start again from scratch excites him.

ABC has only just opened. John had forgotten how early it was. The radio's on and the man's spooning Maxwell House coffee granules into a mug.

'Lillieshall Road?' he says, surprised. 'But that's only just been listed.'

John says he knows that. He fiddles impatiently with his keys. 'What's it on at?'

'Thirty-seven, I think,' says the man, plonking down his mug and rooting through a file. 'Yep, thirty-seven thou.'

John looks at his watch. Football ends in ninety minutes. 'Can I see it today?'

'You can see it right now if you like.'

'Anyone home?' The man from ABC gives a half-hearted shout as he inserts his key and pushes open the front door of 34 Lillieshall Road.

There's a smell of recent frying and something else, a sharp chemical smell – air freshener or cleaning fluid. John follows the man into the dark hall – stairs up ahead, two doors to the left. The carpet looks like it's never seen a hoover. Woodchip paper on the walls.

'Hello, there. Anyone in?' No one answers. 'Must be out. Do you want to just have a look around on your own?' The man yawns. Probably thinking of his Maxwell House, undrunk and cooling on the filing cabinet back in Acre Lane.

'Flats, is it?'

'No, but I think they let rooms out. There are a couple of lodgers or tenants at the top, far as I know. They've got notice to leave.'

'Who owns it?'

'Someone called Reynolds. But I don't think the owner's in the country. Mrs Ricketts is who I've been dealing with.'

'What do you think he'd accept for it?'

'She. You're thinking of offering?'

'I'll make an offer today.'

The man blinks his eyes as if he thinks John's sending him up. 'You haven't even seen upstairs.'

'Thirty-two? Do you think they'd accept thirty-two?'

A plump West Indian woman comes creaking down the stairs. She's wearing slippers, a low-cut top, gold earrings, and she's carrying a pile of dirty towels that she chucks into a corner of the hall. Behind her a teenage girl is standing in the shadows with a metal dustpan in her hand.

'My God, I did not hear the door, I am so sorry.'

'I think we have someone interested in the property, Mrs Ricketts.'

Chapter Three

THE WRONG GERALD SHERRIF, THE RIGHT THOMAS KYLE, AND THE GIRL WHO TOUCHED SNOW

Veronica and Doreen Ricketts, Alvin Reynolds,
Gerald Sherrif, and Thomas H. Kyle
1976–1980

So take a breath, Number 34 Lillieshall Road, and brace yourself, because you've jumped back in time now and – whoosh! – the homely white Leyland gloss from the Pidgeon era is gone. In its place, orange peeling paint and murky dimpled glass. Next door has not yet been attacked with a sledgehammer and surrendered its parts as replacements – that's still a few years in the future.

The hall's lost its airy, family feel and has instead gone back to being the dark, tired, melancholy place John Pidgeon saw on that first day, with its Anaglypta walls and a biro-written notice that says: Thank You For Wiping Your Feet – even though the doormat's worn to nothing and no one ever has or will.

Old cigarette smoke taints the air. Dirt and grit are trodden into the shag pile of the carpet. John Pidgeon was right – this house has never yet seen a hoover. The thick old stair carpet is done on a weekly basis with a brush and dustpan, a Bissell carpet sweeper used in the larger rooms. The dado is thick with grease and dust.

Look, Number 34, you're not so beautiful any more – not so much a house to fall in love with on a breathless late summer afternoon, more a bunch of rented rooms, a place where folk mark time, grateful for a key, a roof, a place to sleep and wait for luck and life to move them on to somewhere better.

Be brave now, Number 34. Say goodbye to the expensive conversions, the sun terrace overlooking the back garden and the terracotta tiles in the kitchen. All those loving improvements – the big glass doors into the yard, the pistachio bathroom with its great big mirror, the louvred cupboards in the bedroom and the giant, low built-in bed – are in the future. The rag-rolling and sponging and the ice-cream colours are gone, the holiday-bought kilims and the halogen lights. In fact, the latter aren't even invented yet.

But the big brick fireplace is back – oh no, sorry, it's not. Not yet. Waiting to be discovered by the Pidgeons, it's currently boarded up, suffocating under brown painted chipboard, a small gas fire with a row of weedy mauve flames lodged in its centre. A flimsy door separates this room from the draughty one behind that contains an old iron bath with a brown stain under the taps, a tumble, twist bathmat that could itself do with a wash.

The water takes ages to heat up but that's not your fault, Number 34: the Ascot boiler's on its last legs. A copy of the *News of the World* from a fortnight ago – its edges frazzled with damp – sits on the old washstand and the door in the corner leads to an old outdoor toilet with rolls of hard, shiny Jeyes Izal paper and a chain you have to pull hard to give a proper flush.

The brightly painted top back bedroom, Lucy Pidgeon's room, with its views over Battersea to the Power Station and beyond – that's dark and gloomy again, floored in lino. There's a narrow bed with nylon sheets, beside it a mahogany bedside table that's seen better days. On it, a bottle of pills, a pack of Rennies, a dusty copy of *Archbold on Evidence*.

Next door, no one's even thought about Spurs wallpaper. The grey speckled pattern on the lino can't really disguise the peppered scorch-marks of a hundred dropped or stubbed-out cigarettes. There's no central heating, just a paraffin heater or two – Andy's Gas delivers the canisters every Tuesday, though sometimes, if it runs out early, a teenage girl struggles back home with one from the petrol station at the end of Orlando Road.

It's a house of discomforts, a house of extremes. In winter ice coats the inside of the bedroom panes. In summer bluebottles fuss at the shabby wood frames. The curtains are grubby white net. What's the point in washing them when every other tenant is a smoker?

Sitting room, you're not sponge-effect apricot and lemon with matching curtains. You're just a dingy, dark room with a maroon-and-gold zigzag paper on the walls, a brown Dralon three-piece suite taking most of the space, the light draining as another crushing November dusk descends. Your antique stripped pine doors are clothed again – panelled over and painted sludge brown. Your carpet is purple with big orange swirls – cheery, someone thought at the time. On the marble mantelpiece, a lace doily or two, a row of Afro hair products, a wooden notice that reads: 'When God Gives You Lemons, Make Lemonade'. But there's not much sign of lemonade being made in here. In fact, let's be blunt. You're not going to be a sitting room for several years yet: right now, you're a lounge.

The tiny room on the first-floor landing – the room where John Pidgeon wrote his lyrics for Island Records and his book about Slade, and where I sit now writing this – serves as both kitchen and bathroom for the upstairs lodgers. It's been like this for thirty years. A bath along the left-hand wall has a wooden counter, which, when pulled down, can take a camping stove and pans.

There's a sink in the corner just big enough to wash up in, but mostly the gentleman lodger from upstairs doesn't bother much with cooking. Instead he just keeps a bottle of milk and some Crackerbarrel cheese in the fridge, a loaf of Slimcea in the bread bin. He'll stand in there, eating his lonely sandwich. Then he'll take a mug of tea back up to his rooms on the top floor.

Garden, get ready to lose your mature magnolia, your yellow climbing rose, your tangle of honeysuckle and jasmine and scented lilac, and your curvy, lovingly dug figure-of-eight lawn. That's still many summers, hours of labour, and eight dozen rolls of turf away. The cat sitting washing itself on the garden shed isn't born yet and the shed's still flat packed in a warehouse somewhere.

It's still some years before bees will hover and sip from your lilies, red admirals tip their wings on your lilac, and little kids will shriek and splash in a blue Early Learning Centre paddling pool while their mothers discuss local primary schools on a canopied swing seat. Sorry, but right now you're back to being exactly what you always knew you were: a scrubby, muddy dumping ground with a concrete path down the left-hand side, an apology for a lawn, and a few straggling clumps of dandelions and groundsel – and the charred remains of a bonfire down at the bottom.

So here you are, Number 34, on a dull Sunday morning in October 1978. Callaghan's Winter of Discontent looms. Downstairs someone is frying a watery slab of gammon. A radio is on – hymns playing, someone singing along. A tall man with greying hair is walking down the stairs, very slow, very erect. From upstairs comes the fizz and crackle of someone's television.

Jonathan has decided that the only way he can help me track down the still-living residents (whether that's Thomas Kyle or Gerald Sherrif or Stanley and Louisa Heron) is to send out massive, optimistic mailshots to all the people of that name in Britain. He's bought something called an Info Disk, the entire country's electoral register on CD-Rom.

'You see, if the name's rare enough, it's worth a shot. I can't try

Mavis Jones or even Vera Palmer – but Veronica Ricketts or Vincent Dias, no sweat.'

'But there must be hundreds.'

'Twenty, thirty of each. We'll get them.'

'So many letters?'

'You give up so easily. I'm telling you, we have the technology. I've spent the last two hours mastering the program,' he says, looking faintly annoyed when I glaze over. 'I think I can export the names and addresses from the Info Disk and then print them straight onto labels. All we have to do is stuff and stick.'

34 Lillieshall Road

Clapham Old Town

London SW4 0LP

ARE YOU THE LOUISA HERON WHO LIVED IN CLAPHAM
IN 1961?
DO YOU KNOW OR ARE YOU RELATED TO A STANLEY OR
LOUISA HERON?

25th April 2003

Dear Louisa,

Please forgive this letter coming totally out of the blue but I wonder if you can help me. I'm trying to trace a Louisa Heron who lived in our house (with Stanley Heron) in Clapham during 1960 and 1961.

I should explain: I'm writing a book which is a biography of our house (34 Lillieshall Road) in Clapham, South London and I'm trying to find out as much as I can about every single person who has lived in this house from the day it was built in 1872 through to the present!

If you are not the Louisa Heron who lived here, then I'm sorry to have bothered you and there's no need to get back in touch. But if you are the Louisa Heron (or if you know Stanley or Louisa Heron) who lived here, then I would love to talk to you – I could obviously travel to see you. I would love to show you the house now and also hear your memories of what it was like to live in then. It may seem like an odd request but anything at all that I can find out will be helpful (and fascinating!) to me. Even better, if you had any photos from that time then that would be wonderful . . . needless to say, you'll get a copy of the book which will be published in 2004.

You can reach me by writing to this address – or else phone me any time on the number above and I will of course phone you straight back.

With very best wishes and hoping to hear from you,

Julie Myerson

The kids help him stuff and stamp envelopes. Raph does his batch in front of the Test Match on television, sitting slumped backwards on the pink telly-end sofa, a bunch of envelopes and labels on his dirty knee, drained banana milkshake glass by his side.

Chloë takes a bundle of envelopes in a Sainsbury's bag and marches up to the High Street to catch the 5.30 collection. Betty goes with her, bouncy with excitement, holding her end of the lead in her mouth. 'Leave it!' Chloë orders and the dog immediately lets go of the lead and then, two seconds later, grabs it again.

The letter we send out is carefully worded. It makes it clear that there's absolutely no need to reply if you're not the one we're looking for. All the same, I come home next day to find thirteen messages on the answerphone from people apologizing for not being the 'right Stanley Heron' or the 'right Thomas Kyle' and wishing me luck with the project.

And then the letters. From a Thomas Kyle:

Regrettably I cannot help you in your search. My father was also called Thomas Kyle (Scottish like myself), as far as I know never left Scotland and Has Been Dead these 33–34 years . . .

A Gerald Sherrif says:

I'm sorry but I have never lived anywhere else but Carlisle and don't expect to as I am now eighty-seven, but I do hope you find the gentleman you are looking for in the near future.

A Stanley Heron goes still further:

About myself: I was born in Coxhoe and have lived here all my life. I am 78 years of age and would have returned your call but am not very clear on the phone and so I apologise for not replying sooner. I am NOT the person you are looking for and I have never been to Clapham ever. I am a retired chartered chemist and the only Louisa Heron I know is my granddaughter. I am sorry I haven't been of much help to you but please understand that I have AT LEAST made this effort to write to you today. If I HAD been the person you are seeking I would have been happy to supply you with any information I possessed but I am afraid I am NOT HE.

I wish you luck in your endeavours to find the RIGHT Stanley Heron . . .

Yours sincerely
Stan Heron

These letters and phone messages are peculiarly and unexpectedly touching. I realize that actually they're a part of what I'm trying to explore: the fact that all of us badly want to be part of a story, to be the Right Person, the One someone's looking for. Don't we all, at the end of the day, just want to connect our lives with the lives of others and experience that satisfying symmetry of time and place that comes from being notified, written to, called to account?

It's touching, but I'm no further on. I wait for the Right Gerald Sherrif or Thomas Kyle or Aston McNish to ring.

A warm evening. Supper over, Jake's loading the dishwasher – 'Do I have to?' – and Betty's rounding up the two younger kids in the hall.

She runs fast at one, then another, three short sharp barks as if she means business, though of course she doesn't. She has no idea what she means. She just likes the chase, the noise, the sense of cause and effect. Like when she rounds up the ducks on the pond in Battersea Park – swimming round and round in a circle, ears flat, until she has a flock of mallards clustered in the centre and then realizes she doesn't know what to do next. It's no good being a Border Collie in central London. Like being a trained heart specialist forced to clean bedpans in A & E.

I pour a glass of wine and wait till nine-thirty to phone a woman in Jamaica called Veronica Ricketts. When there were no Veronica Ricketts on the Info Disk, I remembered that John Pidgeon had mentioned he thought he bought the house from a West Indian. Jonathan looked up the Jamaican phone book on the web and handed me a piece of paper with the name Veronica Ricketts and a number circled in red.

'OK,' I yell down to kids and dog, 'you have to be quiet now!' I dial the number, wait.

The bleep of the phone. One. Two. Three.

'Yeah?'

'Excuse me, is this Veronica Ricketts?'

'Yeah.'

The line's crackly and there's an echo. I explain what I'm doing and ask if she's ever lived in London.

A pause. 'Don't think so, no.'

'In Clapham, London? I mean in England?'

'Nah.'

'You definitely never lived here?'

'Don't believe I did.'

'You mean never?'

'Uh – never, don't think so, nah.'

I apologize for disturbing her and she puts the phone down with a click.

'Well?' says Jonathan.

'She said she'd never lived in London.'

'Damn.'

'But she sounded –'

'What?'

'Kind of – like she was lying.'

He laughs. 'What? Why would anyone lie about a thing like that?'

'I don't know. She just – I don't know – I wasn't exactly convinced.'

'But, sweetie, you can't make a person say they lived here if they didn't.'

'I don't mean that. I just mean – what if she's the right one but she just couldn't be bothered, didn't want to talk to me, just didn't want to play?'

He leans in the doorway and folds his arms and thinks about this. 'Personally I think it's very unlikely. But anyway, even if you were right, what on earth could you do about it?'

I tip back in my chair. 'Offer them money?'

'Oh yeah? And then everyone you phoned would be rushing to agree that they'd lived here.'

'I hadn't thought of that.'

'You know, I keep on thinking about that man Leon in Jake's room,' Raph says a week or so after his visit.

'And?'

'I can't get him out of my head. I even see the wallpaper in my mind.'

I smile. 'Is this because you'd like some Spurs wallpaper yourself?'

Straightaway he shoots me an injured look. 'No, it's not that – except I would like some actually – it's just, um, I don't know what it is.'

'You'd rather you didn't know about him?'

'Kind of, yes. It's like he won't go away now. Even though I liked him a lot.'

I wonder whether to feel bad about this. I know what I've done. In some small way, by bringing the grown-up Leon back to the house, I've messed with the normal order of things and created a ghost: for my own kids anyway. The grown-up Leon may have been and gone, popping in for a beer and a chat – but the ghost of the child Leon is firmly back here now, sitting up under his duvet, kicking a ball around the garden, haunting us, reminding us. That room is one that Raph's taken for granted as his, as ours, since his earliest days, his babyhood. Have I done something terrible?

And is this just the beginning? Is the same thing going to happen with other – maybe less friendly or benign – people from the house? It's true that we stop ourselves thinking about the ones who've gone before. We have to, otherwise how would we ever be able to make our own lives fit those spaces? How would you sleep, cough, be ill, or even (or maybe especially?) make a baby in a room where you could feel all those other people down the years doing it, being it, making it?

'My only worry about if you let me get Spurs wallpaper,' says Raph, warming to the much more important subject now, 'is, I mean, can I trust myself? What if I suddenly switch teams again?'

A Liberal Democrat Councillor has suddenly resigned so there's a by-election down the road in Stockwell Ward. It matters deeply to the local Labour Party, desperate to regain control in Lambeth. Jake has been sent out to deliver leaflets and Jonathan is sitting in the kitchen, phone canvassing, working through each name on the electoral register.

'It may be a silly question,' he says, feet on table and phone to ear, as I come in, 'but I just thought of something. You have checked the electoral registers, haven't you?'

'I don't know. What do you mean?'

'Your big list of names of people who lived here, where did you get it from, originally I mean?'

'It's from Kelly's.'

'And what's Kelly's?'

'It's a kind of old directory of the area, like a telephone directory, I suppose.'

'But you should definitely check the electoral registers too. It might be more accurate for one thing.'

'I think Kelly's is pretty accurate.'

'OK, but you'd get middle names and so on.'

'Do I really need middle names?'

'I think you need every single bit of help you can possibly get, don't you?'

I'm not sure he's right. I'm not sure the electoral registers will tell me anything that isn't in Kelly's – and anyway I've no reason to suppose Kelly's isn't perfectly accurate.

Feeling slightly annoyed at the way he always has to know better, but also knowing that I can't possibly afford to miss a single trick, I go to the London Metropolitan Archives – conveniently just round the corner from the Family Records Centre – which is where you can look at old electoral registers.

But each year's register has to be ordered separately and you can only order five documents each twenty minutes and then wait another twenty minutes for them to be delivered up from the vaults below. I look at my watch. Ten to three. I haven't left myself enough time.

I came here straight from my exercise class and I have to rush back and collect Raph from a school trip at four.

I decide to work backwards from the Pidgeons and just see if I learn anything at all when, suddenly, there in 1980, as well as Veronica Ricketts, is Doreen Ricketts. And next to her name: 'Allowed to vote from July 10'.

Now this is worth knowing. July 10 has to be her eighteenth birthday – which automatically gives me a birth date. Doreen is a year younger than me. I almost run back past the scrubby stretch of park with its Sport for All tennis court, past Exmouth Market and back into the Family Records Centre.

A man moves his bag out of the way and tuts because I'm apparently moving too fast. I don't care. Straightaway I find her birth in 1961. Doreen Josephine Ricketts, daughter of Veronica Ricketts formerly Shirley. Straight to the green marriage registers and after only a few years there's a Doreen J. Ricketts marrying a Mr Webley in August 1984. I order both certificates, pay cash, and run to the tube, making it to school just as the coach pulls into The Chase.

Back at home, I type Doreen J. Webley into the Info Disk and up she comes, an address in Carshalton, though no phone number. Next day I send her a letter, recorded delivery.

4.20 p.m. A power cut. Jonathan and I are looking up random Hinkleys on the Internet – there seems to be an Australian darts player called Peter Hinkley though he lost 3–0 to T. Hankey of England in the 2001 World Darts Championship at Frimley Green. We're just wondering if he might be Isabella and Walter's great-great-something, when there's a huge electrical sigh and everything in the house switches off – *pfling*. Jonathan goes down to the cellar to check the fuses, but it's not us.

It's 6.30 p.m. and the power is still off. Jonathan cooks quiche and sweetcorn in the gas oven and serves it to the kids in the fast-descending gloom. They're dismayed – no Playstation, no TV.

'Oh God, what are we going to do?' moans Jacob.

'Gameboy,' Raph whispers urgently to his friend Seb who came over this afternoon. 'Phone your Dad and tell him to bring that and some batteries.'

Seb has just decided he's staying the night. Raph gets him the phone. I sit on the kitchen sofa, pushing aside school rucksacks, old socks and a tartan blanket covered in dog hair (this even though the dog is not allowed on the sofas).

'Dad, this is Seb. Can you bring my PJs?'

'Can you bring my PJs?' mocks Chloë from the floor where – on Jonathan's orders – she's sitting cleaning everyone's school shoes.

'Shush!' says Raph.

'And, Dad, there's a power cut so can you bring my Gameboy as well as my cricket stuff, oh, and the Tony Hawks PS2 game just in case the power comes on – '

'Thank you,' Jonathan prompts him. 'Thank you beautiful kind Daddy best person in the world . . .'

'Thank you,' says Seb, 'beautiful kind wonderful . . .'

'I really seriously can't see to do this any more,' says Chloë.

'OK. You'll have to leave it and finish later.'

'What if the lights never come back on?' she asks hopefully.

Jake sighs. 'There's nothing to do. This is a terrible day.'

'Oh for goodness' sake, you kids are so spoilt!'

'We're not spoilt, we just need a certain amount of electricity to function.'

'But you're children, not . . .'

'Electrical appliances,' says Chloë.

I get up and call the LEB. They tell me it should be back on by eight.

'Ah,' says Jake, brightening, 'in time for *Big Brother*.'

It's not getting dark but it's not getting lighter either. Jonathan lights six old pink candles he found in the drawer and the kids gaze at them as if they've never seen flames before. The room looks suddenly wonderful – their cross faces suddenly cross in a more intriguing and timeless way. Even the younger boys' nylon football shirts look almost attractive by candlelight.

I snatch the quiche crust on the edge of Jake's plate, and stuff it in my mouth.

By eight, there's still no power. I wander down the road to see whether the men can tell me what time it will be fixed – seems easier than ringing the helpline, which is frankly not that helpful.

It's a warm evening, not as dark when you go out into it – the sky still lavender grey, not quite drained of light.

'10.30,' says the black guy with the grease all over his hands. 'We're hoping 10.30. Don't worry – we'll get it back on for you in time for the Premiership.'

Why does everyone always assume you want to watch football? I look at my watch.

'Two hours?'

'We're doing your end of the road next,' says the blond one with the thin face and an earring.

I thank them and walk back down the road as slowly as I can, suddenly relishing the dark. The street is hushed, just the faint glimmer of a candle in some windows. It looks as though everyone is out even though they aren't. At the Tim Bobbin, long rows of different height candles line the windows. Beyond them, faces move in and out of shadow, laughing, drinking, talking.

Was this how it looked and felt in Henry Hayward's day? I suppose not quite, because they'd at least have had the gas lamps lit. Maybe it's more like the Blitz: total liquid darkness.

Ann at Number 28 seems to be sitting alone in a dark room, so I knock on her door to ask if she'd like to come round for a drink.

Ann has lived here in the road for years, since well before us. She used to work for a religious publisher and is retired now – tall, slender, white-haired, drives a pale blue car and always seems to have heard the whole week's output of Radio 4. She says she'll be with us in five minutes.

Meanwhile the burglar alarm at Number 30 goes off, its peculiar wail puncturing the darkness. The Calmans come out into the street, all dressed up.

'Oh dear.' Frances looks around to see where the alarm's coming from. 'If ours goes off, we're just at the Stepping Stone. Taking our boys out to dinner.'

Ann knocks on our door. Steps carefully into our hall and picks her way round Jonathan's bike in the darkness.

'All I've brought are my hanky, my torch, and my keys,' she announces cheerfully.

'That's all you need.' I hand her a large glass of red wine.

We talk about our house and the road and whether she remembers the people who were here before us – she doesn't. I ask her whether she knows how the road came to be called Lillieshall and she says she did once hear a story that there used to be a farm here and the farmer's wife was called Lily so they named it after her: Lily's Hall. Jonathan points out that there's a place called Lillieshall in Shropshire – isn't it more likely to be named after that?

'I prefer Ann's story,' I tell him.

'Yes,' he says, 'I thought you would.'

I'm on the trail of Lucy Spawton's will. I go to First Avenue House, the Principal Registry of the Family Division, High Court of Justice. A nondescript, government building on the north side of Holborn, just opposite Chancery Lane.

I put my bag through the X-ray tunnel and go past the lockers, where a woman is taking clingfilmed sandwiches out of a briefcase, and into the Probate Search Room – one large yet somehow terminally dingy room with shelves and shelves of hefty maroon volumes. Most people walk past, along to the lifts, to the rooms where divorces are fought and settled, though probably never truly settled.

The girl behind the counter in the Probate Search Room is plump with big earrings. She's talking to a man with food stains down his trousers. I smell the sour unwashedness as he shuffles past me. She eyes me suspiciously. I smile winningly and tell her I'm researching a book and ask her if there's any way you can look up a name alphabetically if you want to discover the year of death – or probate. She rolls her eyes and laughs. 'No way, lady.'

'I just have to go through every volume?'

'Yeah. Well, except on the computer. You know how to use a computer?'

'Of course.'

She rolls her eyes again. 'Plenty of them that comes in here don't.'

She tells me that probates after 1996 are on the computer – you just type in the name. But anything before that, it's a question of going through the volumes. She laughs to herself and retires into a back room, shaking her head.

There are no women in the room, only men, the food-stained one and another who must work here because he has some kind of an identity tag round his neck and fluffed-out white hair, and a couple of improbable-looking young ones in denim. One is chewing gum. 'Please Do Not Bring Refreshments into This Room' says a sign above his head.

I find the volume S–T 1944 and straightaway there she is:

SPAWTON Lucy of 34 Lillieshall Road Clapham Common London died 15 July 1944 Probate Llandudno 29 September to Barclays Bank Limited and Thomas Harlock Beesley Spawton bank clerk. Effects £4289. 3s 3.d.

Again, it's unsettling to see our address printed there. When, I wonder, will it lose its power to shock me? Also the 3s. 3d. It seems sort of futile and unlikely, to see each penny written down like that. I wonder how much £4,000 was worth in those days.

But, armed with this entry, I know what I have to do next. I have to find Thomas Harlock Beesley Spawton, who must be a nephew or brother. It seems pretty straightforward. Assuming he was alive and well in 1944, assuming that Lucy might even have left him the house, all I have to do is go through the S volumes from 1944 onwards, till I find Thomas's death – and see who he names.

The volumes are heavy. I don't care, it will be worth it. Food-stain Man is breathing next to me. I ignore him and press on. Amazingly, I've only got to 1948 when I find him:

> SPAWTON Thomas Harlock Beesley of 34 Park Hill Clapham London SW4 died 5 April 1948 Probate London 12 August to Midland Bank Executor and Trustee Company Limited and Matilda Spawton widow. Effects £5998. 19s. 3d.

That 3d. again. Feeling hugely encouraged – I now know where Thomas lived and even the name of his wife/widow – I go on to look for Matilda. Many volumes and aching shoulders later – 1962 – I have her:

> SPAWTON Matilda of 34 Park Hill Clapham SW4 widow died 12 September 1962 at Chesterton Hospital Cambridge. Probate Peterborough 29 November to Thomas Hugh Henry Stearn retired civil servant. Effects £16447. 7s.

Now I'm feeling quite excited. This means I've tracked Lucy's descendants as far as 1962, which isn't bad. And Park Hill is just past Sainsbury's, alongside Acre Lane – these people may not have lived in the house but they could well end up as part of my story, the house's story. I drop Spawton and start looking for Stearns in the books. Don't care about heavy volumes now – heft them hard and fast, this is worth it.

Sure enough – very soon after Matilda's death – here's Thomas Stearn:

> STEARN Thomas Hugh Henry of 23 Hurst Park Avenue Cambridge died 16 May 1965 Administration Peterborough 18 June to Laurie Stearn widow. £5108

How did Thomas Stearn get through so much money? I wonder. On to look for Laurie.

> STEARN Laurie of 9 Chaucer Rd Cambridge died 3 September 1971 Probate Ipswich 25 October £2071

But there's no one else mentioned, no other name given. A dead end perhaps? I go and sit outside by the lockers, suddenly deflated, oppressed by all these endings. An afternoon spent in this room finally wears you down – flipping through pages and pages of the deaths of strangers.

I eat a Bounty from the vending machine and look at a copy of the *Standard* that someone's left on the seat. Then I go back in and copy out Laurie Stearn's entry and show it to the girl at the counter.

'If you want to know more about an entry,' I ask her, 'what can you do? I mean, is there any further information about the will that I can get access to?'

She looks at me as if I am a complete moron. 'Well, yeah,' she says. 'The will.'

'But can I see that?'

'Yeah.'

'How?'

'You just have to order it.' She hands me a form. 'Costs a fiver. Takes an hour.'

I fill out the form and she checks it for me. Take it to the man, pay, walk out into fresh air and blue skies. I've no idea where I'm going, I just know I have to get out of there.

Outside, it's a normal day. It's reassuring to see living people – men and women in shirts and jackets, black skirts and high heels, walking furiously up and down High Holborn in the afternoon sunshine. I take deep breaths of city air and, after twenty minutes, go back in, through bag X-ray again.

The girl comes over.

'Are you Julie Myerson? Did you pay?'

'Yes.' I show her my form.

She tuts. 'But you're supposed to give that to me!'

I apologize profusely and she tells me the hour starts now. The man with identity tag and fluffed-out hair comes over to me, grinning. I smell his armpits as he moves closer.

'If you don't mind my saying,' he offers, 'the light's very bad in here.'

They shout your name when the will you've ordered is ready.

As the girl shouts 'Meerson!' pain zigzags across my upper back. I've pulled a muscle. I knew it. Too many volumes. Clutching my spasming shoulder, I go over to the desk and collect my will. Scanning it quickly, I see names and addresses – an executor, a witness, a solicitor. Fantastic!

I take it to a table where I can sit and read it properly. The will names Laurie Stearn's two daughters and three grandchildren. The daughters are Audrey Joan Clayton and Margaret Phyllis Askew, the grandchildren Robert Askew, Michael Askew, and Diane Askew.

I sit there and try to decide what's funny about that Margaret Phyllis name. Margaret Phyllis Askew . . . suddenly I know where I've read it before. I've been staring at it on a chart on my wall – it's on the list, the list of names from Kelly's. Margaret Phyllis Askew lived in the house! She lived at 34 Lillieshall Road sometime in the forties, with her husband Peter.

I realize I've just uncovered a fact I could never have guessed at – that the Spawtons and the Askews were related, by marriage anyway.

Which means that if I can find a living descendant of one, then I probably have the other.

Back home, with a bag of frozen peas clutched to my shoulder, I show Laurie Stearn's will to Jonathan, who expresses mild-to-moderate excitement at my Spawton-Askew discovery. He immediately starts looking up Askews on his Info Disk.

'There!' He prints off a list of Diane Askews. The one at the top gives an address in Brighton and there's also a phone number. 'Got to go out to an Environment Scrutiny Sub-Committee,' he says, glancing at his watch and finishing his cold tea. 'If I were you, I'd ring that number now.'

'Now?'

'Yes, now, what's stopping you?'

'But it's seven o'clock on a Thursday evening.'

'Best time to get people. Why do you think all those irritating sales people always ring at this time?'

He gives me a bossy look as he leaves the room.

I sit at the desk and stare out at the hot blue evening sky and bite the ends of my fingers.

If I ring Diane and it's really her, a real Askew relative, then what on earth do I say? I try scribbling a script for myself but it only makes me more apprehensive. I suppose the worst she can do is put the phone down on me. Which would be awful.

I fetch a large glass of wine and gaze at the will. I have to find Laurie Stearn's living relatives, that's certain. And call them. There's no way round it: if I can't do that, then I might as well give up on this whole idea.

Downstairs the children are shouting in the garden and the dog is barking. I shut the window and, coming back to the desk, I see something that even Jonathan hasn't noticed. The will was witnessed back then by two people in Cambridge – E. G. Harrison, housewife and H. P.

Harrison, clerical assistant. And in 1971 they were living at 36 Godwin Close, Cambridge. Could they possibly still be there?

I phone directory enquiries and give that name and address. I hold my breath and wait to be rebuffed. 'Here's your number,' goes the voice.

Feet thundering up the stairs. Chloë bursts in without knocking. Her long blonde hair is plastered to her face with sweat and little bits of grass are also stuck in it. Her eyes are dark with fury.

'Can you please tell those boys to stop kicking their football in my garden?'

I put down the receiver and explain that I've got difficult phone calls to make and must have peace – 'And anyway, are they really doing anything bad?'

She glares at me. 'Well! They've knocked a branch of blackcurrants off my bush and now they're starting on the rocket. So what do you think, is that bad enough for you?' Her eyes widen. 'And they're using a real football by the way, not the foam one you told them to use – just thought you might like to know that.'

I sigh. 'They shouldn't be using a hard ball.'

'You tell them that!'

'Can you tell them? Say I said so. Are they doing the stuff to your garden on purpose?'

She gives me a sulphuric look. 'What do you think?'

'Guess what,' I say. 'I think I've just found a phone number for someone who may know someone who once lived in this house! It's my first real breakthrough to one of the long-ago people.'

She folds her arms sarcastically. 'Well, how fantastically exciting.'

'It is actually – it's really exciting. But I need some peace to ring these people now.'

'Great.' Chloë regards me for a second. 'Thanks for caring about your only daughter's garden! I'll probably have a nervous breakdown when I'm older but at least you'll have got your fucking book written!'

She kicks the door once, before slamming it shut. She's not allowed to say that word. I should call her back. I shut my eyes and wait. She stomps downstairs as loudly as possible. I wait to check she's really gone and soon all I can hear are the boys' shouty-laughs and the small sigh as the house settles.

Before I can think of another reason not to, I dial the number.

'Yes?' It's a female voice, oldish.

'Mrs Harrison?'

'Yes?'

'I'm so sorry to bother you, you don't know me. I'm a writer and I'm researching a book about a house in London – my house – and I found your name on a will, as a witness, and wondered if you used to know someone called Laurie Stearn?'

'Stearn?' The woman sounds nonplussed and a little bit wary.

'Yes, I know this sounds odd but it was her will and I'm trying to trace her granddaughter, Diane Askew.'

'I don't know anything about any wills,' says the woman even more warily, 'and I don't know any Stearns, no, I'm not sure I can help you.'

It's the wrong person or the wrong Harrison or something. Could it be a daughter?

'But you know what,' she says more brightly, 'it's really funny because my next-door neighbour has a niece called Diane Askew. I know she does. Isn't that peculiar?'

'But that's her!' I almost shout. 'That's who I'm trying to contact.'

'What a coincidence,' continues the woman blandly, 'that she should have the same name . . .'

I want to reach down the phone and hug her. 'No,' I try to explain, desperate that she shouldn't hang up on me, 'it's not a coincidence at all. That's who I'm looking for – that's the person, that's her!'

The woman pauses. 'Well . . . Clayton is her name.'

'Audrey Joan Clayton?'

'Yes actually . . . how on earth did you know?'

'Well, it's complicated, but I'm looking for her too.'

'Come to think of it,' Mrs Harrison says, 'I think I might have witnessed Audrey's mother's will a very long time ago.'

'Laurie Stearn?'

'It might have been Stearn. Yes, oh yes, I think so.'

The room's suddenly hot, I'm sweating, my heart is banging crazily.

'Look,' I tell her, 'I'm so sorry to be disturbing you like this, but could you possibly give me a phone number for Mrs Clayton?'

Mrs Harrison hesitates. 'Well, she's not in right now, so you won't get her.'

'Oh, but – '

'But I know where she is.'

I wait. She's going to say she's out of the country or something.

'In fact, I can see her right now,' Mrs Harrison tells me. 'She's just out there in the street chatting to a neighbour. Do you want me to get her for you?'

I wait for what feels like ages but is in fact a moment or two. A sound of rustling and crunching as the neighbour comes to the phone.

'Mrs Clayton?'

'Ye-es?'

I say my bit again. Try to keep it simple. Explain that I'm writing a history of my house which is in Clapham and –

'Lillieshall Road?' asks Mrs Clayton, totally unprompted. 'I went there!'

'You did?'

'Oh yes, dear. When I was a little girl, in the 1930s it would have been, quite a few times. There was an old lady who lived there.'

'Lucy Spawton?'

'That's right, I knew her.'

'You knew Lucy Spawton?' I can't believe what I'm hearing.

'That's right, dear. She lived upstairs, you see, and there was this old couple called the Hinkleys – '

'You knew the Hinkleys?'

'Well, yes, dear, at least I only met them a few times I suppose but – '

Jake comes up the stairs, slumps on the landing carpet in stained school shirt, breathing hard, waiting to complain about Chloë. Furiously, silently, I bat him away, push the door shut with my foot, lock it. I hear him tut and slump for a moment with his weight against it, then turn and go back downstairs again.

'This is just so wonderful,' I tell Mrs Clayton. 'You see you're the very first person I've spoken to who actually knew these people.'

Mrs Clayton laughs delightedly. 'Really, dear? Well, it's nice to be able to be of some use to someone.'

I wonder how old she is. I ask her how old she was when she knew Lucy.

'Well,' she says, 'Miss Spawton lived there for fifty years, she was a spinster, you see, dear. And she lived upstairs and let it out to people, I know that. And when she died, I think it was during the war, she left the house to her nephew Tom who lived somewhere nearby – '

'Park Hill?'

'That's right! And when he died – not that long after Lucy, poor Tom – our Auntie Til sold it to a Mr Reggie Povah – that's P-O-V-A-H if you've got a pen handy and want to write it down, dear. And Reggie Povah was related to us by marriage, and he was sold it a little on the cheap on the condition that he didn't throw the Hinkleys out – they were old by then – but as soon as he'd got the house the horrible man put them in an old people's home!'

'In Hackney?' The day before I had received their death certificates and couldn't understand why, after thirty years spent living in our house, they had died in Hackney a year or so later.

'Yes, well, you see, I think he did it up and let it to Americans and Canadians. Oh, it was a horrible thing he did. I don't think the family really forgave him, you know.'

I think of those names through the forties – the Costellos, Rita

Wraight, the Blaines. I explain to Mrs Clayton that I know Margaret Phyllis Askew lived here in 1947.

'Yes, well, she was my sister, my twin in fact. She's passed on now. And she had three children and one of them, I think Diane, probably lived there with her mother and father. Diane lives in Brighton now. Would you like to talk to her? Shall I get her to ring you?'

Downstairs, Jonathan is back from his committee and has a phone in one hand, a beer in the other. Both boys are sitting on chairs in the kitchen doing a five-minute penalty for deliberately kicking a ball in Chloë's garden. Raph looks furiously sulky but Jake just looks resigned. Chloë is swinging on the swings, clearly relishing the sight of her brothers stuck on kitchen chairs.

'Guess what. I've just spoken to someone who knew Lucy Spawton and the Hinkleys,' I tell Jonathan.

He smiles and tells the boys the penalty's over. They rush out into the garden.

I tell him how Diane Askew may have lived here as a child with her parents Phyllis and Peter. And I tell him about Reggie Povah and Audrey Clayton calling him A Horrible Man and saying he threw the Hinkleys out.

'So we have a baddie?'

'It's a good story, isn't it?' I say – forgetting for a moment that this is all horribly real.

At about nine-thirty the phone rings.

'Julie Myerson?' says a crisp and rather focused voice. 'This is Diane Askew.' Diane says she's had a very excited phone call from her aunt.

'But I'm afraid I'm too young,' she says quickly, as if genuinely sorry to dash my hopes. 'I was born in 1955 and I never lived there. However, I've spoken to my brother Bob – he was born in '47 and lives in Manchester now – and he says he has 34 Lillieshall Road on his birth certificate. Also I looked in my box and it turns out I have a photo of his christening, outside a church with great big white pillars – '

'Holy Trinity? Or St John the Evangelist? That's on Clapham Road. Both have big columns.'

'Well, I don't know – which would it be?'

'This is wonderful,' I tell her. 'I can't say how much I appreciate your ringing.'

'Not sure if I can be of much help,' she says again. I tell her every word is gold dust and that I would love to talk to Bob.

'My aunt told you,' she says, 'about Reggie Povah?'

I say, yes she did, and I ask whether there's any way of finding out more about him.

She laughs.

'Well, he died quite recently,' she says, 'and he was a bit of a – well, let's just say he wasn't too popular in our family. But his daughter Alexa lives near me in Brighton. I see her all the time. I can put you in touch with her easily.'

In a daze, I make the kids tea and burn the fishcakes. Chloë carefully picks the outside breadcrumb bit off. I try to tell them what's happened – that today I've made a breakthrough. I've spoken to people who are related to people who actually lived in the house.

'Great,' says Raph, absently forking peas into his mouth. 'More people cluttering up my room.'

An hour later, Diane rings back.

'Well, it's all very weird,' she says. 'You see I've spoken to Alexa and I don't think she knows much, but when I told her I'd been speaking to you, she said she knows you and she's actually been to the house.'

'What?' I try to do something with this information but it makes no sense. 'Really? How do you mean, been to the house?'

'Your husband is a writer and director called Jonathan Myerson?'

I sit down. 'Yes.'

'Well, Alexa used to be an actress and she came to your house to rehearse something, with Philip Lowrie, who played Pat Phoenix's son in *Coronation Street*.'

'My God, yes, that makes sense, years ago.'

'So, do you see how weird that is? She's been in your house but without having any idea that her father once owned it. Anyway she's very intrigued about the whole thing and would love to talk to you – do you want her number?'

'Funny,' says Jonathan when I tell him, 'I knew there was something odd about that name Povah. I knew I'd heard it somewhere.'

'But what about the coincidence – of her coming here and having no idea about all of this? Isn't it just totally amazing?'

'It's the kind of thing you would say means something,' he points out, maddening in his refusal to be amazed, 'but that I would say is just one of those coincidences.'

'But this very house – of all the houses in Clapham? Of all the houses in just this one particular road?'

He shrugs. He hasn't got an answer to that.

Chloë's response is much sharper. She sits in the bath, pale, blonde, tired, turning the bar of soap round and round in her hands and then dipping it in the water to watch the suds float off.

'Maybe,' she says, frowning down at her wet body, 'maybe it's this: maybe buildings can draw people back to them. Maybe all the buildings we ever go in, our ancestors have been in before us and we just don't know it because we never find out those things.'

She looks up to see what I make of that. I tell her I like it as a possible explanation.

* * *

A hot afternoon. I put the dog in the back of the car and go to the Westminster Archives bookshop in Queen Anne Street. I have learned the lesson of the Probate Search Room and the electoral registers: there could be a whole lot more out there, I have to know where to look, how to look.

I buy six different pamphlets about researching family and homes – genealogy, how to use the newspaper library at Colindale, researching your family history on the web.

'Plenty of serious reading for you there, eh?' says the man with very thin white hands who rings them up on the till.

'Yes,' I say.

'Not that it's any guarantee that you'll find anything,' he laughs.

I get home and try to read the pamphlets but don't understand any of them, so I ask Jonathan if he can make any sense of them.

He gives me a beady look. 'What do you mean, make sense?' he says.

I show him the bit about newspapers on the Internet. Where does it say whether you can look at newspapers on the Internet?

'It says it here,' he says, 'and you can't.'

'Oh.'

The phone rings in my study. I rush upstairs and it's someone called Doreen Webley. 'I used to be Doreen Ricketts,' she says. 'Veronica was my Mum. I lived in that house in 1978 for a couple of years and, well . . .'

She sounds as if she's about to go on. I wait. She laughs softly.

'I remember that house,' she says.

I ask her if her Mum's still in this country.

'She passed away in May,' she says, 'in Canada. She had cancer.'

I tell her I'm sorry.

'I came over from Jamaica when I was sixteen,' she says, 'to live with her. Or that was the idea anyway. I was born over here, you see, but I only lived here about a year as a baby before I was taken back to Jamaica. So living in Lillieshall Road when I was sixteen was really my first memory of England.'

I ask her if these memories were happy and she hesitates.

'Ye-es. But I wasn't there very long. My Mum sold the house and moved to Canada because she was getting married to the owner of the house, you see.'

I take a breath. 'Alvin Reynolds?'

'I never met him though. She married him over there in Canada but, well, the marriage didn't work out.'

This is amazing. Weeks before, Jonathan had, jokingly, wondered whether the mysterious Veronica Ricketts was an Alvin girlfriend and I'd told him not to be silly. Alvin Reynolds was clearly married to Merciline Reynolds, as she appeared in Kelly's, though it was true that, after a few years, Merciline disappears. I ask Doreen whether she'd be interested in coming round for a chat.

'I'd be very interested to see the house again, yes, I'd love to do that actually.'

I ask her if she has any photos of her and her Mum from that time.

'No, none of us together, no.'

'Nothing?'

'I'm afraid not, no. I have nothing of myself at all. I might have one of my Mum somewhere. I'll have a look.'

Jonathan's mailshots – to all the Thomas Kyles and all the Gerald Sherrifs and all the John Costellos – are not producing the desired results. In fact, they have yet to elicit a single response. Jonathan, never one to admit that maybe he has wasted his time, has decided to crank things up a gear. He spends idle afternoons ringing all those who have numbers listed alongside their addresses.

'Hello, can I speak to Thomas Kyle, please? . . . Right, well, I'm sorry to bother you, this is rather a strange call, but I'm trying to trace a Thomas Kyle who once lived in Clapham in South London . . . No, the name Lillieshall Road doesn't ring any bells? . . . Right, OK, thanks, sorry to have bothered you.'

He does this again and again. He tells me that if he finds the right one, he'll immediately arrange for me to ring them back.

But the Info Disk throws up only the one Alvin Reynolds, and he's in Wolverhampton. He's the only Alvin Reynolds in the whole country so unless Alvin stayed in Canada – and, let's face, it he may have done – there's a good chance that this is the Right Alvin Reynolds. Which means I have to dial this one.

'Is that Alvin Reynolds?'

'Yeah?'

'You don't know me, I'm so sorry to bother you . . . it's just that I'm writing a book about our house in Clapham and I think you used to live here.'

'Not interested, sorry.'

He puts the phone down.

The weather has broken, much cooler, rain all night. Walk down the wet pavements to see Jo Bowyer, my osteopath, who's been treating my spinal scoliosis for years. Jo is not only a fencing champion, but also a member of the Bowyer family who owned most of this patch of Clapham for centuries.

Jo grew up in the Pink House – it seems to have no other address, marooned as it is right in the middle of our back-to-back gardens – but now she lives out in the country with her small daughter, husband, and a pack of hunting hounds.

Jo – who has frizzy blonde hair, an intriguingly aristocratic manner, and wears a leather biker's jacket over her whites – is the only person I know who can say 'hot bitch' with a completely straight face. It always feels somehow exotic to lie on her white towelling table in Clapham and hear tales of dead livestock and kennel maids, country schools and fêtes.

Today Jo says that my back feels different from usual.

'I can feel a lot of old, deep stuff from long ago.'

'How do you mean? How long ago?'

She hesitates, her hands under me. 'I would say, the late sixties. Mid to late sixties.'

'You can really pinpoint it to within a few years like that?'

If anyone else tried to tell me this, I'd laugh. But Jo isn't like that. She's honest, no-nonsense, even abrupt at times. If she has nothing to say, she says nothing. Which means that when she does say something I believe her.

'I'm good at putting ages on things,' she tells me flatly. 'I would say this is 1966/67. What was going on in your life then?'

'You mean did I have any accidents?'

'It can be anything – accidents, illness, emotional stress, whatever.'

I tell her – truthfully – that my childhood before my mother left my father (when I was twelve) was really very happy, very settled. They started fighting about two years before she left, so I suppose from 1970 onwards I may have had a tougher time, though I don't especially remember it like that.

'No,' she says, 'this is earlier. How old were you in 1968?'

Eight. I was eight.

I am small, skinny, nervy, wearing corduroy, reading Blyton and Nesbit, hating gym, frightened of the dark, of wolves, of the taste and texture of toothpaste. Frightened of everything, in fact. At school I am so shy I spend each playtime facing the wall in the corner of the playground, gazing at the velvety moss landscape and picking at the crumbly sandstone with my fingernails, hoping no one will speak to me.

We live close to school in a bungalow designed by my mother. There's a swing and a tree house and fairies who live in the bluebells at the shady bottom of the garden, and something my father has always dreamed of having – an indoor swimming pool.

'There was one thing,' I tell Jo. 'We had a swimming pool in our house – just a small one – but I was absolutely petrified of water.'

'Oh?'

I tell her about my daily dread – that we were all supposed to have a swim after school. My sisters couldn't wait to have their armbands blown up and jump straight in, but just the feel of the armbands inflating terrified me. I used to stand in a corner and tremble and cry.

'I thought I would drown,' I tell Jo. 'I didn't think I'd float.'

She asks me if they ever forced me in. I tell her I don't think so, they were very patient.

'I think it was me. I was very

'I didn't think I'd float'

difficult,' I tell her, and I laugh then because I remember other things.

'What?'

I explain to her how, in the same bungalow, my father had a workshop full of chemicals to do with his work (he had a small, two-man plastics factory) and that he once put some polystyrene in a beaker and let it set. Later I tiptoed into his workshop and secretly licked it because it looked exactly like the froth on beer. He then mentioned to me that it was poisonous and I didn't dare tell him I'd licked it, but I was convinced I was going to die.

'What did you do?' Jo asks me.

'I went and sat in the garden with my dog and waited to die.'

After the session, I drive Chloë to tennis practice and we discuss the way fear can affect your body.

'I used to be very scared of the shower,' she tells me, 'but I don't give it any thought now.'

'Hey, I remember that. You used to scream and scream.'

She giggles at the memory.

'And then one day you just didn't.'

'Mmm, I suppose.'

'But do you feel we helped you? Or did we make it worse? Did we used to get cross with you?'

'I can't remember,' she admits happily.

I still remember every moment of the indoor swimming pool. The sunshine wavering over the bright blue water and making juddery patterns on the turquoise tiles. The ominous odour of chlorine, the white ledge you clung to, the decorative dried starfish on the wall – an emblem of terror for years afterwards.

I turn right down Nightingale Lane and ask Chloë how she got over it, the fear of the shower. Does she remember?

'I suppose I just realized it wasn't very rational,' she says, inspecting a scab on her knee.

Doreen Webley is a couple of years younger than me, gentle, quiet, neatly dressed in white shirt and long denim skirt. She comes through the hall and says she doesn't remember it being so narrow. I apologize for all the boxes piled by the door.

'It might be that or it might just be that I've got that bit wider,' she laughs.

We sit and drink tea at the kitchen table. She talks quietly, haltingly, but she offers information without my having to ask questions. I'm impressed by her directness. In the end I put my pencil down and just listen.

'I came in the summer of seventy-eight. I was sixteen. I didn't know my Mum at all – she'd left me in Jamaica when I was two and I hadn't seen her since. I'd been pushed from relation to relation over there, but the aunt I was living with got fed up with me and decided it was time my Mum had me back. So I was sent over here. I'd been in the middle of O levels in Jamaica so I had to try and find somewhere to carry on. My Mum couldn't get me into school anywhere so

I enrolled at Vauxhall College and managed to get a few passes.'

I ask her what her Mum was like to live with and she gazes down at her tea. 'To be honest, we didn't have a very good relationship. I think she resented me being here.'

'And your Dad?'

'He lived nearby. But I didn't meet him at all till I was eighteen. He was OK, his house was a bit more relaxed. I went round there a bit but my Mum got jealous if I went too much.'

'But she didn't really want you here?'

Doreen shakes her head.

'To be honest, my memories of this house weren't all that happy. I was on my own a lot. I had a lot of chores to do. My Mum used to shout at me if I didn't get them done quick enough. She took in sewing and she spent all her time here in this kitchen we're sitting in now. There was a window over there and she'd sit in a chair and sew. She was really just biding her time, I suppose, waiting – to sell the house and go out there to marry Mr Reynolds.'

'And there was no question of you going to Canada with her?'

'No.' Doreen glances shyly up at me. 'I did used to think, Why are you doing this? I mean I only just got to know you and you're going off again. But, well.'

I ask who else was in the house.

'Just my Mum and me. And Mr Kyle upstairs.'

'What was he like?'

'Nice. Elderly man, white, very quiet. He was a solicitor. He helped me out once actually . . .' Doreen hesitates and smiles. 'When I got into a bit of trouble.'

'What sort of trouble?'

'I got done for shoplifting.'

When it finally happens, her belly goes hot, soft. She feels her insides are falling out of her. She can't believe it – that she could be so stupid.

She can't believe that ever in a million years she'd be the kind of person capable of doing something like this.

But Leia isn't either. Or you wouldn't think so anyway. Quiet, pretty Leia, from Mauritius, her first proper friend in this country. Leia cheers her up so much that she realizes how lonely she's been all this time. They work at the hospital on Portland Place together, wheeling the trolleys, taking the food around the wards, chatting all the time.

Right from the first day, Leia decides they're friends and shows her stuff – the best toilet for a quick smoke where you won't get caught, the dodgy drinks machine that sometimes gives you back extra change – jackpot! Leia makes her laugh and Doreen far prefers this to her college life. She's out all day so her Mum can't pick on her. She feels like she's turned into somebody, like she knows who she is.

She has to leave at eight to get the tube to Oxford Circus, but pretty soon she starts leaving earlier and earlier, just to get out of the house. She likes walking up to Clapham Common station in the grey mist – sometimes you can hardly see across the Common and she finds that a bit magical and mysterious. She finds it a real thrill arriving on Oxford Street before the shops are open, walking up and down in the November chill and gazing into windows, listening out for the scrapy clang of someone pulling up a grille, watching the women in their posh coats walking briskly past. Everyone seems to have somewhere to go and she likes that, likes the hurry and certainty of it.

'Hey, you know what, let's meet up, before work,' Leia says, 'have a coffee, look around the shops together.'

Their shift starts at 9.45 and Debenham's opens at 9. As soon as the security man turns the key in the big glass door, they're in – milling swiftly through with the other shoppers. Doreen loves the big stores – the whirr as the escalator starts up, the smells you'd never get in Jamaica: powdery wafts of perfume made sweeter by the cold air, a blueish whiff of bus exhaust from the street outside, the cleanness of plastic bags.

One morning as they walk out, Leia takes her round the corner and leans back against a wall, lights a fag, then thrusts her bag at Doreen.

'What?'

'Look. Inside.'

In there among Leia's familiar stuff that Doreen's seen a million times before – her purse, her ciggie packet, her keys – nestles a silk scarf. Green with horses on it. Price still on: £7.99. It takes Doreen a moment to understand.

'You – didn't?'

Leia laughs and breathes out smoke. 'Didn't see, did you?'

Doreen shakes her head and her heart thumps. She's not sure what to feel. 'Why? Aren't you scared?'

'First few times I was, but I'm better at it now. That scarf, I tell you, I send it home to my Mum and she can sell it just like that.' Leia snaps her fingers. 'Buy something for the babies.'

I pull out a heavy black register, slam it down on the sloping counter, look through the wavering list of typed names, fail to find what I'm looking for and slam it back.

It feels like I've been living at the Family Records Centre for the last two weeks. I've looked for the Costello (Amy and John 1951–58) marriage from 1910 to 1950 and found nothing. I've looked for children born to Aston and Melda McNish (1959–68) and found no one. I've checked the death registers for Salome Bennet and the marriage registers for her as well. Where did all these people go? Quarter after quarter, year after year, I check down the list of names – Blaine, Hibbert, Russell, Wraight – find nothing, heave it back on the shelf.

It's hypnotic. Just half an hour of gazing at births, marriages, and deaths can send you into a fugged trance and you can forget what you're looking for. Amy who? Theodore what? And it's arduous – an hour of standing up and opening and shutting volumes still makes my shoulder hurt. And, sometimes, dull. There are, let's face it, so many dead ends.

Which maybe explains why everyone here seems so bad-tempered. There's not much goodwill. If the edge of your volume touches the edge of someone else's, it's a sharp tut, a look of fury. Register rage.

'Sorry,' I whisper as a steely-haired woman makes it clear I'm encroaching on her death register space. 'Perhaps I'd better go round the other side.'

'Yes,' she hisses, 'perhaps you had.'

Downstairs by the lockers it's worse. There are machines where you can put in money and watch the electronic arm grab you a bag of crisps. There's Max Pax coffee. But most people sit morosely munching their home-made Dairylea and cucumber sandwiches and staring into space. I wonder whether, when they go home, they're any more satisfied with their day's explorations than I am.

The first time she does it, she isn't caught. Rimmel nail varnish from Boots, Cherry Pie. Actually she doesn't even dare take the new one, she steals the tester. Leia cracks up when she sees it, the neck all gunky with dried varnish.

'A used one? What's the point of that?'

Doreen doesn't know. Doesn't know why she did it either. At least Leia's sending the stuff home to help her Mum. She doesn't have anyone to send stuff home to.

Back at Lillieshall Road, her Mum shouts at her all the time. One day, she's doing her chores, brushing the stair carpet for two flights – just their bit of the house, not Mr Kyle's – and her Mum complains that she isn't doing it properly.

Her Mum phones up her sister in Tottenham. 'I can't cope with this stupid, lazy girl,' she yells down the phone. 'Don't see why I have to have her living here!'

Her Mum's sister must have said something to her because her Mum calms down a bit after that, but she doesn't speak to Doreen for a few days.

But two days later she goes into Debenham's with Leia and puts the ring on her finger – just a piece of costume jewellery, nothing really valuable – and just as she's walking out of the store, a woman comes up to her and stops her. 'Excuse me, but can I see your hand?'

Doreen takes her hand out of her pocket and bursts into tears. She looks around for Leia but suddenly Leia's gone. There's only a crowd of people holding onto their bags and staring.

Mapperley Park, Nottingham. A place I lived when I was six, seven, eight, nine. A discreet and leafy area where doctors and solicitors lived, and probably still live. A place my parents moved to, even though my father had left school at fifteen and did vacuum-forming and hot-foil blocking for a living.

But his family had money – money from the hosiery factory his grandfather had established. In fact he'd grown up in Mapperley Park, in a huge house with servants and a heron in the garden. So in 1966, he and my mother bought a piece of land and she designed the exact house they wanted – a long, spacious bungalow with a swimming pool.

I ring the bell and a shadowy figure bends at the opaque glass door, a bolt is slid back and a fifty-something lady with short neat hair stands there. She says she got my letter and would have given me a ring only she'd lost her voice. Laryngitis.

'Come on in,' she says and a moment later there I am, in the hall, our old hall.

It's the same but – what's different? The sheet of opaque glass partitioning it off from the sitting room? I remember it as being a lot more open, bigger, wider . . . but then, like Doreen Ricketts, I was probably smaller. This is the hall where my sisters and I used to run around and chase each other – the space where we'd strip naked and dump our clothes – vests dyed pale pink in the wash, white cotton knickers, thick jumbo cord trousers with elastic waists – and jump up and down the steps and run around the open-plan chimneypiece until we almost sobbed with laughter.

I don't tell the lady this.

'So . . . now we finally get to see your famous indoor swimming pool,' Jonathan teases as we shake hands with the lady's husband.

'I'm afraid we covered it over,' he says. 'It was unused when we came here twenty years ago. But it's still there, underneath – it could certainly be used again,' he adds, as if we might be about to produce costumes and towels.

They take us in and show us that the room is now a hobbies room – computer, easels, filing cabinets.

'She does watercolours, I do oils,' explains the man. 'We came down here from Yorkshire originally – brought some culture to the place!'

He laughs at his own joke, and so do I. Then we all stop and gaze tenderly at the room that has the pool innocently lurking underneath.

'Quite a small pool, then,' says Jonathan, and we all agree that, yes, goodness, it must have been tiny.

'Three strokes of that and you'd be at the end before you'd started,' says the man, and I agree, but the truth is it doesn't look that tiny to me. In fact even now it looks the size I always remembered it – big enough to drown in.

We all go into a little room on the left of the hall, my father's old workshop.

'Now I used to wonder what this room was used for,' says the man, who seems to be warming up and rather enjoying our surprise visit. 'There were all these plug sockets, a dozen or so of them, halfway up the walls.'

'It was my Dad's workshop,' I tell him. 'He had all sorts of equipment in here. Lathes and vices and drills and things. He used to build and fly model aeroplanes. For about two months in 1950, he held the world record for it.'

'You know I thought so!' he tells his wife. 'Remember? I said there had to have been work benches in here, didn't I? Judging by the height of those sockets.'

I look around the room with its calm rectangular view onto the neat garden. A bird table, a row of conifers, marigolds, a rockery.

My father must have spent so many hours in this small room – but there's nothing here at all, nothing left, not even a feeling. This small, white, unremarkable room certainly doesn't feel like the scene of my fake froth incident, my brush with death.

'We had all those sockets taken out,' the man explains, 'the high up ones. They weren't any use to us. I mean how many sockets does one room logically need?'

'By the way,' my father said, appearing noiselessly back in the room, 'it's poisonous, that stuff. So don't go putting it in your mouth or anything.'

A flush of fear lit up inside me. Poison. I had just licked something poisonous. My heart tilted, thumping so hard I felt it in my ears.

'Though I suppose we could have left one or two,' he continues, 'might have been useful sometime. Still, we haven't missed them, I have to admit. And once the wiring's there, you can always put them back.'

I ran to the bathroom and washed my mouth out again and again, then I cleaned my teeth with Signal toothpaste, and then sat in the garden and waited to die.

We walk into the room I shared, aged six, with Mandy – a smoothly tidy room with twin beds and a neat vase of dried flowers and a wash-basin that I don't think used to be there.

'We use this as a guest bedroom, now that our kids are all gone,' says the man.

'When we left this place, I was so sad to go that I kissed these walls.' I show them the place by the door where I remember putting my lips. 'I suppose I thought I'd never see them in my life again.'

'And here you are,' says the man in a voice touchingly bereft of irony.

* * *

Doreen is let off with a caution. Her Mum refuses to come to the station but her Dad is there. He's not too pleased but he's OK about it. He never shouts at her like her Mum.

But her friendship with Leia cools a bit. Leia tells her she's not going to do it with her any more – 'You're hopeless at it, Dorey, you can't hide anything, you look too guilty all the time.' She tells Leia she doesn't know how she looks so level-headed when she's actually nicking stuff.

'I don't think about it. They only see you if you think guilty things while you're at it.'

In the past two weeks, Leia has pinched four pairs of tights, a plastic jar of body cream, a spandex vest, a top, and a pair of bronze leather slippers to send back to her Mum. She even pinched some stamps to post them with, from the handbag of a lady who is in the hospital for her cataracts.

For a while she and Leia don't meet up in the mornings. Doreen still leaves home early but she goes back to meandering the streets, staring into shop windows. Sometimes she gets fed up with that and buys the paper instead – the *Sun* or the *Mirror* – and sits on a bench and reads it, has a smoke. She doesn't like it when the pigeons come pecking round her feet, kicks them away.

One day a drunk man, not that old, comes and sits next to her and she gives him a fag, but then he tries to get too close and she can smell the fumes coming off him, so she has to walk away. But it's nice to talk to someone. Her Mum doesn't like her smoking but her Dad can't see the problem. It's one of the things they do together, have a smoke.

But then one morning she runs into Leia outside Top Shop and Leia says, why don't they go in together? Abba is playing. 'Take a Chance on Me'. After ten minutes in there, Leia gives her two bags to hold and she flinches because she just knows there's pinched stuff in them.

Next thing she finds herself doing – she's no idea why – is she's whipping a tartan skirt off the rails and stuffing it into one of the bags. It may not even be her size, in fact it looks like a skinny one. It's just that she likes the look of it and there's no one watching and there's something about being with Leia again and the big empty shop, the music: it's comforting, it lulls her.

'*Money money money, must be funny, in a rich man's world.*'

She'd been so sure there was no one looking.

She knows before it even happens that they're going to catch her. The hand on her arm. Cold hand, trembling arm. Her stomach moving up into her chest and then falling too fast back down again. And her feeling so sick that she has to sit down right there on the floor, and people all around looking at her and the crackling radios coming closer across the shop floor. And her realizing that Leia is nowhere around and she still has the two extra bags she was given to hold. And she can already hear, clear as anything, the words her Mum will have spat out before the day is over: 'You silly cow. What did I do to deserve you? Why did I ever let you come back here and muck up my life?'

Holy Trinity fête. A bright afternoon, cloudless and warm – the band playing 'Daisy Daisy'. Pushchairs and dogs and kids and women walking slowly in floral patterned dresses. Marmalade and chutney and marigolds and Bizzie Lizzies for sale. It could be a fête of fifty or seventy years ago – except for the displaced chunks of Amstrad and Apple and McDonald's plastic giveaways being sold on the bric-a-brac stall, along with second-hand paperbacks by Colleen McCullough and Joanna Trollope and plastic blonde-haired dolls with crocheted skirts to put over loo rolls.

Our children take one look around and immediately demand money. We give them 60p each and they return five minutes later, hot and sweaty and clutching new bits of junk. Several cheap china ornaments (Raph), red liquorice bootlaces (Chloë), a bag of Haribo sweets (one each).

David Isherwood (vicar of Holy Trinity and our school vicar) comes over and tells me he's seen something amazing in *Country Life* –

something that will help with my research. 'What?' I ask him, intrigued.

'No, no,' he says with a wave of his hand, 'I'll e-mail it to you. There's other stuff too.'

We round up our kids. I buy three pink dahlias at the flower table, even though it's barely worth planting them because the slugs will eat them straightaway.

'Just leave them on a plate,' suggests Chloë, 'with some after-dinner mints and the bill.'

Back at home, there's a message winking on my machine. An elderly, cigarette-scorched voice.

'Hello, dear, are you there? My name's Mrs Creed. That's Creed – C-R-E-E-D. I might be able to help with your book, dear. I lived at 27 Lillieshall Road, you see – I was born there and I left when I married in 1952.'

After that message, another one: 'My name's Lorraine Creed, Mrs Creed's daughter – she saw your bit in the *South London Press* and wonders if you'd like to talk to her. She's worried she hasn't rung the right number – anyway here's her number again just in case.'

I call Mrs Creed back. No reply.

'And Mr Kyle represented you in court?'

'Yeah. He was a nice old gentleman, very kind. I used to snoop around his room sometimes when he was out. And I remember he used to keep his milk in the fridge in the little room on the landing. He came and offered to help me out, do the case. It was in Euston somewhere. I got a twelve-month suspended sentence.'

'Did you ever do it again?'

Doreen smiles. 'No. I don't honestly know why I did it. It was a cry for attention, I suppose.'

I now understand why she has no pictures of her Mum and her together.

'I have one of me, in Jamaica I think, standing on a chair when I was little, about two years old. But no one ever took any pictures of me after that.'

'Never?'

She looks at me. 'Why would they?'

I ask her if she ever saw her Mum again.

'Yes. About ten years later when I'd been married and separated and already had two of my kids, Samantha and Karl, I was talking to my aunt on the phone and suddenly my Mum comes on. I was pretty surprised. We'd sent cards and stuff to each other and that, but I hadn't spoken to her in years. She asked me to come and visit her where she was staying in Tottenham, but I had these young kids and I said, "No, Mum, you come to me."'

'And she came?'

'Yeah. And you know what? I was feeling quite strong by then, a bit older and angrier, I suppose. And I confronted her.'

'What did you say?'

'I can't remember it all but I know I said stuff like, Mum, why did you ever have kids? And she said, Well, you know it just happened, and I said, Yes, sure, but haven't you heard of contraception?'

'What did she say to that?'

'Nothing much. She just shrugged. She hadn't come over to see me anyway. It was some religious convention – she was into Pentecostal religion by then. I didn't see her again till she was dying in Canada and my Dad gave me the money to go and see her. He said, "The way I look at it, Doreen, I haven't given you much in your life, so I don't mind paying."'

We look around the house together and she shows me her old room – our bathroom. She looks around admiringly at our great big white bath and brightly coloured Italian tiles and fitted cupboards and I experience a brief moment of shame.

'My bed was here,' she says, indicating the corner of the room where the loo is now. 'It had a quilted headboard, you know, with lights in it. But lino on the floor and that winter of seventy-eight, my first winter here, I remember being so cold in here. But there was something wonderful, do you know what?'

She turns to our bathroom window – the sash window we leave open in summer for the cats to jump in and out.

'This windowsill,' – she puts her hands on it – 'this is where I first touched snow. I woke up in the night and it was falling and I couldn't believe it and I opened the window and put my hands on this sill here and – oh! – it was the weirdest thing!'

I ask Doreen what she used to do all day in the house, when she was home. 'My Mum would be out a lot, and so would Mr Kyle, and I'd just walk around and snoop. I'd go into their rooms and look out of their windows and, well, you know, entertain myself by staring at the street from different angles and looking at their things.'

She knows the sound of the house – its great yawning silences, its creaks and drips and sighs – the bump of her own heart as she drifts on tiptoe from room to room. She's also trained herself to hear feet on the path, the tiny moment before a key touches the lock of the front door. She can get back down to her own room in three quick seconds of silence if she has to.

Sometimes she goes up to Mr Kyle's room – breathes in the sour-friendly smell of old man, of medication, of unwashed clothes. She runs her hands over the piles of loose change, the shuffle of papers and old fat books with odd titles to do with courts and the law.

Mostly she's careful to leave no traces, but once she did something daring and ran her little finger through the dust on the mantelpiece, leaving a snake's trail of clean paintwork, to see if he'd notice, if he'd say anything. He didn't, and next day the line was still there and somehow that made her feel guiltier than if he'd gone to her Mum and said something.

But she knows he'd never do that. She knows that in some surprising way he's on her side and oddly – she doesn't understand this – this makes her want to go and snoop around his room more. As if she's drawn in there by something – the idea of the friendliness, perhaps, the almost-company.

Her Mum's room is different. Her Mum's room is a bit of a challenge. It has carpet and a wardrobe full of clothes which smell of her – a smell Doreen didn't even know till a year ago and which still gives her a tight, worried feeling inside – and things in the drawers that Doreen's never seen before.

It's also got stuff in it that belongs to Mr Reynolds, the man who rings her Mum but has never once asked to speak to her, Doreen. There's a saxophone in its hard black case, a man's jacket with a chalky line of sweat on the dark inside of the lining, a tin of hair cream.

She tiptoes around her Mum's room and knows that she'd be killed if she was ever found in there.

But she won't be caught, she's too careful for that. She's alone on this dark winter afternoon in 1978 – invisible, unphotographed, unac-knowledged, unrecorded. She just keeps on walking round and looking round. What's she looking for? Something she guesses in her heart she won't ever find, but that's not going to stop her looking.

And one day the house will be sold and that will be it. Her Mum will go off to her next life and she will just quietly slip away into the next phase of her own less real life and no one will ever know she once lived here: Doreen Ricketts, 1978–1980.

Chapter Four

THE FORERUNNER, THE DREAMER, AND THE ONE NOBODY REMEMBERS

The Jamaicans
1959–1975

The strange thing is, Alvin still dreams of the house on Lillieshall Road. Number 34.

Even though he's been back in Jamaica a while now – and in Toronto for twenty years before that – it can still happen. He can still fall asleep after a couple of Red Stripes in the sticky heat of Kingston and find himself back there, under that raw, icy London sky. Overcoat buttoned up to his chin, woollen scarf wound tight around his neck, face stinging with the bitter London cold, there he is again. Pushing open the little metal gate that never shuts properly. Walking up that narrow tiled path after a couple at the North Pole or the Beaufoy.

And in his dream, he'll keep on going, along the hedge and up the single, shallow, bleach-swilled step, pushing his key in the warped lock, turning it. And the front door with its bright new coat of orange paint – his Mum's choice – will creak open and he'll stand there a moment and once again breathe in that Lillieshall Road smell: paraffin heaters, Laurie's cooking, washing on a horse in the back room, milk pan boiling on the stove, fried fish, home.

All three of his kids were born here. Marcia, Michael, Sheryl. Well, the girls were born in the hospital, one at St Thomas's, the other at the Women's Hospital opposite Nightingale Lane, but his son Michael – his son! – was actually born right there in the downstairs front room where he and Laurie slept, would you believe? A cold Sunday morning in February, too damn early. Laurie – thinking she had at least a week to go – moaning and groaning since the early hours, surprised by the sudden slams of pain.

And him telling her it was indigestion. Her telling him to shut up and get her a glass of water or milk or something. 'Right now this second, Al, I mean it, or I'm screaming this whole blinking house down!'

'Don't go vexing yourself, woman.'

'I'm in terrible pain here, I'm telling you, Alvin!'

And him stumbling into the kitchen, wavering a little moment over whether she's really wanting the milk or the water, then, before he can even think, her yelling at him to get a big towel instead – then, no, get the doctor or – no, call an ambulance – and that's before he's even got the water or anything.

And then before he can think what to do – before he can even grumble at her keeping going at him all night, not to mention waking him up so early on a Sunday – there's a flush of blood and water and whatnot and the child's dark head is hanging down there between her open, straining legs. Oh, Christ!

His son. Michael, his son. Proudest and most shocking moment of his whole life. That's it, the pride and the shock coming both together.

And it's so cold in that room, blue-murdering cold, and so they do what they can – they wrap him up in all the blankets they have and wait for the doctor to come, and he does eventually, he comes. He laughs and congratulates her on the speed of it and Laurie says she's not complaining now as she has a beautiful son and he's just perfect, but she would have preferred it slower.

'Bit panicky, I suppose, was it?'

'Even me, and it's my third.'

And they never do get the stain out of the carpet. Christ, what a mess.

His Mum – who'd gone out to work early and was furious to miss the big drama of the thing – eventually puts a rug over it. Making the best of the situation, she calls it, beaming the whole while, because her happiest thing in all the world is when another grandchild comes.

That house was a good place for him. Is a good place. Because he still goes there, you know? You leave a place and travel thousands of miles away, and you think you've gone, don't you? You think you've put a whole load between yourself and that house. But you're wrong, you haven't. The place has the last laugh. In his dreams, he hasn't left it at all. In his dreams, he still goes there.

Four in the afternoon, sky darkening, a storm coming. Dog lying in the hall with ears flat, sound of kids' TV from the back sitting room. Jonathan hurtles down the stairs, yelling, 'I've got one, I've got one!'

He hands me a piece of paper and explains that he just called six Gloria Duncans and the seventh one was her. Really her! The Right Gloria Duncan! 'And now – wait for it – guess what else. Her brother is Alvin Reynolds!'

He stands, hands stretched wide as though making me a cash offer I couldn't possibly refuse (one of his rare Jewish gestures) and waits for me to respond. 'Wow.'

Merciline's husband. Marcia, Michael, and Sheryl's father. This really is a double coup. Actually it's more than double – it's a whole family in one hit.

'Except he lives in Jamaica. Which means he's not the one we phoned in Wolverhampton. That one obviously didn't want to speak to us because he's – '

'Not the Right Alvin Reynolds!'

There's a distant rumble of thunder. I hear the dog bolt up the stairs. I know she'll keep on going till she gets to Jake's room, where she'll cower under the computer table.

The sky's indigo, furiously dark now. The first spots of rain pitter onto my skylight. I race out and grab the washing that's drying on the terrace outside my study. Then, sitting there among the knickers and socks and T-shirts, I get Gloria Duncan on the phone.

She sounds friendly, relaxed, happy to talk. A quietly spoken West Indian lady. 'Yes, mmm,' she says, picking her way slowly and carefully through memory, 'there were lots of us there in that house. First of all there was our mother, Melda McNish.'

This I can't believe. 'Melda McNish! Your mother?'

'Mmm, that's right.'

I explain that Melda McNish is one of the people I've been trying to trace for months.

A smash of thunder. My computer screen flickers.

'Oh,' Gloria says flatly. 'Well, she's dead. She died on Christmas Eve'.

'Oh no ...'

'Christmas Eve '02. Just last year. She gets up in the morning and she's perfectly OK but half an hour later, that's it, she's dead.'

'Oh,' I say, 'I'm so very sorry.'

I am. I'm sad, shocked, disappointed. I can't believe that, as I drove my kids to buy cheese and cookies at Borough Market, bought last-minute flowers, spruced the house up ready for Christmas, the woman I'd been searching for, for four months was just about to disappear forever. Melda McNish. Her name on my pinboard, on my to-do list. The romantic sound of her in my head for months now.

I ask if Aston McNish was Melda's husband. Gloria says no, he was 'my uncle's son'. (Melda's cousin, then? No wonder I found no offspring in any of those big red registers.) 'Do you know anything about the West Indian culture?' she asks me suddenly.

'A little,' I say, then, coming clean, 'well, not much actually.'

She laughs loudly. 'Yes, I can tell. Well, my mother Melda, she was what you might call a forerunner.'

'A forerunner?'

'Yes. If there was anything going then she was always the first one to try it. Anything, you name it, she was up for it. So she came over here first from Jamaica on the boat – the pioneering spirit, if you see what I mean – and then she sent for us all, one by one. Anyone who came over and needed somewhere to stay while they got their feet on the ground, so to speak, they could stay in the house.'

In the house. In our house.

A flash of lightning skids across the sky. A bash of thunder three seconds later. I think of Melda McNish – not Scottish at all, as I'd once assumed, but a bold, spirited West Indian. A woman who could alight in a foreign country miles from home and then house hunt; who could make a sanctuary, a stopping place, a stepping stone – and then send for the rest of the family.

I ask Gloria about the other names, the other people in the house. She says that Florence and Trevor Schloss were a young couple and she thinks they went to the States. Same with the Herons – Louisa and Stanley – to the States, she thinks.

And Salome Bennet?

'Oh, I last saw her about seven years ago, she was in Streatham. Sallee, we called her.'

Gloria then tells me she has a daughter, Yvette – 'grown up now' – who also lived in the house, since she was a baby. 'My Mum looked after her there while I was working, then when she was older and I got a flat, she came to live with me.'

'So she was a child in this house? Did she go to school round here?'

'Oh yes, she went to Macaulay.'

I tell Gloria all my kids have been there and our youngest is due to leave this June. She laughs. I tell her I'd really like to meet Yvette and she says they'd love to come and see the house – they've often passed nearby and wondered about it.

I ask her about the Reynolds children.

'Sheryl? I saw her yesterday actually. Michael's in Canada and he's not at all well – Alvin's been over there, visiting him. I can give you Sheryl's number but I'd better ask her first.'

'And Marcia?' I ask.

Gloria hesitates. 'Marcia lives in Thornton Heath and – well, let's just say, the younger generation . . . they are not how we were. Do you know what I mean? But you want to speak to Alvin? I can give you his number in Jamaica.'

Alvin laughs and laughs when he hears I live here at Number 34.

'You mean you're there right now? In that house? My house! Oh, that's a good one, oh my, oh Christ!'

He tells me he came over from Jamaica in 1954 – he thinks it was that year anyway. He flew from Kingston to New York and then came to Liverpool on a ship called the *North Star*. Or at least he thinks it was the *North Star*. His Mum Melda – 'Oh Christ, I'm still missing her, you know?' – found the house for him because he was too busy travelling around with his work.

'What did you do?'

'Oh, you know, I was a decorator for Bermondsey Borough Council, driving around in a van and that and no time to do house hunting, so she do that for me. And she found this one and she said she just knew I was going to like it and of course I did. I loved it, I really did.'

'Do you remember who you bought the house from?'

'I think a Mrs Blaine.'

'Annie Blaine and her husband Theodore?'

'Annie? Yes, I think so, yes, don't know nothing about the other one though.'

I wish he did know something. The Blaines are proving hard to chase.

Alvin tells me that in those days there were hardly any black people at all in Clapham – 'I tell you, I was the only black in that damn road!' – but it was the fifties and people were pretty friendly to them, there wasn't much prejudice. 'I mean you couldn't call us immigrants. We was all under British rule, if you get what I mean.'

I ask him what it was like, arriving here after Jamaica. 'Frightening,' he says firmly.

'Was it?'

A little moment passes. 'Sure. Like everything else, it was scary at first – the smoke, the cold, oh Christ! – but then I guess you adjust. Worst thing was, there was no bathroom. You know that very little room at the top of the stairs on the first landing you come to?'

I tell him that it's in fact my study and I'm sitting in there now talking to him.

He laughs in amazement. 'You are? Oh, good Lord, no! Well, that was the bathroom, only there was no hot water, not really, and I used to save up my dirt for the weekend and then go down the public baths on Clapham Manor Street and for sixpence you could have a wash and a scrub.'

I tell him the baths are still there – a leisure centre now – my daughter went swimming there yesterday. He laughs again.

'You know,' he says, 'the baths may still be there. But that area has improved so much it makes me laugh. Last year when I was over I passed by the street and I was amazed to see all the cars.'

'We even have residents' parking now.'

'In my time you could park anywhere, both sides of the road!'

I tell him I wish I'd known he was coming: he could have visited and looked around his old home. He says he can't think of anything he'd like more – to walk into the house again.

And I tell him he must promise, when he's next over, whenever it is, to ring the bell. He promises. That's when he tells me he still dreams about the house.

A woman has seen my article in *SW Magazine* and gets in touch. She tells me she lived across the road from our house as a child all through the sixties. I ask her if she remembers anyone from the house.

'Well, give me some names ...'

'Melda McNish?'

'No.'

'Someone called Heron – Louisa and Stanley Heron.'

'No.'

'Well then, the Reynolds ... Merciline and Alvin Reynolds.'

'Oh yes! The Reynolds, yes. My Mum knew her. She was – what did you say she called herself?'

'Merciline.'

The woman laughs. 'Laurie, she was known as. She was a nurse.'

She tells me she used to play with the Reynolds children.

'Let me see ... Marcia, she was the eldest. And then there was – Michael? And Sheryl – the youngest was Sheryl. I think I might have a photo of Sheryl as a baby somewhere.'

The seventies. My mother used to tell us a story. It was supposed to be true but, then again, she always said everything was true. It went like this:

There was a woman and she used to dream, night after night, about the same house, a house she'd never been to, but a wonderful house all the same.

'Such a beautiful house!' exclaimed my mother. 'And in her dream she'd walk all around it – through halls and down corridors, into rooms and out of them again, through the big, beautiful gardens – oh, the gardens were superb.'

The woman actually used to look forward to going to sleep – so she could dream the dream and visit the house again.

And then, one day, she happened to be driving along through the countryside and suddenly she gasped. Because there was the house – the house itself – the exact same beautiful house from her dreams! Only this time, she was wide awake.

She couldn't believe it. Of course she stopped the car. She just had to go and see inside it. With her heart pounding, she walked up to the front door and rang the bell.

A man answered. When he saw her, he looked unnerved to say the least. Amazed. Frightened, even.

'I'm so sorry to call unexpectedly like this,' the woman said, 'but I just had to ask, is this house for sale? Because if it is, I'd like to buy it.'

The man stared and stared at her and finally said in a trembling voice, 'As a matter of fact it is for sale. But I don't think you'd want to buy it, madam.'

'Oh?' she said, unable to think of any possible reason why she would not want it, this house she loved so fiercely. 'Why?'

'Because it's haunted,' he said.

'What?'

'By you!'

At this, the spooky punchline, Mum would give us a triumphant, satisfied stare and we would reward her with a shudder.

Thinking about the story now, though, it doesn't quite make sense. Surely, for instance, the man was wrong to say what he did. If the woman was the ghost, then why would she be put off by the haunting? In fact, wasn't she the ideal buyer for the house? And what happened next? Did she buy it, and did the dreams stop? Are dreams just a manifestation of our longings and do we stop dreaming once we have what we think we need?

These were all questions I wasn't grown up enough to ask but, even at fourteen, I loved the story's seductive logic. It's a story about our relationships with places. The fact that, once the woman sees the house for real, she immediately demands to buy it, is in fact just a measure of the extent to which she already feels she owns it. She is already its possessor.

Even more, I liked what the story seemed to be telling me: that we leave our emotional and spiritual fingerprints on buildings, on spaces. (Do we?) That we can go places when we sleep. (Can we?) That other people can perhaps even see us doing it. (Can they?) That what is to one person a pleasant, tranquil experience can be, for another, a terror, a haunting. (Can it?)

I felt I owned this house from the first moment I saw it. Maybe I'd been dreaming of it all my life without knowing it. Who knows, maybe in our dreams, Alvin Reynolds and I have even passed each other, exchanged a complicit smile.

I used to visit Brooklyn House in my dreams. Or not quite my dreams, but from the awake side of my pillow, in the last moments before I drifted down the slope to sleep.

When my mother found the courage to leave my father in the unhappy summer of 1972, I minded leaving that house almost more than I minded leaving my father. It was a good house, whereas I wasn't sure about my father.

In fact so much misery unfurled there over the following years that it became a much less good house for me, but I didn't know that then, not even a glimmer in 1972. I just loved it, wanted it, cried for it.

I loved my attic bedroom at the top of the house where I had my collection of china horses – eight figures in different colours, some prancing, some grazing, some lying down. I loved those horses – even the green one with the broken fetlock badly glued back on, a hard, syrupy drip of glue hanging down its leg. I dusted them and rearranged them all the time.

I loved the orchard with the henhouse where we pretended to be gypsies in long cotton skirts and bare feet, curtain rings looped over our ears with strands of Sylko. I loved the big, dusty, rat-infested barns where we weren't supposed to go but did, and the high stacks of hay bales for bouncing across, sacks of grain for sliding down, dangerous-looking machinery with its oil smells and stubbed-out cigarettes.

Early mornings, I tiptoed out of the house at dawn and went looking for clay pipe heads among the frozen clods of earth in the magical rosy light. My fingers were stiff with cold but it was worth it. Mostly I just found bits, broken pipe stems clogged up with soil; but once I found a whole pipe head, intact and startling and surely an antique?

I caught a trout in the stream in my net and kept it in a bucket in the shed, where it went mouldy and died and I avoided going in the shed for weeks after that, unable to face the lonely, fetid stew of its corpse. And in another outhouse at the end of the barns, I kept the head of a mallard duck for a week, shut its beak with a rubber band, stuffed a knife up its throat (I was training to be a vet) until the stench finally overpowered me and I buried it with full honours.

One day the farmer abandoned a huge wooden trailer behind the barns and it stayed there, somehow forgotten, for a whole summer. My sisters and I started a stage school on it – singing and acting and tap dancing with only the fields and ditches as our audience. Of course, it wasn't always perfect. In winter we were shoved outside in our anoraks and just stood and bickered in the furious cold. But in summer we were free to plunder the whole ten acres, invisible children, not due back till tea.

The idea that we'd never live there again – that we'd just be visitors from now on – tore at my heart. I cried and cried. When I lay in bed at night, before I went to sleep, I forced my mind to wander round the house, room by room, step by step. I did not want to forget it.

But when we finally returned a few weeks later – when the courts had sorted out custody and visiting – it had all changed forever. My father's revenge. The rooms were unheated and dull with dust. Bluebottles lay dead on the windowsills. The lavatory had a rusty brown stain, uncleaned and unflushed. There were no towels or sheets in the airing cupboard – and those on the beds felt fusty and damp. Even the air smelled unhomely, uncared for.

My china ponies had gone, I never found out where. So had my little transistor radio. And the place was half bare – none of the furniture our mother had taken had been replaced – 'I'm not replacing a stick of it,' he said, 'so you can see how she stripped this place.'

*   *   *

The neighbour who rang me before about the Reynolds family, sends me an e-mail:

> All I really remember of the family was that Alvin and Laurie used to row a lot. That's where my Mum used to step in, when she needed someone to pour her heart out to. I remember once she got her fingers slammed in the door during a row and my Dad had to take her to hospital while Mum looked after the children. Consequently that is why Laurie left the house before her husband. She left him.
>
> I remember she was a nurse, very pretty and kind. She and Alvin were both from Jamaica which is where she trained. I believe she nursed at The Royal Marsden at one time. I recall that once when I was very young Laurie repaid Mum's kindness by cooking Ackee and salt fish for us. I'm sure you can imagine no-one had heard of anything like that in the 60's.
>
> I also remember that Laurie had a friend visit from Canada once, her name was Dilys and I can remember being amazed at the new invention she'd bought over with her, I bet you can't guess what it was, a telescopic umbrella, we're only talking about 30 something years ago, how funny!
>
> For years after Laurie left and then we moved we would have sporadic calls from Laurie. I also remember that after she left Alvin she lived in Tooting somewhere.
>
> Life was hard for a young woman on her own with 3 kids, I was only young myself but I think the break up with Alvin must have hit her really badly because she spent a spell in Springfield mental hospital and then took to the bottle. I believe my Mum visited her in the hospital and I can vaguely remember going to her new home but I don't think we saw much of her after that. Still for many years we'd have an occasional call . . .

Now he's not saying there's anything bad about her but that woman over the road, she's not what you'd call straight. She says things. A stirrer. She'll watch and wait and be there to spring to Laurie's defence at the slightest thing.

Her husband's better, slower to judge or draw conclusions. But their friendship seems to cool a little after the door incident. He's not surprised the kid remembers it – kids remember everything. Such a thing was made of it at the time. And now here she is making it sound like those sorts of fallings-out were an everyday occurrence. Christ.

If he and Laurie ever really let rip with each other – and he's not denying it can happen now and then – it's just a passing thing, they never mean it. He doesn't understand it, can't really bear to think too hard about it, but sometimes it's like they turn into two different people – two types he barely recognises as the man and woman who got it together all that time ago. It's not that he isn't happy to take some of the blame – but it takes two to make a fight, remember. But try telling that to Laurie. And anyway even thinking about all of this gives him so much pain and he can't take it, uh-huh, sorry, no. He is such a soft man down in his deepest heart you see.

He only ever flies off the handle when she and the kids have driven him just about insane with their moaning and shouting. When life seems thankless. When the cold and bitterness bruise him so hard that he'll open that old front door softly softly and creep through the hall, hoping only to crash on his bed and lose himself for a while, and she'll be there in the kitchen and hearing him straightaway and him knowing there's not a chance of getting past her.

'Alvin?'

He stops, holds his breath.

'Al-vin?'

'What?'

'That you, Al?'

'Course it's me, who else is it gonna be?'

'Where've you been?'

'Out.'

(Where?)

'Out where?'

'North Pole. Why? You miss me?'

'Huh.'

'What's that supposed to mean, huh?'

'Nothing.'

He always thought it was a funny thing, that he came to this bloody freezing country on the SS *North Star* and ended up spending so much time socialising in the North Pole. As if his life had slowly and surely gone in such a north-wind direction that it had finally frozen up completely.

He never wanted to make Laurie unhappy, never. She's back in Jamaica now, somewhere in Mandeville, he doesn't know exactly where. No one will tell him, not even the kids. But he still dreams of her – him and her in the house. Fifteen good years he had with her there.

He remembers which door, though. He sees it all the time. The door from the hall into the back room, the room where they slept, the room where Michael came into the world. Sometimes he still wakes at night and sees the door – all the doors of the house but especially that door, the 1974 door – two purple David Cassidy lovehearts stickers on it, put there by Sheryl. A door you can barely see unless you turn the light on. The paint scratched to buggery round the handle. Two splintery bits at the bottom where one night she'd locked him out and he kicked it open and –

That's how big it was for him, OK? He still remembers the door.

Later I drink too much vodka and have an argument with Jonathan that I don't mean to have. I hear myself accusing him of being so practical, being so rooted in the real world, of always needing everything to have a purpose, not understanding the mystery of life, the mystery of mystery. As I say it, I realize two things: that it's an atrociously unkind thing to say; and that I mean it.

'What do you mean?' he says calmly, keeping his temper, forcing me to explain myself.

'Just that there are other things out there, that aren't to do with what you see in front of you.'

'What things? Describe them for me.'

'I don't know. Good things, comforting things. Spiritual things.'

'Be more specific.'

I jiggle the ice around in my glass. 'Oh, I don't know. The colour of the sky, just a general feeling. Like God only not God. I can't really explain it.'

He looks at me impatiently, his mouth hard. 'That's your spiritual side? Noticing the colour of the sky?'

'It's more than that.'

'What then? I'm inviting you to spell it out for me. Educate me.'

'That's it. It's all the stuff you can't spell out.'

'How convenient.'

'There're other things too.'

'What things? Explain them. Really, I mean it. I genuinely want to hear.'

'All right . . .' But I hesitate, wondering if I can. The fact is I look at that sky out there, whether blue or grey, and my heart just lifts. Because it's there. So what is that? It's not God, not to me it isn't. It's about a sense that there's something more out there, something you can never hope to quite grasp or see. A possibility that somehow transforms life.

'I'm waiting,' he says.

'It's a sort of insane self-belief – a feeling of being somehow connected to the world in a way that I'll never understand but I somehow like. It means that when things go wrong for me, I don't feel destroyed.'

'What do you feel, then? When they go wrong?'

'I still feel – like me.'

'So do I. Actually.'

'I frankly don't know how I'd live without this sense,' I tell him.

132

'I seem to manage.'

When I was about twelve or thirteen, I told my Mum that I loved humanity, I loved the world, I just loved everybody. She laughed.

'You'll change your mind about that when you're older,' she said, with affectionate cynicism. Which was understandable, but I knew she was missing the point. I didn't really mean I loved humanity – I didn't know enough about humanity to know whether I loved it or not – but I knew that I felt this ferocious happiness, this wildly exciting sense of possibility.

Sometimes out walking the dog or looking for my clay pipes at dawn, I'd get this urge to stand in the middle of a field and scream with happiness. My heart was buoyant, it floated easily.

It still does. I used to think it was normal, that everyone was like this, but now I'm not so sure.

Jake has it though. When he was a small child, five or six, he used to turn to me all the time and say, 'I lub you, Mummy.'

I knew what he meant. It wasn't that he loved me – though he did, of course – what he meant was, he felt quite blissed out by his childish grasp of what possibilities there might be out there in the world. He felt joy and wanted to express it.

'I lub you mummy'

'It's about joy,' I tell Jonathan, 'about believing in stuff you can't really see, that you just have to somehow trust is there. Something beyond the dark edges of life.'

'Sounds a lot like God to me.'

'It's not God. I don't believe in God, you know that.'

'Faith, then.'

'Maybe faith.'

'Everything's easy when you have faith,' he says.

'Is it?'

'Yeah, you don't have to make an effort, you don't have to get off your arse and do something to improve the world and how so many people live miserably in it, you just have to have faith that it will get better. Sounds a lot like voting Liberal to me.'

'But that's not it,' I tell him. 'You're right maybe, but that's not what I'm talking about at all.'

'What is it, then? What are you talking about?'

I sit on the sofa and shut my eyes.

'I don't know,' I tell him, 'I don't know what I'm saying.'

www.ancestry.com is the virtual Family Records Centre. It's horribly American, but for $39.95 you can access the US phone book. And it shows only two Louisa Herons in the whole USA. And only one in her seventies. She lives in Queens Village, New York State.

I call her and explain about the research I'm doing and ask her, did she by any chance live in Lillieshall Road in Clapham in London in 1960?

'Mmm,' she says cautiously, 'I did.'

I push my study door shut. 'You did? Oh, that's wonderful. Do you mind if I talk to you for a few minutes?'

'Mmm, mmm. But I have nothing to say.'

'But it was you? You lived here at Number 34 Lillieshall Road? You remember the house?'

'Oh. Yeah.'

I can't suppress my excitement but I can't have her hang up on me.

'I'm so sorry to ask you all these questions but you see, do you remember a lady called Melda McNish?'

'Mmm.'

'You do?'

'Well, she was the landlord, mmm. Nice lady.'

'Was she?'

'Yeah, mmm, mm. Like a mother to me that lady was.'

'I'm afraid she passed away last year,' I tell Louisa, unsure of whether this is the right thing to do or not.

'Mmm.'

'I'm sorry.'

'Mmm.'

'Do you remember which room you lived in here?'

'Huh?'

'Upstairs? Was it a room upstairs?'

'Could be. Yeah.'

'Do you know if it was the first floor?'

'Maybe.'

'Or the floor above?'

'I'm old. I can't remember.'

'Do you mind if I ask you a few more questions?'

'I don't want to answer, you see, because I don't want my name in no book.'

I explain to Louisa that I could change her name if she wants. She tells me then that she came over to study nursing at Orpington and then she went back to London. It's not clear whether this was when she lived in the house or not.

I ask her if she remembers Gloria Duncan. She brightens.

'Gloria? Mmm.'

I tell her Gloria and her daughter Yvette are coming to tea tomorrow. Her voice springs to life.

'You tell Gloria to give me a ring, OK?'

'Can I give her your number?'

'But – you have my number already!'

'Yes, can I give it to Gloria?'

'Oh. Mmm. Yeah.'

The Public Record Office at Kew – state of the art and with its own glossy brochure – could hardly be more different from the buzzing, brown-carpeted space that is the Family Records Centre or the battered bureaucracy of the High Court Probate Room.

You drive in past the Kew Retail Park – shiny new Next and M&S and JJB Sports – and there's even a car park. Then a huge open space with a fountain and a pool of greenish water about the size of a football pitch. And the building is brand new and purpose-built – blond brick, smoked glass, and air-conditioning.

I know what I'm after: until the mid-sixties, the Board of Trade insisted that all ships arriving at British ports submitted 'Returns of Passengers brought to the United Kingdom who embarked at Ports out of Europe. (Passengers in each class of accommodation should be entered in separate groups)'.

For each month of each year there's one box for ships arriving at London and Liverpool and another box for all the rest. I decide ships from the Caribbean would dock at Southampton, Plymouth, or somewhere on the south coast. I order 1957 and 1959.

The first three boxes arrive in the Map Room, huge flat cardboard boxes, each bigger than a breakfast tray. Inside is a folder for each port. And inside each folder, A2 sheets of flimsy paper, typed, and numbered names. A huge number of the ships seem to come from New York – most of them in fact – but I turn through them until I find a ship from Jamaica. I don't know what these lists will tell me, but I feel it would just be so exciting to find one of our people, to see the written evidence – to glimpse him or her walking down that gangplank and into a new life in freezing, foggy fifties Britain.

I run my finger down column after column: Glendora Ifill from Barbados ... Archibald Barbour from Antigua ... Delsie Panton from Kingston. And then, almost immediately and rather unbelievably, there he is – one of ours – Stanley Heron, passenger 290. It's got to be him, hasn't it? Arriving on the SS *Irpinia* at Southampton on 24 August 1957 along with over a thousand other passengers. He embarks at Kingston, heading for 23 Swallow Street, Yorkshire, a cabinetmaker, carrying a British passport issued in Jamaica. The next listed passenger, number 291, Gerald Powell, also gives Swallow Street as his 'Address in the United Kingdom'. Which makes me wonder whether Stanley just offered it to his cabin mate who was in need of an address he could cite confidently as they stood in front of the Customs Officer.

I scrutinize the lists. Stanley is otherwise alone. So has he yet to meet Louisa, or is she waiting, following him on a later ship, ready to join him once he's settled in Yorkshire?

'I run my finger down column after column ...'

Gloria and Yvette Duncan are here at Number 34 for tea, from Selhurst and Brixton respectively. First time back in this house in twenty-five or thirty years.

Gloria – a really attractive, smiley woman of sixty or possibly more – is wearing a white top with a heart-shaped neckline and holding an old-fashioned snap-clasp handbag. Yvette's about our age, denim-jacketed, shoulder-bagged, friendly and straightforward. She tells us she works with refugees as a vocational guidance counsellor – 'it's just a fancy new job description' – in Deptford.

'I can't believe it,' she says, unable to stop looking around her. 'To be here again, I just can't really take it in, you know?'

Gloria tells us that her husband Raphael Duncan was in the RAF in England, but hated it. They got married out in Jamaica but Gloria left soon after and came to England 'because the marriage was in a state and because I wanted to be with my Mum'.

'That was Melda? The forerunner?' I say.

She smiles at me. 'Yes.'

She's young, skinny, sad – a girl in her best, thin summer dress. She's left her husband in Kingston and come over here with just the one suitcase. The boat is a big adventure, quite fun really; but when she arrives in Southampton, it's cold, rainy, miserable, just as she'd imagined.

The shock of no sunlight: the air is grey. She's never seen air like it before and she doesn't have the clothes for it, she doesn't have much of anything, but she doesn't care: she'll soon be with her Mum. Meanwhile, she can taste an odd silvery taste in her mouth like metal and she's sick – sick with the boat and nerves and the newness of it all, but that's to be expected, isn't it?

'I didn't know it then but I was pregnant. I must have conceived just before I left Raphael. Yvette was born about six months later.'

'I was the first child in the family to be born in this country,'

Yvette proudly tells us. 'I came first – and then there was Marcia, Michael, and Sheryl.'

'the marriage was in a state and I wanted to be with my mum'

Gloria gets a job as a seamstress in the rag trade district on Mortimer Street. Long hours, the commute to Oxford Circus, a whole winter of it. After that she decides she's had enough and she trains – like Laurie – to be a nurse. St George's Hospital in Hyde Park and later in Tooting. She lives all over the place, but she can't manage with the baby as well so her Mum – Melda – keeps Yvette with her at Lillieshall Road. Almost a decade later, when Yvette's nearly ten, she finally comes to live with her Mummy in Selhurst.

Mel loves that child. Yvette shares her room and bed and goes to school at Macaulay. 'There were just three of us black kids at Macaulay, can you imagine? Just three!' There's a nice woman called Pearl Oag down the road and when Mel's out at work, Pearl's granny, Nanny White, sometimes takes Yvette till she can get home.

It's 1960. They are the only black family in Lillieshall Road.

* * *

So many of them in that house, 1960 to 1963.

Uncle Alvin and Laurie in the downstairs back room and their three little kids in the smallish first-floor room next to the bigger front one where Yvette and Aunt Mel ('I always called her Aunt Mel even though she was my granny') share a big double bed. The bed is in the alcove on the far side and there's a pinky-brown settee against the wall as you come in, the telly – 'very important the telly!' – just in front of the window.

Yvette and Mel are just mad about *Coronation Street*. Addicted. Every evening without fail at 7.30 they sit on the settee together and tune in to life at the Rover's Return. The exotic ordinariness of Ena Sharples, Minnie Caldwell, Elsie Tanner.

Sometimes, if Mel's not around, Yvette goes upstairs and knocks on Salome Bennet's door and goes and watches with her. There's a big double bed in the corner and they'll curl up on it together – 'we all watched telly all the time!' Sallee Bennet is a quiet woman, very pretty and kind. She works in a factory somewhere in Streatham and keeps herself to herself. If she wants to cook she uses the little stove outside her room on the narrow upstairs landing. Or else the one over the bath in the little room on the floor below. Both landings always smell of cooking – boiled rice, fried fish, patties, tea bags.

In the room next door to Sallee are the Herons – Stanley and Louisa. And, later on, the Schlosses – Florence and Trevor and Ivo. Trevor works as a mechanic at a cabbies' garage at the Oval and Ivo is the baby, but he's not quite all there. Or that's what Aunt Mel says. The Schlosses are Jamaican like themselves but frankly they are a bit of a nuisance – bolshie and no one likes them much. In fact they have a bit of a falling out with Melda and after less than a year, they leave.

After that, Yvette and Mel move into the smaller room next to theirs – the one the Reynolds kids slept in – and their own room, the bigger room, is rented out.

'Could it have been rented to Vincent Dias?' I ask them.

They both look blank. 'Vincent who?'

'Dias. There was a Vincent Dias listed in the house around that time.'

Gloria shakes her head. 'Don't remember no Vincent Dias.'

The smaller room is not as easy to be in as their old room. They have to shuffle round each other, though Yvette is glad to be able to look out at the garden, the trees and squirrels: it's tons better than the view of the street they had before. The bed takes up almost all the space, that and the big old wooden wardrobe and the oil heater that stands on the floor. You have to wiggle round it to get anywhere and Yvette still has the scars on her bum where she burnt herself on that heater – 'not once but twice!' There's also a big old sideboard in there with one of those old phonogram things in it and sometimes her aunt lets her listen to stuff on it, old jiving music, 78s, the sort that gets Mel going.

Melda – the forerunner – is queen of the household. There's a chair on the left of the kitchen fireplace where she always lords it – she likes to see exactly who is going in and out of the front door. She might have on her slippers or she might have on her shoes, and she might be peeling sweet potatoes or preparing okra or she might be mending an old shirt of Michael's, but no one gets past her.

'Alvin?'

'What?'

'That you, Alvin?'

'Uh.'

'Alvin?'

'Yeah, Mum, it's me.'

'Don't grunt when I'm speaking to you.'

'What is it, Mum?'

'Where you been?'

'Down the North Pole.'

'Not for too long, I hope?'

Laughs. 'Not for too long, no.'

'Hmm. You're never here, you know that?'

'I know it, Mum.'

'So, what you going to do about it?'

'Don't know, Mum.'

That was then. No one asks Alvin that sort of stuff any more. Mel passed away on Christmas Eve, her slippers on, carols playing on the radio. And the rest of them, they're spread out all over the world now, gone their separate ways forever.

Clarence Hibbert was Melda's cousin. He lived in the house in 1959 – worked as a guard on the Underground – but he's in the States now. As are the Herons. Laurie is said to be living in Mandeville, Jamaica. Alvin's in Kingston and Michael's in Toronto, and Yvette herself is a grandmother. Her son Darren has a two-year-old son.

But no one remembers Vincent Dias.

'Are you sure he lived here at the same time as us?'

'Pretty sure, yes.'

'Weird, huh? Doesn't ring any bells at all.'

As they leave, I write down Louisa Heron's phone number in New York for Gloria and pass on the message about phoning. She seems genuinely pleased and says she will do it definitely, she will phone her. Yvette walks into the sitting room, throws her head back, folds her arms.

'That corner there,' she tells me, indicating the space to the left of the sofa where we have our CD player, 'there used to be some big doors there, didn't there?'

I tell her that we took them off to open the two rooms up, but that we still have them in the cellar. 'We'll probably put them back on one day, when the kids get too loud and horrible and we want to shut them out.'

'That's another place my Aunt Mel used to sit all the time. Her old armchair. I can see her there right now, chatting and smiling. I've got a photo of her sitting there in that corner with me on her lap when I was a little kid. I could drop it in some time if you like.'

* * *

142

Same corner of the same room, four decades and three families later. The walls are magenta – would Melda have liked them? – and the sofa is dark chocolate, a colour chosen to hide the dog hairs, but it only hides half of them because the dog's both black and white. The floors are stripped and varnished. The rug was bought in Marrakesh. We hoped we were getting a bargain but we hadn't learned to haggle and I think we were fleeced. Helen, my mother-in-law, has come for lunch and we're sitting and drinking coffee and talking about how she came over on the boat from Australia in 1949. She's tall, slim, blonde and older than she either looks or likes to admit. She's just spilt the tiniest drip of coffee on her white linen trousers and is dabbing at it with a damp napkin.

'I was running away from a disastrous love affair. He was Jewish and much older than me and he said he couldn't possibly marry me. I was broken-hearted. And I came to England and almost straightaway met Jonathan's father and thought, Oh my God, not another Jew! I've done the same thing all over again.'

I never met Aubrey. He died only a few months before I got to know Jonathan properly. In fact I later realized I fell for Jonathan while he was grieving for his father. I remember him – thin and tired-looking, wolfing down a plate of food at the National Theatre where we both worked, and I remember wondering why he looked so shattered and I felt an unexpected rush of tenderness for him. I had no idea then that he'd just lost his father.

Helen tells me how she was supposed to have a room in a bedsit in Tedworth Square – 'Just off the King's Road, it had all been arranged' – but it turned out when she arrived that the previous girl had decided to stay on after all – 'Changed her mind just like that!' – so she was told she could only have it till the Monday and after that she'd have to find something else.

'I almost cried. The woman whose house it was cooked me some frozen spinach with an egg – she told me how hard eggs were to get hold of. This was not long after the war, remember. Then she asked if I had any duty-free cigarettes and I had bought two hundred on the boat – and she took them all! For one lousy egg! Later I was so hungry I bought a half-pint of milk from the dairy on the corner of Sydney Street and drank it and cried all over again.'

Helen sips her coffee. The walls behind her head pulsate with red.

Amy and John T. Costello lived in Number 34 from 1952 to 1958, forced to find new lodgings, presumably, when the Blaines sold the house to Melda McNish. I see them as a quiet, married couple – Irish perhaps. They live in the front room at the top, keeping themselves to themselves, walking carefully up the stairs when they come in from work, hoping they won't disturb Mr and Mrs Blaine.

I see Amy as blonde.

'Why?' Jonathan asks me.

'Because it's a blonde name.'

'Oh now look, I didn't want to get you going on your synaesthesia again.'

I only discovered recently that I have this – and it's true that I'm rather excited about it. When I read or say or hear words, I see colours – sometimes one colour per word and other times a whole series of colours laced through a word. I thought it was just something everyone had.

Amy is a yellow word and therefore somehow a blonde name. Jonathan thinks my synaesthesia's funny, but Chloë takes it seriously. She thinks she has it too.

'Monday's blue, Tuesday's yellow, Wednesday's mauve,' she says, counting the days of the week off on her fingers.

'No, green. Wednesday's definitely green.'

'You two,' says Jonathan, 'can we get back to the slightly more urgent matter of the Costellos?'

At the Family Records Centre, I start looking for their marriage from 1930 onwards. By the time I get to 1950, eight John Costellos have married in England – from the John Costello married in Bilston in 1935 to the John Costello married in Paddington in June 1949.

A certificate from the Family Records Centre costs £7 and the bills are mounting. But for £3 apiece, they will check each register entry and only produce the certificate if it corresponds to a specified detail. So I order a reference check on all these John Costello marriages – did any of them cite Lillieshall Road as their home address?

A week later I know that none of them did. And why should they? Amy and John probably got married in Ireland, came over here to make a go of it. Or else maybe they weren't Irish at all but some of Reggie Povah's Americans and Canadians.

I try the Probate Search Room and find the will of John Thomas Costello of Bexleyheath who died in 1958 with a son and heir called Desmond Thomas Hadican Costello. Hadican is grounds for hope but most people don't put their middle names in the phone book. He is untraceable. As is John's Aunt Agnes, who is to be the beneficiary of £25 – only to have the bequest revoked in a codicil made three weeks later. Whoever you were, John Thomas Costello of Bexleyheath, you seem to have boasted quite a fiery temper.

'What colour's Hadican?' Jonathan asks me.

'Brown, definitely.'

After almost thirty years, back to Brooklyn House. 'Brooklyn House, Caythorpe, Notts' – the address on all my envelopes from nine to twelve, a somehow vast and crucial three years of my life, strangely skewed and overshadowed by the years that followed. The years when we no longer lived there, visiting our father every other weekend in a sad deteriorating house that we could no longer call home.

Actually there was more to it than that. He made us promise not to call where we lived with our mother 'home' – or not in his presence, anyway. If we did so by mistake, speaking without thinking (we were twelve, ten, and eight) he'd flinch and his jaw would go rigid. He frightened me, this man with all his rules, his constant burning anger. I realized even at that age that it was a bonfire he wanted to keep burning. He'd fuel it with anything – his daughters' hearts if necessary. I tiptoed around him carefully. 'When we go back to The House Where Mummy Lives . . .' 'Oh, I left my book at The Other House.'

All houses have contained grief. But Brooklyn House has contained more grief than most. Though it was also the house of the blissful summers of fishing in the beck and dressing up as gypsies and poking around inside the fascinating corpses of dead animals, it was also the house where my father began to hate me, to list the reasons why I was no longer lovable to him.

We drive over the humpback bridge and park on the left. 'It's smaller than I imagined it,' Jonathan remarks. There's a pink clematis wrapped around the front door – we never had plants like that – and the wishing well is still there, but the gravel looks fresher, whiter.

And it's on the market. Though I doubt anyone's going to stop and beg to buy it because they haunt it.

Pam Barker and her husband show us in. The house feels done up – light, creamy colours, soft rugs, thick pile carpet, gold frames that wink in the late afternoon sun streaming in at both ends. On the right of the hall, the TV room, which used to be our dining room. The white-painted windowsill where our phone was – 'Hello, Lowdham 2539, who's speaking please?'

We stand there in the room that was our dining room – though for a while it's true we did also have a little television in here and I'd watch *Coronation Street* (while Mel and Yvette watched together in my future home) followed by *The High Chaparral* (Manolito! Vittoria!) with my Mum.

We go into the kitchen. 'Same boiler,' Pam's husband points out to us.

'My mouse Millie had her babies right there on that actual boiler,' I tell them. 'Her cage was there and one morning I came down to hear this squeaking noise.'

Eight blind pink faces with a graze of whitish fur. The smell of mouse droppings, sawdust, and kerosene.

The house feels different, though. It's been extended all over, especially at the back, so the stairs and landing have shifted into quite different spaces. It's disorientating: they seem to extend too far back, making it feel like a place I've never been before. I realize how strongly that sense of space stays with us. Whether a memory springs from childhood or adulthood, we do actually remember how far away walls felt, how long corridors, how wide landings.

The garage where we put on plays each summer – forcing our father to wire up speakers, spreading sawdust on the floor and subjecting neighbours to an hour of acting and dancing – has been replaced by a completely new double carport. The shape of the lawn has been altered entirely, extended, smoothed, the gravel drive up the side a much posher version of what used to be an old dust and shale farm track.

'You'll find the orchard changed too,' Pam's husband tells me proudly. 'We took a JCB to it, filled in that Victorian pond.'

'Oh!' I try to hide my disappointment. 'The one with the rickety wooden bridge?'

Not so much a pond as a deliciously mysterious sunken place in the orchard's long grass. A pit in which to keep prisoners, a trench in which to squat down and hide from Indians or Germans. We fired arrows from the bridge, which was strong enough to take our weight but rotten and creaky enough to feel dangerous.

We climb the stairs to my old bedroom.

Here's where I lay and listened to my parents fighting, and then one night my Mum came and slept in the spare bed next to me and told me she was going to leave Daddy. I lay up here and heard my father creak around his study, heard his feet coming heavily up the stairs. Sometimes, if I couldn't sleep, I was allowed to go and sit in his workshop on a high stool and watch the little flickering black-and-white Sony television.

'We found some of your writing on the walls downstairs, you know, under the paint. I think you'd signed your name.'

'Sweet,' says Jonathan. I shiver.

The room next door to mine used to be a kind of junk room – windowless, a mess. I didn't like to look in it – there was just blackness, the red eye of some kind of water heater, the sigh of pipes. Now it's a little bathroom – neatly fitted out. Towel rail. Shower. Soap dish.

Before we leave, they take us out to the barns, past the orchard. I can barely look at it – a smooth green lawn with trees. Gone is the hut where I kept the dead duck. And the chicken shed that was, for a brief, frenzied summer, the headquarters of the Caythorpe Ghost Club.

'The Ghost Club?' says Jonathan. 'But where were the ghosts?'

'Not ghosts exactly. We used to creep up on suspicious-looking people, anyone we didn't like the look of.'

'And then?'

'And then report back. We had meetings – with biscuits. We made badges.'

But Mr Barker has levelled it all – the Ghost Club HQ, the wonderful bumpy terrain, the hidden pits, the old damson trees, and half of my childhood.

'Wait till you see what we've done to the barns,' he says.

The Barkers are selling Brooklyn House itself and are going to live in the barns. Only the cast iron pillars look Victorian and familiar.

'There was a trough here,' he says, pointing to the clean white walls with their views over the flat Notts fields. And suddenly I know where I am. I'm in the corner where Sparky chased a rat and got stuck down behind the sacks of grain for a day, unable to move or jump out until Mum finally heard her yelping. Here's where our truck stood – the talent contest truck. Here's where Jimmy Hughes, the farmer's son and farmhand, offered us fruit gums in the sunshine. We could take the fruit gums because he wasn't a stranger. But we knew we weren't to trust him otherwise. It was said that he'd once got a girl in the village pregnant.

The Barkers tell us that Jimmy Hughes died, just a year or so ago in fact.

'But – how old was he? Only ten years older than me or something?'

'That's right. It was awful. He just dropped dead on his doorstep. In fact, he'd just finished doing the orchard for us. He was the one who did it all.'

Every time we ask someone from the house if they remember Vincent Dias they frown and say No. No one has any memory of a man called Vincent anything. Even Alvin, who let out the rooms, can't remember a Vincent. Could the electoral register be wrong?

There is only one Vincent Dias listed on the Info Disk in London and last year I wrote to him (the phone number was ex-directory). No reply. So I assumed he was simply The Wrong Vincent Dias. But having found no others many months later, Jonathan drives to the address in Catford.

'Your letter came,' his wife Shirley tells him, 'but we'd just got back from Eastbourne and it got lost among the junk mail so we never replied.'

All over the country, people are bothering to write and tell us they aren't who we're looking for – the wrong Vera Palmer, the wrong Thomas Kyle. And meanwhile the Right Ones just forget to get back to us.

Now they come to tea.

A hot Sunday, the street dusty, kids shrieking in gardens, the ice cream van jangling by, the hydrangea outside the front door greyly parched.

Vincent clutches a bunch of car keys. He's a tall, slender, ferociously good-looking man with grizzled grey hair and clipped beard. A light denim shirt and denim jeans – several chunky gold rings on his fingers

149

and several matching gold teeth. His wife Shirley is a much larger lady with high tight cheekbones and a low, slow, gravelly voice.

We've made tea and put out a plate of biscuits, but Shirley says she won't have anything – she had a drink before she arrived. 'If I want, I'll ask.'

Vincent accepts a Coke and pulls a couple of cracked, black and white photos out of a crinkled plastic carrier bag. One has three young men in smart clothes, facing the camera purposefully dressed up for a night out. 'That's me in the middle,' he says, 'I bought that hat for two and six at Cecil Gee.' I don't tell him that no one remembers him but I run some names past him – people who were here in his time – and he remembers no one, though he adds that he might have known the faces. 'We didn't know names back then.'

'He used this place just as a bed,' his wife explains.

Vincent arrived from Jamaica on 2 September 1956 on a boat called the TN *Castel Verde*. He was nineteen years old. He took the boat to Genoa, stopping off at Barcelona, Madeira, and Venezuela on the way. From Genoa, he took a train to Calais – 'we must have been through thirty tunnels!' – and another boat to Plymouth and then the train to Cannon Street Station in London. The one-way trip cost £75.

He was alone but he didn't feel all that lonely. It wasn't so tough – his mother was already in the country, living on Larch Road in Balham. And then there was his Uncle Lester and Aunt Ena Townsend on Elspeth Road, just off Lavender Hill, and he went there for just about all his meals, so he was well fixed up. Unlike Shirley, who came over on 3 August 1959 and knew absolutely no one. 'It was terrifying, you know?'

He met her on her second week in the country and it turned out they'd grown up in the same neighbourhood in Kingston and even had friends in common – just that they'd never met. They got together at a party on Larkhall Rise – 'the first house on the right after the hump-backed bridge' – and three weeks later they went out together to another party and Vincent got so drunk that Shirley had to bring him back home here to Lillieshall Road.

'He knew where he was going and he had his keys, but I had to come up with him and put him to bed. I sat in a chair all night in that room of his and I watched him tossing and turning, and I didn't dare leave him because I was afraid he would vomit and choke, you know? My mother was furious because she didn't believe me. "Tom is drunk but Tom is no fool," she used to say. That was her saying in those days. Turns out this Tom was just drunk.'

That was the only time Shirley ever came to this house, that night in 1959. I ask her if she can remember where Vincent's room was? 'Of course I can,' she replies hotly – and leads us unhesitatingly straight up the stairs to our own bedroom.

Vinnie finds the room at Lillieshall Road through a friend of a friend. You ask around. Something usually comes up. Actually the rent is not too dear. Between about 20 and 30 shillings a week – he knows plenty who are paying more for shared rooms where you have to queue up with your pan in your hand if you want to use the kitchen. He gets about eleven quid a week in his job as a shunter on the railways, so he feels lucky. He's just nineteen and new in the country, and anyway there are plenty of landlords who won't rent rooms to coloured people. They'll say, Yes, the room's available, then change their minds when they see you. Or else you'll get a notice on the front door saying 'Rooms to Let. No Coloured Men'.

This house is pretty rare because it's actually owned by Jamaicans. He pays his rent to a man called Alvin who plays the sax and lives downstairs with his family. They seem nice enough people, though he doesn't take much notice of the kids.

He's just in and out anyway. He barely uses the kitchen, since he eats most days at his aunt and uncle's and he'll have a bath sometimes in the back kitchen if he feels like it and there's some hot water – though you have to get in quick or it cools down before you can do anything about it.

He has the front room on the first floor that looks out over the street. The sun comes in every morning and now and then the sunny brightness dazzles him, almost makes him feel he's back in Kingston. Sometimes this is a good thing, other times it makes his heart ache. The room's not bad at all – furnished with a wardrobe, bed (which is just inside on the right as you come in, facing those windows), table, and a little two-seater sofa by the window. The wallpaper is flowery and the floor is lino – some greyish pattern. There's a paraffin heater and white net curtains on the window and sheets are also provided. The trouble with paraffin heaters is the smell. Sit on the bus next to someone and you can tell straightaway if they have one in their room. He has to dry all his clothes in front of it and sometimes even he catches the pong of gas as he pulls on a shirt or vest.

Vinnie's life is pretty much the same every day. He just gets up and goes to work in Kingston – which is nothing like the Kingston he grew up in – then goes and has a drink at maybe the Wycliffe Road pub or the Beaufoy Arms where he's getting to know a few more of the locals. They're not bad there, not much against coloureds. One man he knows had to be escorted to the pub by police just to make sure he got there safely. He person- ally hasn't had that experience. After a few pints he'll go back home to bed and out again the next day. He barely sees anyone else in the house – just pays his rent and gets on with it. Maybe sometimes he'll go out dancing to Brixton Assembly Rooms or Battersea Town Hall – he even has an English girlfriend for a while before he meets Shirley.

'I bought that hat for two and six at Cecil Gee'

Shirley is working as a laundress at Hampton Court. She's a slim, nice-looking girl with a quick smile and wide cheekbones. He notices her straightaway at the party. They all go to parties all the time – it's the only way to meet other people from Jamaica. Shirley's not drinking but she's joining in all the same. She tells him she knows hardly a soul in London but she's not going to let it stop her having a good time. He says maybe he could show her a good time and she laughs him off and then goes quiet on him.

Later, when he knows her better, he finds out this is just her way. She can be outgoing and she can be shy and he likes this, the way he's not sure where he stands with her. She tells him she was so very lonely when she first came over. He knows what she means: he's had his lonely days, lonely nights. Even if, like him, you have family over here, there's nothing like the shock of that mean bitter climate. The cold is so limiting, it stops you doing things, depresses your mood. In Jamaica you can at least get dressed up and go out and relax in the evenings, and it's hot. Here the weather can stop you in your tracks – make you give up all your plans and do nothing.

Shirley discovers this to her cost. She considers doing an accountancy course at night school to improve her chances in life, but she goes to catch the bus and sees her first frost – a hard glitter of whiteness over everything, the lampposts, the railings, the edges of buildings. It's pretty but it makes her breath hurt. She can barely move her fingers and her feet sting and go numb, one sensation after the other. She gives up and turns back, huddles in bed at home and just cries with disappointment.

'We seen snow in the cinema and we thought it looked like clouds . . . but then of course we feel the real thing and it's nothing like.'

Shirley's rented room is so cold that she can make Chivers jelly and put the bowl out on the windowsill and it's ready to eat – cold and set – in the morning. And then the smog – sometimes you stretch out your hand in front of you and it disappears just like it's not there any more. One time she and Vin are walking back from the pub and she can hear his voice quite clearly but can't see him in front of her. She almost panics. He holds her tight and laughs, but her heart thuds and she feels like getting straight on that boat back to Jamaica.

By early 1960 Vincent is pretty much going steady with Shirley and ready to move out of Lillieshall Road. In the Beaufoy Arms one night he tells her they should get married and he can tell she's pleased. They marry at Battersea Registry Office on 5 November 1960, with a reception afterwards at his uncle and aunt's on Elspeth Road. It's Bonfire Night and all around them rockets and firecrackers are popping and snapping. The wedding cake – three tiers – is made by a Mrs Daly and costs £7. 10*s*., with the cake stand hired from Arding & Hobbs.

'The wedding cake. . . costs £7.10s with the cake stand hired from Arding & Hobbs

Vinnie and Shirley begin their married life on Rushill Road, but when their eldest child is seven months old they move into the downstairs back room at Number 2 Broadhinton Road.

'Number 2?' I say. 'But that's amazing because that's where Isabella and Walter Hinkley lived with their sons before they moved in here.'

Shirley – who of course has never heard of the Hinkleys – seems unmoved. 'Well, we moved a hell of a lot when we first got married, right up until we could afford a house of our own.' She tells me they have four children, nine grandchildren, and a great-grandchild. Vincent is going to be sixty-five next Tuesday and they're having all the family round for a proper party.

They've been together forty-three years, her and Vincent – 'we've had our ups and downs but we've stuck together and that counts for a lot. Though sometimes I could strangle him of course.' She laughs, Vincent looks less convinced.

As we come downstairs from Vincent's old room (now our bedroom), Shirley says she's sure the landings have got narrower. I tell her it's probably because we've got so much junk lying around at the moment and she agrees.

Meanwhile Vincent says he can't get over how different the street looks – a lot smaller. Maybe because of all the cars, or the larger trees.

Vincent drove buses after the railways. He started at Stockwell on the 177 and 168 then moved onto the 37, which goes to Brixton. Then he drove the 53 from Plumstead Common to Oxford Circus. But he stopped in 1994 due to ill health and now, as of Tuesday, he's officially retired.

I ask if they ever think of going back to Jamaica. 'We've been here so long,' Shirley says firmly, 'and my children and grandchildren mean a lot to me. Why pull up all these roots? In Jamaica we'd have to start over – what would be the point?'

'And anyway,' Vincent adds, 'I've got plenty of friends over here and I don't need to go over there and buy myself some more.'

* * *

Raph is getting undressed for a shower. It's a hot evening and the window is wide open and Dinah the kitten is washing herself in the window box. I wish she wouldn't sit right inside the box, because she then jumps into the bathroom and flicks soil over everything.

Raph pulls off his T-shirt and tells me that when he was out on the Common this afternoon with his new best friend Caz, a man came up to them.

'A really dodgy man, yeah? With a manky kind of vest and trousers and he came up to us and started saying stuff like, Please allow me a kick of your ball.'

'What did you do?' I ask him. He takes off his boxer shorts, walks to the other end of the room and fires them into the dirty clothes basket as if he's shooting a goal.

'Well. I look at Caz and I mouth No, and then we both start saying No to him, and Caz says it too, out loud, and he starts saying to us, Look, I won't take your ball, I just want to have a kick of it and give it back to you, and I kind of believed him because he didn't look like a ball-stealer as he had about seven shopping bags, in fact he looked more like a paedophile than a ball-stealer.'

'Goodness,' I say. 'But there were plenty of other people around, right?'

'Oh yeah, but they were all lying down on the ground with their eyes shut.'

'So what happened then?'

'I said, Look, I'd love to give you a kick of my ball but my Mum won't let me give stuff to strangers, and he goes all kind of mad and starts saying, What? What does your Mum say? Tell me what she says, and he's smiling and trying to be charming but, you know, Caz and me can take a hint and so we walk quickly away and then we start to run.'

'Good boys, that was the right thing to do – did he leave you alone then?'

'Well, um, no, he comes after us but we say we gotta go and we run a bit faster and then he leaves us. Anyway we pretend to go far but in fact we

only went a couple of trees away and I say to Caz he seemed like a paedophile and Caz says, Yeah, and I say, Does your Mum go through all this
all the time with you? and he says, Oh Yeah, and we both agree that Mums
Are So Funny, always worrying that we're going to go off in people's vans.'

I drive through a sweltering Streatham traffic jam and out to Sussex to
see Mrs Bennie, now ninety-six, who lived next door at Number 32
from 1941 to 1983. A key witness. I'm hoping she'll remember things.
In Streatham High Road a whole lane's closed and there are fire engines
and the wrecks of two burnt-out cars. No casualties presumably
because the firemen are sitting around eating ice lollies.

In the end I stop at a garage for a bottle of water. My clothes are
soaked with sweat, the hair at the back of my neck is wet. 'Too hot,' says
the man who serves me. 'I come from Sri Lanka you know, and I tell
you it's not as bad as this there.'

'Different kind of heat?'

'Uh huh. Cool heat.'

I drive off with Nina turned up loud – 'Mississippi Goddam' – and
finally the road turns green and leafy and there's air to breathe and the
light is sweet and clear and dappled with shadow.

Colin Murhall, who grew up next door, has given me very precise
instructions for finding Vine Cottage. 'You'll see two sets of traffic
lights followed by a general store and a post office. That means you're
here basically. We're the one with the two tall white chimneys . . .
there'll be a navy-blue car outside. We'll leave you a space to park.'

He comes out and directs me up the very steep slope.

'Use the handbrake and put it in reverse,' he advises, 'just to be on
the safe side.'

Inside, the cottage is deliciously cool. Gwen gets me a drink of squash.
There's a huge black Newfoundland taking up half the room and on the
other side Mrs Bennie – small and slim and wrinkled but looking

much younger than ninety-six – is sitting meekly and shyly in a chair.

'She's been a bit worried,' Colin explains. 'At first she said she didn't want to get involved. She thinks she won't be any use to you.'

I shake her hand and say it doesn't matter at all and that I'm just so pleased to meet her.

'Very nice to meet you, my darling,' she says and proceeds to tell me how good her accommodation in Uckfield is and she has no complaints whatsoever, thank you.

'Aunt, can we talk about Lillieshall Road?' Colin says loudly.

'Lillieshall Road? Oh yes, I moved there in 1941 just after I was married. I was born in Battersea, you know, went to school on Tennyson Street. Our school was opposite the Cripple School. We felt very sorry for those cripples.'

I tell her I want to run some names past her and Colin says I have to shout, so I kneel on the floor next to her and proceed to shout names into her ear.

'There was a dark family in there,' she tells me when I get to Reynolds. 'Very dark – dark people, you know?'

'Aunt,' Colin says, 'that's not very politically correct.'

I laugh. 'Tell me about the dark family, Mrs Bennie!'

'Very dark, they were. But nice people even so. Except for him. He was awful to her, really awful!'

'Really? In what way awful?'

'She was a nurse, you see, such a lovely woman, really lovely, and when she married him his mother was so pleased. His mother was a very nice woman too.'

'Melda McNish?'

'That's right, yes – very nice lady, though very dark she was too.'

Colin and Gwen are laughing. 'Auntie, you've got to find another word instead of dark.'

'It's OK. The dark man,' I shout into Mrs Bennie's ear, 'what was he like?'

'Oh well there were fights. Terrible fights. We used to hear them. Such a noise, shouting and all that. She came out crying into the street one day and I said, What is it? and she said, That man, my life is over with him. And his mother was on her side, she was very against him for it. Why couldn't he just settle down and make this nice woman happy?'

Mrs Bennie folds her hands and gazes at them for a moment.

'What was he like, the dark man?' I shout.

'Wicked. A wicked man. Though you'd never have known it to look at him – well dressed, charming, nice-looking, smiled all the time. Wicked man.'

When I first spoke to him, Alvin Reynolds was the charming dreamer, sitting in Jamaica, longing to be back in his Clapham home, a good man, the head of the family, a man with a true sense of home. In less than a month, he has become a much more tempestuous character – the Wicked Man.

'Tell her about the gambling, Aunt,' says Colin.

'Gambling?'

'Oh yes, a gambling den, on the top floor. People coming and going all the time, such a noise ...'

'What?' I ask her. 'Cards or what?'

'Cards, yes, anything – such a going-on.'

'She used to hear it,' Colin says, 'because she had rooms on the top floor of Number 32, you see – the noise would have carried.'

'I saw them get married,' Mrs Bennie continues.

'What? Alvin and Laurie?'

'Yes, the nurse. They got married there at the house and we watched from the upstairs window. The bridesmaids were all different colours. Lots of different-coloured bridesmaids they had, every shade you can think of, my darling.'

I ask Mrs Bennie whether she remembers anything about the Blaines, the people who were there before the Reynolds.

'Blaines? Yes?'

'Do you remember what they were like?'

'I'm getting old, darling. I can't remember. I know they kept the garden nice, they were well off. The dark people let the garden go, such a shame.'

I ask if she remembers Mavis Jones-Wohl and her little boy?

'Tommy?'

'No, Rodney.'

'Rodney, yes! My husband used to take that little boy for walks.'

Mrs Bennie tells me she used to go dancing at the Locarno in Streatham and that she liked her shoes to match her dress – 'pink dress, pink shoes, black velvet dress, black shoes. I wonder what happened to that black velvet dress.'

Back home, we have supper in the garden. Candles lit, the sprinkler turning lazily, Dinah playing with a moth under the magnolia tree.

Raph, separating out the various components of his salade niçoise so he can eat them in ascending order of preference, says, 'Gambling! Wow! In Jake's and my room?'

'It might not have been actual gambling,' Jonathan says. 'It might just have been a bit of partying that she heard, surely?'

'She was pretty certain about the gambling.'

Raph carefully forks the blue-yellow yolk out of a hard-boiled egg, puts it on the edge of his plate, eats the white. 'Did he win money do you think?'

'Was it legal?' asks Chloë, taking a sip of pink squash.

'Mummy,' Raph says, 'you know you want a mobile phone?'

'Well, I'm not sure I do actually.'

'Well, but my question is, would you mug someone to get one? If they'd already mugged you, I mean?'

'Raph?'

'Yuh.'

'Run that one by me again.'

* * *

I call Alvin in Jamaica again, with a few more questions. 'It's you!' he says, laughing. 'Oh my, this is getting to be a habit.'

I apologize for disturbing him – 'No, it's fine, it's fine' – and ask him if he remembers anything at all about a Patricia C. Reynolds, who from my records seems to have been in the house a few years before him. He doesn't.

'So you're not related? That's all I was wondering.'

'Oh no, not related, no.' So just a coincidence, the name.

I then ask him if he remembers anything at all about Thomas Kyle or Gerald Sherrif.

'Kyle was an elderly English guy, can't remember much about him. Gerald Sherrif, he was black and I think he worked for London Cabs – you know, down by the Oval.' Like Vincent Dias – is this just another coincidence?

'And I also wondered whether I could perhaps speak to one of your children? Maybe Marcia or Sheryl?'

He laughs. 'Hmm, well, we have nothing to hide, I don't see why not. Sheryl, she lives not far from you in Mitcham, you know. Marcia – let me see, she's in Thornton Heath.'

'Do you think they'd mind talking to me?'

'Well, I don't know, as I say, we have nothing to hide . . . I'm just looking for the phone number now as a matter of fact. Or maybe, hmm, maybe you could ask my sister for the number.'

'I know, perhaps just tell me Sheryl's last name and I can maybe get it through directory enquiries. Is she married?'

'Married? Hmm, no, not as far as I know. I don't think she has married at all. So she's probably still just Sheryl Reynolds.'

He can't be very much in touch with her if he's not that sure. Finally I ask him about Veronica Ricketts. I don't say anything about having met Doreen. I don't say I know Veronica was his wife.

'Veronica Ricketts?' he says in his laidback drawl. 'Hmm, yes, let me see, she was a tenant of mine. She passed away this year as a matter of fact, in Canada, you know. I rented her a room in the house for a while, yes, hmm.'

'But you said he was so nice,' Jonathan reminds me when I tell him about this conversation. 'You really liked him when you first spoke to him.'

'Well, he does sound nice. He's very warm and open, you know, on the phone.'

'Warm and open but doesn't tell anything remotely connected to the truth.'

'Apparently not. And anyway all this stuff about having nothing to hide, that's always suspicious isn't it? He can't really be in touch with his daughters, not if he can't give me their numbers and doesn't even know if they're married or not.'

'For all we know, he is related to Patricia Reynolds. For all we know, she's yet another cast-off wife,' says Jonathan. 'Cast-off sister, aunt, anything.'

I tell him that would be neat, but I doubt it actually because she was there before Melda even, and I do believe Gloria about Melda being the first.

'But he's our second real baddie, isn't he?' I say. 'Just like Reggie Povah the spiv.'

'Only a bit more alive.'

'Maybe he's lying about that too. Maybe he's speaking to me from the other side.'

'You just got seduced by the bit when he said he still dreamed about this house.'

'I know,' I admit, 'I did. I liked that. I'd been waiting for someone to say that.'

Jonathan tips back in his chair. 'Alvin just talks a good script, that's all.'

Gloria phones to say she called Louisa Heron in New York and that she's crippled with arthritis now and her husband Stanley died five years ago, but they were so pleased to talk again after all these years. 'Thank you so much for putting us in touch,' she says.

Meanwhile Yvette drops round a crinkled plastic carrier bag that contains something wonderful. It's the photo – a large, framed, black-and-white picture of her aged about two, sitting on Aunt Mel's lap. It's taken in our sitting room, the old pine double doors entirely recognizable behind the armchair they're sitting in. The carpet's one of those laboriously fussy sixties patterns, all geometrical flowers and zigzags, and the armchair's shabby, worn, and threadbare – possibly peachy pink with a criss-cross pattern – way past its best, for sure.

Melda's wearing a sleeveless, flowery print dress and looks about forty, blazingly pretty, eyes lit up with a hot, happy smile. Her feet are stretched in front of her, ankles crossed – hard to see whether it's slippers or shoes on her feet – and her fingers grasp the stuff of Yvette's little white dress, as if to somehow display it to the photographer, as if to show what a precious jewel her small granddaughter is. Yvette, matching white bow tied in her hair, is glancing off in another direction, one small

hand lifted slightly, as if contemplating any moment a swift wriggle down off her grandmother's lap.

It's just a single moment in an ordinary room in a terraced Clapham house in the early 1960s. One of the people in the picture is gone, the other grown up, a grandmother herself.

But it seems to contain in one heart-shuddering flash every single thing I'm attempting to divine and explore: family, affection, love, generosity, hope, and – however fleetingly – home.

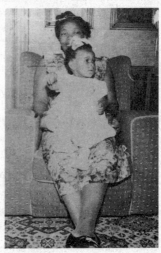

'eyes lit up with a hot, happy smile'

Chapter Five

THE WEDDING IN THE BEDROOM, THE BOY IN THE BATHROOM, AND THE LITTLE GIRL WHO SAT VERY VERY STILL

The Blaines, the Bartolos, the Costellos, Patricia C. Reynolds,
Rita Wraight, Olive Russell, and Mavis Jones-Wohl
1948–1958

In 1959, Melda McNish and her son Alvin buy 34 Lillieshall Road from a couple called Annie and Theodore Blaine. They have a daughter. They might be American. Or Canadian. More people have said Canadian. That's all we know.

'Do you by any chance remember anything about the Blaines?' I ask Alvin on the phone.

'Not much, no.'

'Do you remember the Blaines?' I shout in Mrs Bennie's ear. 'Annie and Theodore Blaine?'

She gives me a lop-sided smile. 'Think so. Blaine. Yes.'

'What were they like? Were they Canadian?'

She tips her head on one side and smiles even more sweetly. 'I'm old, my darling, I don't remember anything.'

The Info Disk offers us several hundred Blaines. Most of them appear without phone numbers. We enlist the kids' help and send letters out to all the Anns and Annes and Annies. Almost mercifully there are no Theodores.

'You ought to say there's a cash prize,' Raphael suggests as he stuffs and sticks. 'That would get them ringing you, sure as anything. Say there's a thousand pounds or something.'

'Mummy already had that idea,' his father tells him, 'and it's a stupid one. They'd all get in touch instantly.'

'People will do anything for money,' Chloë adds airily.

Three days later, a lady rings up: 'I'm Mrs Blaine.'

'How nice of you to – '

'Well, the thing is, Charlie's mother was called Annie Blaine.'

'Really?' I pause. 'And – who's Charlie?'

'My husband. Late. He's gone now, of course. She was from Ireland though and that's all I know. We're the only Blaines in England now.'

I wonder about this, remembering the several hundred letters. 'Really? How do you know that? Are you sure?'

'Absolutely sure. There was this newsagent you see – or do I mean estate agent? – anyway he got in touch with us a few years back and said he was trying to trace a Sidney Blaine because someone had left him a million pounds.'

'Gosh,' I say.

'But it wasn't us. Sadly. That's how I know, you see, that we're the only Blaines. Don't know what happened to Sidney though.'

Actually, I'm wrong. We do know a little bit more about the Blaines. We know that – according to Mrs Bennie from Number 32 – they keep the garden nice. Unlike the 'dark people' who 'let the garden go'.

But do the 'dark people' really let the garden go? Or is it perhaps tempting, if you're white and live in Lillieshall Road in the sixties and have the only black family in the street move in bang next door, to imagine that they must, at the very least, be chaotic and untidy people?

Even if they don't beat their wives (and there seems to be evidence that they do), even if they don't carouse and gamble into the night (and there seems to be evidence that they do), are they really going to be the types to tend their marigolds and keep the blackfly off their tea roses? If the definition of middle-class respectability is keeping your shirt collar Daz white, your kids off the streets, and your grass trimmed, then aren't the 'dark people' just bound to be the sort who let the nettles grow?

I don't believe Mrs Bennie is prejudiced. Or no more prejudiced than anyone else in that street at that time anyway.

'We all had manners,' she tells me when I visit her on that sweltering afternoon at the Murhalls', 'we were well brought up. My father, he was ever so strict.'

She points to a huge sepia photo of him on the Murhalls' wall – a wonderfully imposing-looking gentleman, severe and attractive, dressed for riding, and brandishing, yes, a crop.

She talks about the street in the forties and fifties – the Tim Bobbin pub where they all used to go and drink – though Mrs Bennie's husband didn't actually like to sit outside. 'He wouldn't drink out there on the street.'

'He wouldn't drink out there on the street.'

I ask her if she went to drink there too and she gives me a quick, prim look. 'Oh no,' she says with a little intake of breath and a quick flutter of her hand up to her mouth, 'not me.'

'She did! You did!' Colin and Gwen cry together, laughing.

She twinkles at me and I catch sight of her long, crooked brown teeth. 'Well, maybe just a bit then.'

But isn't that just it? If you have manners and you're well brought up, if your face is white and you don't go down the Tim Bobbin (or not much), if you keep your path weeded and your beds mulched – then isn't it a bit of a pity if, however nice and friendly they might seem, a 'dark family' moves in next door?

I guess the Murhalls must have really missed the Blaines.

Swing back to a bright Saturday morning in May 1948.

A pretty, young, dark-haired woman – smiley, with good English but spoken with a lilting middle-European accent – sits in a Notting Hill estate agent's office with her four-year-old daughter.

Dorothy Bartolo has on her one really good dress – pale blue merino wool, short sleeves, buttons down the front and a neat, thin belt with a round buckle. She made it herself. She's especially proud of the little pearly buttons along the edge of the pocket – with dressmaking, it's the details that count, make something ordinary feel fine. To tell the truth, she's slightly hot and perspiring in this dress – the sunshine here in Kensington is hazy but unexpectedly warm. They told her England would be colder. Everyone had warned her it would be chilly as anything. Wrap up, they said, you won't believe it after Egypt.

Her daughter Winnie is also dressed up smart – a plaid dress with puffed sleeves, also made up on the sewing machine by Dorothy (those sleeves were murder!) in salmon pink and pistachio, with a crisp white Peter Pan collar. Crisp and white because it was laundered and ironed back at home in Alexandria and carefully packed by Dorothy in layers of tissue paper. Wilfred laughed at her, but she knew what to do. She knew that if they were going to make a good start in London, they were going to need Clothes That Make a Good Impression.

She met Wilfred, who's Maltese, in Alexandria. His family specialized in working as lighthouse keepers. They'd be sent off for nine-month stints and then come home for three months off. Once he'd met Dorothy, he had to settle down and get a job as a cashier at the electric and gas company. But it was a good job and they were very happy there and didn't especially want to leave, but the British Consul advised them that they should. So much unrest since Nasser took power and no one knew which way the situation was going to go. Some days you let yourself think about it, some days you didn't. They weren't that worried for themselves but they had to think of Winnie – you can't have a child out there when everything's so raw and unpredictable.

The voyage took twelve days past Malta and Gibraltar – where Dorothy longed to get off, feel her feet on solid land, and Wilfred wanted to see his family, but it wasn't allowed. She'd lie awake in her berth at night, butterflies in her stomach, and listen to the boat creaking and crunking on the swollen water – sometimes it sounded as though the seas would pull it apart, literally tear it limb from limb. As it turns out, she wasn't far wrong. When the SS *Askania* reaches Liverpool, it's scrapped – it's too old, on the verge of falling apart.

Now Wilfred's out at the labour exchange and Dorothy and Winnie are sitting and waiting to see what rooms are available to rent. There's a list apparently, but the man says he's sorry but he thinks everything is currently taken. He seems a friendly man and says he'll do what he can if they don't mind hanging on. So they've been ages in this hot, airless office, waiting to hear. At least in Alexandria they'd have had a fan to cool them down. Dorothy has told Winnie that if she's good they'll ride on a tram afterwards, maybe see the ducks in Kensington Gardens, and when she hears this Winnie drums her heels in excitement. She's always good though, the promised treats are barely necessary. Dorothy can't remember when she last played up.

Dorothy stifles a yawn and watches the younger man behind the desk nearer to them. He's wiping postage stamps over a wet sponge and slopping them on envelopes. Even he looks so uncomfortable in his suit, great dark bags of perspiration under the arms. He probably wishes he didn't have to work Saturdays. He'd probably rather be reading the paper in Kensington Gardens too.

'Mu-mmy,' Winnie begins.

'No, sweetie,' Dorothy says, kissing the top of the little girl's dark head that somehow still seems to hold onto the scented, blossomy heat of home, 'shh.'

She tells her to shush because she's busy listening to a conversation on the other side of the office, at the desk over by the window. A couple have come in – oldish, twangy voices, American maybe? The woman has on a well-cut suit and has her hair done in a French pleat, a style Dorothy likes. The man has a stick and a frowny look on his face, but he speaks with a kind voice. Dorothy strains to listen without looking impolite. They're saying something about 'tenants' – a house – she thinks she hears the word 'South' and then 'Clapham'. She's heard of Clapham. She's heard of the Clapham Omnibus but has never been absolutely sure what it is.

Suddenly the friendly man behind the counter catches her eye and smiles. He comes over to where she and Winnie are sitting. He rubs his hands together and glances back at the old couple.

'Now, madam, this lady and gentleman are called Mr and Mrs Blaine, and they're looking for tenants for a nice and sunny double room in their house in Lillieshall Road in Clapham,' he says, 'and guess what I just said to them? I said, well, you see that lovely lady over there? I can't recommend her highly enough. She's got a daughter but the child's been sitting absolutely still on that seat for an hour!'

'If the house was here in Clapham,' Jonathan says, 'what on earth were the Blaines doing in an estate agent's in Notting Hill?'

'I know, it's funny, isn't it? But Dorothy insists it was Notting Hill. Maybe they owned another house in Notting Hill?'

Either way, they definitely let a room to Dorothy and Wilfred and their little daughter Winnie on that morning in May 1948. I know this because I manage to track Dorothy down in Guildford on a warm summer morning in May exactly fifty-five years later. It isn't very difficult. She's the only Dorothy Bartolo on the Info Disk.

She has a warm, lively voice with a Germanic accent – she was from Austria but her daughter Winifred has never been there – the kind of voice that hovers always on the edge of laughter. She tells me her husband Wilfred's been dead now a few years but she remembers the time at Lillieshall Road very well, clear as yesterday.

'those sleeves were murder!'

'I think it was May,' she says, 'because we were on a farm near Ipswich before that. I know we planted potatoes in March. So maybe it would have been after that. Summer. May, June? That kind of time.'

'On a farm? Then all that stuff you wrote about Winnie's dress with the crisp cotton collar from Alexandria is all wrong,' Jonathan points out. 'They came to England off the boat, stayed on a farm somewhere and only then came to London to look for a room.'

I dither for a moment. This has occurred to me too.

'But look, Dorothy gave me a photo of Winnie in that dress. I didn't make up the dress. And Dorothy told me she used to make up curtains and cushions and blinds for Heal's, so I bet she did make their clothes. And we know the story about the Blaines coming into the estate agent's office and Winnie sitting absolutely still for an hour is true.'

'Hmm.'

'Come on, you know what I mean. My story's fine. It's true in all the most important ways.'

'We rented the room for not a lot of time – only about three months,' Dorothy tells me on the phone. 'My husband Wilfred was Maltese . . . I was born in Egypt, my father was English, my mother Austrian; between us we had lots of languages, you see. Wilfred got a job with the telephone exchange, and our daughter Winifred was four years old when we lived there, all in the same room. The one at the top, on the front.'

Raph and Jake's room. The Tottenham Hotspur Room – the one that had a snooker table in 1977, the one I painted bisque when I was pregnant with Jake, the one where I sat and wrote my first novel. Suddenly the room gets younger, older. The year 1948 shudders into view.

I tell Dorothy she must have been very young in 1948 as she doesn't sound so very old now.

'My daughter Winnie's sixty now! And I'm eighty years old, would you believe, and I have five great-grandchildren!'

171

I ask her whether she remembers anything about Mavis Jones-Wohl who was there at the same time.

'Oh yes, Mavis. And her friend Olive. They'd been in the army together, I think, and they both worked at Lyons Corner Houses, in the catering, you know? Mavis was a cook and she knew all about cooking but only on a catering scale. You asked her for a recipe and let's just say you got the amounts in pounds, not ounces, if you know what I mean! But she got a lot of left-over food cheap, which was great as there were still coupons then. She was quite generous with it.'

'What did she look like?'

'Mavis? Very nice-looking, pretty and lovely, a lovely person. Always smiling and kind.'

'And what sort of age?'

Dorothy hesitates.

'Well – I was twenty-four and she was maybe a little older than me. Olive too, she was probably about the same age as Mavis but she wasn't very nice, not at all. Oh yes, she could turn round and be really quite nasty.'

'And did Olive have a boyfriend?'

'My goodness, not with that character! Mavis was the nice one, definitely. But Mavis had an American husband, I think, to start with – and a little boy, he was called Rodney or Ron. Something beginning with "R" anyway – about Winnie's age or maybe a year younger, three years old perhaps. But his father wasn't around any more. Don't know what happened to him. But Mavis married again pretty quickly. The wedding reception was there in the house, you know, in her room. We went to it.'

'What? Here at Lillieshall Road?'

'Oh yes, that summer it was. We were there and so were the Blaines. And Olive. And Winnie and the little boy running around.'

'Which room?' I ask her quickly.

'The one under ours – the room at the front on the first floor.'

* * *

Jonathan and I lie in bed on a Saturday morning, in the room where we've been sleeping and waking for the last fifteen years. The room where, several decades ago, Vincent Dias woke to ice on the inside of the window and dried his vest and pants in front of a paraffin heater; the room where, more than half a century ago, a clutch of bright, merry, laughing people stood in their best clothes toasting Mavis Jones-Wohl and her brand-new husband – a handsome American serviceman . . . in his army uniform? Tony? Or Eddie? Or . . .?

'You don't know who she married?' I ask Dorothy. 'You don't remember his name?'

'Oh no, we were only there that one summer, you see. We didn't know them all that well, to tell the truth. It was very nice of them really, to invite us down for a drink. The only thing is, I seem to remember he might have been a friend of her husband.'

Eddie or Tony or Larry, hair slicked back, big grin on his face. How long has he known Mavis? Did he always have the hots for her, even when she was still married to his friend? And is the groom nervous? Or can he relax now the registry office bit is over? Does he swoop down and affectionately grab little Rodney, his newly acquired son, tossing him up in his big strong khaki arms? And does Rodney squeal as everyone stops to watch for a moment and laugh?

Clearly such a good thing, for the little lad to have a man in his life again. And such a strong, handsome one too – another serviceman. Mavis has made a bit of a thing of liking army boys, especially the Yanks, makes jokes about it being because they're away a lot, off your back so she can get off hers. But Olive knows it's not that. Like a lot of girls, Mavis has a bit of a thing about the Yanks. Won't admit to it because it's too obvious, but civvies just don't do it for her any more. Give her a uniform any day – and that accent straight out of the pictures. Got a taste for it in the war and it's shaped her desires ever since.

And Mavis – pretty, happy, eyes glittering, her new cream-coloured hat with the little veil just ever so slightly endearingly askew – does she glance up with a rush of tenderness at her new husband, grateful for this unexpected and sudden show of genuine affection for Rodney?

Either way, it's a grand, sweet occasion – loud lively talk and laughter, whiff of Brylcreem and pinks (a great bunch bought this morning by Dorothy in the High Street and presented to the bride, now standing in a brown smoked-glass vase on the dressing table), cigarette smoke, chink of glasses, music from a gramophone, sun streaming in. Even the Blaines join in. Mrs Blaine, handbag over her wrist, sipping a glass of Asti Spumante, listening to Dorothy ask Olive how to make plum jelly. Mr Blaine explaining the finer points of bridge to Wilfred – he ought to learn.

Or maybe it's not like that at all. Maybe it's a more sedate and restrained affair – people shy and tentative with each other, the bride nervy and worrying she looks fat, the groom a little tense and cross, wishing there were more booze, sick of the bloody racket made by the two kids. Maybe it's a dullish day, disappointing weather, grey oppressive skies, mizzling summer rain. Maybe everyone's aware that Mavis is simply covering herself, going for second best – to give the boy a father and herself a little security.

Maybe Winnie and Rodney rush around too hard and boisterously and smash a glass and splash sherry all over the Blaines' second-best furniture? And that doesn't go down too well of course and Dorothy is mortified because they've only been here a month and don't know any of them all that well, and it's no good her saying it's just not like Winnie to break something: it's done now and she feels awful.

And maybe Mavis – leaning forward to let her nameless, faceless hubby light her cigarette – is really narked because it's her wedding day and she'd have thought that Mrs High and Mighty Bloody Blaine could have let it go just this once. They're only kids after all. Four years old and been on their best behaviour all day. What does she expect, the silly uptight cow?

* * *

I read the paper while Jonathan sits up in bed with the phone and rings up total strangers from the electoral register, ticking them off the list as he goes.

He's set himself to find Rita Wraight or Amy Costello – they both lived here with Mavis, Dorothy, and the Blaines.

'Ring some Olive Russells too while you're at it,' I urge him, 'you never know.'

'It's too common a name, there's no point.'

'Wonder if she married.'

'I thought you said Dorothy said she was too horrible to have a boyfriend?'

'Horrible people find partners sometimes too.' He looks at me hard. 'Yes, I do mean you.'

'Hello,' he says, suddenly getting an answer. 'So sorry to bother you. I'm researching the history of our house in Clapham, London, and I'm trying to contact a Rita Wraight who would have lived in the house in 1948.'

A beat.

'It's not you? Oh, so sorry then for wasting your time.' A little laugh. 'Thanks.'

He rings off.

'Funny how they nearly all wish you luck with your research.'

Others try to keep him on the phone – start telling him about their own family backgrounds.

'That's really interesting about your grandfather but, it's a shame, I don't think he's the one we're looking for,' he says. 'Sorry to have taken up your time. Yes, thanks so much. Yes, I'll bear that in mind – yes – thank you. Gosh, how fascinating, thanks, goodbye.'

He rings about thirty people. He crosses them off with a felt tip. Sometimes he makes a note to himself to say he's left a message.

'Not a single hit,' he says with a sigh.

'Make sure your notes are clear,' I tell him. 'We don't want to come back to them in a month and not be able to remember who we've rung.'

I sip my coffee and lie back in bed.

'You know something?' he says. 'When I talked about helping you like this, I'm not sure I pictured you lying in bed doing nothing while I worked.'

'I'm not doing nothing,' I tell him, 'I'm looking at the ceiling rose. I've just realized it's the same one that would have been up there on the ceiling at Mavis's reception.'

'Yeah, well, so are the window frames, so are the walls, so is the floor.'

'I know, but there's something about a ceiling rose. It's more like a piece of furniture, isn't it?'

Mavis's ceiling rose, Vincent's ceiling rose, Melda and Yvette's ceiling rose, its once sharp floral detail now blurred by decades of paint. And how many others have woken in their beds in this room to gaze at its central lumpy sunflower with the extra burst of daisy petals around the edge? I lie there and keep my eyes on the flower until it wobbles and shudders and I can almost see the 1940s light swinging from it and pick up the shimmer of laughter, the odour of cigarette, the quick, gay, throwaway sound of a once-upon-a-time party.

Back to the Probate Search Room. I've given up on the Costellos. It's quite simply too common a name. So now I'm on to the Blaines and not feeling much more confident.

It's different in here today – kind of buzzing. Then I realize what it is. People are actually talking. To my left, a man with grey sticky-out hair is explaining loudly to a shambling man how to go about searching.

'You can't trust the volumes,' he says, 'that's the number one rule. It's all very complicated. I've been doing this for a very long time and I'm lucky, you see, I have a highly unusual surname.'

He gives the man a lot of bossy advice very loudly. This goes on for maybe ten minutes. That's a long time in the Probate Search Room.

The fat man in a red Lacoste polo shirt, who is searching the volumes next to mine, starts to harrumph and sigh and tut, clearly resenting the distraction. He tries to catch my eye to lodge a mutual complaint, but I'm not in the mood to join forces.

I reckon that if Annie and Theodore Blaine were already oldish when they let the room to Dorothy and Wilfred in 1948, and we know that their names are still on the electoral register until 1958 (well, Theodore's disappears two years earlier in 1956 actually), then it's worth checking for their deaths from then onwards. I must find a descendant and maybe trace someone who can tell me about them. The Blaines were important – they owned the house – it's driving me mad that we know so little about them.

When Shambling Man goes away finally, Lacoste man turns to Grey Sticky-Out Hair. Clearly bursting to lodge his complaint: 'Well!' he says. 'That certainly went on a bit.'

Sticky-Out sighs dramatically but appears not to get the point. He doesn't see it as a complaint but as an expression of solidarity. 'Not that it will do any good, of course.'

Lacoste eyes him nervously but with a faint flicker of interest. This wasn't the response he was expecting. He cracks. 'No?'

Sticky-Out rolls his eyes. 'Won't make a ha'p'orth of difference – '

Lacoste, keeping a fat finger in the volume to mark his place, decides to enter into the spirit of the thing and agree. 'I noticed that. Didn't take in a word, did he?'

'Hopeless case.'

'I wondered why you bothered frankly.'

'Ah well. I've been doing this a long time, you see,' Sticky-Out says proudly.

There's a pause while both men continue flicking through the volumes. The room settles back into silence. Temporarily though, because it's clear Lacoste doesn't want to let go now.

'You say you have an unusual surname,' he begins – and Sticky-Out brightens, apparently ready to do some more talking about himself. 'Well,' Lacoste continues, 'you see I have a very normal surname. Very normal indeed. But I'm unusual in myself.'

Sticky-Out decides to ignore this. 'I've been doing this for months,' he confides, 'coming down all the way from Stoke-on-Trent. It's a ridiculous system. It ought to all be computerized.'

'I'm doing this for an old tutor of mine,' says Lacoste. 'University tutor actually.'

'Goodness,' says Sticky, refusing to be impressed, 'I wouldn't do this for anyone else, I can tell you that. Too bloody boring. Too bloody hard work.'

'Oh, I'm not doing it for nothing,' says Lacoste, smiling fatly. 'I'm getting paid.'

'All the same,' says Sticky weakly.

I'd expected to find Theodore's will first, since his name disappears from the register two years earlier than Annie's and I'd assumed he'd died. But no, here in fact, all of a sudden, is Annie:

> BLAINE Annie of 64 Mount Pleasant Biggin Hill Westerham Kent died 26 Jan 1965 at Farnborough Hospital Kent Probate Nottingham 29 March to Theodore William Blaine retired master greengrocer and florist.

It's funny, even though I know almost nothing about her, and even though a part of me is getting used to this sometimes coldly speedy process – births, marriages, and deaths of strangers flicking past in a day, an hour, a minute – still, seeing it, the actual written-down evidence of Annie Blaine's death, gives me a small snag of pain.

I wonder why probate was granted at Nottingham. Is that a clue to anything?

And Theodore was a master greengrocer and florist. Maybe in that wedding room it wasn't bridge he so enthusiastically discussed with

Wilfred Bartolo, but the price of carrots, the perfect, twirled beauty of gladioli and dahlia blooms, cut as crops from Kent fields and stacked into vans at crack of dawn on hot June mornings. Maybe Wilfred replied, telling him about the reality of lifting potatoes in the whipping wind of Suffolk. Maybe the scented, fray-petalled pinks in the vase weren't from Dorothy Bartolo at all, but taken from Theodore's shop, snatched from a metal bucket that morning and wrapped in a paper doily by Annie before being thrust into Mavis's manicured hands.

Meanwhile Lacoste and Sticky-Out are still talking, fingers now permanently lodged in their volumes. They've gone beyond research now, moved on to other topics. 'All these Kurds,' says Lacoste with real fer-ocity, 'do they really think we want them?'

'Politicians,' agrees Sticky-Out, 'I don't believe a word they say.'

'We don't need any of these refugees,' affirms Lacoste, 'except perhaps Chinese. Chinese are very industrious, you know, fingers to the bone, I'll give them that.'

'Well, so are the Asians in point of fact,' agrees Sticky-Out, 'but I can't be bothered with politics. When election time comes round I don't even bother, you know.'

'Ha! Me neither,' agrees Lacoste. 'Who do they think we are? I'm short enough of time as it is. I just say, No thank you, and that's that.'

'As soon as they produce a printed card,' says Sticky-Out, 'I do the same. I just say, No thank you.'

'No thank you! Ha! Stops them in their tracks.'

'That's right, that's it. In their tracks.'

I order Annie's will and then find Theodore's three years later in 1968. Needing to escape from the ever more jubilant certainties of Sticky-Out and Lacoste, I go out for a coffee, but forget how hot it is out there. The thing about research is that it's nearly always air-conditioned. Maybe that's why so many researching types wear nylon.

* * *

Theodore Blaine leaves everything to his daughter Annie Jennings and her husband Armand Jack Arthur Jennings.

You'd think that Armand was a hopeful sign, but it turns out there isn't a single Armand Jennings in the country.

'A name like that, you'd change it or risk getting beaten up,' says Jake, and he's probably right.

'You can't look for their wills, too many Jenningses,' says Jonathan. 'But if you checked through all the Jennings births looking for mother's maiden name of Blaine . . .'

'I'd probably have to be sectioned at the end of it.'

It's Sunday and I finally get around to digging the beds where the old laurel hedge used to be in the front garden. I dug it up with Jake's help because it was all gnarled and only half a hedge anyway and I want to plant a lavender like the one down the street. Once this was all lavender fields: it was Lavender Hill.

I dig deep by the crumbly old front wall and find three things: a little old bottle saying Booth's Distilleries on it. Not a modern miniature but an old one, definitely. Also, more interesting, a wizened, squeezed-out tube of Gleem toothpaste, the writing on it still readable. The word Gleem written in a curly fifties logo, like the 'That's All Folks!' at the end of Warner Bros cartoons. And an old brass button with an anchor on it. Did Mavis like a sailor too?

Later I do a search on Google for Gleem toothpaste and it says the brand was first manufactured in America in the forties. Could this actual tube have belonged to Mavis's new husband? I get a sudden image of him, frantically cleaning his teeth before the wedding – white froth spilling out of his mouth – before flinging the tube out of the window into the front garden.

I'm ringing every Wohl in the phone book. But given what Dorothy told me about Rodney or Ron, I start with R. Wohl, Southend. Run the usual introduction (writer, book, house) and then: 'Sorry to bother you, but does the name Mavis Jones-Wohl mean anything to you?'

Man's voice, hesitant, guarded. Ye-es, his mother was called Mavis Jones-Wohl.

'She was? That's wonderful! I can't believe I've actually found you.'

He hesitates. Then says he hasn't seen her in years, has no idea of where she is. 'I probably can't help you,' he says.

I explain again what I'm doing, researching this house. He sounds nonplussed.

'Well, I wouldn't have ever known I'd lived in London.'

'Really?' I can't quite take this in. Even if he doesn't remember, he must surely know.

I tell him about Dorothy – that the other day I spoke to an old lady who remembers him as a little boy, about three years old, running around at his mother's wedding reception. In our house.

Silence.

'I wouldn't know anything about that.'

'But – you were here . . . ?'

'I really wouldn't know.'

I struggle to think of the right thing to ask next. I can't let this man go – because this is him, the little boy who played with Winnie in our bedroom in 1948!

I ask him if he has an address for his mother.

'Sorry, I don't.'

He doesn't say it in a hostile way. Just final.

I ask if he minds telling me how long ago he last saw her. He gives a little cough.

'Well, let me see, I was born in '46. In '54 she remarried and she put me in a children's home. I was eight. I never saw her again.'

I sit there with the phone in my hand and I feel my whole body go still as I realize that this is not like any of the other calls I've made. This isn't like anything. This isn't something I expected I'd have to do. Tell someone something they didn't already know about their own life. Don't already know. By the way, you lived here. This was you.

In chilling slow motion, the scene at the wedding reception changes. Mavis leans forward, smiling, and lets her new husband light her cigarette. She holds it between shiny red-polished fingers, keeping her eyes intently on him as she inhales, breathes out on a laugh at something someone behind her is saying.

She's a little bit tiddly, she must be. Blast. Going to have a rotten headache tomorrow, that's for sure.

Meanwhile, noticing that Rodney – who's been getting on her nerves all day with his whining and his forever pulling at her best clothes – has slunk back into his bedroom, she pops out onto the landing and quietly turns the key in the lock. He'll find enough to do in there. He'd better. He knows if he rattles the door, he'll get a good hiding later.

There, now. A grown-up party, finally. Apart from the Bartolos' little kid who's easy to ignore. They can have a bit of peace, relax, let their hair down. It's her wedding day, after all.

Mavis sucks on her ciggie again and the end burns hard and a tail of hot ash falls on the Blaines' scuffed brown lino.

I tell Rodney Wohl that I'm so sorry. It's just dawned on me what a shock this call from a stranger must be.

'It is a bit of a surprise, yes.'

He tells me he never tried to find his mother, never.

'Why not?'

'Well, I suppose you see these programmes on the television and you think, do I really want to go there?'

I tell him that I was estranged from my own father, that when I was sixteen he told me he didn't want to see me any more. But even though it's true, as I hear the words slip out, I feel ashamed. It's not the same.

I'm used to what happened with my father – and I wasn't eight. I'm just trying to win his confidence – make him feel I understand these things. And how can I, and anyway is it even any of my business to try?

'I'm sorry,' I say again, 'this must be a lot to take in. Maybe you didn't even want to know all this?'

He says nothing, but he doesn't contradict me.

I realize I too am shocked. You don't expect to have to phone someone and find yourself telling them who and what and where they were in a time they know nothing of.

I wouldn't have said I ever lived in London. The words make perfect sense now. I'm revealing a whole new self to Rodney – a self he knows nothing of. This house may be crammed full of ghosts, but mostly the ghosts know who they were. Even Alvin, even Vincent Dias – they all know they were here.

And yet here's the ghost of a small boy running between people's legs at a wedding reception he doesn't know he even attended.

He asks me if I know who his mother married when she lived here. I tell him that as far as I know – from what Dorothy has told me – he was an American serviceman.

'Oh, my father was an American serviceman too,' he says, 'but I didn't know they ever got married.'

He tells me his mother was the black sheep of the family – a 'rebel'. I ask him how he knows that.

'Just – I think relatives said so.'

Are these relatives still around? He says no, they were old back then, they'll certainly be dead now. He says his mother came from Grimsby and the family name was Cribb. He has 'no photos whatsoever'. I ask – very hesitantly now – whether he thinks he'd ever have any interest in coming and seeing the house where he lived when he was so small.

He is silent for a long moment. 'No. I don't think I'd have any interest in that. A house is just a house after all, isn't it?'

I tell him that what I'm really trying to do is find out about how we feel about the spaces we live in – that impulse we all have, wherever we live, to reach back and wonder who was here before.

'Oh, we all do that,' he says with a little laugh.

I ask if he has any kids. 'Yes.'

'Would they be interested, do you think?'

'I don't know. Maybe.'

I leave him with my phone number. I tell him I completely understand if he never contacts me ever again, but if he did I would so love to hear from him. We say a very polite, almost warm goodbye.

Afterwards, I go and stand in our bathroom – his bedroom – and look out of the window at the wet garden. The magnolia leaves glow greenish. I try to imagine Rodney standing there, looking out of that window in the summer of 1948. What would he have seen?

Then I realize he would have been far too small to see out. Three years old. His head would barely have reached the sill.

'It's funny that one ordinary little room has had two lonely children in it. We know that now.'

'Which room?'

'Our bathroom. First, in 1948, little Rodney Wohl. And then in the seventies, Doreen Ricketts. Neither of them were wanted by their mothers. And you know what's even stranger?'

'I can't imagine.'

'What I keep remembering is how John Pidgeon told me that he tried to use that room as a study but he just couldn't settle, so he moved to the smaller room and made it into a bathroom instead.'

'That was just sensible. It makes a really big comfortable bathroom. Anyone would have done that, if they could afford to and had the space.'

'Even so. You don't think it's funny that he said that, without knowing anything about either Rodney or Doreen?'

* * *

I find a Mrs Cribb in Scunthorpe on the Info Disk. Rodney had said the family name was Cribb and she came from Grimsby. Could she be related to our Mavis Jones-Wohl? Could she even be our Mavis?

'Hello? Is that Mavis Cribb?'

'Yes, dear.'

I explain who I am, what I'm doing. 'I'm just about to sit down to a meal, dear. Can you give me a ring another day?'

If Annie Blaine was born in 1895, then her daughter Annie could have been born any time from 1911 to 1940 (I decide that sixteen to forty-five will be my research limits of fertility). So at her youngest, Annie Jennings could have given birth in 1927; at her oldest, born in 1940, she could have given birth any time from 1956 to 1985.

So I search fifty-eight years of Jennings births, looking for a mother whose maiden name is Blaine. And I find no one.

My last lead on the Blaines is gone.

I know our house was built by 1872. I have an 1870 map of Clapham that shows a cricket ground where our house now is, and another map from two years later, 1872, that shows the road clearly existing.

And the earlier map shows that half our road – the bit with the Tim Bobbin and the cottages – already existed in 1870 and was called Orchard Street. Which means it was extended and renamed Lillieshall when the next raft of houses – ours and the larger ones further down – were built.

But why were they built, and by whom? And why the name change? Why didn't they just extend Orchard Street and continue to call it that?

'I know why The Chase is called The Chase,' says Raph, whose topic last term was Clapham History. 'Because they used to chase things there.'

'Who did?'

'People. It was their front drive and they used to go hunting right down it. A man called Samuel Pepys lived there but I think he died.'

185

It seems almost like a backward step to drive back to the Minet Library, home of the Lambeth Archives, but I realize there are still depths – and drawers and card indexes – I haven't plumbed.

The librarian points me at the index drawer for streets and there's a clutch of pink, scrubby-edged Lillieshall Road cards. LBL/DCEPS/ SW/2/62 offers something called an apportionment. What's that?

'You'll have to wait,' says the librarian, who has taken up his post behind the desk. 'My supervisor's downstairs at a meeting and the other person who should be here is off sick.'

Forty minutes later, a large out of breath man brings it to my table. He has a look of resigned incredulity on his face, as if he can't possibly imagine why anyone would want to look at these basement-stored papers.

It's a folded parchment-like bundle of ten sheets or so. The copperplate on the front reads 'Dated 6th December 1876' and below that 'Order of apportionment of cost of paving'.

I open up the wide double-foolscap sheets. The first is a standard printed form, the first word in Gothic script:

> **Whereas** we, the Board of Works for the Wandsworth District, being the Local Authority within the said District for the execution of the 'Metropolitan Management Act, 1855' and the several Acts amending the same and incorporated therewith, deem it necessary and expedient that so much of a certain New Street called *Lillieshall Road* as is a continuation of what was formerly called Orchard Street situate in the Parish of Clapham within the said District should be paved.

It goes on:

> Now we do hereby, in pursuance of the power and authority for that purpose vested in and imposed upon us by the said several Acts, charge and assess the respective owners hereunder named of

the several houses, land and premises, situate in the new said
street called Lillieshall Road within the said District to the
payment of the several sums of money apportioned by us and
hereunder set opposite the respective names of the said Owners,
being the apportioned cost of paving the said Street and the foot-
paths thereto. Sealed with the Seal of the said Board of Works for
the Wandsworth District, as such Local Authority, as aforesaid, at
a Meeting of the Said Board, held at their offices, Battersea Rise, in
the Parish of Battersea, within the said District, the Sixth day of
December, One Thousand Eight Hundred and Seventy-Six.

The seal is now a blob of greasy red, the signature of the secretary
indecipherable. It's strangely exciting to read of Lillieshall Road being
called a 'new street'.

I turn to the next sheet – a list of owners: Bennett, Robert;
Quickendon, Thomas; Williams, Harriet; Maslin, Edward; Whittingham,
Walter William; Millne, George William; Liddicoat, Edwin; Armitage,
Edward . . . and on. But no Hayward, Henry.

But hold on, this is actually 1876. Five whole years before the 1881
census where I first read the names of Henry and Charlotte and Arthur
and Frank and Florence Hayward. I realize that all this time I've simply
– naïvely? – been assuming that my Haywards were the first owners. Yet
maybe they weren't.

I shuffle quickly through the rest of the papers. There are lists of
accounts, more lists of the same names, and then, almost the last sheet, a
map of the street. It shows each house with its owner's name neatly and
clearly written alongside. I count them down, working out which is which
and once I have my bearings . . . Number 34 is owned by E. Maslin.

I cross-check against the list of costs apportioned and, yes: 'Maslin,
Edward, Helena House, Lillieshall Road, 1 house, Number 15, 18 foot 5
inch frontage'. And at a rate of 7s. 4d. per foot, Edward Maslin was
being asked to pay £6. 15s. 0d.

But why is it listed as Number 15? And why is it called Helena House? Am I sure this is the right house? Yes, I am because next door, Number 14, occupied by Harriet Williams, is listed as 'Saville House'. That's the definite proof – those two words are still gold-painted in an arc above the door of Number 32 next door.

So in 1876, our house was owned by Edward Maslin and was called Helena House. But did he name it that, or was it the builder? And, more crucially, did yet another person own it between its construction in 1872 and Maslin buying it in 1876?

The final sheet shows how the costs were calculated. Arthur Southam, Surveyor of Clapham, has drawn up immaculate accounts. He wants to spend £52 on flints, £9 on gravel, and £4 on hoggin. Three days' rolling and watering will cost £6, three gullies at £5 each will cost £15, and the asphalt itself will cost £203. 10s. 0d. That and everything else totals £317; with 5 per cent added for collection (£15. 17s. 0d.), the total cost is £332. 17s. 0d. The total apportionment demanded from the owners comes to £332. 12s. 6d.

So now I know that every last house in this new street had been built before the road was even surfaced. So for how long did Walter Whittingham and George Millne and Harriet Williams and Edward Maslin turn off the hard surface of North Street and then trudge along through the mud, avoiding the wagon ruts, finally shaking and scraping the clods of London clay off their boots before they dared enter their brand-new houses?

Did Edward Maslin, noticing the fringe of mud round the bottom of Mrs Maslin's skirts, take out his pen and a sheet of his newly embossed 'Helena House, Lillieshall Road' paper and write to the Board of Works for the Wandsworth District to demand that, without delay, the road be paved, whatever the cost?

By the summer of 1972 my mother is very unhappy with my father. But whenever she tells him she wants to leave, he says she's free to go but can take nothing but a suitcase. That's how she came to him – with nothing – and that's how she'll go, with nothing.

She spends a month planning behind his back. Gets herself a job in a nearby printing factory – the boss is a friend and he gives her an advance against her salary. With this she gets a mortgage, buys a large but cheap and shabby Victorian terraced house in the red-light district of the city, gets it ready.

Twenty-three Balmoral Road is so close to our school you can see the science block from my bedroom window. I can sit on my bed and make out the thin dark hoses of the Bunsen burners that I used in a chemistry lesson earlier in the day.

Prostitutes walk up and down the road all day and night. You know they're prostitutes because, though they walk and walk, none of them ever seem to be getting anywhere. One of them especially intrigues me. I think of her as My Prostitute. She always wears head-to-toe purple and her long blonde hair has a bald patch at the back. Mum says she's a transvestite. She's always smoking but she has a sympathetic face.

The week before we move in, a woman is murdered in the house opposite. According to neighbours, a bloodstained mattress stands propped against the Bulwell stone wall for eight days before the refuse men finally remove it. But Mum doesn't tell us this till years later. Instead, she arranges our dolls and teddies on our beds, gives us corned beef salad with Hellmann's salad cream and tinned Yeoman's potatoes, followed by Jamaica ginger cake with butter on it.

We don't have a television, so we play It and Sardines and Charades. Sparky's with us and so is Caspar the budgie and Alice our duck, waddling

'and Alice our duck'

and shitting happily round the yard. 'One day,' says Mum, 'you'll look back on this as an adventure.'

'I know my street was originally called Orchard Street,' I tell the librarian at Minet, 'so how can I find out when the name was changed? Maybe even why.'

'That's easy,' he says, maybe meaning he won't have to fetch another parchment from the dusty shelves in the basement. 'It's all in here.' He scoots his chair backwards and pulls a large green volume off the shelves under the desk. 'This is a gazetteer of all London roads. Lillieshall Road, you said?'

He looks it up for me. 'Here you are.' There it is:

> Lillieshall Road, formerly Orchard Street, 1–61, 1871, Borough of Wandsworth

'So I suppose I need to order this document in the card indexes. This one that says "Renaming".'

'That won't tell you anything that isn't here.'

'It might.'

'No, don't think so.' He sees the dusty basement beckoning, digs his heels in.

'It'd be great to see it. I like looking at old documents. Can I? Please?'

I hand him the pink slip I've filled in: LBL/DCEPS/SW/1/135.

He reads through the numbers disdainfully. 'These are right along the corridor, in the back room. Might take a few minutes.'

'No problem.'

Mummy has fallen in love with someone else. This is one of the reasons why our father hates her.

Uncle Gordie has moved in with us, but he has a camp bed at the top of the house. Daddy says we shouldn't let them pull the wool over our eyes like this and urges us to check whether it's actually been slept in. We never do.

Gordie's nice anyway. On cold winter mornings he comes in and lights the little gas fire on our wall and we put our school uniforms on in bed, staying under the covers as long as possible.

In this house I make my first cake – lemon drizzle, out of a packet. Because our mother and Gordie are Living in Sin, other kids aren't allowed to come to our house. Or at least they're allowed to come and play for an hour, but never to Stay the Night. Instead they're collected on the doorstep by pinched-looking parents who always decline my Mum's offer of a cup of tea.

At Balmoral Road I turn thirteen and start spending more time in the bathroom. One day I put so much Boots Strawberry Bath Foam in my bath that Gordie comes home to see great wafts of fruit-scented bubbles floating off down the street.

LBL/DCEPS/SW/1/135, the Street Renaming Document, arrives from its basement fastness in a large dirty cardboard box. The librarian hands it over and returns to his desk. I can tell he's itching for the moment an hour from now when he can turn the sign on the door around: Library Closed.

Inside the box, there are other documents – about other, unimportant streets. I lift each out gingerly, form a new pile on the desk beside me until the one with the typed rubric 'Re-naming and Re-Numbering Orders' lies at the top.

In the centre of the page, large curly copperplate, a thin nib: 'Orchard Street, Clapham, renamed'. Then, double underlined, 'Lillieshall Road 5th May 1871'.

Inside this folder, in quick, feminine handwriting, a large sheet of paper, red seal at the bottom: 'Metropolitan Board of Works. Extract from the Minutes of the Proceedings of the Metropolitan Board of Works at a meeting held at the office of the Board Spring Gardens on

Friday the fifth day of May One thousand eight hundred and seventy one.'

Then, written slightly larger: 'Resolved and ordered on the motion of Mr Fowler. That the line of thoroughfare known by the name of Orchard Street, in the Parish of Clapham in the County of Surrey, be renamed "Lillieshall Road", and that notice of this order be given to the Board of Works for the Wandsworth District, pursuant to the 87th Section of the Metropolis Management Amendment Act 1862. Sealed by Order, Clerk of the Board.'

This is brilliant, I think. Lillieshall Road has an actual birthday – the fifth of May.

But my street truly comes of age on 16 February 1877 when the numbering is sorted out.

> It is hereby resolved and ordered on the motion of Mr. Selway, seconded by Mr. Carr. That for the purpose of distinguishing the same, the several houses and premises in the line of thoroughfare known by the name of Lillieshall Road, in the Parish of Clapham, in the County of Surrey, be marked with the numbers, as shown by red figures on the Plan now produced, marked 1914, in lieu of the existing numbers, as shown on the said Plan, the odd numbers commencing with 1 and ending with 61, being assigned to the houses on the Southern side, and the even numbers, commencing with 2 and ending with 66, to those on the Northern side . . .

I turn straight to the red-hatched plan. There it is: 15, now marked 'Helena House 34'. Our house's christening – with Messrs Carr and Selway as godparents.

The librarian wanders past, looks down, purses his lips approvingly, and mentions, almost nonchalantly, completely forgetting his earlier obstinacy: 'Oh, by the way, if that has the date, there's nothing to stop you popping off to the London Metropolitan Archives, to look up the

Minutes of the Metropolitan Board of Works and see why they decided to do it. Who organized it, stuff like that.'

I write a carefully considered letter to Rodney Wohl, apologizing again for the shock I must have given him. I explain that I quite understand if he feels he doesn't want to, but that he'd always be welcome in our house, to see the room where he lived as a little boy all those years ago.

I tell him it's now our bathroom – and that it has a lovely view out onto the garden where there's a magnolia and a lilac tree.

'What makes you think he wants to come and look at some old trees?' Chloë asks, reading the letter over my shoulder.

'Will he come?' Raph asks with a slightly worried face. 'Will he have to look in our bedrooms too?'

'Don't worry, she just wants him to go in the bathroom,' Chloë says, 'so she can make him cry and write about it.'

'Chloë, really, that's not true!'

She laughs and runs upstairs before I can grab her.

'Is it true?' I ask Jonathan later. 'Am I too hooked on the story? Do you think I should just leave poor Rodney Wohl alone?'

'Well, you're not forcing him. No one's forcing him to do anything. And I don't think you're doing anything wrong by offering information that you happen to innocently come across.'

'Innocently!'

'You didn't know what you were going to find.'

'But he never asked to be offered it. The poor man was just minding his own business in Southend.'

Jonathan looks at me.

'All I mean,' I tell him, 'is should I be looking more closely at my own motives here?'

He smiles.

'I just mean,' I say, digging in deeper, 'that these are people's real lives we're talking about here. It's easy to forget that . . . it's just, when it gets exciting, you sort of lose sight of it.'

'So what are you saying? That you wish you'd never managed to find him? That you're not bursting to know more about Mavis's story?'

'Well, I'd like to find her, I really would.'

'You think he wants that?'

'Don't know. No. Not really.'

'And what about her?'

'I don't know.'

'Yes, you do.'

'OK then, I do and no, she doesn't. But – people can change.'

He says nothing, just smiles again.

I call Mavis Cribb again.

'Is that Mavis?'

'Yes, dear.'

'Sorry to bother you again but is now a good time? Have you got a moment to talk?'

'Oooh, I'm ever so sorry, I've just popped something in the microwave, dear. Could you give me half an hour, say?'

From: Rodney Wohl
To: julie.myerson
Subject: Letter and Book

Dear Julie

I must apologize if I gave you the impression I was shocked or disturbed by your phone call. Intrigued would have been nearer the mark. I did not know my mother had married another time, I wonder what happened to him?

My Mother was a woman ahead of her time I suppose would be one way to put it, she enjoyed the company of men and was not inclined to fidelity (so I have been told). Mother was a charmer or how else could she have married three times in an era when marriage was supposed to be for life? Yet for all that she brought me up to be self-reliant and did her best for me.

My earliest memories do not include a regular male in the house, so maybe the marriage did not last very long. Olive Russell was my mother's friend and they shared a house together in Grimsby for a few years before parting and going their separate ways.

I do not regard myself as a victim in any way, life for me in a children's home gave me stability and the chance to go to the same school from one term to the next. You said you had not talked to your father since you were sixteen, and I assume that was what coloured your thinking as to my situation. But as I grew older things at home became more and more fraught and with hindsight life in a children's home was the best thing that could have happened.

As to the invitation to visit your bathroom, I will keep it in mind if ever I am caught short going through Clapham Old Town! (I promise not to leave the seat up) but truth be told the only time I am south of the river is when I get caught in the wrong lane and have to go over Tower Bridge. I enjoyed talking to you and do not think you should feel the need to apologize in any way at all.

I should be very interested to read your book when it's published, and to see how my mother and her friend fit in to your tale.

Best Wishes
Rod Wohl

Dorothy Bartolo and Winnie come to look around our house – first time back here in fifty-six years: a bright and sunshiny day, boys in hooded tops on skateboards. Shouting, clatter of wheels. A faraway car alarm going off.

Dorothy is wearing a grey woollen cardigan and clutching a tissue in her hand. She stands on the pavement looking small and daunted while Winnie parks the van. Finally, Winnie jumps down – an impossibly small, slim person in pale cotton chinos. The van seems a comical touch. She looks like a fairy at its wheel.

'Hello, I'm Win.' She puts out a hand.

'The four-year-old!' I say.

She throws back her head and laughs.

'She's sixty!' Dorothy says, beaming.

'Thanks, Mum,' Win says with feeling.

We approach the front door of our house. I'm worried. I don't know what Dorothy's going to make of our Dulux Sexy Pink hall walls and I'm suddenly acutely aware that the mat may smell of dog pee.

Dorothy, who's ahead of me, stands for a moment looking in – as if it's not her place to go – as if she's not invited. She purses her lips and then steps purposefully over the threshold and glances back at me with a little smile.

I feel tight inside. 'Welcome back,' I say.

'Goodness. Never thought I'd come back. After all these years.'

'Does it feel the same?'

She puts her head on one side. 'Don't know. Can't tell yet.'

Winnie meanwhile is glancing around her.

'Do you remember it at all?' I ask her.

She shakes her head and smiles. 'Not at all, no. I was too little, I suppose.'

Dorothy peeps into the sitting room, shakes her head. Takes a step back. 'I never went in there, you see – that was the Blaines'.'

So that was where they lived.

I warn her that the kitchen will seem entirely different, since we extended it over the yard. 'It was a long narrow room,' says Dorothy, 'with a great big fireplace in the middle.'

I ask her if there was a bath in the back room by the garden. She thinks so, but she seems uncertain. This, too, was the Blaines' territory. 'They were quite elderly, you know, they lived downstairs.'

We go upstairs to the first half-landing and she seems a whole lot happier. We all crowd into my tiny study with its computer and books and framed posters. All my books, telephone, piles of old toys and grown-out-of clothes waiting for the charity shop.

Dorothy folds her arms, suddenly businesslike. 'OK, so ... these were not here' – she indicates the French windows onto the terrace. 'Here there was a window only. A small window, you could not see much. Here' – she points to the front of the boiler cupboard – 'there was a grey gas cooker with a white door, on four legs.'

'Goodness, Mum,' Winnie says as I laugh, 'so much detail!'

'Oh, I remember it all. Next to it a washbasin. Over here' – indicating the radiator – 'a small table.'

She looks around, almost satisfied. 'And here' – where my desk is – 'the bath. With a lid you put down if you wanted to cook or prepare food. You could not take a bath if someone was cooking, obviously.'

We walk down one step and up three steps and across the landing into our bedroom. She strides across and takes stock immediately.

'Ah, Mavis's room. There was a sofa here,' she says, pointing to our old white radiator, 'and a round table over here' – she gestures to where my dressing table is – 'with chairs all around.'

It's an odd thing, hearing about the furniture – especially having imagined Mavis's wedding reception in there. I realize that I'd pretty much imagined it with simply older versions of our own furniture in there – bed, chest of drawers, dressing table – when actually it has to have been entirely different.

As Dorothy speaks, the room slowly changes shape. She says that Olive and Mavis worked shifts, she thinks, and that after Mavis got married she moved upstairs (to Chloë's room this would be) with her new husband and Olive looked after the boy downstairs. They swapped rooms in other words.

'Really?' I say, surprised. 'Rodney lived with Olive.'

'They were newly-weds!' Win points out.

I tell them about Rodney being left in a children's home. Dorothy looks shocked and upset.

'No! That lovely little boy?'

I tell her I spoke to him last week – that he never saw his mother again.

Dorothy shakes her head. 'But Mavis was such a lovely person.'

'Obviously not, Mum,' Winnie says.

'And yet you say Olive looked after him after she married?'

We both glance towards the bathroom, Rodney's room: we can't help it.

'Yes, she loved that boy, Olive did. She played lovely with him.'

'But she wasn't as nice as Mavis?'

'She was . . . let's say rather rough. Rough-looking.'

I tell her that we think Mavis came from Grimsby and that her maiden name might have been Cribb and that I'm trying to get in touch with them now.

'That's funny,' Dorothy says, 'because I had relatives from Grimsby. My father, you know – in 1888 when he was thirteen, he walked from Roxby to Grimsby and got on a trawler and ran away to sea. He didn't want to work on the farm. If she'd ever told me she came from there I really do think I'd have remembered it. Funny that she never said anything.'

I ask her if Winnie and Rodney ever played together. 'They played out there in the garden. The Blaines would keep an eye on them for us.'

'Do you remember that?' I ask Winnie.

She smiles and shakes her head.

Dorothy says she thinks Theodore Blaine had a sister living somewhere nearby. She'd come around a lot and chat to Mrs Blaine in the garden. They didn't work by the time she knew them – definitely too old, retired by then.

The garden is long and narrow, neatly kept with a smooth lawn and beds full of shrubs and flowers, red and yellow and pink roses mainly – and a gravel path down the left-hand side.

Rod and Win like to creep up on the butterflies and try to catch them between finger and thumb but they're never quick or quiet enough, and they've never caught one yet. It makes Mrs Blaine laugh.

Theo Blaine used to be a florist and he tends his shrubs with care and knowledge, pruning and mulching and planting according to the season. He grows flowers from seed and bulb and sometimes he'll cut huge blooms and put them in the house.

Some days in that first hot summer of being in London, Dorothy will come in the door and the whole house will be pulsing with the warm bright perfume of roses. She stands a moment and breathes in. And she'll leave the door of their upstairs room open deliberately for a while, hoping to catch that scent. Though once Mavis and Olive start heating up their stews in the kitchen on the landing, it will be obliterated by the smell of old mutton and she'll have to shut the door.

One day Annie and her sister-in-law are out in the garden, walking up and down and peering into the flowers, and they call Dorothy over.

'You don't let Winnie on the Common, do you?' Mrs Blaine asks her.

'Well, yes,' she replies, 'of course I do – to run and that.'

Mrs Blaine places a hand on her throat where a single row of pearls rests creamily against her old skin.

'But you don't let her go in the paddling pool, do you? Only, little boys do all sorts of business in there.'

Later, Dorothy tells Wilfred what she said and they have a good laugh. 'She should try living in Alexandria,' Wilfred says. 'You get a whole lot more than little boys' business in the water there.'

*　*　*

Finally, we go up to the boys' room, Dorothy and Winnie's old rented room. I apologize for the dreadful mess, but Winnie seems oblivious. Instead she walks over to the window, looks out, and then turns back to face us.

'In here,' she says in a steady voice, 'in this room, was the first time I ever saw my mother cry.'

Dorothy nods and says nothing.

'You sat on the bed which was facing the window,' Winnie says, pointing to the wall where Raph's football posters of men called Postiga and Acimovic are currently blue-tacked, 'and you opened a letter and you cried.'

'That's right,' Dorothy says. 'It was my mother. She was ill and I'd just found out.'

'She had to go into hospital,' Win says, 'and I sat over there by the fireplace and I watched you. I saw you cry. You don't forget a thing like that, seeing your mother cry for the very first time.'

Dorothy pulls her cardigan around her shoulders and the room's very quiet but we can still hear the skateboards clattering outside in the street.

A letter comes in response to our mailshot to All Annie Blaines Everywhere:

> *Dear Julie*
> *Can't help you but small sub-plot here . . . My husband's family name was Bernstein. Like many Jewish families in the late 40s and 50s, the family decided to adopt an anglicised name. They decided to do this when their first son was born (1946ish). They did this by turning to the Bs in the London phone book and sticking in a pin! They came up with Blaine – apparently simple and only one or two in the phone book. I wonder if Annie and Theodore Blaine were in the book at that time? Sorry we can't be of more help, good luck with the book.*
>
> *Jean (and Rod) Blaine*

* * *

I forgot to call Mavis Cribb back the other day, so I call her now – a week later. It's late afternoon, can't be a mealtime, and I'm just going to have to hope there's nothing about to go ping in the microwave.

I apologize for the delay and ask whether this is a good time.

'We-ell,' she goes, 'it is *Countdown* . . .'

'Would you rather I called back?' I say, heart sinking.

'No, love, you're all right, fire away.'

She confirms that her husband and Mavis were cousins. Great! But that she knows nothing of the family nor of anyone alive who knew them. 'They're all dead, that lot.'

Mavis Cribb's mother was a Clara Cribb and she married a George Jones. Mavis had a brother called Byron, she thinks. Good name, Byron – shame about the Jones.

She takes down my number and says she'll ring me if she thinks of anything else (but she doesn't sound hopeful) and then she goes back to Richard Whitely.

Another door slams in my face.

I know I should go to the Family Records Centre and resume the job of ploughing through endless volumes to locate – who? The Costellos and Blaines have consumed weeks of my life and offered me precious little.

Time to move further back in time – surely one of Arthur, Charlotte or Florence Hayward had children. I know Lucy Spawton died a spinster but she certainly had a nephew, so how many brothers or sisters did she have who had children? And Lucy's lodgers, the Hinkleys, did they have children and did their children have children? And then there's Edward Maslin, my new discovery. I know nothing about him at all, haven't even started.

But I'm shattered and it's hot and I'm beginning to feel that, although I may have the names, I'll never find out enough about the Hinkleys or the Haywards, the people from longer ago in the house.

And even if I do, where are all the photographs? Will I ever know what Henry Hayward or Isabella Hinkley looked like? Images of these people are so easily lost. Romantically, you imagine photos lie waiting in a box in someone's attic, but they don't. They end up destroyed by mildew, eaten by mice, or abandoned at some car boot sale in the middle of Wales – ownerless and placeless.

Rita Wraight lived in the house in 1948 – the same time as Dorothy and Winnie, but they don't remember her. Maybe she took over their room. A couple of weeks ago, Jonathan discovered at the Family Records Centre that a Rita Wraight married a Kenneth Leek and had two children, Janet and Stephen. So he's written to all the Stephen and Janet Leeks in the country.

'Has anyone ever written back to you to say they're the right one?' asks Jake as he trudges off to post them.

'I wait in hope,' says Jonathan.

We stand outside 23 Balmoral Road, Nottingham. Thirty years since I lived here and the road looks far shabbier and sadder even than it was back then. Now many houses are boarded up, empty, or squatted. Far away a radio blares Avril Lavigne and two kids kick a can down the street. You can still see the High School science block though – clean blond brick and shining glass, smartened up since my time.

A jolly-looking lady with red cheeks opens the door. Wearing slippers and an old grey track suit and holding a tiny schooner of what looks like sherry.

She beams when I tell her who I am and why I'm here. 'Yeah,' she says, stepping back to make way for us, 'I got the letter, I just – you know, never got round to ringing – but it's fine, come in. It's a mess but just help yourselves, walk around. Go anywhere you like.'

She tells me their name is Eastwood, she's Jean, and they've been here for years and her husband is the caretaker at the Nottingham

Boys' High School next door. But he's retiring so they're going to be leaving soon. The house is a tied cottage.

'It's been great,' Jean says. 'We were lucky to have it. It's a lovely house and we've been really happy here.' She looks like she's always happy – as determined and bright as my mother was when she moved us in here.

I walk into the sitting room where we had our first TV-less Christmas. I remember my mother's sofas and armchairs and yellow curtains, her knack for optimistic, feel-good decoration, for making things feel like instant home.

Jean says we're welcome to go on upstairs and look at anything we want. Touched by her kindness and trustingness, I do exactly as she says.

I show Jonathan the room that was our bedroom – the piece of wall next to the window where my bedhead was. My satin ballet shoes hung here – next to the same window where I glanced out that night and saw my father's car, waiting, watching, then driving away.

The room is stacked with boxes and piles of clothes. I try to stand for a moment and realign the space, get it back to how it was. But it doesn't work, it's gone – all the years in between are there, pushing me away. I show Jonathan where the gas fire used to be – the whoosh of the flame as Gordie stuck a match in first thing in the morning.

'I think you had to be there,' he says kindly.

Upstairs is our old playroom. I put on a puppet show for Debbie's ninth birthday in here – a big success, a dozen little girls giggling. We had big pine shelves with our farm animals very carefully arranged. Even though I was twelve going on thirteen, when we came here I regressed into a kind of last-gasp childhood, playing games I hadn't played in years with a fury and intensity I would never find again.

Two boys are in there watching a Harry Potter video.

'Hello. I'm just looking round because I used to live here when I was a little girl. Do you mind if I come in? This used to be my playroom.'

The older boy frowns. 'When?'

'Years and years ago. Before you were born.'

They stare at me. One is about eleven, the other about five.

'Was it just like this?' says the five-year-old.

'Almost,' I say. 'We had some shelves here. But we didn't have a TV.'

'No TV?' He looks horrified. 'Wasn't it invented?'

'It was invented. We just didn't have one. Couldn't afford it for a while. No videos either – they actually weren't invented.'

The small boy, who is wearing just a vest and knickers, very grubby and stained, comes over and looks at me carefully.

'Was this here then?' he asks me, indicating the door.

'We had a door, yes, probably the same door.'

He walks out onto the landing. 'And this?' – indicating a pile of magazines and a hairbrush on the stairs.

'Not that,' I say, 'but we used to leave things on the stairs too.'

He takes my hand and walks me round, showing me pictures, windows, beds. I know what he's doing – he's trying to take in the impossible fact that another child lived here once – the sheer unlikeliness of other lives, in other times.

'Did you have carpet when you were here?'

'Yes, but not this one.' The stair carpet is orange, swirly. 'We had a different carpet.'

'What was it like?'

''Fraid I've forgotten. It was such a long time ago.'

'How old are you?'

'Forty-two. I'm forty-two.'

He rolls his eyes. I understand. How can all those years be somehow squashed back into this box of compacted time, into a single reality?

* * *

From: don sherman
To: julie.myerson
Subject: No 34 – Book

Dear Julie,

My stepson Stephen passed on your letter regarding my wife, Rita Sherman, nee Leek, nee Wraight. We married in 1982. She has asked me to get in touch with you regarding 34 Lillieshall Road, as she leaves the 'scientific' side of our activities to me.

We are both in our late seventies now (I am nearly out of them), so memories do not come easily. The fact is that Rita cannot remember her sojourn in Clapham at all, so on the face of it, she cannot help you. It would be interesting to know the dates of her occupation, she says, just out of curiosity as to where it fitted into her life at that time. You never know, it might start a string of memories . . .

By way of explanation, Rita had a quite unhappy life up to her early twenties, with parents who moved house very frequently whilst she was a child. Consequently, her education suffered with the subsequent stream of different schools all over South-West England and into Wales. She left school at 14 to work in a fish and chip shop in Newport. By the time she was 17, she found herself in the NAAFI. Leaving that to come 'home' to Lisson Grove, where her mother had lodgings while Dad had decamped to South Africa, after a better job. Shortly after, mother followed him, taking younger daughter. Leaving Rita and her eldest sister to find lodgings as Mum had terminated their tenancy. There followed a period of job and digs-hopping, during which the stay in your house must have occurred.

In the circumstances, photos of the period are non-existent I fear. Sorry.

Good luck and best wishes with the book in any event.

Kind regards,
Don (& Rita) Sherman.

Unsure how excited I ought to be about this faintly confusing but at the same time quite promising e-mail, I ring Rita Sherman and ask her if she thinks she actually is the Rita who lived here in 1948.

'Well, I think maybe yes. It does sound a bit as though it probably was me, doesn't it, dear?'

I run some of the names of the people then living here past her, but she says none of them rings a bell.

'Sorry, dear, can't help you there. Don't remember a soul to tell you the truth. I was quite a lonely girl.'

So I ask her if she minds telling me how old she'd have been in 1948.

'Twenty-two. I was twenty-two. By the way, do you know which room I had, dear?'

'Well, the thing is, I suppose I was actually rather hoping you could tell me that. I mean, do you think you do remember the house, then? Lillieshall Road – a street in Clapham, not far from Clapham Common, about five minutes from the tube?'

'Was it the room on the ground floor? On the right as you come in?'

I tell her there's no room on the right as you come in, only on the left.

'That could have been it. Yes, the left. I certainly never went up any stairs, I can tell you that.'

She explains that she went to hospital at the age of fifteen – 'acute appendicitis and an abscess on my lung' – and then left home at sixteen because her Mum made her go out and earn a living. She lived in flats and bedsits all over London, moving on every time she got a new job or the money ran out.

'I know one time in one place I had a lot of trouble with American soldiers – following me home and that. One night my father hid behind the hedge to try and catch one of them, but you'd think if he could do that he'd have maybe bothered to come and meet me, walk me home, wouldn't you?'

I ask if I can take her phone number, if I think of any more questions. Of course, she says and gives it to me.

'01784,' I say as I write down the code. 'So where's that then?'

I hear her take a breath.

'Gosh, dear, let me think, where is it? You know I can't remember – aren't I awful? Hold on, it'll come to me, it's . . . I know it's near the airport, somewhere like . . . oh goodness, yes – Ashford. It's in Ashford. You'd think I'd remember a thing like that, wouldn't you, dear?'

Rodney Wohl's birth certificate, ordered from the Family Records Centre, arrives.

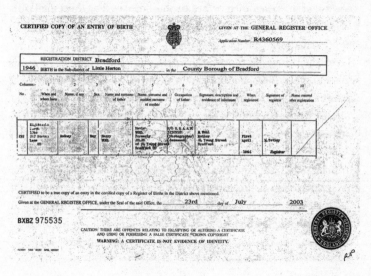

It tells me that he was born on 18 March 1946 at 217 Horton Lane, Bradford, to Mavis Wohl, formerly Jones, of 24 Young Street, Bradford, and that his father was Harry Wohl, a photographer in the US Army Air Force, P/O USAAF 32309581. And it says that Harry was dead before his son was born.

So did Mavis really marry him? Or did she just take the name Wohl? And was he really dead before Rodney was born or did she just say that to make it sound better when the Registrar asked for the father's name? And if he did die, was it in action, just before VE Day? To be born in March 1946, Rodney must have been conceived no earlier than May 1945. Or was Harry Wohl posted to the continuing war in the Pacific? Or maybe he died in some more mundane way, just after the end of the war.

Most importantly of all, what do I do now? Do I e-mail Rodney and tell him I have some information about his family and ask him if he wants it? But that sounds too self-important, too ominous. And it might make it sound worse than it is. On the other hand, if he's never known that his father died before he was born, well . . . And the information I have is, after all, in the public domain. Anyone could get it. But does that make it better or worse to tell him?

And there may be more information coming. Now we have his service number, Jonathan has sent off to the Pentagon for Harry Wohl's service record. Are we about to find out how he died?

Three weeks later, the reply comes from Stephen Rowland at the National Personnel Records Center in St Louis:

> The record needed to answer your inquiry was lost in the July 1973 fire that destroyed millions of records here at the National Personnel Records Center. The records stored in the area which suffered the most damage in the fire were those of :
> - army veterans discharged or deceased between November 1, 1912 and December 31, 1959.
> - Air Force veterans discharged, deceased or retired before January 1, 1964, whose names come alphabetically after Hubbard, James E.
>
> WHAT YOU NEED TO DO:
> ? Fill out Page 2 of this form (NA FORM 13075) as completely as possible, as well as any other form(s) you may have received with this one such as a Standard Form (SF) 180 and NA Form

13055. Please note that if the *only* document you need is the
Report of Separation (DD Form 214, WDAGO Form 53-55 etc), it
may be available from a former employer from the recorder's
office of the city or county where ...

But with the simple information we have from Rodney's birth
certificate, let alone a WDAGO 53 or a DD 214, it turns out we cannot
answer a single one of these questions.

So another day at the Family Records Centre, looking for Mavis Jones-
Wohl's marriage certificate. Dorothy has told me it was during the first
half of 1948 – she's very definite about that as it coincided with the
precise and short period she and Winnie and Wilfred were at Lillieshall
Road.

So I check from 1940 to 1950. I check under Wohl and Jones and
Jones-Wohl. There is no marriage registered.

Wasn't it a real wedding reception after all?

Chapter Six

WHY WON'T HE WRITE?

The Povahs and the Askews
1944–1948

It's 1948. At breakfast, Margie tells Reggie something pretty damn interesting. The house on Lillieshall Road is going to be put up for sale. He looks up from his toast and marmalade, licks his lips, tries to keep an even and uninterested expression on his face. 'Who says?'

Marjorie feigns a yawn and says: 'Peter.'

'You sure?'

'Mmm. He and Phyllis were round at Aunt Til's and apparently she says she's been thinking of selling all along but now she's decided and feels so much better about it. So it's definite. She's getting onto agents today. That's what he said anyway.'

Reggie blinks to keep himself calm. Touches his moustache. Puts the spoon carefully back in the marmalade jar. He's been waiting for this to happen.

'Til should just go on renting it out,' he says quietly. 'She'd make a packet, you know. In this climate. That area. Mad to sell if you ask me.'

He licks a finger. Marjorie sniffs and pours more tea.

'But she can't. She's got Peter and Phyll in there already. And there's the old couple.'

Reg makes a face. 'Peter and Phyllis pay almost no rent. She should turf them out, get Peter to stand on his own two feet. Get some proper tenants in, charge a full whack.'

Marjorie peers at him over her glasses. They don't suit her, those glasses, make her look too old and frowsy.

'You're sounding so horrid, darling. Peter is family. He and Phyll were in a fix. Uncle Tom stepped in and helped. You'd have her throw them out?'

'I don't mean that,' he says quickly, 'just, she needs to talk to someone with some business nous, that's all. Someone who could manage things for her – collect the rent, sort of thing.'

'No, my darling, you are being dense – don't you see? She doesn't especially care about the money. She's just getting too old, old and tired – it's all too much for her, since Uncle Tom went. I'm frankly surprised you can't see that. I'm not sure she'll stay in London much longer anyway.'

Reggie gets up, pulls on his coat. He's chuffed, he can't help it: this is what he wanted to hear. He bends, plants a dry kiss on the top of his wife's unbrushed head, but she pulls him down to her and they kiss on the lips.

'You're a good girl to tell me this,' he says, 'good little Marge. Let me have a word with Til, see what I can do. See if I can wangle things.'

Marjorie frowns.

'How d'you mean, wangle things? Why do you even need to get involved, my love?'

'Don't you worry about it, my great big baby girl. Trust your Reggie. Povah will sort it out.'

Nine o'clock at night. The thick relentless heat of Jonathan's study. Until a few years ago, this was the loft – how I wish I'd been able to poke around in here in Lucy Spawton's day! – now it's a sisal-covered space from where you can see the whole of Chelsea spread out and twinkling.

But it's a mess. A drum kit, two televisions (Playstation), three large floor cushions, two computers (one for the kids), books and papers falling onto the floor. Stuff that no one knows what to do with ends up here. As well as suitcases, boxes of archives and old toys, half-defunct objects, gadgets that might be worth repairing one day. It's still a loft, in other words.

I've come up here for some peace, to phone Alexa Povah. A tabby lies on her back on the desk, paws flung out. I have to work the phone out from under her soft striped body. After first making contact with Alexa, a few weeks ago, through Diane Askew, I said I'd leave it a few weeks – I needed to learn a bit more about the Spawtons and the Askews first. Now it's time to reconnect.

Alexa's husband, Glyn Sweet, answers the phone. He's an actor, like Alexa.

'That's an amazing coincidence,' he says in a friendly, honeyed voice, 'about Alexa actually having been to the house to rehearse and having no idea that her father had owned it – my God, we simply can't get over it. The spookiest thing, don't you think?'

I agree that it is. 'It's the kind of thing you'd see in a film and just not believe.'

'You'd never get away with it,' he laughs.

He fetches Alexa. He says she's been dying to talk to me.

'Daddy died two years ago,' she begins immediately. 'He was eighty-eight. And Mummy died back in '76 when I was twenty-three. And her best friend, my godmother, died last year. And I was born in the Hospital for Ladies near Clapham South – and we lived in this big old vicarage in Leigham Court Road in Streatham and my Daddy was a racing driver at Brands Hatch and then he bought and sold cars and he had a garage called Acre Autos on Streatham High Road in, I suppose, the fifties and I never knew anything about him owning a house but, oh dear – is it true? Diane says he got someone thrown out.'

I pause, struggling to write down this sudden unleashing of information. I tell Alexa the truth – that I only know what Joan Clayton told me – and I deliberately leave out the bit about her calling him 'that horrid man'. It feels strange and slightly wrong to be telling one family member what another has said. Especially about her own father.

'It may not be entirely true,' I tell her carefully. 'I only have it from one person after all. These stories get passed around and distorted. In any family they do.'

'No, the awful thing is, I can sort of believe it,' Alexa says. 'It does sound a bit like my Daddy. You see he was – how can I put it? – a bit of a wheeler-dealer. He had lots of money-making schemes. If he could see a way to make a bit of cash, he jumped right in there.

'Peter is family. He and Phyll were in a fix . . .'

'He was from a wealthy family, you see, and he was sent to boarding school and while he was there his Daddy upped and left and I think that sort of toughened him up. Poor Daddy. And anyway, he was a Blackshirt, marched with Mosley's Fascists.' She laughs a small laugh of amazement. 'And then as soon as war was declared he joined the RAF and, well, oh dear, I really wouldn't be surprised if he did do something like that. It sounds so very like my Daddy. But why?'

* * *

Reggie puts the telephone down and lights a cigarette, picks up the heavy pewter lighter and weighs it in his hand. It's just as Marge said, just as he'd hoped, Til's pretty keen to get shot of the place.

The house has been in the family since way back – they say Tom's Aunt Lucy was there for more than fifty years and her family before her. But now that poor old Tom's gone and keeled over – 'so soon after Lucy, a terrible thing really,' Til tells him with a catch in her voice. 'I just can't be worrying about renting and all that palaver.'

'Of course, you can't,' Reggie says soothingly.

'It's a big house too, three storeys, big garden,' Til tells him, 'needs a bit doing to it now of course. Aunt Lucy just couldn't manage the garden in the end, and Tom wasn't well either and she wouldn't get anyone in to do it. Have you been there?'

He tells her he hasn't – not strictly true: he had a furtive snoop around once before when Tom's Aunt Lucy died and left it to Tom and Til. He tells her that he knows the street. He remembers the Tim Bobbin on the corner. Popped in for a snifter once, must've been just before the war. That lovely hot summer.

'Well,' Til drones on, 'it's virtually empty now – only Peter and Phyll and the baby, and the Hinkleys of course. I'll need to have a word with you about the Walter and Bella situation actually.'

Reggie's quite surprised at Til mentioning the baby – bit of a family sore point for a while, that baby – but maybe it's all sorted now.

Peter is his wife's brother, not a bad chap – ulcers on his legs but knows everything there is to know about cooked meats. Bit of a loser though, and a temper too (never a hit with the women, a temper like that; he doesn't know how Phyllis puts up with it). Peter's wife, Phyllis – and quite a looker if you ask him – is Aunt Til's niece. That's the connection.

Bob Askew – Diane's brother, Peter and Phyllis Askew's son – calls me.

He tells me that 34 Lillieshall Road is on his birth certificate and that his parents were living there then. That they got married either just before or just after he was born. 'Either way it was a bit of a close-run thing,' he says.

I tell him that Mrs Clayton – his aunt – told me they were given somewhere to live in a hurry because they were in a bit of trouble.

He laughs but he sounds wary. 'I think the bit of trouble was me coming along.' He adds that he was born in a nursing home in Wimbledon but came home to Lillieshall Road for the first year. After that they moved to Thornton Heath, which he remembers much better – went to school there and everything.

Despite all this information, Bob seems ready to hang up, as if he's done his bit. Desperate to keep him talking, I apologize and say I'm aware that there's something intrusive about delving into someone else's family history.

'I looked you up on the website,' he says by way of reply, and then he tells me he's a bit of a family historian himself.

'Oh, really?'

'Well, I take an interest.'

I ask him whether he'd be at all interested in coming to see the first house he lived in – because he'd be very welcome here any time and I'd so love to meet him.

'To tell the truth I don't leave Manchester if I can help it.'

'Not even to see where you lived as a baby?'

He laughs. 'A house is just a house, isn't it?'

Funny, I think, that's exactly what Rodney said.

'I know what you mean though,' he adds more warmly. 'I didn't used

'I think the bit of trouble was me coming along'

215

to be interested in any of this family stuff, but recently I just started thinking a bit about roots and the past and so on.'

He tells me that a great deal of family memorabilia – photos and so on – were lost. 'Because of my mother's illness,' he says and hesitates. 'You know my family's rather chequered history?'

'I don't,' I admit carefully. 'What illness? What history?'

'Well, in 1963 my mother fractured her skull and became a paranoid schizophrenic.'

'Goodness, I'm so sorry.'

'She fell down the stairs – it was suggested that my father pushed her, in fact he may well have pushed her – anyway we lived in caravans and very much all over the place. Until I went to university. I'd get sent off all the time to my grandma's in Cambridge.'

'Laurie Stearn?'

'That's right. They were good memories, with my grandma. The loss of all that stuff, photos and all that, didn't bother me till recently. And then we had an aunt as well, who lived in Clapham, I don't know where . . .'

'Matilda Spawton? At Park Hill?'

'That's right.'

'Known as Til, married to Thomas Spawton.'

'Park Hill, is that close to you then? She used to have me over and feed me up,' he says, 'Auntie Til did.'

I ask him how his mother and father met.

'Well, he was her second husband actually – she got up to all sorts of things with Americans during the war.'

'What sort of things?'

'She was just . . . a bit of a lass.'

'She was just – let's just say a bit of a lass – and anyway she married one of them. My father was a grocer, possibly in Clapham but definitely in Chelsea and later Wimbledon, and when she met him I think he was ground crew in Cambridge because of his legs.'

I ask him about Reggie Povah. Did he know him well?

'He was a right rogue he was. He's dead now. His daughter lives in Brighton – she's the actress.'

'Alexa?'

'Caroline, you mean. Don't know when she became Alexa.'

'So hold on a moment,' Jonathan asks me, 'what exactly was the relationship between Reggie Povah and Lucy Spawton.'

I have to think about this. 'They were related – but only distantly, by marriage. In the middle you've got Peter and Phyllis Askew. And their children were Bob and Diane Askew.'

'Yes, I've got that.'

'And Phyllis was Matilda's niece. And Matilda was married to Lucy's nephew.'

'I'm lost.'

'No, you see, Peter's sister was Marjorie Askew and she married Reggie!'

I draw him a family tree in green felt-tip on the back of an envelope. Then it goes wrong so I cross it out and he redraws it better, with enough space to put all the names. We finally work out that Reggie Povah was Lucy's nephew's wife's niece's brother-in-law.

The walls of the Reading Room at the London Metropolitan Archives are clothed in rows and rows of bound committee minutes, many going back over a hundred years – School Boards, LCC, GLC, Cemetery Boards, and the Metropolitan Board of Works. On all my previous visits, they never seemed worth touching, they looked like an unbreakable wallpaper. Now I lift 1871 straight off the shelf and flick through to May. The meeting of 5 May at Spring Gardens SW1 – a site now occupied by the London Eye.

It's so simple. Look through each agenda item until the word Lillieshall springs out. And there it is: Item 23. But it's not what I'm looking for: it seems to be something about drainage and sewers.

I keep going, more in hope than expectation. And then, eventually: Item 97, the Board reads a report dated 17th April on the application of Mr E. B. I'Anson for the formation of a new road, to be named Lillieshall. It's all so clear – clear yet dry. Not much more than the official notice. A Mr Fowler moves the motion and it's passed.

I take the volume through to the archivist's desk in the main room: 'Is there any way of finding out any more about this, the plan maybe?'

She stares in horror at the volume as though it is on fire.

'We don't like those to be taken out of the Reading Room.'

'Oh, I'm sorry,' I say, glancing back at the Reading Room, which is a full ten feet away. 'I just . . . I thought it would be easier to show you.'

The archivist speeds round the corner of her desk and steers me by my elbow back through the arch into the Reading Room. We lay it on a table and instantly she relaxes, all smiles.

'Yes, of course, you could ask for the supporting documents. Each item will have supporting material.'

She looks up the reference, even fills out the pink chit for me – maybe doesn't want me touching anything.

'I'll see if the plan is available. A lot of them were weeded out, so it's hit and miss, I'm afraid. Mostly miss.'

The supporting documents turn out to be a book almost as fat as it's wide. The dark brown binding is battered, crumbling like treacle tart. Stick-on label reading a copperplate 'MBW May 1871' on the front. Inside, the papers are crumbling as well, the corners fragmented, the occasional tear, the whole thing dusty and grimy, filth coming off on my hands.

I see an army of clerks assembling it after each week's meeting and then constantly referring back to it as the Board's decisions are checked, rechecked, and challenged. But everything presented at that meeting of the Board of Works seems to have been painstakingly inserted – sometimes even the tiny doll-sized envelopes addressed to the Chairman. And in the top right-hand corner of each, there's a blue crayon number referring back to the agenda item number.

'Inside, the papers are crumbling . . .'

Spring Gardens, 5 May 1871 – a sticky day in early summer – and the Metropolitan Board of Works settles down for its weekly meeting.

All around them London is growing, taking shape at a furious rate. In fact, it's one big building site – the biggest city in Europe is getting bigger. But there's no grand design here, no fevered Haussman tearing down terraces and ploughing roads wherever he fancies. No, this is being done the proper British way – each citizen free to make his own application, free to do what he thinks is right. Which means red tape: everything needs permission, everything needs another report read, another document signed. Not a brick must be laid or a piece of ground dug without the signature in place.

Sometimes Fowler wonders why they bother. Sitting here in Spring Gardens, he doesn't know why they're pretending to make decisions when so much of this is simply going to happen.

Item 9 is a perfect example. Joseph Bazalgette – not that someone as high and mighty would ever turn up in person – wants permission to lay some more of his sewers. Permission? They know he'll get it, so why go through this rigmarole each time?

Fowler sighs and looks out of the window as the Secretary reads: 'I beg to report that plans of the following proposed district sewers have been submitted for your approval by the several District Boards and Vestries hereinafter named, and I recommend that the execution of these works be sanctioned by you.'

Why does Bazalgette send in these weekly reports? If he just got on with it and dug his blessed tunnels, what then? Would any of them be any the wiser? They're all underground, aren't they? Who's going to know apart from a bunch of fat London rats?

And now Selway is asking questions. He's new enough, poor man, to imagine there's some purpose to all this. He's querying the twelve-inch pipework requested by Wandsworth. Why, when Chelsea, Kensington, and Westminster all want Mr Bazalgette's brick tunnels?

'It says here that these pipes in Wandsworth are being laid along a set of roads – Macaulay, Lambourn, Orchard Road,' says Selway. 'Seems a perfectly normal state of affairs but also listed here, if I read aright, is the Cricket Field Clapham Common. I can't for the life of me understand why a cricket pitch requires subterranean drainage.'

The assistant riffles through his papers, makes some mumbling

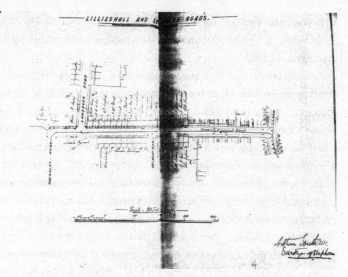

'the plan shows a new street 50 feet wide . . .'

noises. But he's saved by the Secretary: 'If I might refer members to Item 97, concerning the requested extension of Orchard Road. I believe that all will be made clear once that matter is tabled for consideration.'

Selway shrugs, annoyed that there should be such a simple answer to his question. Meanwhile, the Chairman lifts his pen: 'Mister Bazalgette's request – pipes, sewers and the like. Anyone wish to speak against?'

Please God no, thinks Fowler as throats are cleared. But silence reigns. Dinner is another ten minutes closer.

'Nem con,' says the Chairman. The Secretary scribbles.

By the time they reach Item 97, they've all forgotten pipes and sewers. Fowler's nodding as the Secretary reads: 'Tabled, Committee, is an application from Mister Edward I'Anson of 7 Laurence Pountney Hill in the City of London for your approval to the formation of one new road and two continuation roads on Clapham Common Cricket Field Estate, Clapham Common, as shown on the accompanying plan, numbered 16306.'

Some look up and wait for the plan to be placed on the easel. But not Fowler. He shuts his eyes and listens – or tells himself he does – as Edward I'Anson steps forward to read out the tabled report: 'The plan shows a new street 50 feet wide joining an extension of Orchard Street (40 foot wide) by which direct communication between Clapham Common and Clapham Old Town would be formed.' He points at the plan: 'Here . . . branching from the latter street is a new street forming a continuation of Lambourn Road. That's here . . . No, sorry, here.'

Does anyone notice that I'Anson's fingers are trembling as he taps the diagram? Maybe they just imagine he hasn't done this before, thinks it's all much more serious than it really is, or that there's a real chance he could get turned down. But how often do they do that? More trouble than it's worth, the appeals, the investigations.

I'Anson drones on. He has a lisp – unfortunate for a man who needs to say 'street' so many times. Thtreet.

> The plan also shows another side road about 170 feet long leading towards the land belonging to the same owner – that's Colonel Bowyer – but which has only one entrance until the adjoining land, leased for a period, should come into possession. The application for approval of this latter road has, in consequence of objections raised by the District Board, been withdrawn. The remainder of the scheme seems unobjectionable and I therefore recommend that the application be granted upon condition that no barriers or obstacles to free access to and use of the several roads by the Public be at any time erected or caused.
>
> The name 'Macaulay Road' is proposed for that road leading from the Common. 'Lillieshall Road' for the road leading into North Street, the name Orchard Street being cancelled.

'Lambourn Road' for the continuation road into Lillieshall Road,
are unobjectionable.

The District Board approve the Plan as amended.

I'Anson finishes speaking and crosses his arms in front of him.
Then, almost immediately, he puts his arms behind his back.

'Any questions for Mr Lanson?' asks the Chairman.

'I'Anson,' the Secretary quietly corrects him.

'Exactly so,' says the Chairman, unaware of his error.

There's perhaps three, four seconds of silence. Then, inevitably,
Selway: 'I'm not wholly clear. Is it Orchard Street or Orchard Road?'

'Is this genuinely important?' asks the Chairman. 'Will it truly influence your deliberations?'

'Chair, we have approved pipework – if I might refer the committee
to Item 9 – for Orchard *Road*. Yet here we are being asked to permit the
extension of Orchard *Street*. Any inaccuracy might cause our former
order to become null and void.'

Enough is enough, Fowler can smell his dinner drying out in the
oven. They've been in this room for three hours and there are still
forty-seven more items to be considered. 'Might I move, Mr Chairman,
that we grant the application? Subject to the usual conditions about
barriers and obstructions, free public access. Usual stuff, order to
Wandsworth District Vestry.'

'Seconded.'

'Anyone against?'

Selway folds his arms but says nothing.

'Item 98, then, Committee, concerns the reallocation of . . .'

I'm still trying to find John and Mary Spawton's marriages. John was
Thomas Harlock Beesley Spawton's father so he has to have married at
some point. But by 1906 (by which time he would have been in his late
forties), the only John Spawton who gets married is in Grantham.

Could be him. Why not? But I don't have the right feeling about it. I suppose I should order it anyway to check.

Meanwhile, Mary doesn't seem to be marrying either. Did she die young? Or remain a spinster like Lucy? I decide that tomorrow I will probably check for her death from 1881 onwards.

I move to births and find, while looking for Mary, another Spawton birth, in July–September 1865: 'Catherine A. Wandsworth'. Is she related to my Lucy? Could she be an older sister who died or moved away by the time of the 1881 census? Or were there simply other, unrelated Spawtons in Wandsworth?

I'm in Alexa Povah's cosy, bright, front sitting room in Brighton – well, me plus a huge, slobbering yellow Labrador, Alexa, Glyn, their teenage daughter Henrietta, and Diane Askew, who sits quietly on the edge of the sofa clutching a box of photos. I can't quite believe that I'm looking at Reggie Povah's daughter. Alexa – pretty, blonde, bubbly – isn't much older than me. She tells me she's about to do a play at Cheltenham but in between she's a 'trolley dolly', an air hostess. The two careers fit very well together. 'I don't rest. I just fly!'

Coffee is served in thin china cups. I balance mine carefully, anxious to get on with drinking it so we can get to the photos. But first we talk about Reggie.

'Bit of a character,' Glyn says, laughing.

Alexa tells me that Daddy – Henry Augustus Reginald Povah – was born in Streatham in 1912. Married in 1940 to Mummy – Marjorie. I ask what Reggie was like.

Diane blinks and takes a sip of coffee. She seems to be waiting to see what they say.

'He was one of the most . . . positive people I've ever met,' Glyn says very carefully.

'Did he like you?'

Glyn smiles and looks at Alexa. 'No. No, he didn't.'

Alexa explains that she was married before. And then she met Glyn and they lived together. This didn't go down too well with Daddy. When she told her father – 'at the age of 34' – that she was expecting Henrietta, all he said was: 'So you like him then?'

'"Of course I do," I told him, "and we're getting married."'

'"Not again!" he said. "We went through the big wedding thing last time."'

'"Don't worry," I said, "you're not coming."'

'"I'm not? Well, that's OK then."'

'He was the kind of man who was anti a lot of things,' adds Glyn. 'He was anti-Semitic, anti-gay, anti-Labour.'

'Anti-you,' says Henrietta.

'Anti-me!' Glyn laughs self-deprecatingly at this memory. Does it hurt him to remember or is he as placid as he appears? 'He was a real Alf Garnett.'

'One Christmas I gave him Mao Tse Tung's Little Red Book as a joke, as his under-the-tree present,' Alexa says, 'and he said, "Alexa my darling, you have sold your soul!"'

'He had great energy,' Glyn adds kindly.

'Mummy used to have to manoeuvre him into doing nice things, a sort of bribery. She'd say, Reggie if you do this good deed, you'll end up with ten times the profit – and he believed her. She always stuck up for him. She used to say, "Your Daddy's a gentleman inside." I do think she believed it. He was under a car first time he saw her – noticed her legs going by.'

September 1939. He's there, on his back under the Lagonda, fiddling with the sump, fingers thick with oil and dirt, sweat pouring under the overalls.

It's the hottest afternoon and the pavement of Streatham High Road is only a matter of yards away from his face. Trams, bustle, women – especially women. From time to time he takes a break and tries to see up someone's skirt.

Next thing he knows, a fine pair of legs walk by. Tan shoes, high heels, good ankles, calves – clip clop – really top-notch legs they are, alpha minus he'd give them, certainly best of the afternoon so far. He cranes his head out and round to see if he can see the body they're attached to, but no, she's already been sucked off into the crowd. On an impulse that surprises him – pure Povah skirt-chasing impulse! – he pulls himself out from under the vehicle, stands up and takes off after her.

She turns around, surprised. He looks her straight in the eye: usually works.

'Wondered if you fancied a drink sometime?'

'What?'

He likes the nervous way she bites at her lip. Dark hair, brunette, slight gap between her front teeth. He can't tell what her breasts are like under the coat, but she's got nice hands, small wrists – he likes a small wrist. Usually a good sign. Her nails are a bit ragged though – the thumb bitten right down on one hand. He pretends not to notice as she quickly covers one hand with the other. But he's glad she does it – means she likes him, means he'll have her blouse buttons undone within the week.

'Well?' he says. 'Are you seeing anyone or aren't you?'

'Goodness. You're a bit bold, aren't you? You don't even know me.'

He shows her his hand. 'I'd shake and say How Do You Do and all that but you probably don't want to get covered in muck and oil.'

'Too right,' she says. 'You a mechanic?'

He laughs loudly.

'I own Acre Autos down there.'

She glances, smiling now, flustered as if she should know.

'But mostly I race cars – Brands Hatch, you know, that sort of thing.' He tries to be as nonchalant as he can.

'A racing driver?'

He lifts his shoulders and sighs as if it's nothing.

'I was under a car actually,' he says.

'What?'

'Just now. Under a car. Lagonda. Saw your legs go past.'

'My legs?' She screws up her eyes, half suspicious, half amused.

'Just your legs. Stockings. Thought I'd ask if you'd like to go out, on the strength of the legs, I mean.'

Marjorie laughs, more warmly this time, and bites her lip again. 'But I might have been hideous!'

'Hit lucky, didn't I? You're not. I know a good bit of body work when I see it.'

'You're very forward, I'll give you that. I don't know where you get your cheek from.'

But he knows. He knows exactly where he gets it from. He gets it from them all trying to crush him – his family always down on him, all the time. It just so happens that when his father ups and goes, runs off with another woman, leaving his poor dear Mum in the lurch, then the cash runs right out. Being the youngest, he gets taken out of school just like that before a single thing has sunk in. Unlike his sisters, who are now all posh and educated. Or so they like to think.

Never mind. Always one to think on his feet, he gets himself a job at fourteen, in a garage, and they sneer at this, his sisters. At first they sneer because their bro is a mechanic. Then, later they sneer because he moves up fast and makes a bit of money – Reggie the wide boy, the one who's always been 'a bit East End'. Not good enough for them, they make sure to put him in his place. People always have, it's always been the way. He's never been allowed to forget the time his grandma Clara had him to stay as a small boy and wrote a postcard to his mother saying he was 'a terrible child'. As a baby they thought he was ill, they said, he was that fractious. Brainstorms, they called his tantrums.

Brainstorms – well, he still has them. Only now there's a difference:

now he makes a pretty packet out of them. Just give him any old thing – car, pram, jalopy, and he'll renovate it and sell it for twice the price. Whatever he does in life, he comes out at a profit. Profit Povah, that's him – that's what they hate. Let them laugh at him all they like, see if he cares a jot.

They stand there talking on that pavement for three-quarters of an hour on that day in September, until the shadows lengthen and the butcher starts to pull down his blinds. She says her name is Marjorie and she lives in Gracefield Gardens. He tells her how he tried to get out of the RAF, how they rumbled him and he's got his papers anyway. She says it's all very funny. She says, 'Well, at least you had a go.' She says he's a character. She says yes, maybe she'll go out with him.

They agree to meet at the Locarno, perhaps go dancing, take it from there. Reggie feels himself perking up. Never mind that the country's at war and he's covered in oil and business isn't so good. He's got himself a date.

Povah pulls it off.

As we sit and talk about Reggie I'm very conscious of Diane on my left, silent and tense, sifting through a shoebox of black-and-white pictures of her family.

Then, all of a sudden, she shyly leans forward and puts one in my hand and I look down at it and here it is – about four inches square – the exact thing I've been imagining for a very long time.

A thickset man in a pinstripe suit, frowning slightly, holds a small baby in white knitted bootees high and awkwardly in his hunched-up arms. To his right, you can see the front of next door – 32 Lillieshall Road. To his left, not quite visible, our house, Number 34. Meanwhile, a hedge runs along behind him, barely reaching his waist. This is the hedge that's now above my shoulders. The hedge that I pruned last Sunday before the rain came down.

'It's my father, Peter, holding my brother Bob,' Diane explains.

'Outside our house!'

'That was July 1947. Bob was about three months old.'

She then shows me photographs of Bob's christening – a group standing with the vicar in front of Holy Trinity Church, the white columns so familiar to me from all those Macaulay School end of terms. 'Christening of Robert Peter, May 1947, parents and godparents.'

'the hedge I pruned last Sunday.'

I turn and ask Diane – as tactfully as I can – about the story her brother told me of her mother falling down the stairs.

'Yes, that's right. I was very small when it happened.'

'And it made her ill?' I don't say what her brother told me about her father possibly having pushed her. I'm not sure, after all, whether or

'the white columns so familiar to me.'

229

not he was joking. But I do say that Bob said something about schizophrenia and Diane hesitates – and not for the first time I'm highly conscious that I'm wading through the tragic, personal lives of total strangers.

'They were never sure whether it was that or something else that caused it,' she says. 'In those days they didn't know. But yes, she was certified at one point. She had ECT treatment.'

From there, we get on to her father's ulcerated legs. She tells me it wasn't just that. Her father also had a genetic disease called Anderson-Fabry – it's a rare renal condition that creates intense discomfort in the hands and feet and can lead to blindness. It's carried by women who are barely affected by the symptoms. Suddenly I remember that her brother had mentioned a family disease.

'That's why we know our family tree. We had to research it, because of the disease.'

Alexa says she wants to know more about her Daddy turfing people out of the house.

'Those poor old people! Why would he be so keen to do it?'

I explain that, as far as I know, once he got the Hinkleys out, he let it to a whole bunch of people – Americans and Canadians. We're not sure whether Annie and Theodore Blaine owned it or rented it from Reggie and then sub-let to Mavis and Dorothy and Olive and so on. Or maybe they eventually bought it from him and took the rent themselves.

'Ah well, there were always lots of Turks and other foreigners staying with us in the house in Leigham Court Road,' she says. 'Maybe there was some kind of a war connection there?'

'I'll tell you a really sad thing about Daddy,' she says then. 'Do you know what the last thing he did before he died was? He took me into his garage and said, "I've got something to show you, darling." And you know what he'd done? He'd swapped his brand-new X-reg car for an electric shopping trolley! Can you imagine? It was so sad.'

Alexa then jumps up and goes behind the sofa, coming back with a very old, thick, brown cardboard box saying '2 dozen small tins Heinz Cream of Tomato Soup' in scuffed black letters on the side.

'Do you know what this is?' she says – and she shows me the side of the box where *LOVE LETTERS TO BE DESTROYED UNREAD. DO NOT BREAK OUR TRUST IN THIS* is scrawled across the cardboard in grey pencil.

'My God,' I say. 'From him? From them?'

I can hardly believe it. Alexa looks pleased. 'Just before my Mummy died she gave me this. She made me promise never to read them and I never have because, well, you know, it was a promise and I don't feel I can break it. I think they're love letters between my Mummy and my Daddy, mostly written during the war and before they got married, so before he bought your house, I'm afraid. But, well, I can't imagine why she wouldn't want me to read them, can you?'

I shake my head. I can't take my eyes off the box. Made in Canada, Heinz 57.

'But anyway, the way I see it is, you didn't make that promise, so in a way there's nothing to stop me letting you read them, is there? And Glyn didn't make the promise either – so I got him to look at a few of them.'

Henrietta, kneeling on the floor, fair hair falling over her shoulders, has already whipped out a faded and stained blue envelope and opened it. 'Hey, Mum, listen to this: it says "24 Sept 1940 – The Start". What's "The Start", I wonder?'

> *24th September 1940*
> *The Start*
>
> *My Darling Reggie*
> *I don't know if you remember it but it is exactly a year ago tonight that I first went out with you . . . remember? Darling it really has*

been a lovely year knowing you and although there has been a
million things against us I think we've got a lot out of it don't you?
When I came down Gracefield Gardens this morning I thought of
this time last year when I stood talking to you for about an hour and
a half – you told me how you had tried to wangle your way out of the
Air Force under false pretences and how you went through your sight
test by memorising the letters.

Henrietta giggles and so does Glyn. Alexa and Diane say nothing. I take a breath.

'The thing is,' I say as carefully as I can, 'these letters would be just amazing to read, even purely just because of how much they'd tell me about your father's character. And he's important to me because he owned the house and – well – I mean, you probably don't want me to take them away, but I don't suppose you'd let me come another time and spend a morning just reading them, would you? I'd be ever so careful.'

'Oh, take them!' Alexa says, taking the 24 September letter back from Henrietta and closing the flaps of the box. 'Take them away and read them. I can't, but as a matter of fact, I'd quite like them read by someone.'

'You're sure?'

'There's a diary of my mother's in there too, I think. No, really, you're very welcome.'

I leave the house quite astonished by their trust and generosity. Under my arm, letters, diaries, evil landlords and false pretences. A whole archive falling straight into my lap. And all opened up by that first phone call to Joan Clayton in Cambridge. It's all suddenly seeming far too colourful, far too easy.

Next morning, two messages on my answerphone. The first:

'Hello? Hello? This is Mr Humphrey – Humphrey Eric Spawton of 33

Cherry Park Road, – I repeat: Cherry Park Road – Beeston, Nottingham N923 8RT. That's N923 8RT. Would you like to ring me back this evening please? I repeat: would you like – would you like – would you like – would you like to ring me back this evening please? I'm going to repeat that address . . .'

Second message:

'Hello? I haven't given you, I haven't given you. I haven't . . . given you my number. It's 0115 628 334. I repeat . . .'

Three minutes after I pick this up, the phone rings again and I answer.

'Hello, my dear, been back long?'

'Who is this?'

'It's Mr – it's Mr – it's Mr – '

'Mr Spawton?' My heart sinks. 'Thanks so much for ringing.'

'My name is Humphrey Eric Spawton – have you got that? Humphrey Eric – I was born on July 13th 1932 in Nightingale Gardens, Nightingale Gardens.'

'And – er – do you think you might be related to Lucy Spawton who lived here in our house?'

'I was born in Romford, so what do you think?'

'Well, she came from Clapham so, perhaps not?'

'But I think I must be related somewhere along the line, don't you? Aren't we all related to each other somehow in the end?'

'Well, OK, in the end maybe. Yes – if you go back many years.'

'But that's it! That's what I'm saying – years and years and years and years and years and – '

'Thanks so much for calling, Mr Spawton, but I'm afraid I don't think you're the one I'm looking for.'

'But I am, I am, I am the one! I'm asking you, I'm asking you seriously now – do you think I am related to that woman?'

'Um, seriously – no, I think probably not.'

'Look here, young lady, my brother was born in the county of Berk – Berk – Berkshire.'

'Huntingdon?'

'How did you know? Do you know my brother?'

'Thanks so much for your time, Mr Spawton.'

'But wait! Don't you think?'

'I'm so sorry but I have to go now.'

'Oh. Very well then, my dear.'

I march straight up to Jonathan's study. 'I wish you'd told me you'd written off to a whole load of Spawtons too.'

He looks at me. 'You didn't seem to be making much progress at the Family Records Centre. I thought it was worth a try – it only takes a couple of hours to download the names and mail-merge them. Jake and I did it yesterday, while you were out.'

'You could have warned me.'

'You told me Lucy had sisters and brothers. If we just get one direct descendant, then we're laughing. Has someone rung?'

The second post brings a letter from Joan Clayton – Diane's aunt – in Cambridge. Joan's mother's sister was Matilda Scott, who married Thomas Spawton, Lucy's nephew.

'Joan's mother's sister . . . married Thomas Spawton, Lucy's nephew.'

As I open it, two old sepia photos fall out. I make a point of not looking at them, force myself to read the letter first.

> *I'm afraid I have no further details of your house apart from a couple of things about Lucy Spawton which I will enlighten you in the letter. I've told you most of it on the phone but here goes!!*
>
> *Lucy Spawton (spinster) once owner – her nephew Thomas Harlock Beesley Spawton (what a name) married my mother's sister Matilda Scott on 12 April 1912. On Lucy's death the house was left to the said T. H. B. Spawton – then on his death my Aunt Matilda became the owner – about 1947/48 my sister Margaret Askew (deceased) and husband lived there and their first child Robert was born during this period – and I've only just learned the address is on his birth certificate.*
>
> *For the whole of this period Lucy had the Hinkleys (in their 70s and 80s) in a ground floor flat and after my sister & family left, Aunt Matilda sold the house to a Reggie Povah (my sister's brother in law) on condition he didn't evict the Hinkleys – but sadly he did just that and turned the whole house into flats and let it to Americans and Canadians – not living in it himself. From then on I lost touch of the whole situation once my aunt sold it.*
>
> *The two things I forgot to tell you about Lucy was in her younger days she became Head Buyer for the renowned firm in London of Derry and Thomas (hope I spelt this right) – it was on a par with our today's Harrods . . . I'm enclosing two photos, one of Lucy in the Group and one of Uncle Thomas and Aunt Matilda together – you are very welcome to keep the photos, thanking you once again,*
>
> *Best wishes*
> *A. Clayton*

I pick up the photos. The first one says 'On Holiday in Felixstowe'. Thomas Harlock Beesley Spawton and Matilda Spawton (*née* Scott) stride purposefully arm in arm towards the camera in that self-conscious way people do when paying to have their photo taken by strangers. The background's bleached out almost to nothing, but you can make out some holidaymakers, a packed prom and a solitary black dog.

Thomas looks about thirty-five and paunchy, with oddly shortened (or ill-fitting?) trousers and a buttoned-up jacket. I think he has glasses and maybe a moustache, but it's hard to tell from the photo as the facial details are very faint. He looks anxiously happy. Happy, yet anxious. Anxious to please?

Aunt Matilda, Til, looks older – fortyish at least, solidly built, strong, handsome face and big feet in pointy strap-buttoned shoes. Thomas seems aware of the camera – intent on getting his money's worth? – but his wife is glancing away at something in the far distance, a half-amused expression on her face. Hard to tell if she's really looking at something or whether she just prefers the idea of herself looking away.

The other photo is taken in Eastbourne. There's no date. Crowds of summer people, rows and rows of beach huts, and in the foreground a family lined up and posing for the camera in deckchairs. 'Aunt Til,' Mrs Clayton has written on the bottom, 'my Dad, Aunty Lucy, my sister Margaret and myself.'

Aunt Til leans back, eyes shut, white cloche hat on, dress with white tie at the neck. A big, hand-some, no-nonsense woman enjoying the sunshine. Mrs

'on holiday in Felixstowe'

236

Clayton's Dad is tense, unsmiling, dark-complexioned, with a cigarette (is it a cigarette?) in his hand. Tie-less, legs slightly apart, the bloke on holiday, his deckchair wedged uneasily between two women. Did his wife take the picture? Was he telling her to get on with it?

'Did she come back here to 34 Lillieshall Road at the end of that hot day in the photograph?'

In the front, sit two small, short-haired girls – maybe three or four years old, Joan and Phyllis. Bare feet and big knickers. Scowling at the camera, just as bored as their Dad, perhaps, at how long the photo is taking. And then, the best bit. Next to Dad is Aunt Lucy – my Lucy! – the most striking person in the photo by far. Tiny, beady, dark-faced Victorian woman – deliciously, spookily out of place in this sunny beach group. She has on a high-necked, sacklike dress, mannish black shoes, white stockings, hat with fruit on the front. No hair visible. Dark, shadowy eyes. She clasps her hands and stares directly at the camera, unapologetic.

She's Lucy Spawton – that's Miss Spawton – Clapham spinster, department store Head Buyer, Eastbourne holidaymaker. Just down for the day and Good Lord, this sun is stifling hot, isn't it?

'Take something off, Auntie,' says Matilda. 'For heaven's sake, you're going to fry.'

But, of course, she won't. She dresses with an almost aggressive primness, she knows that, but then she's never been a looker, never wanted to be. The things she's gone after in life – a satisfying job, a little financial independence – aren't the kinds of things that are bought by looks, and she knows that too.

She isn't all that interested in fashion actually but, working in quality womenswear as she does, she's developed a taste for good things, for a pleasing weave on a piece of fabric or supple bit of leather: sturdy well-made shoes, fine cotton and linen, stuff that will last. She doesn't want to buy things twice over – she'd prefer to hold on to her money. In fact, she never wanted the hat with the fruit in the first place, to tell the truth – Matilda persuaded her into it, leaned on her to buy it.

'You'd look ever so nice in that, Auntie. A bit of brightness – it'll suit you.'

'Not my sort of thing at all, Til.'

'Try it, that's all I'm saying.'

She doesn't mind. It's just the one hat and she can afford it and she knows Til means well.

Maybe she lives at the top of the house in Lillieshall Road, in the room where Jake now paints his goblin models and listens to Linkin' Park, where Leon Pidgeon slept under his Spurs duvet, where Winnie Bartolo saw her mother open a letter and cry, where Thomas Kyle stacked his lonely law books and Doreen perched on a corner of the bed and told him about the shoplifting.

Or maybe she's right here in our bedroom. Maybe she strides up and down this smallish, creaky room and hoicks up the sash window, which always sticks a little on the left, and hears the blackbird singing his hopeful one-note song at dawn as I do.

There she is, Lucy Spawton, caught by the camera for a split second on a summer's day on the coast sometime after the First World War.

Did she come back here to 34 Lillieshall Road at the end of that hot day in the photograph? Did she walk up our front path, brushing against the baby, ankle-high privet hedge on her right, and turn a key in this actual front door? And did she unpin her fruit hat in front of a mirror in the hall and, leaning towards the glass, notice a freckle on her face where somehow, despite her best intentions, she'd caught the sun?

Raphael looks at the photo of Lucy and shudders.

'Looks like the wicked witch of the West,' he says, 'the one where the house falls down on her and only her shoes are sticking out.'

He's right, of course. There's something about Lucy's dark, pointy, old-fashioned face. A fierce old woman furiously pedalling her bicycle past just before the hurricane.

'She is a very funny-looking lady, I agree.'

'Did she have your room?'

'No idea. Maybe.' I can tell he's fervently hoping she didn't have his.

I'm wrapped in a towel, just out of the shower. Raphael looks down at my bare feet and smiles to himself.

'What?' I ask him. 'What's funny?'

'I was thinking that witches have square feet,' he says.

I look down at my big feet, not my best feature, misshapen from years of ballet and an accident with a cast-iron bath when I was twelve.

'My feet aren't square, are they?'

He says nothing. Just looks at them and smiles to himself.

907042 R Povah AC
Hut H3.3T Wing
RAF St Athan
Glam. S Wales

8 June 1940
My Darling Marjorie

I have got tons to tell you in this letter but before I start I should like to point out that I was very annoyed at finding you out last Sunday at 11.45, also very worried. Where the devil did you get to? I hope your mother is prepared to tell fibs for me if ever it be necessary.

Anyway darling there's nothing I can do about it except trust you . . . Dink and I always maintained that the worse you treated a girl the better they were in return and if one ran after them the less they thought about you . . . I cannot possibly get leave to be married but have found out it can be arranged for you to come here to marry me. Also dearest I made a mistake about our money. We shall be worth exactly £3. 2s. 0d. per week but as you know I shall need nothing in the way of clothes or boots and in fact all I need is fags providing I have you with me.

Anyway the last two weeks have been the most thrilling part of my life . . . I should love to explain and tell you all tons of things about what we're doing here but I cannot because all letters are censored. Well tell Dinkie to try and remember the most thrilling moment of his life and then magnify it umpteen times and then he might be somewhere near it. Anyway it suits my character beautifully in fact it really has made me feel different altogether. I must be the type that thrives on thrills and excitement because I am putting on weight visibly and am as happy as a sandboy.

I am always thinking about you dearest, sometimes I dream about you too and their [sic] such lovely dreams I couldn't possibly write on paper about them, but I'll tell you about them sometime. Well darling, big baby Margy, give my love to your mum and all at home and be a good girl, don't give anyone the slightest chance to tempt you out with them, I wouldn't stand for that if I were home, in fact you know you would never be out of my sight if I could help it, cheerio my own sweetheart

Love Reg

(Darling I don't know whether you realise it or not but I shall only be able to sleep with you every other night. Sorry I thought maybe you didn't understand)

[undated]
Dear Povah
Business is not too bad, could be a lot worse. Lou as you know has been at Streatham for a few weeks but there is not anything doing. Have not sold a car yet, one or two almost, but you know what car salesmen are. I think a car is sold when the money is in the till.

Well I trust the girls of [illegible] are as pleased with you as the Streatham virgins and that you are keeping up the true tradition of the motor trade and not always dealing with used and partworn articles.

Arthur D. Whitely

28 August 1940
Reggie
. . . well now dear about your marriage. Your letter came as a great surprise to me as I thought you had given up that idea for the time being anyhow. Please do take your Mum's advice just a little. Remember that no marriage is happy unless there is love especially from the man's side. Pressure brought on you from Marjorie is not sufficient, but as I have told you before you must please yourself.

As far as Marjorie being scared of me – Rot. She is afraid I might influence you and I should be sorry for you if you were married because by the mere fact in telling you this shows that she would not hesitate to come between us and try to stop you seeing me.

I was so sorry to hear about that poor chap who did not come back, it is terrible and I know dear you felt it. Of course the other chaps who took it so coolly perhaps are made of tougher material . . .

Well my dear son did I tell you that your Pa came over to see us, he refers to Lena as his little sweetheart here, the soft old fool. Some men get like that when they are no longer young . . . I called to see the dear old Bentley it was placed in a good position back away from the door and I asked the man to put a sheet over it which he promised to do. I am going in again tomorrow to see if this has been done, if not God help him,

love
Mum
X

Yesterday the temperatures in London broke all records – 100 degrees F in Gravesend. Two boys in two different parts of the country have jumped into two different lakes and drowned. Meanwhile a man on a motorway turned the air-conditioning in his car up too high and got frostbite in his foot. Today feels even hotter than yesterday. We sleep all night with all the windows and curtains open but it makes no difference.

The heat seems to make people angrier than usual. Two days in a row we've woken to shouting in the street. First time, it was a family from down the road. 'I'm telling you for the last time, get in the bloody car!' screamed a mother. This went on for ten minutes and was painful to hear. We agreed it could easily have been us.

Today, it's the turn of the refugee hostel across the road. A woman in thick, dark clothes and a veil leans from an upstairs window in the already oppressive heat of 8 a.m. and listens to the fracas below.

'Call yourself a man!' shouts a burly West Indian from a downstairs window. 'Do you? Do you? Come here, let's have you – call yourself a man? Come here then, let's see you, mate! Show yourself!'

The basement windows of the house are all boarded up – a recent measure – which gives the place a sad look, like a person whose eyes are shut forever.

One night a few years ago we went to bed late after a party and I looked out of the window to see smoke coming out of this house. I called the fire brigade but they were already on their way. By the time they'd arrived, someone had thrown himself from an upstairs window – Jonathan saw the dark shape fall into the basement-well below.

Spotlights were set up and the paramedics worked for hours to get the person on to a stretcher. I watched, I couldn't help it, couldn't tear myself away – the eerie blue-white lights and the hot night and the people walking briskly to and fro and the incessant pumps of the fire engine chuntering on.

It was five in the morning and almost light before all the emergency vehicles had finally gone and the street was quiet, empty. You looked at the house and there was no sign that anything had ever happened, no trace of the drama that had just that night unfurled.

The fire, we heard later, had actually been a modest one, easily extinguished. The person on the top floor – fresh from a war zone – had simply panicked.

Jake stands in our room and sweats. He is desperate to get out and join his friends but will only go in blue winter jeans, thick socks and heavy trainers.

'You don't make any effort to understand,' he bellows, sweat dripping off him. 'This is what all my friends wear! Exactly this outfit! Their parents don't interfere with them!'

'OK, you're grounded, then,' Jonathan says, 'simple as that. Unless you put on a pair of shorts and get a bottle of water, you're not going anywhere.'

Jake looks near to tears. Wetness stands out on his face, his neck. He pushes out a shiny, purplish bottom lip, unsure of what the next line of rebellion should be. Weeping or shouting? Toddler or teenager? His face has changed recently, as if each feature is growing independently and too fast – as if his nose and mouth are in some race to the death and have temporarily lost sight of what sort of face they're actually supposed to be in.

'You guys!' he blurts out, flinging his hot body down in the armchair. 'You want to ruin my life, don't you?'

'No,' I tell him as gently as I can, 'we just don't want you to end up in hospital with heatstroke.'

'Oh heatstroke! But shorts aren't in fashion, you stupid woman, and I can control my body temperature and – '

'Of course you can't,' Jonathan interrupts, 'don't say such a ridiculous thing, boy.'

'How can you possibly control your own body temperature?' I ask him. 'If people could do that, they would never get heatstroke.'

'I'm telling you, are you deaf? I – won't – get – heatstroke!'

'I don't care. You're going nowhere unless you change.'

'Oh my God!' Jake sinks further down in the armchair, shattered, tears running down his face.

'You're boiling already, darling,' I tell him.

He stomps up to his room. Jonathan and I look at each other as he slams the door hard enough to make the whole house shudder.

I have a sudden fascinating thought. 'I'd give anything to know how many times all the doors in this house have been slammed since 1872,' I tell him. 'Seriously. Just imagine if you could find that out.'

I'm almost a regular here at the London Metropolitan Archives. The archivists nod at me as I enter. Before I left the other day, one of them mentioned the land tax records. Before there were electoral registers, apparently, there was land tax.

After twenty minutes, the box arrives in the Reading Room. It's a little larger than A2 and the Clapham land tax records are tied together in a simple white tape band, about thirty years' worth. Each year's tax returns are detailed in a single purpose-printed booklet, an extract from the Act of Parliament at the top. I start at 1870.

The booklet names each street – again that exquisite copperplate, street names in purple, double underlined, everything else in curling black script. There's the name of the occupant and the name of the owner, the house number, and then the amount taxable and the amount payable. I turn the page, there's The Chase; turn the page again, there's North Street and Lambourne Road and Orchard Street.

Lillieshall Road does not make its tax-paying entrance until 1872. There are only fourteen houses in all and Mrs Williams owns four of them, all empty, and Mr Jenkins owns two. By 1873, these houses are starting to show occupants. And written alongside the Lillieshall Road entries, sideways up the page: 'Formerly the Cricket Field Estate, the remainder of the land was redeemed in June 1872'.

This is the cricket field into which Bazalgette carved his pipework. This is the grass at the end of Orchard Street that was swallowed to make more houses for London.

And at Number 15 – as Number 34 was known before the 1877 renumbering – there is Edward Maslen's name. Proof, then, that the first occupant was definitely Edward Maslen, paying his ten shillings and twopence land tax in 1873.

But, skimming back through my notes, I realize that he was listed in the 1876 road-surfacing apportionment as Edward Maslin. Which one is the correct spelling?

I pull out the 1874 booklet – I know where to find Lillieshall Road now, the order remains unchanged each year – and he's Edward Maslin again.

In 1875 he's Edwin Maslin.

In 1876 it's Edward Maslem. It's getting worse.

Whatever his name is, he's the first occupant of 34 Lillieshall Road, but not the owner. The house still seems to be owned by Mrs Williams, who also owns the four three-storey houses. Who was she?

'*Maslin . . . he's the first occupant of 34 Lillieshall Road.*'

I turn through each year's booklet, watching the number of tax-paying houses in Lillieshall Road grow each year. Then, in 1881, the house is empty and in 1882 it is suddenly owned by Edward Maslem and occupied by Henry Hayward. So did Henry pay his rent to Edward or Edwin Maslin or Maslen or Maslem?

In fact, I discover that Maslem owned it until 1898, with Elizabeth Spawton – Lucy's mother – paying him rent until she bought it from him in 1899.

I go back and take a last look at 1873. It is such a beautiful document. Did the collector go from door to door, or did he send more copperplate letters and graciously await payment? Did he notice Lillieshall Road was starting to come alive, taking shape as a little community between North Street and the Common, or was it no more than an extra set of figures for him to calculate?

I am just closing the booklet when I notice, listed at The Terrace, Victoria Road – now Victoria Rise – Edward I'Anson. And suddenly, the picture shifts. As he addressed the Metropolitan Board of Works, his fingers were trembling and Fowler took this for nerves, for naivety. But it was a liar's tremble. He had given his address as Pountney Hill in the City, but in truth he lived just round the corner, in a row of grand houses on the edge of the Common.

Had he noticed this stretch of land, then? Had he had his eye on it for a while – hearing that the Bowyer family were quite keen to sell off the cricket pitch? And then, having landed the post of District Surveyor, could he engineer the land sales, placing himself neatly in the middle?

I wonder whether, standing in Spring Gardens that afternoon in 1871, being quizzed by the Board, he kept this particular secret close to his chest? That Lillieshall Road was his baby.

Tintagel, as it's been romantically named, looks like something out of a horror movie: gothic turrets, stained-glass windows, monkey puzzle tree in the garden.

Mum's excited because it was built by Mr Liberty of the famous London department store and has 'all the original features'. There's a billiard room, a cool, dark, tiled hall, stained-glass windows, stables and tack room out the back, and, best of all, a Victorian grotto. Stalactites and stalagmites, dripping water, moss and ferns. We keep it for a couple of years but no one ever goes in there and it makes the sitting room and billiard room hopelessly dark. In the end, we have it knocked down and settle for a patio instead.

I'm thirteen when we move into Tintagel and sixteen when we leave, but a lot happens to me there: I have my first period, write my first poems, start my first novel (on the small manual typewriter I wheedle out of my grandfather, who collects all manner of junk), and kiss my first boy. The boy is my French penfriend's older brother, Serge – skinny, blond, serious. We are so mad about each other that we never speak or even make eye contact.

But the night before he goes back to Brittany, he kisses me in the hall, which is deathly quiet except for the wicker-creak of the dog in her bed. I remember nothing about the kiss except his smoke breath and the fact that in the morning I don't look like the same person any more. Even my clothes look different on me.

'a lot happens to me there'

Tintagel is also the house where I get the letter from my father saying it will be better if we don't see each other any more. I stand in the garage – the only place, in a house of sisters and stepbrothers, where a person can go to be alone – and I sob. Then I stop and I never cry about it again. Each day that I don't have to see him feels lighter – all my weekends are suddenly my own. I am sixteen. I begin a new novel about love and death in the 1920s. It's incredibly self-conscious and arch. It fills an exercise book.

From Marjorie Askew's Diary

Tues 2nd Jan 1940
Came to the office. Miss Holt lost her ring. Wrote to R. Don't feel very well. Throat still hurts me. Wish the war would end and things return to normal.

Fri 5th Jan
I hate this war. He gets further away.

Sat 6th Jan
I stayed in bed until late. This is the first weekend in ages that I have had nothing to do. Can't even write to R. Hope he hurries with his new address.

Sun 7th Jan
Miserable Sunday. Guessed it would be. I hate weekends spent at home. Peter took me to the pictures. He's a good kid.

Wed 10th Jan
Had office to myself again. I felt much better. I wrote to R. I hoped that I should have had a letter from him. Had lunch with Mr Lewes. Funny world. Saw Betty in evening.

Thurs 11th Jan
Miss Holt's back. Had lunch with Beryl. Damn nice kid. Glad she's happy. Still no letter. Peter and I took Mummy to the pictures. Saw The Crazy Gang. Personally I feel fed up.

Friday 12th Jan
Received letter from R. It's a lovely letter. He even asked for a nail
file. I'm so pleased . . .

I phone Joan Clayton and ask her if she remembers which bit of the house Lucy Spawton lived in.

She says, as far as she can recall, she was in what she calls the 'first-floor flat' – the rooms that are now our bedroom, the bathroom, and my study with the loo next door. Joan says she doesn't know which one Lucy actually slept in but the front room (our bedroom) was a kind of a sitting room with a little upright piano in it.

I ask Joan whether she knows why Lucy never married and she laughs. 'Just take a look at her in that photo I sent you, my dear! She was a typical old maid, wasn't she? Look at how she's dressed on a boiling hot day to go to the seaside!'

It occurs to me that maybe Jake is also heading for Old Maid status.

I ask her if she knows why Tom and Matilda Spawton's address is given as 34 Lillieshall Road on Lucy's will.

'I don't think they ever lived there, dear, but I think they used to go and sleep over during the bombing and that. She was an old lady by then, remember.'

Joan tells me her sister Phyllis worked at Dolcis in Cambridge before she came and lived here in the house. 'Funny girl she was, she's dead now so I suppose I can say that. You'd never have known she was my twin. She led her own way of life, if you know what I mean.'

'In what way?'

'We-ell. She got married to this man, Frank, at eighteen – Mother didn't approve of that at all. Then war came along and he went into the RAF and they drifted apart. Then she worked at Shorts, which was a munitions factory in Cambridge, and there she met Peter Askew. He was a grocer.'

'The one who specialized in cooked meats?'

'That's right, dear. That man knew all there was to know on the various ways of cooking meat. He worked on the cold cuts counters of all sorts of high-class grocers.

'*That man knew all there was to know on the various ways of cooking meat.*'

'But Phyllis could be wild. Really very selfish and headstrong. Do you know, during the war, my own husband was in the RAF and I went down to live in Cornwall for several months. I left all my clothes in London and guess what, she – that girl! – wore my best coat so much it was nearly worn out to a thread! And she never apologized! Can you imagine? I'd never have done that to her, never!

'And then, after our poor mother was dead, I once mentioned to her, "You know today's Mother's birthday?" and she said, "Oh, who cares? I never think about these things, I live for the future" – can you imagine saying that?'

Joan tells me that she always felt there was some mystery about her Uncle Tom. 'We were never sure where he came from, originally I mean, whether he came from London. One day after he died we came across an old watercolour with the initials AS on it and we asked what the picture was of and Aunt Til said, "Oh, that was where Uncle Tom

251

used to live once." Which was funny because I suppose we assumed he'd come from London like the rest of them.

'Anyway, for some reason Lucy took him under her wing, paid for his education – he was very close to Lucy, there was only about sixteen years between them, you see.'

'Funny,' I tell Joan, 'I mean if his father was still alive, then why would Lucy need to take Tom on like that?'

'Really couldn't say, dear. Only I know that was the case. The other thing is – oh no, this is silly . . .'

'What?'

'Well, there was something amiss with Tom, to be honest, dear,' she suddenly says.

'How do you mean?'

She sighs again. 'Well, I don't know really, there just was.'

One day Joan and Phyll are round at Aunt Til and Uncle Tom's and he's about to go off, not on the tube to the Midland Bank where he works, but to pay a visit to his cousin Fanny, who he's pretty thick with, always been dead fond of.

And Joan's watching, pretty bored, sitting on the little fence at the end of the garden swinging her legs in their blue sandals, and Phyll's off crying in the bushes somewhere, being a rotten cry-baby as usual, and Joan sees a funny thing. Uncle Tom has on this little black hat – he calls it his homburg. He always wears one – sometimes a black one, on other occasions a grey one. He takes his hats quite seriously. 'Anyone seen my homburg?' – that's what he tends to say, because it always gets put down somewhere strange in the house and it's a famous thing that he can never find it.

Anyway, on this day he says 'bye to Til and toddles off down the path and has just got as far as the garden gate when Aunt Til shouts at him to get back. 'Tom! Tom! Come here, I need you over here a minute!'

He turns around quick and looks at her. And then, meekly like a dog or something, he goes scuttling straight back up the path to her, obedient as anything, and Aunt Til whips the hat right off his head and gives it a quick brushing over, just briskly all over like that with a clothes brush she has in her hand, and then she hands it back to him.

'I don't want Fanny to think I'm not looking after you,' she says.

'Sorry, dear,' says Tom.

And Joan can't think why he's apologizing when Aunt Til's surely the one being bossy. And she giggles to herself and Uncle Tom winks at her as he scuttles back down the path, as if to say it's all fine and there's nothing funny about what he just did. But it doesn't wash. She can't quite see him in the same light after that.

But then again, Aunt Til, she's the really barmy one. Their Mum says so. One day she's standing outside their house in Cambridge in her fur coat, waiting for the taxi to take her to the station, and Mum comes rushing in and says, 'Does anyone know where Til is?'

And Phyll laughs her naughty, stirring-up laugh and says, 'Mother, would you believe it, she's outside cleaning the windows!'

And their Mum, she's quite angry. They hear her talking loudly to Til. 'What'll the neighbours think if they see you doing that, Tilda? What on earth were you thinking of? Think they're grubby, do you? What exactly are you saying? That I can't keep my own house clean enough?'

Aunt Til looks quite taken aback. 'I was only making myself useful in the time I had, Laurie,' she says, and her lips go all bunched up like she's ready for a fight. 'Better than standing around.'

'What do you think you look like, standing there all got up in your fur anyway? For heaven's sake, Til.'

Yes, Til's the barmy one. When she dies they find that fur coat of hers in her bedroom cupboard with a note pinned to it, a note which says, 'TOUCH THIS COAT AND YOUR FINGERS WILL DROP OFF!'

'Just in case a burglar broke in, you see, dear.' But then Joan breaks off a moment. 'Is this really interesting, dear?' she asks me anxiously.

253

I reassure her and she chuckles. 'At least I'm interesting to someone, then,' she says. 'Actually,' she goes on, 'although Tom worked at the bank in London, he did go up for a vacancy in Cambridge, but he didn't get it because of his health.'

'He was ill?'

'His heart. He was Church Warden at St James's Church in Clapham, which was near Park Hill where they lived. And he was getting ready to go to church one Sunday morning and he collapsed on the bathroom floor.

'Poor Aunt Til was downstairs getting herself a hot drink and she heard the thud. I don't know how soon after that he died, but he was never conscious again.'

The photos of Lucy, of Tom and Matilda, of the group on the beach, even Peter Askew holding baby Bob outside our house, all come in shades of black and white and furry yellow tones of grey.

It's tempting to imagine these lives lived out in these colourless shades – to think of these men and women and children pulling on dark grey clothes and walking down black streets against a white sky, holding white babies against blackish hedges, spending their time with grey-faced people with sepia ideas and moods.

But, of course, it wasn't like that. Daily life for them was as colourful as it is for us. Yes, the poster billboards and shopfronts didn't shout quite as loud, but there were still the easy primaries and pastels. The fuzzy yellow light that comes after rain. The acid brightness of a blade of grass or a dandelion head. The hectic pink of a baby's teething cheeks. The molten blue of a summer sky.

I drive past Clapham South tube to fetch the boys from cricket and I glance towards Clapham Common where the trees are bending softly in the wind. Black trees, white sky, invisible wind. Some boys are kicking a ball. A dog is running. A pushchair is being pushed. It's the same scene, with just a few details modernized. The design of the pushchair, the Nike logo on the ball, the starkly modern electricity poles.

But the fast-moving sky with its patches of blue and cloud, the green grass beneath, could be any sky, any grass. 2003, 1880, 1947.

Edward I'Anson's job is somehow to bring some method and control over the building frenzy that has exploded in this part of London.

When he moved to Clapham Common, it was quiet. Just the canter of horses or the lowing of cattle on the Common and, occasionally, when the wind blew from the north, the whistling screech of the new train line that runs from Clapham Junction to Waterloo. Now it's more like how he imagines the Klondike Gold Rush, everyone wanting to stake their claim for a chunk of Clapham soil.

'It's impossible,' he tells his wife almost every morning at breakfast and again at supper. 'They're supposed to apply for a licence, but hardly any of them do. They just start digging without a care in the world. We'll be lucky if half these houses are still standing in ten years' time. I can't possibly check up on them all.'

Does his wife, recalling his enthusiasm for developing the old cricket pitch, the endless meetings with the bailiff from the Bowyer Estate, how they suddenly seemed to have that little bit more spending money, sympathize? Or does she just wish he didn't have to spend his days walking round building sites, muddying his boots with the clayey Clapham soil, demanding to see the gaffer?

I'Anson's annual returns have just arrived for me in the Reading Room and they tell the clear story of this man's daily working life. A constant process of inspection, discovery, note-taking. The return for 1871 shows that on 5 December he 'discovered' Thomas Williams in the process of building two four-storey houses on Lillieshall Road, each thirty-eight feet tall. No notice had been submitted to the Vestry and Williams is promptly charged £2. 7s. 6d.

Not that he seems at all cowed because on 13 December, I'Anson 'discovers' Williams building another two houses. The same day, he 'discovers' Edward Armitage of Old Town building two four-storey houses. They are deemed to be forty feet tall and he is charged £2.10s.

In a way, doesn't I'Anson have only himself to blame? Didn't he encourage the District to lay the drainage, spur Bazalgette's interest, push it through the Metropolitan Board of Works? Can he really be surprised if all the builders in Clapham Town are now snapping up plots of land, building a couple of houses at a time? And anyway, the Bowyer Estate seems only too keen to sell. He's heard that they want to buy some manor house in Northamptonshire.

On 18 January 1872, he discovers – that's his word, marked in the ledgers as 'Discovery' – Thomas Williams of North Street, 'owner and builder', erecting two three-storey houses on Lillieshall Road, each twenty-seven feet tall. Just over two months later, on 28 March, Thomas Jenkins of 13 Orchard Street is also building two three-storey houses on Lillieshall Road.

Number 34 is a three-storey house – there are only seven of them in the street, everything else is two- or four-storey. Thomas Williams goes on to build another pair, as does Thomas Jenkins. Which means that one of these men is the man who built our home!

But which? It's just as I'm beginning to wonder if I'll ever know that I remember the land tax returns. Harriet Williams owned numbers 14 to 17, all empty in 1872, rented to Maslin and Whittingham and Mapleston by 1873. Williams is a common name but the coincidence is too great.

But if Mr Williams of North Street built our house, why did he name it 'Helena House' if his wife was called Harriet?

Jonathan and I park outside Tintagel, close to Nottingham's busy Forest Road. The same tall wooden doors, the high, brownish wall. Whenever someone mentions the long hot summer of '76, I think of this wall. It shimmered in the heat, looked like water. Elderly Miss Gisborne, who lived across the road, used to tell my mother how it cheered her to see five pairs of feet appearing over the top of it – as my sisters and stepbrothers and I spent hours trying to do cartwheels and handstands in the garden.

We open the gate and walk up the drive. All the curtains are drawn and I'm just about to knock on the door when a woman comes hurrying in from the street, closely followed by an older woman. 'Excuse me, but what are you doing?'

I apologize and explain that I wrote a letter, that I used to live here. The woman, who has dark hair and a foreign accent, looks unimpressed. She never got any letter (has anyone received any of my letters?) and no, it wouldn't be convenient to show us round right now – 'My husband is in the Gulf'.

I apologize and ask whether it might be possible to come another time? Maybe, she says. We are walked off the premises.

Tuesday 30 January 1940

Lots of sad days, heavy falls of snow, letters, nothing doing at office, getting on my nerves. Hope Reg and I will be married soon.

Thursday 1 Feb

Miserable day. Thaw has started in real earnest. Mr Lewis had too gay an afternoon. Saw Max Miller. Borrowed her chauffeur. Peter took me to Astoria. No letter.

Friday 15 Feb

Same old routine. Feeling a bit depressed. Throat doesn't get any better. Wish R would write to me every day.

Thursday 22 Feb

Quite [sic] day nothing exciting. Received rather upsetting letter from Reggie – wish he would not get funny ideas. If he was going to be away 30 years it would be the same.

Friday 23 Feb
Lunch with Stinker. Nothing happened. Wrote two letters, destroyed them both. Feel rather worried. People keep talking to me about getting married and I feel awful. Wish R would write.

Sunday 25th
Weekend spoiled because R did not write.

Monday 26th
No letter. I feel terribly worried, why doesn't he write? Received letter when I got home. Feel much happier.

Tuesday 27th
Wrote to R. I don't know whether we are getting married or not before he goes to the East. I want to but somehow, reading between the lines, I don't think he does.

Sat 2nd March
Bought coat, hat and wool for gloves. Feel pleased with them. Should look quite soignée.

Mon 4 March
I received another letter from R. I cannot possibly let him have any money as I'm broke. That part is worrying me more than anything.

Wed 6 March
Nothing exciting happened. I am feeling rather worried.
[This is followed by a mark: a circle with a cross in it.]

Sunday 10 March
Everything's OK.
[Another circle with a tick in it this time.]
I wrote to R and told him.

11th March 1940

Dear Reg
Oh darling my own sweet silly evil-minded Povah I can hardly wait
to see you again . . . oh by the way I nearly forgot a very important
thing and that is that everything in the garden is lovely. You know
what I mean. When I think of how you have loved me I think you are
undoubtedly very clever.

M

The thing is, she wants to love him completely the way he begs her to
let him love her. He doesn't believe her, she knows that. He thinks she's
fobbing him off when her being 'unwell' seems to coincide exactly with
him coming home on leave. It always seems to get on his nerves when
she's 'unwell', but the timing's hardly her fault, is it?

But because they're as good as engaged, and because everyone else
(Beryl-at-the-office included) frankly seems to be doing it, then a large
part of her gets reckless and thinks, What the devil, let him get on with
it. The thing is, when they're together, it's all so beautiful and she loves
him dearly, and he's so clever with the ways he finds to love her that,
well, it's easy to trust him too completely. There was that time in front of
the gas fire when his mother was out for hours and hours. She got a
carpet burn from the rug but she didn't much care, though she could
feel it under her stockings next day. Reg said he liked that – the idea that
she could feel it after, but him saying that made her blush, it really did.

And then there was the time when his Ma had taken cough medicine
and was so very sound asleep that they risked it – though she couldn't
relax that time, her heart was thumping so, listening out in case the
snoring stopped. But in the morning she found the evil cow had been
in and stripped the bed. Just to show them that she knew.

Another thing that hacks her off is that it's OK for Reg. All he has to do is go back to the airfield and his mates and wait for the next time. Doesn't occur to him to worry – in fact, he doesn't even write sometimes when he's sworn to God he will. Unless he wants money of course; then he suddenly seems to find the knack of putting pen to paper. But it's different for her. She has nothing. She has to go back to the dreary old routine of that blasted office and Beryl and Miss Holt going on at her and nothing at all to take her mind off the worry.

And it is a worry. She draws her little circles in her diary and then she waits. Waits and waits and waits. Her head is numb with waiting. And sometimes she thinks that all she does all this freezing winter is wait for those two things. Sometimes she doesn't even know which one of them she wants or needs more urgently: a letter from Reggie or the curse.

Reading Marjorie's diaries is getting me down, rubbing me away, making me sad. She misses Reg so much.

I can't quite decide why I feel so battered by them. There's almost a sense of déjà vu, as if I too have been in that place where you wait and wait and it's cold and tiring and tears seem to collect behind every single thought you think. The heart-bruise of being at the mercy of someone else, at the mercy of a life that contains very little else except the constant expectation of that person. When did I feel like this? I try to remember. Nottingham as a teenager? Bristol, when I was a student and the boy I loved was in another town?

'But it's not sad,' Jonathan reminds me, 'because you know the ending. You know they're going to end up together – that even though she's desperate for a letter from him here in January 1940, she ends up spending a lifetime with him.'

He's right of course, she did. But she doesn't know in those letters and diaries what I know now.

'But they're both dead now,' I say. 'All those letters, just a Heinz tomato soup box. That's all that's left of them.'

'Nonsense. Alexa has memories. You said she was very close to them.'

'Yes, but their love. All her longing, all that aliveness and brightness – it's just, look, it's just an old cardboard box.'

Jonathan laughs. 'You're spending too much time with dead people.'

Maybe I am. That night I dream that Lucy Spawton is playing 'My Baby Just Cares for Me' on a black upright piano in the far corner of the room. She has her back to me and I shout at her again and again to turn around so I can see what she looks like, but she doesn't; she just keeps on playing – a small, rigid, square-footed person making music in my bedroom.

Friday 8 March

Hoping R will phone this evening. I wonder whether he will go to [illegible]. Reggie did not phone. I sat up until 2 o'clock. Was very worried. Could not sleep. What could have happened?

Saturday 9th March

Reggie explained why he did not phone. He certainly let me down very badly. I feel hurt. I even doubt whether he loves me. I couldn't hurt him like that. I love him too much. We went to Beryl's.

Sunday 10 March

Somehow although we had quite a good weekend, the beginning cast a cloud. R tells me he's sorry. I'm afraid I'm hardly in a position to think straight.

Monday 11 March

Feeling rather miserable. I hated to see him go last night. I felt so lost. I don't think he realises what it means to love a person. Will he ever? Only time will tell.

Tuesday 12 March

Had letter from R. Asks me to forgive him. I do. I wrote him, sent him dictionary. I believe he really does love me only he's led such a peculiar life.

Wed 27 March

Reggie and I feel awful. We love each other so much. He cried and so did I. He must truly love me. Mrs Pratt died.
[This page seems blurry and tear-stained.]

Monday 22 April

Had one lovely letter and one horrible one. Sent it back. He must surely realise I truly love him. Sent letter in morning. 8 pages. Wrote again in evening and sent R black tie. Hope he likes it.

Friday 10th May

Hitler has invaded Holland and Belgium. Wrote to Reggie. Why won't he write? Lent Beryl 10/-.

Friday 17 May

Reggie did not phone as promised.

Tuesday 21 May

Wrote to R. Quiet day. L did not come in. Not feeling too good. Auntie Carrie has shingles. Very queer.

19th July 1940

Dear M

Oh boy am I going to make a fuss of you, of course that's if you'll let me. I remember you saying at Waterloo that I have to marry you first before you will let me love you. Does that still go?

I hope you will make an exception this time because I can't marry you this next weekend can I? And I shan't have enough time to look round for a bit of fresh in the short time available unless of course Winkie can fit me up with something a bit lively. It's about time he found me a good woman.

I hope darling you can stand a joke but I feel very humorous this perfect Saturday afternoon. It may be due to the raid going to my head. I enjoyed every moment of it although my heart was thumping like fury as the explosives got nearer and nearer, but honestly darling I wasn't the least bit frightened, do you believe me?

Just think darling, next Friday I shall have you all to myself for hours and hours – isn't it wonderful? Roll along Friday. Darling borrow some of those things from Beryl I should love to try them, aren't I awful? Give my love to your mother . . .

R

I take a train to Cambridge to meet Joan Clayton for the first time. It's a warm, blowy day and the carriage is full of clean and hopeful-looking young men reading novels and eating crisps.

The taxi drops me in Godwin Close, the place where I first spoke to Joan's neighbour on that amazing evening that now feels like a hundred years ago. It's a semi-circle of pebble-dash houses with decent sized front gardens, conifers, dark clipped hedging. Diane Askew – who's told me she's staying with her aunt over half-term – opens the door. Joan is hovering just behind her, half obscured by Diane's elbow. She peers over the top: 'Come in, my dear, do come in.'

She's wearing a smart dress, pearl earrings and necklace, and blue nylon housecoat over the top. We shake hands warmly. I'll never forget that Joan was my breakthrough – the first person I ever tracked down who actually knew someone from the house.

'I've been knitting squares,' says Diane, moving her needles off a chair. She goes into the kitchen to make coffee.

Joan smoothes her skirt over her knee, a nervous-excited look on her face. We glance down at our feet and then tilt our heads to listen to the noise of Diane in the kitchen – both desperate for her to come back in and rescue us from each other.

'It must be lovely for you, to have Diane here all week,' I tell her. 'Did she come up on Monday?'

Joan makes a face. 'It's only because of you coming. She wouldn't normally. Hasn't stayed here since 1985.'

Diane brings the coffee in.

'Put it here,' says Joan bossily, moving a table over.

'I've remembered another story about Lucy,' she says before I can even pull my notebook out. 'I was telling Diane just now. Once, when she must have been getting to be quite an old lady, Aunt Til took Lucy to the Bank of England for a visit, you see – it was all grand, with marble pillars and that, and do you know what? Lucy's knickers fell down! The elastic must've gone! Aunt Til told my mother, she said she didn't know where to put her face. Can you imagine, dear?'

I laugh and tell her it's a great story. I tell her I think she's the only person left in the world who actually knew Lucy. 'Ah well,' she says, 'she was a funny old lady. Mind you, so was Aunt Til. A bit round the twist. And the annoying thing about Uncle Tom, dear, was he used to take so long to eat his food.'

'Really?' says Diane, rolling a cigarette in the corner of the room.

'Well,' says Joan, 'you see he'd read somewhere that it was healthier to chew each mouthful forty-eight times or something. I'd sit there waiting for him to finish so he could actually answer a question or say something. It was so boring!'

She shows me a photo of Tom dressed up to go to war in 1916. He looks faintly camp, faintly comical, like a boy who's been in the dressing-up box. On the back he's written, 'Dear Hugh, Do I look fierce or ugly enough to frighten the . . . '

'like a boy who's been in the dressing-up box'

We squint at the word.

'Hun?' says Diane.

'Have it, dear,' Joan says to me when I pass the picture back. 'Do you want it? I don't want it back.'

I tell her I couldn't possibly keep it but I would love to borrow it.

265

She shrugs. 'No one else in this family is the slightest bit interested.'

'Oh, Auntie,' says Diane.

'No,' says Joan, 'my son says that when I go he'll just chuck the lot away, into a skip.'

I look at Diane, who says nothing and just picks a strand of tobacco off her tongue. I tell them that I'll take great care of all the pictures, then in the end make sure I return them safely to Diane.

I show Joan the original estate agent's details of our house from when we bought it in 1988, photographs of all the rooms looking spick and span and rag-rolled. Sponged.

Immediately she points to the bedroom.

'That's it! That's Lucy's sitting room, the one where she had the upright piano. One time, we were all in there at Christmas singing carols, and my goodness it went on for ages! The piano was in the corner of the room over by the window, a little black one, it was. And Lucy played and we all had to sing. I was bored to death and I just wanted to sneak under the table and hide. I was about thirteen and there would have been me and Mum and Dad, Tom and Til, Lucy – and would your Mum have been there?' she asks Diane. 'I suppose she must have been.'

'Well, they wouldn't have left her somewhere on her own,' Diane says crisply.

'I remember the room quite well,' Joan says, ignoring the comment. 'It was very Victorian in furnishing, even though this must have been 1929 or 1930. There were all these tables with maroon chenille type cloths on them with these tassels hanging down. I liked those tassels.'

Diane says she thinks she remembers Tom and Til vaguely, but Joan seems not to want to hear about that.

'They were joined at the hip, Tom and Til,' she says. 'Like I said to you on the phone, dear, we never knew much about Tom's other family. I don't know for instance if he had brothers or sisters or what happened to his mother.'

Outside the sun has started to come out. We get on to Diane's parents, Phyllis and Peter Askew. 'I don't think Diane will mind if I say this,' says Joan, throwing a quick glance in her direction, 'but he was a very aggravating man, Peter was. There was one time, soon after Bob was born and they were living there at Lillieshall Road and our Mum – who wasn't much of a traveller, as you might know – came all the way from Cambridge to stay the night and baby-sit so they could go out properly.

'They were going to the theatre. Phyllis had the tickets all arranged, and she'd got on a nice outfit and got her hair all done, and Peter just came home and said, "We're not going." Just like that. And then he reached out a hand and messed all her hair up to show he meant it. Our Mum was so cross. She went all the way back home to Cambridge the next day. I mean she'd come for nothing. Can you imagine?'

'The thing about my father,' Diane says quietly, 'is he always had these terrible ulcerated legs.'

'Yes, and you know what?' says Joan.

'Excuse me, Auntie, this is my story,' says Diane. She leans back and tells me that her father would have thirty-six yards of bandages around his legs. 'When he was ill, he'd lie under the covers and shiver and just not be able to get warm.'

'It must have been terrible,' Joan agrees. 'Peter wasn't a well man. And he'd always do lots of jobs at once. As well as the cooked meats he went and did bar work for Reggie and Marjorie at the various pubs they had in the country. I think it suited him, to do bar work and get away from my sister.'

I ask if Phyllis and Peter used to fight a lot.

'He was very patient with her actually,' Diane says.

'Why then?' says Joan, turning to Diane with an astonished expression on her face. 'Why did he hurt her? I always used to wonder that.'

'Mum was the one who'd make it physical,' Diane says, 'not him. She used to kick him on his legs, his ulcerated legs! He never hit her back.

He always stood up for her. I used to have some terrible fights with my Mum and he'd always say to us when we were fed up with her, it's not her fault, she can't help it.'

'She was erratic all her life,' Joan remarks quickly, 'even before she fractured her skull.'

Diane asks if I'd like more coffee.

'Bring the biscuits, please, Diane,' commands Joan. 'The cream biscuit barrel. The one next to the cooker, on the left-hand side.'

Joan takes my hand. 'What time do you have to go, dear? What I mean is, I don't want you to go at all. I really like having you here, it's really nice talking to you.'

Phyllis is already spoken for, a married woman, when she meets Peter in the public saloon of a pub in Histon where she's been evacuated during the war.

'My name is actually Margaret,' she tells him when he bends to light her cigarette and asks her name, 'but my second name is Phyllis and that's what I'm called. All of my friends call me Phyll.'

He puts his lighter back in his pocket and looks at her. She likes his grey eyes, cool and steady.

'Can I call you Phyll?'

She twists her mouth to one side and peers at him over her glasses. Wishes she'd left them off.

'Sure. I don't mind. But I'm married actually.'

'Is there a law, then, against calling married ladies Phyll?'

She smiles, says nothing. He edges closer on the bar stool. She can tell there's something wrong with his knees or his legs – she noticed when he came in how he moved a little too carefully, edged his way stiffly through the low doorway of the bar.

'Where's your husband then?'

'Back home.' She puts her head on one side and looks at him.

'Oh? Where's home?'

'Cambridge. My Mum's there too. I've got a sister – she's my twin. She's in Cornwall right now. This is her coat actually.'

She nicked the coat from Joan's wardrobe when she went back last weekend. If she doesn't need it, well, it can't hurt, can it? Though she knows Joan'll probably be mad at her. Any opportunity to have a go.

'Nice coat. What you doing here then?'

She wrinkles her nose. 'We're in a bit of a state actually, my husband and me are. Trying to sort things out.'

'By being apart?'

She shrugs. It's not a question she knows the answer to herself. She asks him what he does and he says he's currently working at the Short's factory in Madingley.

'Short's?' she says. 'But so am I!'

But, he tells her, his real profession is grocer. He specializes in cooked meats. Brisket and tongue and great big sides of glistening pink ham with their white streaks of fat . . . Or maybe he doesn't talk about meats at all. Maybe he just sticks with grocer.

Or maybe by then they've got on to other, more important things – like how pretty he thinks her eyes are and how much twaddle other people talk about the war and how many raids there have been in Streatham, where his sister lives, and why she and her husband haven't got any kiddies yet. And whether she'd like to meet up after her shift and go out for a drink sometime.

'But we're out for a drink now.'

'Properly, I mean.'

'A date?'

'If you like.'

'I don't know.'

'Well, think about it.'

'But she came back to Cambridge to try and make a go of her marriage,' Joan tells me, 'even though she and Peter were involved by then.

It was the spring. And I remember that Peter suddenly turned up at my mother's house in Cambridge with all these presents they'd been given, you know, given to the two of them together. And when he got there he saw that my mother and Phyllis and her husband were out and he put the presents on the table and just sat down and waited.'

'Peter!' Phyllis stands there in her specs and a flowery cotton dress buttoned up the front with a small gap just showing a chink of her brassiere and stares and stares at him. Her cheeks are flushed but she looks pretty put out. Or crazy. Or both. Her mother comes in the door behind her.

'What's he doing here, Phyll?'

'Shut up, Mum. I'll handle this.'

Peter looks up at her. 'Where's your husband, Phyll?'

'Peter.'

'Where is he?'

'Not here. He's out.'

Phyllis looks down at the kitchen table where Peter's laid all the stuff she left behind with him in Histon – bits and pieces that have been given to both of them by friends and relatives last Christmas when they thought they were an item, when he thought shé was going to get a divorce. When, for a while, she thought so too.

Peter takes a breath. 'I thought these were rightfully yours, Phyll, so I brought them. Thought you might want to have them, sorry, that's all.'

Phyllis looks at him and doesn't know what to say. Puts her hand on the door to steady herself.

'I'm leaving now,' Peter says. 'You don't need to worry yourself. I'm going.'

But he doesn't move. Instead he goes on sitting there and he looks at her, and after a moment he lays his head in his hands right there at her mother's kitchen table and sobs.

* * *

'And maybe that changed Phyllis's mind, because a few minutes after that she just walked out of the garden gate with nothing, no luggage or anything, not even a jacket. She walked out and went after him.'

'Just like that? She followed him?'

'Just like that. Our mother, she called her back, begged her to at least sit down and discuss it like a rational person, but Phyllis wasn't having any of it – she just wasn't hearing – she just walked out of the house and followed him. Kept on going. There was no calling her back, her mind was made up. It sounds romantic, dear, but in fact it was a whole lot of trouble that she was walking into, if you know what I mean?'

Diane says she can't find the biscuit barrel. Joan finds it for her.

'It wasn't where you said.'

'Right there, by the cooker? Have one, dear. Go on. Have a ginger nut.'

Joan tells me she's a great believer that in this life you reap what you sow. 'And after you die,' she says, 'I think there's somewhere good we all go. It's just that if you've been bad you take a whole lot longer to get there.' She pauses, frowns: 'Hitler, for instance, I think he's maybe not even there yet – or if he is, he's only just got there.'

She leans back and touches her pearls, thinking this one through for a moment.

'And I'll tell you another thing about my sister. There were these builders working near our house and this builder, Norman Gissing, he was a good ten years older than her and he had a fiancée. He was engaged to her for nine years, took the best years of that woman's life but never married her. And my sister was seeing him and she had this secret sign that if she left her bedroom window a little open then that meant she'd meet him later – imagine it!'

Diane is lighting another roll-up. She crinkles her eyes at me. 'What's so strange about that, Auntie? I think that's pretty normal, don't you, Julie?'

Joan sits up straight. 'Yes, but look, Diane, let me get to the point. You see one day our Mum closed the window by mistake and she didn't know and of course there was such a to-do. Phyllis was furious, she really was.'

Diane chuckles to herself, blows smoke out. Joan shoots her a glance.

'And anyway in the war,' she says, 'do you know what happened to Norman Gissing? He had his head chopped right off by one of those propellers off a plane. Died instantly.'

'What a horrible way to die,' says Diane.

'Exactly!' Joan looks triumphant. 'You reap what you sow.'

Morning slides into afternoon. I tell Joan I ought to get going soon, get a cab back to the station. Immediately she takes me by the hand and walks me round the room and shows me her watercolour paintings. Chaffinches, daffodils, holly leaves, a tiger's roaring head. 'I'm self-taught, dear, I just do them, you know.'

Diane smiles at me and Joan sighs and sits back down again, adjusts the doily on the back of the chair.

'Can I tell you one more story, dear? It's nothing to do with your house but I'll tell you anyway.

'My poor first husband Bill, it's his story really. It was a winter day in December '67 and he went to work on his moped as usual and came back and I thought he should have a warm supper, so I did him this bacon roll, bacon and tomato, and afterwards he said, "Joan, I've got a bit of indigestion, I'm going to lie down for a bit", and he went upstairs and I remember thinking he didn't look too good.

'But he came downstairs again and watched a bit of telly with me and Mum, who was staying. And there was something about the Duke of Edinburgh on and we thought we'll just watch it to the end, but he stood up and he went through that door over there.' She points to the white painted door. 'And he said, "Joan, I'm going to bed for good" – and what he meant of course was, he was going up and going to sleep this time. But you know what? He didn't know it then but he was right, it was true, he ended up going for good.'

I slide the cap on my pen and sit forward and Joan takes my hand.

'Well, in the night, I woke at about 1 a.m. and he was sitting there on the edge of the bed and perspiring so much and he said the pain in his chest had got worse and he had pain in his neck and arms. He looked awful. And I said, "Bill, I don't care what you say, I'm going to call the doctor." And I called the doctor and he said it's probably indigestion and not to worry. And I said, "But can you really perspire so much with indigestion?", and he said, "Oh yes, definitely, you can do, yes." And I said, "Doctor, I'm sorry but I'm asking you to come out here right now." And so he said all right, he'd be there as soon as he could.

'And half an hour later he arrived and he went in to look at Bill and I went into the room next door where my Mum was and I remember hearing this gurgling sound. And I turned to Mum and I said, "Mum, I think he's going." "Going where?" she said, and I said, "I think that's it. I think he's going to die. Right now, I mean, die now."

'And I went back in and the doctor was taking his stethoscope off his ears and he had tears in his eyes and he looked at me and he said, "I'm sorry, I'm afraid he's gone, I really am so sorry."

And I said, "Would he have lived if you'd got here sooner?" and the doctor said, "Maybe, but he'd have been a vegetable." And I said, "Well, I know he wouldn't have wanted that. Not my Bill."'

The room is still and silent.

Joan turns to me.

'That was 1967,' she says, 'more than thirty years ago. He was only fifty-two.'

She lets go of my hand. Tears are standing in her eyes.

'That's nothing to do with your house though, is it, dear?'

My Darling Girl
I hope you weren't nervous during the storm in London last week but
I know my Marjorie is not the nervous type, she's got all the courage
in the world and audacity too. But I love her for it so much and I feel

273

*that if we can get together some time we shall be able to make quite a
lot of money.*

    *I cannot think of any reason which will affect our happiness, by
the fact of you being a big girl, although I should not like you to be
much bigger if you can possibly avoid it, because as you know darling
I'm not a very big chap myself and it is possible I suppose that I
might become uncomfortable if you did eventually outweigh me and
make me look undersized. I hate the hell having to write this stuff but
as you know it appears to worry people which might in time include
myself, so darling Marjorie you will have to study your diet and do
some exercises . . .*

I'm sitting with Marjorie and Reggie's Heinz soup box and the dog is
barking and Chloë and Raph are huddled in the garden with their
heads close together. I go out on to my terrace to ask them to put the
dog in her pen and they spring apart guiltily.

'What are you two doing down there?'

'Um – oh, we're just trying to set grass alight with a magnifying
glass,' says Chloë brightly.

I go back to my letters.

Seconds later, Chloë appears in my study, blonde head sweaty, eyes
blazing, grass stains on her halter top.

'Excuse me but did you hear a single word I just said?'

I look up from wartime Streatham. 'What?'

'Er – hell-o? We're setting fire? To the garden?'

'Just be careful, please,' I tell her, 'and don't let the dog bark too
much. And shut the door after you.'

Thursday 27 June
No letter this morning. It's so awful never hearing the postman stop.

Monday 1 July

At last letter from R. Says that things will not be too bad out there for me. I shall certainly go because I love him so much.

Saturday 6 July

What wonderful news this morning. R is coming home. I'm so terribly happy. He wants us to be married.

Monday 8 July

Came home early but R did not phone. Had drink with L.

Tuesday 9 July

Went to pictures on my own. Saw Mae West. R did not phone again tonight. Feel very disappointed.

Friday 19 July

Reggie came home. So happy to see him. Had new uniform. Thought he looked marvellous. We went out and had drink.

Saturday 20 July

Reggie and I had lovely day and have decided to get married on my 21st Birthday!

Tuesday 30 July

No letter from R. Cannot understand what has happened.

Sometimes she really could strangle him. Why does he have to make her worry like this? Why can't he just stick to what he says? Why can't he pick up the phone when he's promised? Why can't he stick to the weekend he originally said, when she knows she can sleep with him because she's arranged to stay somewhere – a very complicated and inconvenient arrangement if truth be told – instead of asking to come next weekend when, as she wrote to him yesterday, 'to crown it all I shall not be well . . . and I do so want you to enjoy your weekend to the fullest extent'.

Meanwhile, everything's gone wrong at the office too. The boss and Miss Holt have come back, which means she has to start working again and it's nearly driving her crazy. She's so sick of that place.

Yes, all right, she'll admit it. She's fed up. She doesn't understand why the blasted war can't be over and her and Reggie married and, more than anything, why he can't be better with money instead of borrowing a quid off her and pretending he's going to post it off that day but always claiming to find himself flat broke instead 'without even a fag or anyone to borrow off'.

Still, she did her first job for him. Sold the Lagonda for £15. Played dumb, pretended she didn't know what she was doing. He said he was very proud of her, said he couldn't have lied better himself. She likes that.

> Povah, believe me we shall be successful, as I said last weekend,
> your graft, my brains and our money.

She did well, his baby girl did, selling the Lagonda for him just like that. Frankly, though he didn't let on, he was a bit surprised. His Marjorie, with her little typing job and no nous or experience whatsoever when it comes to selling cars! It shakes him up, the idea that she can do a thing like that.

Sometimes she really surprises him. She's tougher than he thinks, his little baby girl. She laughs loudly when he told her how, as a boy on one of his motorcycles, he used to go absolutely crazy and streak up the Brixton Hill in the centre tram line at well over 70 mph, and sometimes perhaps get a scare or a near-shave, knowing full well that if he hit anything it would mean curtains. He expects her to be a bit shocked, but no.

'You really did?'

He nods and strokes her knee. 'My heart used to thump away but if I screamed out as loud as I could I felt better straightaway. I was steady.'

She goes quite still and looks at him. 'I know what you're talking about, Reg. I've done that.'

'You've what?'

'Not the bike, of course, but the rest. I've gone where no one can hear me and I've screamed my head off. I've done it – I mean it, I have.'

22 Oct 1940

. . . Darling, I'm writing this from the shelter.

You write in your letter written on Friday – don't judge me by what I've been – well my darling you know full well that I don't care twopence for what you've done. You know that I've got you to tell me about your different escapades and then had a darn good laugh. It's only been things that you've done since I've known you that have hurt and I minded about. And I don't care what you've done before so long as you never let me down – and I feel you never will.

Well darling I'm still feeling 'very well'. I say a prayer every night but I guess I'm too wicked for an answer. Still you don't want to worry dear. I'll do something about it, even if I have to use gunpowder.

Glad to hear about all your physical training. It will certainly do you a lot of good, you know, get the tummy down. It will also keep the 'other' down but of course, this is no time to talk of the other . . .

Jimmy – you know the fellow that sleeps near me with his young lady – lent me this fountain pen and it's running out I believe. Everyone down here is fast asleep and now a baby has just started howling . . . better close now.

I love you darling

Marjorie
XX

The last few words are almost too faint to read as the ink runs out.

* * *

I'm driving back from Chelsea with Chloë and Raph – heading over the Silverthorne traffic lights and on to North Street, when I almost crash the car.

'My God!'

'Mummy, what?'

I've just seen something that's always been there, but that I've never noticed or looked properly at before.

'That is – just – so – incredible.'

'What? Tell us, Mummy, what?'

'Sorry, kids, we've got to go round again.'

I turn right on to Lillieshall Road, right again at Lambourn Road, and right on to Broadhinton. Continue along Broadhinton till we're almost on North Street, then pull in and turn the engine off. I get out of the car and so do the kids, cross the road to the opposite pavement, and look back.

'That's all?' says Chloë.

'No,' I tell her, 'look. It's terribly exciting. I don't know how I've missed it all these years.'

It's hard to read – old black paint, mostly worn out now, only legible on the dirty brick if you stand right back and half close your eyes. But it's definitely there and I can read almost all of it:

W JENKINS BUILDER AND DECORATOR
SOUTH LONDON
ESTAB

Not our builder, Mr Williams, but the other one – the man who built half the houses on Lillieshall Road. Here he is, here's his sign. It must be almost a hundred and fifty years old. And I've driven past it almost every day for the past fifteen years.

They stand in the fusty old hall at Number 34 and he puts a protective arm around her fur-coated shoulder.

'I'll give you a good price, Auntie Til,' he says as convincingly as he can.

But Til's no fool. 'I know what it's worth,' she tells him, 'but I'm not after making anything much out of it. So I'll give you a good deal, Reg, but there's a condition.'

He removes his hand, sticks it in his pocket.

She points a gloved finger at the door on her left – the one that leads into the front and back rooms and is shut. He can hear a wireless, faint sounds of someone moving about.

'The Hinkleys, I told you – dear old couple – that's their room, two rooms. They use the kitchen down here and the bathroom out the back, too. Walt and Bella have been here nearly as long as Lucy was – since the First War, I think.'

Reg makes an effort to nod and stretches his mouth into what he knows will pass for a smile. 'But Til,' he says, 'I don't see where this is leading.'

The old lady sighs. 'They're old, Reg, they don't want to move, not now.'

Reg scratches his head, leans an arm on the banister rail. Notices how shabby the wallpaper is, how pocked the lino on the stairs.

'Of course, Auntie,' he says, 'I can understand that.'

'So what I'm saying is, you don't make them go, all right? They get to live out their time here, where they feel comfortable. They pay a decent rent, Reg – they've paid it all these years and they'll pay it to you.'

Reg rubs his hands together, he can't help it. He'd been worrying the 'condition' would be something much less easily kicked into touch.

'My dear Aunt Til,' he says in the voice he uses for selling cars that he's a tad doubtful about, 'let me put you straight on one thing. If you think I'd turn an elderly couple out on the street, then I'm shocked. Offended even. You just don't know what sort of a man I am.'

Til studies him for a single hairy moment. Then she smiles and puts out a hand. 'This has worked out really well, Reg. I'm grateful to you. You can't imagine how worried sick I've been about this place.'

They walk out down the brown tiled path and into the street, stand together and look back at the house. The upstairs windows are filthy. The hedge is newly planted, waist high, but could do with a trim.

'Don't you worry about anything,' he tells her. 'You just leave it all to old Povah here.'

As soon as he gets home he starts looking through the directory for the nearest old people's home. There's one in Tooting but the woman he speaks to tells him about their other place, much cheaper as it turns out, in Hackney. Rogate Road. He gets straight on to them. The man who runs the place is out, but would he like to leave a number and they'll get him to telephone?

He thinks about this for a moment. 'No,' he says, 'don't worry yourself, my darling. I'll give you a bell a bit later on.'

Chapter Seven

SOME DIE YOUNG, OTHERS LIVE TO NINETY

The Spawtons, the Hinkleys, Vera Palmer, and Beatrice Haig
1894–1944

When she hears the front door open and then shudder shut, when she recognizes that man Povah's wheedling tones, followed by Mrs Spawton's softer, more hesitant voice, when she can feel that they're standing there in the hall just on the other side of the frail pine door, then Isabella sits right up in her chair and peers across at Walter. Breathing quietly, mouth open, teeth slightly off kilter, hair flattened up against the antimacassar. Good. Let him stay like that. She doesn't want him upset by this.

Because she knows what's Going On. She has felt This coming for a long time.

She gets up carefully in her stockinged feet and moves across the floor as quietly as a mouse, barely a skitter, just the wool of her stockings catching on the rough wood boards, and turns the wireless on. Rotates the dial just enough. Then takes her stick and moves on grimly towards the door and presses her ear against it.

She barely needs to listen. She's been waiting for this. Walter, given half a chance, will pretend it's not happening – let himself be pushed around rather than have any upset. But she'd rather know. And Lucy, God rest her, did not trust that Povah man an inch. Neither did

Beatrice for that matter – all those stories about his shenanigans in Streatham, and Bea said there was worse that did not bear repeating and Isabella can easily believe that.

But maybe Mrs Spawton doesn't know it. Or maybe she's heard everything but just needs to sell the house. Turn a blind eye – it's what they all do these days. It's a trick they all learned in the war.

Isabella listens.

'Know what it's worth . . . Hinkleys . . . nearly as long as Lucy . . . pay it to you, Reg . . .'

'Let's get a grip here. Isabella Bloomfield Hinkley was born in 1859,' says Jonathan, 'and so was Walter Allen Hinkley. 1859. We've got their birth certificates.'

'Yes. I know. So?'

'So in 1948, when Reggie turfed them out of the house and into the old people's home, they were almost ninety.' He waits for me to get the point. 'And you're giving her the sharp hearing, quick-wittedness, and physical agility of a twenty-year-old!'

'C'mon, not a twenty-year-old.'

'OK, but there's no way Isabella would've been creeping around and eavesdropping. She'd more likely have been sitting in an armchair dribbling.'

I think about this. 'Some ninety-year-olds are very fit.'

'Sure. But their death certificates say that one of the causes of death – just a few years later, remember? – was senility.'

'What's all this about?' I ask him. 'You're suddenly on Reggie Povah's side?'

He laughs. 'I also don't think it would have been wooden boards. I think it would have been lino or heaps of tatty rugs, in 1948.'

'This is pedantry.'

'And one more small but crucial point.'

I sigh.

'How come, if she can hurtle unaided across the room to turn on the wireless like that, how does she then suddenly need to turn around and pick up a stick?'

He's right. It doesn't work. I'm stuck – gazing into darkness here.

Flicking backwards in time, leaving 1948, leaving Reggie and his crocodile smiles to Aunt Til and taking off another layer; unpeeling, moving swiftly backwards, entering the final stages of the Second World War, and then folding back the years right into the thirties, the twenties. One by one the little lights I've been relying on are extinguished, fading away for simple lack of concrete fact. Everything darkens, slows, and comes to a kind of stop. Narrative standstill due to lack of information.

I want so badly to imagine these people and reinvent, conjure up, their real lives. But so far I've been building stories almost entirely based on tiny gobbets of fact. I've been quite lucky. Even the dialogue is real – remembered and reported conversations and anecdotes, second- or third-hand perhaps, filtered through the attitude of the teller – but still actual words spoken by actual strangers, whole decades ago. You gather a handful of these small recollections and it's not so hard to fill in the rest.

But I don't have even that much for these new people. Lucy Spawton, yes. But the Hinkleys, her lodgers. And Beatrice Haig, her friend, her companion. I have no first-hand accounts, not even any of Joan Clayton's crunchy, second-hand accounts. I still don't know who they were, what they looked like, how they talked.

I know that Reggie Povah broke a promise made to Matilda Spawton and that he made the Hinkleys leave this house. And that his name has been mud in the Askew family ever since. And I know that the Hinkleys were extremely old by then and that they had two sons, Walter Stephen and Charles Edwin. In fact, it now occurs to me, did the sons try to stand up to Reggie? Did they complain on behalf of their ageing parents? I wonder if I'll ever know. So what do I know about the Hinkleys?

Her birth certificate: Isabella was born in Billericay in 1859, daughter of a letter-carrier. I know that her surname at birth was Bloomfield but that by the time of her marriage she'd become Isabella Bloomfield Mills. What does this mean? That her father died and she had acquired a stepfather, perhaps, a Mr Mills?

She's a nineteenth-century Essex girl, a dimply black-eyed baby, her father's open favourite, the one who can get him to say yes to anything. 'Our Zizzy's going to be a stunner' – is that what he tells the blokes down the Rose and Crown in Billericay, his proud heart set on her going places, making waves in this world? Until his accident. Knocked down by a hansom cab, confined to bed aged thirty-six, weakened lungs and muscle atrophy, dead within the year.

Or maybe not. Maybe our Bella's a skinny, tetchy, clever girl. Clever, but not so easy to love. Dirty blonde hair that's hard to pull a brush through – pimples and a cough that won't go away. Maybe her mother died giving birth to her and her father's never forgiven her and the sooner she can get out of Billericay the better. Because she's unwanted, a virtual orphan until the Mills family take her under their wing, teach her to read and write. Maybe . . .

Meanwhile, Walter Hinkley: he was born the same year, 1859, in Council House Street, Dover, the son of a dairyman. His mother is given as 'Ann Hinkley, late Hood, formerly Palmer'. Does this mean her maiden name was Palmer, but that she'd married a man called Hood who was now also dead? Did Hood beat Walter, taking a stick to the boy whenever he'd had a bad day? Did Bella and Walt meet, finally, in London and find they had their sad, splintered childhoods in common, as well as a fierce attraction for one another?

And Beatrice Mary Haig, Lucy's friend, what about her? She lived here from 1926 at least up until 1939, and possibly longer (Kelly's has no listings for the war years, nor are there electoral registers), but by 1945 she's gone, slipped off the edge.

Who was she? Did she die during the war? We do know she was a good friend of Lucy's – a good enough friend to have 'the sum of two hundred and fifty pounds' left to her by Lucy when she herself died in July 1944. But Beatrice is gone from the house by 1945 – Kelly's Directory is back in print but her name is gone. Where did she go? Did she even live to enjoy this measured bequest from Lucy?

'Maybe they were in an accident together,' Raph says with unsavoury relish. 'Both of them on the motorway, splat.'

'In 1944?' says Jake with a smile. 'Moron.'

'Or maybe a suicide pact?' Chloë eagerly suggests. 'Maybe they both loved the same man and couldn't have him so they killed themselves?'

'Why would they do that?' Jake points out. 'If they both loved the same man, then one of them should have just killed the other one.'

I tell them it's easy enough to find out. I need to find Beatrice's death certificate or will and trace her living descendants.

'But I'm afraid she sounds to me like a spinster with no kids,' Jonathan says, 'just like Lucy.'

And he's right, of course. That's what I've been thinking. Far more likely than that she and Lucy swigged mutual poison or held a gun to each other's heads. Two things I've learned to dread in the course of unravelling this house: women with good, unusual names who suddenly go and marry a man called Jones. And people who die childless. So very selfish of them. Couldn't they have spared a thought for their future biographer?

It's a humid and cloudy day. Chloë, Raph, and I walk the dog on Clapham Common – watching her hurtle across the dry, brown grass in pursuit of crows. Then we drop Raph at cricket coaching and Chloë and I get on the Central Line to Holborn to return to the Probate Search Room. Chloë – already in a bad mood (because she's twelve) – asks me why she has to come.

'Because it's your home too. It's good for you to get involved in this.'

'You know I hate going out in the heat.'

'It's not that hot. And it's a nice little trip.'

'I don't want a trip. I just want to stay in my room.'

'With the curtains drawn and the light on?'

'It's cool and dark in there. The way I like it, OK?'

'You know, your room might have been Beatrice Haig's room all those years ago. Whoever she was. It's pretty likely actually, because we know Lucy Spawton was in our room and the Hinkleys were downstairs.'

'Hmm. Who do we know so far who's had my room?'

I think about this. 'Well, OK, working backwards . . . Lucy Pidgeon. Before her, Mr Kyle, the old solicitor who helped Doreen Ricketts, and, let's see, before him Salome Bennet for a while, and before her Olive Russell.'

'Who's she?'

'We didn't find much out about her, except she was rather ugly and charmless, worked in catering and was Mavis Jones-Wohl's friend.'

'The one who got rid of her little boy?'

'That's right. But Olive was nice to that poor boy and really cared about him apparently. In fact when Mavis got married to her American GI, I think Olive and the little boy were downstairs and Mavis and her husband moved up to your room for a bit.'

Chloë rolls her eyes. 'To have sex?'

'Well . . .'

'It's OK, Mummy, all rooms must have had sex in them, that's just something you've got to face. So who was in there before that?'

'That's where we've got to. We don't know. I'm hoping maybe Beatrice Haig.'

We get off the tube and walk out into Holborn.

'Do you mind it?' I ask her. 'Knowing all of this about your room now?'

Chloë glances in the window of Pret A Manger. 'Why should I? It feels like my room to me. And I bet none of them painted it emerald green or had a bunk bed. Anyway it was Jake's room before it was mine and I mind much more about that. I hate the idea of him in it – his smell and all that. Can we get a drink and a snack later?'

'I'm going to look under H for Haig and start searching for Beatrice's death from 1939 onwards,' I tell Chloë in the Probate Search Room. 'because we know for sure she was listed as being in our house in that year.'

She makes a non-specific guttural noise.

'Don't you think that's interesting?'

'If you want me to be honest, not really.'

'It is. Think about it. You like history and this is the best sort of history – about real people's real lives, rather than battles and politics and dates and all that.'

'I like politics and battles,' she says quickly. 'And dates. Just because you don't understand them. And, anyway, it's just that it seems to take so long to find anything out in these places.'

She looks around disparagingly at the room, with its people flicking volumes open and shut, and yawns.

'No, it doesn't. I've found loads so far. And it's what you have to do if you're a researcher. It may be boring but it's totally worth it for that moment when you suddenly find something.'

Chloë harrumphs. 'Can I ask you a question?'

'What?'

'Will you put every little thing I say in the book?' She scowls. 'Is that why you want a child with you? Is that why you've been asking me all these questions?'

'How d'you mean?'

'I know you, you're going to write: "'Oh I wonder who lived in our house?" said Chloë, standing naked in the street reciting poetry.'"

I laugh. 'Why on earth would I say that you were naked?'

'I know the way you write. You'll put anything in for effect.'

* * *

287

She sits at the big table in the centre of the Probate Search Room and reads *Rebecca*. She is fully dressed.

In fact, in her red cotton combat trousers and pale pink Hennes T-shirt she looks like a strange exotic bird in the middle of all these research people, irritable in their black and grey, their man-made fibres. The only child in the room – deep in her book, oblivious to everything, a slight frown puckering her forehead, fingers slightly curled under her small round chin.

She's recently taken to looping her long blonde hair in a kind of ponytail-cum-bun, held in place with a silver spangled elastic and it suits her. She looks timeless, a face from any century – lovely in its gravity and plumpness and far curvier than I was at her age. I know she won't look like this for long – smooth and blossomy and perfectly poised on the ledge that is adolescence, but with no particular impulse – yet – to jump.

She notices me watching her and gives me a withering look. I start on the volumes, beginning at 1939. There's nothing for a few years then, suddenly, there she is in 1944. Beatrice Mary Haig. Died 16 September 1944 in Eastbourne. That's only a couple of months after Lucy.

I order the will and try to explain to Chloë why this is quite exciting. She puts a finger in her book.

'So . . . let me get this straight. The Lucy woman died in July and left her friend £250 and her friend died two months later. I bet she never even got a chance to spend the money.'

I agree it seems strange and sad that they died so close to one another.

'Maybe Beatrice died of grief?' says Chloë. 'Maybe they were lesbians.'

I admit to her that the thought had crossed my mind.

'Cool!' she breathes, suddenly more interested. 'Gay people in the house!'

While we're waiting for Beatrice's will, I show her how you can feed people's names into the computer to see if their wills have been probated since 1996. Random checks.

'Do you want to do it?' I ask her.

'No, you.'

I type in a name.

'Who's that?' she asks me.

I explain that it's the name of a relative of the Hinkleys – I have his address but he hasn't replied.

'So if people don't get straight back to you, you immediately assume they're dead?' She gives me a beady look. 'Don't you think that's rather horrible?'

Beatrice Haig's will confirms what I'd suspected.

That she was indeed a spinster, that she died at a hospital in Eastbourne, that probate was granted to her brother-in-law, Jonathan Huddart. That she left small sums of money to a variety of sisters and sisters-in-law and nephews and nieces, as well as 'the sum of ten pounds to my friend Lucie Spawton'.

'Which she never got,' says Chloë, 'because she was dead. What happens to money if someone's left it but they're already dead?'

I tell her I don't know. I expect it's distributed among the other people.

'Ten pounds? Wouldn't go far.'

'It was worth more in those days.'

But now I have a list of nephews and nieces, so all I have to do is establish who is dead and who alive, and then start writing letters. I'll start with Gordon Bird and Sidney Bird, Sidney Huddart, Edwin Huddart, and Alan Huddart – one of them will surely still be alive?

'Info Disk,' says Chloë promptly. 'As soon as we get home we can try the Info Disk, right?'

She's suddenly interested, involved. I pretend not to notice. She would hate it if I showed her I was pleased.

But before we go, there's someone else I want to track down. Lucy Spawton's will, which I've had for a while now, contains an interesting and perhaps revealing 1941 codicil:

> This is a codicil to the last Will and Testament of me Lucy
> Spawton of 34 Lillieshall Road Clapham Common in the
> county of London Spinster dated the thirteenth day of June One
> thousand nine hundred and forty one . . . in addition to the
> legacies given by my said Will I give and bequeath to Mrs
> Millicent Jane Beverton of 34 Lillieshall Road aforesaid the sum
> of fifty pounds free of legacy duty provided she is in my
> employment at the date of my death and not under notice to
> leave given or received . . .

'Millicent Jane Beverton. She's a new name – someone who clearly lived in the house but we didn't know about,' I tell Chloë. 'She must have been a housekeeper or companion of some sort, or maybe a live-in nurse. And Lucy mentioned her in her will, though she obviously only wanted her to have the money if she was still working for her.'

As I tell Chloë this, I notice that the irritating man with a cord and laminated card round his neck and dandruff down the back of his jacket who has been eyeing me constantly, hovering near the 1940s section and acting as if he and I should be making urgent contact, is moving closer. He's the one who's always staring at me – even now it's taking all my concentration not to catch his eye.

I go on checking for Millicent Jane Beverton from 1945 and keep going until, some fifteen minutes later, I discover her death in 1966.

> BEVERTON Millicent Jane of the Aged Pilgrims Home Hazellville
> Road, Islington London died 5 September 1966 at Whittington
> Hospital St Mary's Wing Islington Probate London 22 November
> to Eva Mercy Haggar married woman and Reginald West legal
> executive £826

I feel I should search for 'Eva Mercy Haggar married woman' but I'm tired and the constant leering is beginning to get me down.

I tell Chloë I think we might call it a day and she places her bookmark in her book and scrapes her chair back, eager for Pret A Manger. But before I can even get my bag, Nutter Guy moves swiftly across the room, pushing past several people and says, 'Hello!' very loudly as if I should remember him.

'Um – Hi.' I pick up my bag and pretend to look for something.

He stands in front of me, waits. I don't look at him.

'Are you – working for one of the companies that researches wills?' he asks me.

'No. Just for myself.'

'Ah. Aaah. You see, it's just that I've seen you here before, you see.'

I say nothing. What can I say?

He stands for a moment and looks at me hard and then, without a word, moves away.

'He's weird,' says Chloë

'Yes.'

'I suppose if you spend your whole day with dead people and wills and stuff like that, it drives you completely mad in the end.'

She sighs and undoes her ponytail, then deftly loops it up again, pulling a few strands out to make it prettier.

The archives for Derry & Tom's – the department store on Kensington High Street where Lucy Spawton worked as a buyer – are lodged at Glasgow University. The archivist says she'll have a look and see if they've got anything that mentions her and send it to me.

Ten days later, a jiffy bag arrives in the post. There's a photocopied sheet with some general stuff about the store – and a photo of a tea room and roof garden that Barker's opened in 1921. Barker's was actually next door to Derry & Tom's (where it still is).

I study the picture – the huge fig plants, the decking, the overhead awning and the director's chairs could actually all be part of any Kensington café today. Only the men's straw boaters and the slump-shouldered waitresses with their bandeau style caps give it away. Would a Head Buyer from Derry & Tom's next door have popped in for tea? I like to think so.

Derry & Tom's was set up to cater for 'good middle-class lines', as opposed to Barker's which was for 'high-class lines'. But by 1922 Derry & Tom's was beginning to show trading losses and a gulf was 'emerging between managers and buyers'.

And now I turn to Lucy's employment contract. It says she was employed in Haberdashery and Trimmings and Bijouterie – except that last word has for some reason a thick black ink line swiped through it. Did they close down Bijouterie as losses started to mount? Her employment commenced on 15 March 1888 – which was before she moved into Lillieshall Road – at a salary of £350 with commission. It also says that in February 1923 her salary was raised to £400.

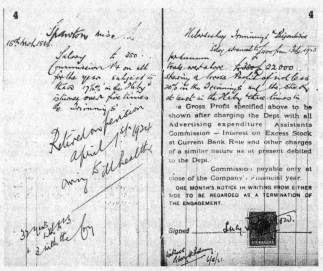

'she was employed in Haberdashery and Trimmings and Bijouterie.'

'Interesting,' Jonathan says, 'when you bear in mind that from 1907 onwards her mother got a special reduction in land tax on the basis of low income.'

'How do you know that?'

He pulls out the photocopy we ordered of the land tax booklets. 'Look, here at the bottom: "Land tax remitted, under exemption 1509, income not exceeding £160 per annum."'

'She was earning well over that.'

'Then either they lied to the land tax collector or I suppose it's possible it was only assessed on the income of the actual named owner, old Mrs Spawton.'

I also have a piece of paper with Lucy's name typed on it, along with what must be other employees of Derry & Tom's. And the last document shows that Lucy retired on 1 April 1924 'owing to ill health'.

Thirty-six years at Derry & Tom's. Lucy is a career woman – unusual, surely, for her time? What are those last days and weeks at the store like? Are the heydays over? Has her once-beloved store become a shabby and fractious place, dragged down by backbiting and cost-cutting? Does she look forward to the day when she can wake at home in Clapham and yawn and stretch and roll back over to sleep, knowing she doesn't have to get the bus to Kensington?

Here it is, then, the last written record of her working life, the last visible trace, the final account of her salary-earning hours. I stare at the paper for a long time. Alongside Lucy there's a Mr F. V. Crisp, a Miss A. Chapman, a Mr C. S. Bodger. The forgotten staff of Derry & Tom's. Is there anyone out there who remembers or cares what they did?

Colin Bodger? Well, she does have a brief acquaintance with him, actually. He lives not far from her in Wandsworth – Jeypore Road, one of those narrow streets of Edwardian terraces that slope down towards Wandsworth Common. He's a kind, quiet young man – lives with his mother Kathleen now, since she's been a partial cripple and far too poorly to look after herself.

They get talking one cold February day in the Larkhall Tea Gardens, where she's biding her time waiting for Beatrice to turn up. Beatrice said half past and it's already twenty to. Punctuality has never been one of her strong points, but then Lucy knows that well enough by now.

'They get talking one cold February day in the Larkhall Tea gardens'

Lucy herself, she's not like that – never late for anything. Wouldn't dream of it. In her book, tardiness amounts to a kind of hoity-toitiness: what's so special about her that she should expect anyone to wait? Lucy spends her life in an agony of fretting that she'll get left behind by the world.

Unlike Beatrice. Beatrice is warm and giving towards the world and expects the whole world to be warm back towards her. She never doubts it for a moment – never watches her back or looks for a snag in anything. Sometimes this trait of Beatrice's makes Lucy smile. Other times – once or twice anyway – it has reduced her to tears. There's something about Beatrice's warmth – all those Huddart nephews and nieces who love her and write to her and make her laugh (unlike poor dear Tom, who is nothing but a worry to Lucy) – that makes her feel she's missed out on something, that she'll always be on the outside looking in.

Now, in the tea rooms on Larkhall Lane, a piano's playing – 'Lovely Boating Weather' in lilting out-of-tune tones – and she plays with the grains of sugar glued to her teaspoon and notices him glancing over her way. Why? She's not used to being looked at, but he seems a pleasant enough young man – wavy-haired, clean-looking, a good few years younger than her.

Lucy raises her head and looks over. The one thing she's never been is reticent. Why bother with all that? She's never sure where her bravado comes from, but she imagines it comes from never having been thought of as feminine or pretty by anyone, of never having known what it is to be desired. There's a kind of freedom in that, isn't there?

So if someone looks at her, she doesn't blush: she just looks back. Simple as that. What does she stand to lose? Nothing. That's her reasoning. Same reason she always spits the words straight out, tries to say what she means. 'I say what I mean and I mean what I say.' That's her motto – ever more pertinent as the years go by.

'Do I know you?' she asks the young man, who has come over now and removed his hat. She gently pulls at a chair, indicating that he's welcome to sit.

'No,' he admits, 'but I think I know you. Didn't you used to work at that millinery place on The Pavement?'

'About a hundred years ago, I did!'

He smiles and stretches out a hand. 'I'm Mr Bodger by the way. Not that long ago, surely?'

Lucy shakes her head in disbelief. 'Oh, more than twenty years. I was a snip of a thing. My parents ran it. Tom and Lizzie Spawton. But you – you must have been a little kiddy, hardly more than a baby?'

Mr Bodger puts his hat down on the table. She notices that his nails are clean and square, his hands pale with the blue veins standing out in relief – like a marble statue. Like a girl. She can't take her eyes off his hands.

'I'm thirty-six and you . . . you must be a little younger,' he says politely.

Lucy wants to laugh. She's forty-three years old, but she's hardly going to tell him that.

'I went in there with my mother all the time,' Mr Bodger continues. 'So what happened? They close you down?'

Lucy shrugs. 'My Mama got too old, had to retire. And Mrs Harrison kept putting the rent up.'

'Do you still live round here then?'

'We moved into Lillieshall Road. And my brother's married – we don't see much of him – and, well, my sisters . . .'

She breaks off suddenly. Does she really need go any further?

'Catherine?' Mr Bodger's face lights up. 'Don't you have a sister called Catherine? Catherine or Katie or . . . And wasn't there a Mary too? I'm sure she used to fetch me lemonade from the back. I always looked out for her because of that.'

Lucy smiles and stiffens. She doesn't know what to say.

'I'm sorry,' he says, perplexed, 'I just wondered . . .'

'It was probably Mary with the lemonade,' Lucy says firmly, hoping he'll leave it at that.

Mr Bodger looks suddenly stricken. This embarrasses Lucy; her nose stings and she blinks away a tear, hoping he doesn't see. She wishes Beatrice would walk in the door, right now.

'I'm so very sorry,' he says quietly. 'It's my fault, it's none of my business, I shouldn't have asked.'

Lucy shrugs and looks across the busy tea rooms, away from him, anywhere but at him. She doesn't know what to say. She wants to tell him it's all right, that it's all in the past, all of it, that she doesn't dwell on it. But she can't quite get the words to come.

'I went to work at another store actually,' she tells Mr Bodger.

'Oh? Which one?'

She tells him. He looks impressed. Rightly so – Derry's is one of the best. He starts to tell her about himself then – that he used to work in the men's outfitting department at Arding & Hobbs and that he had a nice room too, went with the job.

She bites her lip and looks at him. 'Ilminster Gardens? Oh my goodness, but – the fire?'

He looks down at his hands. 'I lost everything – job, home, everything, all in one go. You wouldn't think it could happen.'

You wouldn't. And no one in Clapham can forget it – that terrible, black afternoon of 20 December, still less than a year ago, when Arding's began to burn. It was 4.20 p.m. – already dark and crisp, the Sally Army band playing carols in St John's Street. 'The Holly and the Ivy, when they are both full grown . . .'; a man with chestnuts in paper cones; an organ-grinder with a sudden stash of sugar bonbons for the little ones.

The store was busy, fully stocked and gaily decorated for the busiest Saturday of the year. And it had been a good day too, tills tinkling, rosy-cheeked women worked off their feet.

Someone in the linen department said they smelled smoke – and reported it, Mr Bodger tells her, but they were all told to carry on, it was nothing.

'No fire bell sounded, nothing like that. They sent us back to work – told us to stay behind our counters and get on with it. We knew they were wrong, but what could we do?'

Lucy knows the rest. By the time the blaze has engulfed linen and fine china and ripped through the flesh and bones of the vast store, eight lives have been lost to smoke asphyxiation. Four are staff, four customers – one a five-year-old, intent on experiencing the magic of the Christmas Grotto for the first time. The store band – hired for the Christmas period – plays 'I'm Afraid to Go Home in the Dark' while the store is evacuated, Mr Bodger tells Lucy.

'You mean that was true? I always wondered about that story,' she says, frowning slightly. 'I thought the papers might've made it up.'

He assures her it's true.

'They all trooped out to that music, it was eerie,' he says. 'A most peculiar mixture of calm and panic. I think they thought the fire would be put out in minutes, you see.'

The fire engines pump continuously, but they don't really have the fire under control until nine o'clock that night. Mr Bodger tells her that two details of that night will always haunt him, stay in his memory: the constant crash of glass as every single window in every building in the vicinity folded in the intense heat. And the smell of cooked turkey.

'Cooked turkey?' Lucy echoes, sitting forward in her chair. 'How come?'

'You know Francis & Son's, the men's outfitters opposite?'

Lucy nods. She knows the shop well. Her mother used to know old Mr Francis. That place was more or less destroyed in the blaze as well.

'You know Francis & Sons, the men's outfitters opposite?'

'Well, they'd got hold of thirty or forty birds and they'd hung them in front of the shop.'

'But they don't sell food.'

'Special offer for Christmas – Mr Francis's idea. The blaze just simply roasted them.'

Lucy laughs, she can't help it. The idea of all those Christmas dinners ready in advance!

She never saw the actual fire as she was at work herself that busy Saturday – the last Saturday before Christmas. But the news spread quickly and next morning she and Beatrice had joined the crowds who made a special trip to survey the damage. People stood stunned. Some wept or turned away. Others bowed their heads or gasped in amazement.

Because nothing could prepare you for it really. A grand and gay and lively building like that, melted down in a single night, reduced to rubble. At the height of the blaze, the store had simply caved in on itself – its breath sucked out. The twisted steel supports – somehow hideous against the chill morning skyline – and piles of charred and blackened brick were all that remained.

'The store was busy, fully stocked and gaily decorated for the busiest Saturday of the year.'

'She'll never forget all those beds'

Such a fine, elegant place it had been – the smartest and grandest south of the Thames. Lucy remembered going in there with her mother when just a tiny girl and being lifted up to look at the ladies' gloves in their glass cases – row upon row of slim, kid fingers pointing in all directions. It made an impression, filled her with a sense of excitement about retail trade that she never forgot.

And so much merchandise lost as well, it punched at her heart. She'll never forget all those beds from the bedding department – soot-blackened frames and posts with their knobs still on – scorched and warped and greasy, hanging from steel girders.

Even that morning, firemen are still hosing the smouldering ruins and across the road a man is hammering boards over the cracked windows of the Falcon. Meanwhile, Ilminster Gardens – where three hundred of Arding's six hundred-strong staff have rooms – is also gutted, their personal belongings all gone.

Many large London stores give donations to help them – Harrods,

Gorringes, and her own, Derry & Tom's. Because if you work in retail, you felt for those poor folk. After years in a department store, the place is more than a livelihood – it's family. It's the thing that keeps you rooted and sane, the thing that ties you to the world.

With this in mind, she tells Colin Bodger she'll put in a word for him at Derry's. She's quite a friend of Mr Crisp who runs the menswear department. He'll see you right, she tells him. It's a great place to work. I couldn't recommend it to you more highly. If there's an opening.

Mr Bodger says he can't thank her enough.

'But that's made it rather difficult for me to ask you what I was going to ask in the first place.'

Lucy turns her beady gaze on him. 'In the first place?'

'When I came over just now. I was going to ask . . .'

Lucy waits.

'Whether you'd mind if I called on you sometime?'

'Another thing about Lucy,' Joan Clayton tells me on the phone. 'She didn't know anything about people, what made them tick and that, and she certainly knew nothing about children. It wasn't that she was cold exactly. She just always got it wrong, if you know what I mean.

'One time my sister and I were staying at Auntie Til's. We were about ten and we both contracted the mumps. Aunt Lucy came round to see us and she thought she was being kind, she was quite a generous person really in her deepest heart. But do you know what she brought to amuse us? She brought us each a copy of some highfalutin newspaper – the *Telegraph* or the *Financial Times*, something like that. She really thought we'd like that. We were so disappointed!'

Lucy colours straightaway when he says that, about calling on her. She doesn't know what to say at all. What can the man be thinking of? She's forty-three years old and, well, she's never had a young man in her life.

'forty-three years old . . . and she's never had a young man in her life!'

Oh, it's quite ridiculous, quite awful. She's not used to being approached like this, not by men, not in tea rooms.

Mr Bodger looks at her and he really is very pleasant-looking, but far too young for her of course, the silly chump.

'Well?' he says, and there's an openness in his eyes, a lack of guile that seems to imply he doesn't think it's an odd request at all.

'I don't want to offend you,' Lucy replies crisply, 'but I think not.'

'Tea sometime then?'

'It's just – it's not a good idea.'

'But you're in here now.'

'I'm waiting for my friend,' Lucy says, annoyed at having to provide so much private information about herself.

Mr Bodger looks a little stricken. 'I do apologize. You already have a –'

'Miss Haig. I'm waiting for my friend, Miss Haig.' Lucy's feeling really aggravated now, aggravated and embarrassed by this conversation. But Mr Bodger stands up and takes his hat, bows his head.

'I'm so sorry. I really had no intention of offending you, Miss Spawton, and it's been so very nice talking to you and, well, of course, I'll leave you in peace.'

'I didn't mean . . .' she finds herself saying. And he stops, turns around. Suddenly hopeful.

'What I mean is, it's been most interesting, yes,' she says and tries to smile, but her mouth won't stretch and the moment's somehow gone and, well, he just nods politely and walks out of the Larkhall Tea Gardens.

When Beatrice finally arrives, she tells her about the extraordinary encounter and her friend fiddles with the little flower brooch at her throat – a nervous habit, something she does when a thought is especially taxing – and looks carefully at Lucy.

'Why extraordinary?'

'Well,' Lucy says, 'I ask you, how could he?'

Beatrice laughs and takes the brooch off and inspects the pin. Begins to clean her nails with it.

'Sometimes I don't understand you at all, Lucy.'

'What don't you understand?'

'He was an attractive young man – you say so yourself. And he lives nearby. And all he was asking was to call on you. A pleasant friendship. What are you so afraid of? What could possibly be wrong in that?'

Lucy sniffs as if it's obvious. 'Why on earth should he be interested in me for a start?'

'Why shouldn't he? And anyway, no need to worry yourself about that – the fact is, he was. He liked you. He wanted to, I don't know, talk to you.'

Lucy picks irritably at a loose thread on her glove. It shouldn't be coming apart. It's Derry & Tom's best. She'll make sure to write to the manufacturers in the morning.

'I don't do that sort of thing,' she says, lamely. But even as she says it she's falling out of kilter with herself, asking herself the simple, obvious question that she can't quite bear to answer: Why Not?

Why not? Women of her age have married, made late marriages. Two ladies from the church got married very recently and they're in their forties. 'Someone to put dinner on the table for,' one of them said, and Lucy had smiled into her hymn book.

And yet . . . why not?

She's lain awake with that question ever since, night after night. She's watched it move around her small narrow room, dipping in and out of the shadows, accusing her, rousing her, laughing at her in her loneliness.

Well, never mind that, no time to dwell.

She's true to her word, meanwhile. She speaks to Freddy Crisp on the Monday morning and by the following Thursday Colin Bodger has a new job in menswear at Derry & Tom's: £350 per annum, which is a great deal more than he would ever have got at Arding & Hobbs. He's extremely grateful and he writes her a letter – shy, yet heartfelt and well expressed – to show his thanks.

Lucy acknowledges it and says she was glad to be able to help. And she means it. Help is what she's good at. Putting a word in, giving a step up to someone who deserves it. But that's where it stops. And always after that, when she glimpses young Colin Bodger across the clatter of the staff dining room or getting into the lifts, she turns her head away. She can't quite bring herself to return his eager, open gaze.

By the time of the 1881 census, Lucy Spawton's father, Thomas Harlock Spawton, is dead. He dies in 1872 – when Lucy is only four years old. Not that she need be lonely. At 55 Old Town she is shown living with her older brother John, her older sister Mary, her mother Elizabeth, and her grandmother Mary. There's an assistant milliner called Louisa also living above the shop and a domestic servant called Eliza Dodson.

The land tax records reveal that they were renting the shop from Charles Poole. But from 1878, the owner is registered as a Mrs Harrison. Did she put the rent up? Because the Spawtons pull out of 55 Old Town in 1881. Elizabeth doesn't move the family into Number 34 Lillieshall Road until 1894.

But by the time Lucy's mother dies in July 1914 – in her room at 34 Lillieshall Road – she leaves everything to Lucy. Everything. Why? What's become of John and Mary? Are they dead or disgraced? And what's happened to Catherine Annie Spawton, another older sister of Lucy's, whose birth certificate I have but who seems to have disappeared by the time of the 1881 census, though she reappears in the census of 1901?

I walk up to Number 55 Old Town, to see what it looks like now. A pretty, early Victorian terraced house, two storeys, smallish. The ground floor is now a Winkworth's Estate Agents. Three young men and a woman, all in striped shirts, are sipping Starbucks coffees and talking on the phone.

Edwin Huddart rings me. I found his address on the Info Disk and he's the right Edwin Huddart! But he sounds extremely old.

'I receiv-ed your le-tter . . .' he says very slowly.

I run upstairs with the phone, trying not to sound too out of breath, trying to find a quiet room away from the children – struggling, too, to place him into a mental family tree. It's Beatrice Haig. And Edwin was mentioned in her will. He's one of the nephews – Sidney or Edwin.

'I received your letter,' he says again in a voice I can now hear is charming, warm and well educated. 'I'm ninety-six, you see.'

'Goodness,' I lie 'you don't sound ninety-six.'

'I'm very deaf I'm afraid. I do apologize for that. I do so very much hope I'm making myself understood?'

I tell him it's extremely kind of him to ring, but I'm not sure if he hears me. It's like talking to someone long-distance.

He goes on: 'Yes, well, she was my favourite aunt, you see, Auntie Bea.'

Beatrice Haig . . . Auntie Bea! So this is it, I've got her.

'Well, you see your aunt lived here in our house,' I begin.

'Oh well, Lillieshall Road, yes, my twin brother Alan and I, we were always visiting.'

'You came here to the house, her house?'

'she was my favourite aunt, you see, Aunt Bea!'

'Oh yes, oh yes – do you know something? The first thing that springs to mind is, we listened to our first crystal set radio in that house on Lillieshall Road.'

I tell him that's wonderful and ask if it would be possible to come and see him sometime and talk about his aunt.

He doesn't seem to hear me. 'I got your letter, you see.'

'I know, that's so kind of you – to ring – '

'We came all the time. I'm not sure how much I can tell you. But I live in Sussex, you see.'

'I can easily come and see you there, Mr Huddart.'

'I'm ninety-six, you see. Ninety-six and frankly rather deaf. I don't mind owning up to it, you know. I'm not much good on the telephone, am I, my dear?'

Beatrice Haig shudders into view, takes human shape at last. I can't see her, not really, not yet – will Edwin Huddart have a photo? Oh please let him have a photo – but she's somehow warming up for me, she's there. Auntie Bea.

In fact, the conversation with Mr Huddart has told me very little really. Except that she had a radio, and twin nephews, and that she was their favourite aunt. But it's brought her to life, made her exist beyond my piece of paper, beyond the list in Kelly's Directory. Someone who is alive and here on the planet right now remembers her. Loved her, even.

Someone in Sussex who is ninety-six. I must see him immediately.

I sit down and write a note to Mr Huddart, thanking him again for ringing and asking if I can make a date to see him 'at his earliest convenience'. I make it clear that anything at all is convenient to me. I feel a note is safer than calling him and I sense that he is a polite and kind man who, having taken the trouble to ring, will probably reply straightaway.

As I walk downstairs with the letter, hoping to collar a child and send them to post it, the house is suddenly flooded with Auntie Bea's newly benign presence: Lucy Spawton's friend, Edwin and Alan's favourite aunt, proud owner of a crystal set radio.

'What was a crystal radio exactly?' I ask Jonathan later.

'An early wireless,' he says. 'You put a little thing in your ear, I think. You could probably find something about them on the Internet.'

'I just love it,' I say, 'that this house has such resonance for him. He's ninety-six – almost a century old! – he still remembers that experience so clearly.'

'Well, it'd just be so exciting, wouldn't it? Especially for a young boy at that time – to hear your first radio. People speaking somewhere else and you can hear them, like they're in the same room.'

'I thought they always had radios, even in the olden days,' Raph says.

'Oh, so the Elizabethans had radios, did they?' Chloë asks him.

She dives under the kitchen table to pick up a ping-pong ball. She and Raph have recently discovered table tennis, which they play enthusiastically at our big round kitchen table. 'It's a more challenging game when you don't have corners,' Chloë insists.

307

'I remember when I first saw colour TV,' I tell them, 'at my granny's. She always got gadgets as soon as they came out. It was after school – we all went over specially to watch it. We had strawberry Nesquick and we watched the Test Card for ages.'

'The girl with the long hair and the blackboard,' says Jonathan.

'And wasn't there a puppet or a clown in it somewhere?'

Jake is staring at us. 'You sat and watched a test card?'

'They were more innocent times,' I tell him. 'We still had the capacity to be amazed by things like that.'

'Anyway, that test card was famous,' his father says. 'Everyone remembers it. Everyone our age anyway. By the way,' he says to me, 'I meant to ask you, all that stuff about Lucy Spawton and the Bodger guy. Is it real or did you make it up?'

I hesitate. 'Does it make any difference?'

'You made it up.'

'She just makes it up!' shouts Chloë, smashing a ball down so hard over the net that it bounces up on top of the kitchen cupboards.

'Made up isn't quite how I'd put it,' I tell them.

After a while, I lose track of what's real and what isn't. After weeks and months, these people are filling my head, my dreams, taking up so much space in my imagination that I feel I could turn around and explain them to anyone.

Three nights in a row I've dreamed about Bea and Lucy. The dreams have told me nothing and moved me no further on – just given me poor sleep, and almost made me wish I hadn't conjured up these new and urgent ghosts, who, let's face it, have been at rest for years.

But Lucy's job at Derry & Tom's, that's real. I have the written evidence, as well as all the anecdotes from Joan Clayton. And C. Bodger's name is definitely there on the staff list that Glasgow University sent me – typed by a faint, wobbly typewriter, the script sloping ever so slightly to the left: Mr C. S. Bodger, 7 Jeypore Road, Wandsworth Common. Below Miss L. C. Gething and above Mr E. Smith.

I picked him on a whim actually, deciding to write about him because I liked his funny name; and then I found, when I checked again, that of all the thirty-odd staff listed on the page, he was the only one who actually lived fairly near to Lucy. But then I'm getting used to these serendipitous coincidences by now.

And certainly there really was a terrible fire at Arding & Hobb's that Christmas Saturday in 1909, and, yes, it gutted the store, which didn't open again until the following December. I've seen the photographs – grainy black-and-white, shot with light and wet and the spikiness of burned metal. Jagged shapes against a freezing white sky.

And Lucy's spinsterhood is real, we all know that – I've seen the photo where she fixes the camera with her fierce virginal gaze. Lucy Spawton – Head Buyer at Derry & Tom's and spinster of this parish. And yet I know from Joan Clayton that she was also kind and well intentioned (and intelligent, if she read the *Telegraph* and *Financial Times*), if socially awkward.

Not too socially awkward, though, since Bea – kind, favourite Bea – was her friend. And Lucy worked for thirty-six years in a job where she must have dealt with people all the time and which must have required a love and understanding of beauty and comfort: fine fabrics and well-made clothes. And the Larkhall Tea Gardens really existed, that's for sure. I wish they existed now.

But did Lucy ever meet Colin Bodger in there? And did he ask to call on her and did she fix him up with a job? Did she, in fact, ever meet him at all? Well, I have no evidence whatsoever for any of that and, frankly, I doubt it. My only defence is that possibilities are my only currency here – the possibilities that grow out of small, carefully discovered, and lovingly nurtured facts. How else am I supposed to bring these people back to life?

So, it goes like this: if Lucy had happened to be sipping tea in there one afternoon while waiting for Bea, and if it had so happened that she'd been approached by Mr Bodger of Jeypore Road in Wandsworth, who used to work in menswear and lost all his prospects in the Arding & Hobbs fire, then would she have been moved to help him out? Knowing what I know of Lucy, I like to think so.

And if he'd meanwhile taken a shine to this intelligent, abrupt, yet somehow enticingly blunt, dark-eyed older woman, and if he'd found the courage to ask to call on her, then would she have rebuffed him? Sadly, I think yes.

But, in the thick dark of the night in her small bedroom – now our sisal-floored, glass-shelved family bathroom – would she have lain awake and wondered why she hadn't said yes? Or would she have slept soundly, her mind uncluttered by self-doubt, clothes neatly folded on the chair, preparing herself for the onslaught of work the following day?

The honest answer is, I don't know. And I think by now you're as well placed to decide as I am.

And maybe I should have said – Lucy's sisters and her brother, they're real and I know now what happened to them. I have the certificates of where and when and how to prove it.

Dr Hill still remembers the day in late September, almost thirty years ago, when he attends the Spawton girl.

Late September 1881. An unexpected reprieve from autumn, a string of warm, golden, mauve-skied days, people suddenly going hatless in the streets again – shop doors all through Old Town are standing open, despite the brown curled leaves blowing in the gutter. Children flying off to Cock Pond, coatless, to throw pebbles and float their twopenny boats.

Mary Elizabeth – eighteen years old and rather lovely. Many a time he's passed the shop at Number 55 in the early morning and seen her scrubbing the step for her mother, sleeves rolled to reveal fine, slim, pale arms, black hair twisted on her head to show a pale, fine-boned throat and neck.

'Morning, doctor!' she'd cry out, not the least bit coy. Mind you, none of those Spawton girls were – straight as a die, direct as you like, all three of them. It made him smile to see girls who looked you straight in the eye and spoke back to you as if it was the most ordinary thing in the world.

'Morning, Miss Mary. Why, if you don't mind me asking, aren't you in school?'

He knows the answer. He just says it to twist her temper a little.

'I'm fifteen, Dr Hill, and so I don't go to that place any more! Why aren't you there yourself, pray?'

He laughs.

'Oh, well, I'm older than I look, Miss Mary.'

'Oh. Is that a fact?'

'How old do you think I am, then?'

She can't think of an answer to that – not one she'd dare give anyway. She doesn't know enough about men to know what age they might be, though she knows it's rumoured that young Dr Hill – could he be twenty-eight? – is courting a nurse called Theresa but Theresa won't become engaged to him till he has his own surgery. Her brother John heard that down at the Bull.

Dr Hill doesn't know this is what's going through young Mary's head. But he likes the way she stands and cocks her head on one side for a moment, considering, then waves him away with an impatient hand and continues with the step.

Hard to believe it's the same girl now, lying here in this bed, which has been pulled away from the window to avoid the draughts. Though they needn't have bothered – the weather's so unseasonably warm that the air feels soft on your face.

The table next to her is piled with tonics and tinctures. Her face is the colour of lead, her skin hot, dry. She holds the sheet bunched up in one hand whose claw-like aspect points to the fact that she's held it like that, unmoving, for a long time. Hours or even days.

The room smells sweet. He knows that smell. He's smelled it a thousand times and he'd like to say it's a smell that doesn't necessarily mean anything. But it wouldn't be true. He knows the smell, and it's the smell of death.

'Hello, Mary.'

She doesn't stir.

'How are you today, my dear?'

He places himself in her line of vision, but she looks right through him. She stares at the window, as if she might divine something in that cloudy, greasy pane that can't be seen by the naked eye, that can't be seen by all the rest of them who aren't sick, who are laughing and chatting and bobbing in and out of doors on this bright, blowy day.

'Can you open your eyes a bit, Mary?'

Her eyes are small tight slits, the lids blueish, and some swelling and pussing at the corners.

He asks Mrs Spawton whether she's taken anything in the last day and night.

'Toast and water,' her mother says. 'She took a little of that off a teaspoon yesterday morning. I heated and strained it and gave her the water. I couldn't get her to have the toast. She won't take anything solid at all.'

'Nothing since then?'

'She won't, doctor. If I try to get near, she turns her head away. She's very weak, coughing all the time. I tried an embrocation, but it does no good either. Is it her lungs, do you think?'

One of the younger daughters inches forward – a tiny girl, a smaller, thinner, uglier version of Mary. Beetle-browed, crook-shouldered, barely out of childhood. This little girl raises her hand to make herself seen.

'She's burning up, doctor, she told me so. Can you do anything to make her colder? That's what she wants, I know it. She's crying out to be made cold.'

Her mother waves her away. 'Goodness' sakes, Lucy, nip downstairs now and put the kettle on. And tell that Eliza to shut up the shop till John comes back. I need her up here now.'

But the child is undeterred. She hovers by Dr Hill's elbow, clearly used to ignoring her mother's instructions.

'Should we sponge her, doctor? Cold water or warm? Please . . . just tell us what would make it better for her.'

He's not sure whether the girl simply means to make her sister more comfortable or whether she believes a cure is really possible. He knows the mother doesn't when she kneels suddenly at the foot of the bed and begins to weep and pray.

Dr Hill leaves a draught and some powders – not that he has any confidence they'll get her to take it – and he tells Mrs Spawton to call him straightaway if anything changes. He says he'll send his boy with a bill for this visit but not to worry as he won't charge them for a subsequent one. He feels a flush of guilt when Mrs S thanks him profusely for this generosity. He knows it's not that – it's because next time he visits will be a formality – a case of form-filling.

As he leaves, the mother's still weeping loudly and he sees the Dodson girl – Eliza, is it? – who helps out in the shop and who they say the son, John, has taken a shine to. She's heaving with all her might to pull down the awning on the shop. She leans the hook against the wall and turns and raises her hand to him, and he nods to her as he climbs back in the brougham.

Outside the air is bright, sparkling. It's not a time to catch pneumonia – not in the middle of an Indian summer when you're eighteen and no one even knew you had weak lungs until a couple of months ago.

MARY ELIZABETH SPAWTON. FEMALE. EIGHTEEN YEARS. ACUTE PNEUMONIA AND PHTHISIS 2 MONTHS. CERTIFIED BY MR B HILL MRCS. ELIZABETH SPAWTON, MOTHER, PRESENT AT THE DEATH. 55 OLD TOWN CLAPHAM. THIRTIETH SEPTEMBER, 1881.

'Outside the air is bright, sparkling.'

Eight years after Mary Spawton died, Walter Stephen Hinkley, eldest son of Isabella and Walter, was born at 2 Broadhinton Road, a small terraced cottage just around the corner from Lillieshall Road, to where the family would eventually move.

I know this, but it still takes me hours and many black volumes at the Probate Search Room to finally discover Walter's death.

> HINKLEY Walter Stephen of St Anthony's Nursing Home West
> Hill Rd, St Leonards on Sea (Essex) died 17 November 1988.
> Probate Brighton 13 December. Not exceeding £70,000
> 8851318126N

He lived to be ninety-nine. No wonder my arms are aching. I write off to one of the beneficiaries, Philip Lloyd. I think he's a nephew. Almost immediately, I get a reply. Very exciting, a living Hinkley descendant: two sides of tissue-thin A5 airmail-type paper, perfect curly handwriting. I have to hold the letter up to the light to read it.

I did have an Uncle Wally – he married my Aunt Lettie just after the end of the First World War (about 1920) and the wedding was in North London and Uncle Walter Hinkley and my Aunt lived in North London and had a daughter Muriel who married a Lewis Jones but both are long gone.

I was at the wedding of Walter and Lettie and remember his parents dimly and he the father was a shipwright in Deptford but I have no knowledge whatever of where they lived – it could well have been Clapham. Walter Hinkley the son was a customs officer in London Docks but I believe also worked in Deptford shipyard and studied in evenings and became a civil servant.

The last I saw Uncle Walter and wife Lettie was at St Leonard's (an old people's home) and Lettie died soon after Uncle Wally in 1988 in St Leonards. I have no photos and I am 93 years old and I don't get about much now. One point: I have a sister Beryl Lloyd slightly younger than me who might know more. I enclose her address. You could contact her if you think this worthwhile.

Yours sincerely
Philip Lloyd

PS Walter Hinkley had a brother who was at wedding and he was a civil servant and lived in Harrogate but I never met him again.

I write off straightaway to Beryl, but get no reply; so after a week or so I write back to Philip Lloyd, mentioning that I've heard nothing from Beryl and adding that I would love to come and see him for a brief chat sometime if he didn't mind.

I would say that my sister Beryl generally takes an extended summer holiday – a cruise or trip abroad and you could certainly try phoning her.

I have told you everything I know and as my family and my self always lived away from North London – we only saw Uncle Wally infrequently whereas my sister was in the Civil Service and lived in North London and would have seen WH more often. There are no other family members left (my son Keith is 58 and would not have met Uncle Wally as he was born in Chelmsford and now lives at Eastleigh (Southampton)). I don't think it would help for you to see me as I've told you everything I know and I hope my sister might be able to help.

Yours truly

Meanwhile a woman called Eleanor Bingham – who has the tiniest voice I've ever heard – leaves a barely discernible message on my machine. She says Beryl has put her in touch with me. She might be able to give me some information about her Uncle Wally.

It's like listening to Tinkerbell talk to an answerphone. I play it three times with my ear to the speaker and finally manage to write down a number.

We know that on 15 October 1882 – the year after Mary's death from pneumonia – John Howell Spawton married Eliza Dodson, from Great Paxton in the parish of St Neots. And we know that, at the time of her marriage, Eliza had for some years been employed by the Spawtons as a domestic servant. But we know little else. Maybe Mrs Spawton was quite fond of her servant and was understanding – even happy – about the union. Maybe Eliza was considered so much a part of the family by then that – far from there being any resentment or bitterness – there was a celebration, kissing, congratulations.

Yet by the time of her own death, Mrs Elizabeth Spawton, widow of Thomas Harlock Spawton, master draper, left everything to Lucy, cutting John out completely.

Anyway, the marriage is doomed from the start. They move to Camberwell and on 23 January 1884, two years after their marriage, John and Eliza are delivered of a son, Thomas Harlock Beesley Spawton – future husband of Auntie Til, future smoker of pipes and wearer of homburgs, future frightener of the Hun! But within a month of Tom's sixth birthday, his mother is lying in her grave.

> ELIZA SPAWTON. FEMALE. THIRTY YEARS. WIFE OF JOHN HOWELL SPAWTON, BUILDER'S CLERK. ASTHINIA & EXHAUSTION 9 MONTHS, 12 DAYS. PHTHISIS 4 YEARS. J DODSON, MOTHER, PRESENT AT DEATH, 118 UPLAND ROAD, CAMBERWELL. TWENTY-FIRST FEBRUARY 1890.

Evening, light rain. I drive to Mitcham to see Joyce Creed, the only person who ever responded to my plea for help in the *South London Press*. Mrs Creed lived across the road from our house for years and years. When she first rang me in the spring, I knew almost nothing about the Spawtons and the Hinkleys and Reggie Povah and Peter Askew and Alvin Reynolds. I have been postponing my visit until I knew enough to ask her the right questions. Now I'm here to examine my last living witness. The little metal gate squeaks twice. A dead straight concrete path leads past rows of cheerful red and yellow bedding plants. Mr Creed – big, white-haired, smiling – lets me in through the glass screen door.

'Joyce!'

The room he ushers me into is brown-painted and looks on to the back garden. More rows of plants. The tang of old cigarette smoke.

Mrs Creed beams at me and orders Stan to make me a cup of tea. Her fingers are yellow and her face is a mass of tiny lines like tree bark. Stan brings in a mug for me then lights a cigarette.

She tells me that her father and grandfather were both born in 27 Lillieshall Road – 'my family's been there over a hundred years' – which means they'd have lived there before our house was built, when Orchard Street was next to a cricket ground. Their neighbour would have been Mr Thomas, who built half of Lillieshall Road and made Edward I'Anson's life such a trial.

Mrs Creed frowns when I tell her this. 'They never said nothing about a cricket ground,' she says.

She says she went to Clapham Parochial School (this later became Macaulay), which back then was in the middle of North Street, just at the end of our road.

'Very strict,' she says. 'Miss Lode was the Head and then Miss Bassom came next and later Mrs White. We wore velour hats in winter with a black headband edged in red and with CPS – Clapham Parochial School – embroidered in the centre.'

Mrs Creed sits forward in her chair with her hands folded in front of her and shoulders back, as if she's being interviewed on television.

'We had a red long-sleeved woollen jumper and stockings and navy-blue knickers and a drill slip. And then in summer a panama hat with the same headband. And we went to church once a month, to Holy Trinity – boys on one side, girls on the other. And do you know what, I still remember my first day of school. I came home afterwards and Granny Potter who lived with us said to me, "How did you get on, Joyce?" and I told her it was all right except I didn't like the sums. "What sums?" she said. "The ones on the board in the church," I said –'

At this point Stan claps a hand on his knee and stubs out his cigarette.

'She'd been reading the hymn numbers! Thought she had to add them up!'

We all rock with laughter. Stan lights another cigarette.

'You left school at fourteen in those days unless you passed a trade scholarship. My sister Betty did pass, you know, except we couldn't afford to send her off to train. A pity, she was such a clever girl. I was the dunce of the family.'

I ask her if she remembers an old lady called Lucy Spawton.

'Lucy Spawton? Now then, it does sound familiar – was she very little and odd-looking?'

I tell her I think that yes, she probably was.

She shakes her head. 'I don't remember no one like that. I remember the church people. There was Canon Durrell and Reverend Nye, and then Reverend A. C. Raby – he married us – and Deaconess Dora.'

'Deaconess Dora?'

'Deaconess Dora Gallop! She was a funny one – she rented rooms on Orlando Road and – '

Mrs Creed looks suddenly coy. Stan blows smoke out through his nose.

'Tell her,' he says on an outbreath.

'No!'

'If you won't, I will.'

'All right then. We called her Deaky Dora. She ran the Sunday school. And she used to come down the street, down Lillieshall Road, in those great big cassocks and we were all playing games on the corner of Orlando Road against that great big wall – '

'What did you play?' I ask as the car-free road of sixty years ago flashes into life in my head.

'Oh, spinning tops, throwing a ball up the wall.'

'Marbles,' adds Stan.

'No, not marbles, we didn't play marbles – we liked to worry old ladies. So if there was one coming down the road and it was getting, you know, dusk, we'd say, "Oh please, miss, mind our cotton!" And we'd pretend we'd got a piece of cotton stretched out between the lampposts and she couldn't see it and she'd have to step over it – we laughed so much.'

'Tell her about Deaky Dora,' prompts Stan.

'Well, we were so naughty – she used to come down the road in these great cassocks, you see, and she was always losing her keys and she'd shout, "Children, children, come over here! I think I've lost my keys!" and we'd have to grope around in the bottom of her cassock, you see, because they'd have got lost. And while some of us were doing it, the others used to go round the back and lift up the skirts to see what colour.'

Stan looks at me and laughs, checking. I laugh too.

'We were terrible back then,' says Mrs Creed. 'Terrible we were. And it was mean, too, because she were a good one, that Deaconess – always popped round to see how we all were, or if she heard you were poorly or anything like that.

'Sometimes, Granny Potter used to have fetched her pint of ale in a jug from the Tim Bobbin and she'd stick a red hot poker in it to warm it up, and she'd be just about to drink it and the knock would come on the door and she'd say, "Quick, Joyce, put the jug under the table!"'

Mrs Creed also tells me she remembers the beautiful big rectory in Macaulay Road – now long demolished to make room for the LCC estate that is Macaulay Square.

'The Holy Trinity fête was held there every year and we could all go, and it was so beautiful and there was strawberries and cream in the garden – this beautiful lawn with an enormous great shady tree right in the middle. And the 5th Clapham Scouts were there playing their band

'the car-free road of sixty years ago flashes into life in my head.'

320

music, and there was nothing we loved so much as the rectory toilet, which had the most beautiful decorated bowl and handle we'd ever seen!'

Stan chuckles.

Mrs Creed and I both agree it's a shame the rectory's gone.

'Some monstrosity of a council block they've put in its place,' she mutters.

It's true, I think, it's a sad, drab place. I delivered leaflets there for Jonathan during the local elections and later, on election day itself, went round trying to knock people up. I didn't get anyone to come and vote Labour. Aimless kids tried to trip me up in the concrete stairwells, broken furniture and cardboard boxes were piled up in people's doorways.

'But did you know the tree's still there?' I ask Mrs Creed. 'A huge great spreading tree, a chestnut, I think it is. I've often noticed it. It's enormous. It must be ever so old.'

Mrs Creed widens her eyes, suddenly six again – small enough to be impressed by strawberries and rich folks' toilets.

'There it stood in the middle of the rectory lawn, it was big even then. Big enough for three or four of you to hide behind – we was all skinny in them days – and no one would've known you was there.'

Kids still dodge behind it now. I've seen them. In the middle of the scorched and scrubby wasteland, strewn with discarded toys and beer cans, that passes for a lawn. On a hot summer's day they'll be out there, on their rusted bikes or micro-scooters, while their mums spread a blanket on the ground and smoke and chat and listen to the radio.

Sometimes they hide behind the old tree and sometimes they try to climb it, frantic trainers scrambling up its peeling sides. But not a single one of them realizes they're sitting bang in the middle of the old rectory lawn. And not a single one of them would care if they knew that the 5th Clapham Scouts once played 'Down at the Old Bull and Bush' while people queued in awe to use a flushing toilet with a handle that was decorated with blue and golden roses.

* * *

Catherine Annie Spawton cares.

The last time she ventures outside into the open air is to visit that tree. Catherine Annie Spawton: thirty-six years old; slim, adventurous, and robust. She's an outdoor girl. Illness doesn't suit her. She used to be a jolly, bouncy girl – the big-boned, healthy one in the family, the one on whom, since Mary went, all the hopes of the future were pinned. Unlike Lucy, whose nickname used to be 'Bird' on account of her frail little limbs and her beaky face. Lucy was the one they were always half-ready to lose – ever since her birth: born early, weedy, bawling babe.

But Lucy's fit and strong and wedded to her job, her retail life – fourteen years she's worked in haberdashery and trimmings. Whereas Catherine is dreamy and bookish – before her sight begins to go, anyway. Cathy notices things like trees. Until she gets ill, almost nine months ago now, she's an infant teacher at the Parochial School. She'll take the little ones off to the Common to collect pine cones, empty robin's-egg shells, feathers, twigs, acorns. They'll tear around, sturdy little legs tottering over the grass, bringing back treasure after treasure to show her.

One little girl brings a curl of silver paper and they reckon it must have fallen from a magpie's nest.

'Does it count, Miss?'

'Of course it counts,' Catherine tells her, and it goes on the table with the rest.

Miss Spawton is famous for her splendid nature table. Then she has her first fainting fit and the doctor asks for some of her urine. When it tastes sweet, they know that that's that. She can't work, her energy goes up and down, and when the weakness comes upon her, she's helpless – devastated. Up until the time of her illness she had still cherished plans of finding a husband after all and maybe having a couple of little ones of her own. She'd like a boy and a girl, one of each. The boy will be William and the girl will be Rose. Rose or Lily. She likes Lily, but she thinks at the end of the day she prefers Rose.

Their mother, too, would have liked her to have produced a child –

a square, bouncing boy babby for her to cherish and love. There's poor Tom, of course, but he's never quite right, because of his mother, the way John went off and married that Eliza Dodson. Only Lucy cares about Tom. Of course, there's Jane and Laura, the children of John's second marriage. But they're girls and her mother has a thing for boys.

Now Catherine lies in her narrow bed in the top room of Number 34 and sweats and trembles and, when she dares, lifts her nightdress to see her pelvic bones, her bruised ribs, the swollen nub of her stomach where no food will nourish her, and she knows there'll never be a little Billie or a little Rose. There won't be anyone in fact – she won't get a sweetheart now. Not now she can barely walk. Not now that Lucy even has to help her to the toilet, in case she falls on those two steps on the landing. Imagine that on her wedding night! Being helped on and off the toilet. She doesn't let herself think of it, for when she does she shakes with grief and self-pity.

But today, a chill, bright February day, the sixth of February, she pulls at Lucy's dark merino sleeve.

'Please Lucy, please my love, let's walk down Macaulay as far as the rectory. The old tree might have some leaf on it by now. It'd give me such a lift to see it.'

Lucy hesitates, wondering about this; some days Cathy can't see much at all. 'Right round the corner? Won't you be tired?'

'If I am, we'll turn back.'

Lucy's concerned because last week, a bitter January day, they tried walking the other way, up into Old Town towards the Sun pub, stopping along the way to watch the building work where the new fire station's going up, and Catherine ended up so breathless she had to sit on a bench for more than half an hour.

They got colder and colder.

In the end, Dr Hill drove past and, seeing them sitting there so forlorn and Cathy trembling with the cold, he insisted on putting them in his brougham and driving them home. There, he came in and took Catherine's pulse, felt her muscles, and looked at her eyes and then told her firmly that she should be in bed. That she needed to be warm and wait for her energy to return.

Catherine laughed, though in truth the laugh came out as more of a sigh. 'It won't return, Dr Hill. Why should it return? Where exactly do you think it's gone, that it might decide to turn on its heel and come back to me?'

Lucy looked at her with interest. Her sister isn't any cleverer than her but, being a teacher and having read such a lot of books, can always come up with a flowery little idea that makes Lucy take notice. Dr Hill laughed and teased her sister back. He was always good that way. But down in the dark hall, pulling on his gloves, he turned to Lucy with a look that chilled her. 'Move her down here,' he said. 'She shouldn't be climbing stairs.'

Lucy tried to think what else she should ask him, but the doctor was looking away now and wouldn't catch her eye. This fact alone squeezed at her heart. Warren Hill was renowned for his inability to beat about the bush.

'Will she . . .?' Lucy couldn't finish the question. Dr Hill looked at her then.

'Keep her down here,' he said again. 'Don't let her do anything. Not a thing. Make her comfortable. Keep her warm.' He moved towards the door to let himself out. 'And keep her laughing,' he added soberly as he took his leave.

Now Lucy shouts up to their mother that they're going out. She's not sure Mama hears – a good thing, maybe. Cathy pulls her scarf and gloves on and asks whether Tom is going to send anyone a Valentine's card.

Lucy laughs. 'How should I know? Poor Tom. Somehow I very much doubt it.'

'He's eighteen,' Catherine insists.

Lucy thinks about this, but doesn't know what to say. 'There's plenty of women would love Tom,' Catherine says, and Lucy notices that she has to stop and get her breath back after saying that.

'Oh, my dear, are you up to this?'

Catherine ignores her. 'You must stop calling him poor Tom,' she says. 'Everyone does it and after a while it starts to stick. He's not poor, he's perfectly good and ordinary.'

They've been calling him that since Eliza Dodson died and he was sent to live with them in Clapham. John hardly ever visits him any more, and Tom has only met his half-sisters the one time.

'I'm going to ask him if he's sending one,' Catherine continues. 'I'm going to encourage him.'

'You mustn't! He'd hate it.'

Catherine smiles. 'Lucy. Don't be a dunce. You know I wouldn't dream of it.'

They walk carefully down the front path with its brown and cream tiles and into the street. The air is still frozen, the sky dark, a glimmer of sun coming from behind a cloud.

'Spring,' Catherine says softly.

'I don't think so.'

'Come on, Lucy. Spring has to come eventually.'

Lucy walks slowly, feeling how heavily her sister leans on her, how fragile she is, how much weight she has lost, given that she's taller. Or is she? She certainly used to be.

'If you want to know, I hate this time of year,' she tells Catherine, who smiles.

'You hate too many things. Hating takes energy. Save your energy.'

Lucy wonders about this. Sometimes she thinks it's the sheer force of her feelings for and against things that keeps her going, keeps her alive and healthy. But she doesn't say this.

It takes them a very long time to get to the rectory, twice as long as usual. Finally, they stand and look at the chestnut tree. It's dark and empty, a winter skeleton, bereft of bud. Dusk is coming down and they haven't lit the lamps yet. It's very hard to see much of anything at all.

But Catherine, who's breathing very fast now, her throat rasping as she slides each breath in and out, tugs at Lucy's coat sleeve. 'Look, there!'

'Where? What?'

'Little buds – don't you see them?'

'Where?' Lucy squints hard into the dark criss-cross world that is the tree.

'All over!' Catherine says. 'Tiny shoots of green, very pale – you must be able to see them. This time next week, it'll be in leaf, I'll bet you.'

Lucy shakes her head. She really can see nothing and her eyesight's good, she knows that. She can read at night by candlelight and not strain her eyes. But she sees no sign of bright green in that great big tree. All she feels is her sister's sour breath on her cheek, the swoosh of her blood pulsing in her thin, thin wrist, and the certainty that they should not be out there in the bitter cold.

A week later, Catherine's dead. She dies in the downstairs room, her arms open wide – reaching out towards their mother who has been with her all this time but has turned away just for a quick second to get a glass of water from the kitchen.

'Mother!'

Tom does send a Valentine as it turns out – to Norah James who works at the bakery on North Street. But she makes no attempt to find out who it's from, and he's too awkward to tell her.

And that very day, St Valentine's, Lucy has to walk down Macaulay Road to the church to make arrangements for the funeral, and she passes the tree and catches her breath. Every tiny twig of every tiny branch of every larger branch boasts a tender, baby-thin shoot of acid green.

CATHERINE ANNIE SPAWTON. FEMALE, 36 YEARS. DIABETES 6 MONTHS. ELIZABETH SPAWTON, MOTHER, PRESENT AT THE DEATH. 34 LILLIESHALL ROAD. THIRTEENTH FEBRUARY 1902.

* * *

I call Eleanor Bingham, the Tinkerbell-voiced woman: a Hinkley descendant, though I don't yet know quite how. She tells me, in the faintest, flutteriest voice, that Walter Hinkley's wife Lettie (Lettie Maddams – Walter and Isabella's daughter-in-law) was her mother's cousin.

'And do you know what? She had only one eye. Poor kid. She lost an eye at the age of seventeen! There was some kind of a game being played with an ebony walking stick and the silver knob flew off and hit her in the socket of her eye and the eyeball slid down her cheek!'

'How awful!'

'And it was such a shame because, prior to that, they were such a good-looking family and it meant she had to give up her embroidery. But in the hospital she just said, "No good crying over spilt milk", and got on with it. You had to in those days.'

'That's quite a story,' I tell her. 'Do you think it's true?'

'How can you doubt it? She died at the age of ninety-nine, by which time she was totally blind – the other eye had also gone by then, you see. And I went to her ninety-ninth birthday party and I brought her some pink carnations. She had pink wine and a pink dress and she groped around for the carnations and held them up to her dress – even though she couldn't see them – and then she took a sip of the wine and toasted everyone and said, "I wish we could have wine this colour every day!" She was a jokey person, you see, dear, full of sparkle, full of fun.

'And, well, she was blind and he – Uncle Wally – was stone deaf by the end – he died when he was ninety-nine as well, except that he was nine years younger than her so he died nine years later, if you see what I mean – well, he was deaf and he used to say, "I can see, but it's Lettie who keeps me perpendicular."'

They must have been quite a pair.

Eleanor tells me that she only knew Wally in the latter part of his life – 'Not when he was in your house, I'm afraid.'

I tell her it doesn't matter, that I just want to get a picture of these

327

people. She says she used to transfer him from guest house to nursing home and back again.

'Yes, they moved all the time. They roved around like Wandering Jews! After they gave up their house, they went to stay with some friend in Wales who ran a guest house and their only possession that Lettie insisted on taking with her was her frying pan! Anyway, sometimes they helped out – being left in charge of the place when the owners went on holiday. And after that they bought a flat in Dover – his father Walter had come from there originally I think – but that was too much for them, so they went to a series of guest houses in St Leonards, but there was always something wrong with them and then they'd move on.'

I ask her what her Uncle Wally was like.

'He was a chatty man with beautiful handwriting. He wrote me all these letters and I've still got one of them which I'll send you.'

'And he had a daughter, is that right?'

'Just one child, yes, Muriel. She died at a fairly young age of Parkinson's, I believe. She met her husband Lewis on a fellowship holiday and they were an odd couple really – he was this sprightly little man with quite a juvenile wit, but there you are.'

'And Muriel?'

'She was – well, she was retarded by her illness. It was awful for him, for Lewis, when she died, because he came home one day and he was so looking forward to retiring, and he came through the door whistling and there she was . . .'

I wait a moment.

'What – dead?'

'Just like in a horror film or something. Oh well, but this is off the subject.'

'Not at all,' I tell her. 'Please go on.'

I ask her what Wally did for a living and she says she knows he was an exam vigilante.

'An invigilator?'

'Yes! An invigilator. I know he was one of those by the end. He was a very clever man. He got two degrees while working – scientific or something – but he worked at Chatham Dockyard and it was hard and he didn't like it. He didn't have any of the advantages that this generation has. And he met Lettie during the war I think, in Leith. He said that several ladies came down the stairs in overalls and he looked them over and he saw Lettie and he thought, That's her, that's the one I want!'

I ask again whether there are any other members of the family I could talk to, but she says they're all gone and there were no other children.

'No one left of that line, I'm afraid, dear.'

I say I think it's so sad, the way whole families can just fizzle out and disappear. But she says that, personally, she doesn't look at it that way at all. She's more interested in the current scene.

She laughs again. I wonder how old she is but don't dare ask.

We say goodbye and she promises to look out a photo if she can, and send me the letter, and I wonder whether that will be it. Whether all that's really left here on earth of the Hinkleys is this – Eleanor, the tale of the deaf and blind couple roving the guest houses of the south coast with their one frying pan, and that single, dramatic story of an ebony knob and a sliding eyeball?

But then I remember there was another brother, Charles.

A hot, hot day. I'm going to Steyning in Sussex to see Mr Huddart, the 96-year-old nephew of Beatrice Haig. Ninety-six seems too old to be a nephew.

His daughter Sue has offered to drive me – in fact, I can tell she wants to drive me as he is clearly too old and frail to see me alone. I arrive at her flat in Putney Heath as instructed at exactly 9.45 a.m. and find her ready in the beige-carpeted hall with a bunch of plastic carrier bags.

We're shy with each other.

'Lunch,' she explains, as she picks up the bags. 'I thought going to a pub might be too difficult with Dad's hearing.'

Her car is clean and smells new. As we drive, she tells me that her mother and father lived most of their lives in Brazil. Her mother was part-Brazilian, part-French, and quite a lot younger than her father. While in Brazil they had two babies, both of which died. 'Two full-term babies,' Sue tells me, keeping her eyes on the road. 'Imagine it.'

When they retired, they came to the village of Steyning – chosen by her mother. 'But she wouldn't become a part of village life, she wouldn't join in. And though she was a lot younger than Dad, she got Alzheimer's. He nursed her through it without any real help. Changing her and washing her – he was eighty-five by then!'

Sue says that her mother used to shake him awake in the middle of the night – at eighty-five – and that she once got up and somehow went up to the attic and got one of his old dress suits and put it on and said, 'Come on, let's have breakfast.'

I feel very touched that Sue tells me all this. She doesn't sound like someone who trots the stories out easily for anyone she meets. I sense that she hasn't said some of these things aloud in a long time.

Then she tells me that, shortly after her mother finally died, so too did her own husband.

'Only three months after her. We knew he had a bad heart but no one expected him to die then.'

Sue's voice falters. 'It hit Dad especially very hard.'

She shakes her head and glances back, ready to overtake. I tell her how sorry I am.

'He just got this pain in his chest – classic, of course – and he rubbed it, thinking it would go away. We both rubbed it. I still worry that if we hadn't rubbed it while we waited for the ambulance to arrive, then he wouldn't have died. I think it broke up the clot and sent it to his brain. It haunts me, you know, that we rubbed it like that.'

* * *

Steyning is a picturesque village with a lively high street – thatched cottages, gables, antique shops crammed with china cats and copper warming pans and old, dark, barley-sugar furniture.

Sue's dad – 'He's Edwin but he's always known as Ted, you must call him Ted' – doesn't live in the really pretty bit, but up a few winding streets where the houses are more modern.

At ninety-six, Ted Huddart still lives completely alone.

'It terrifies me,' Sue admits. 'He has one of those alarm things round his neck but he always either forgets to turn it on or else presses it by mistake! One time he was out mowing the lawn and forgot to turn it on and I had to send the police to check he was OK. He doesn't know how much I worry about him.'

We park and get out of the car with the carrier bags. Immediately a very tall thin shape darkens the frosted glass of the porch door.

'There he is!' Sue says, as if a sighting was a rare and delicious thing.

Straightaway the door opens. Ted Huddart is a very tall, very thin, very good-looking man – shock of white hair, smooth skin, a kind face alight with pleasure and anticipation.

He shakes my hand while Sue hurries into the kitchen to make coffee. In the living room, a large table is covered in a vinyl cloth. On it is my letter to him and some photos. I can't wait to look at them. Ted sits me down on his left – 'that's my good ear' – and we beam at each other.

He is fairly deaf, but he has a hearing aid, and it's clear after a moment or two of talking that I don't have to shout, just look at him and speak clearly. I can tell by his face, his huge, stooping, blue-eyed presence, that he is an extremely gentle man. I realize he's probably the oldest man I have ever met.

He says he came and stayed with Beatrice – 'my favourite Auntie Bea!' – when he was seventeen or eighteen and doing his Matriculation in London. Accountancy exams. He says this would make it 1922 or 1923. I quickly realize that I have Beatrice Haig down as living in the house from 1926 – but never mind, I can clear all this up later.

I ask him if he remembers Lucy Spawton. He says he does. He screws up his eyes. 'A strange kind of person. Small, very short legs. Too short for her body, if you know what I mean. And very talkative, but in a strange way.'

I ask him how. He thinks about this. 'She tended to agree with everything you said. She agreed straightaway, and that made you run right out of conversation. I think she was shy actually. An awkward little person. She wanted to say the right thing yet didn't know quite what it was. Didn't fool Alan and me. Children pick that kind of thing up right away.'

Sue brings in the coffee. She tells her Dad that she is going out to post his letters, do his lottery ticket, get his prescription. Is there anything else?

Once Sue has gone, Ted hits his stride. His Auntie Bea was one of six daughters – 'Six girls, can you imagine! She was the third eldest and my mother was the fifth. She worked all her life in a millinery shop, I think. She was born in 1870, I know that – she was a nice woman, small and slender. We loved her, she was very kind.'

He says he remembers meeting Tom – 'Lucy's son' – I tell him Tom was actually her nephew, the abandoned child from an early, mistaken marriage.

'Ah yes. Nephew, that's right. But she bossed him about and cared for him, didn't she? Always worrying over him. But he was a good chap – he had a great sense of humour, Tom did. I remember him sitting there in the kitchen in your house smoking his pipe, and I remember being surprised when I heard he worked in a bank.'

'Why?'

'Well, you know, he had this distinctive deep-throated laugh and a rather countrified accent – he didn't seem like he would care a jot for money – a very friendly chap, very friendly indeed.'

'Did he come from the country?' I ask Ted.

He frowns. 'Not from London anyway. All I know is there was

heart surgery in those days. He had a leaky valve and this was probably what killed him.'

Ted gives me two photos: 'You can borrow these, take them away with you. I haven't looked at them in a long time.' One is of Auntie Bea with her arm around each of the twins – they look about eight or nine, blond, sweet, good children. Auntie Bea looks pleased and proud to be photographed with them.

The other is of Ted's mother's wedding – three women dressed in white sitting in a garden, two men and an old lady in black standing behind. 'That's my grandmother, the very old lady, and my father on the left, and his best man who was called Robert Graves. They were all from Cockermouth.

'That's my grandmother, the very old lady . . .'

'My mother's mother was from Suffolk. And we spent school holidays on a farm run by my mother's uncle. It was near Monks Eleigh. Their surname was Vince. Three of those boys were killed in the First World War. It broke their mother's heart. And I remember a very hot summer in Suffolk and we contracted mumps while staying there and we'd go and cool off in the river. And I was sent to fetch some marmalade from

Lavenham – this was during the war – and I took the coupon to get the ration of marmalade and they gave me some. And I went out of the shop and thought that was easy and went in and asked for some more. And the girl in the shop said, "Hey! He's already had some!" – and I had to give it back.'

Ted laughs, but lunch is nearly ready and I can see he's getting tired.

'You know what Auntie Bea used to say to me? "Don't think you know everything, Ted." She used to call me Mr Why because I asked so many questions.'

He shows me the family bible, which has an entry for Bea's birth in 1870. Beatrice Mary Haig in sloping italic script.

I ask him if he thinks Bea was happy.

'She was a happy person, yes. But she knew her own mind and she wouldn't be ordered about, not by anyone. She was one of six daughters – did I say that already? – her father took to whisky rather too liberally after they were all born. But can you blame him?'

We sit and eat meatballs in the kitchen. They don't know I'm a vegetarian and I would always rather swallow a little meat than embarrass a host. My kids would be appalled. It was only quite recently that they stopped calling out 'Poor, poor animals!' when passing the meat section in Sainsbury's.

In the kitchen, Ted and I sit next to each other on one bench and Sue sits opposite.

Bea dealt with, we talk mostly about cricket – Ted's big passion. He tells me he played cricket with Brian Johnston when he worked in Brazil. I tell him my youngest, Raphael, would love to hear about that, that Raph's doing coaching today in fact – and that if I'd known he was so mad about cricket I'd have tried not to come on a day when the Test Match was on.

He laughs and says it's perfectly all right and that when we go he'll have to decide between a snooze or the cricket. 'These days, all too often the snooze wins.'

After lunch, Sue washes up and I dry the plates and Ted insists on getting down on his hands and knees to put them away in the lowest cupboards. Every time a Pyrex dish is handed to him, he laboriously leans his walking stick against the counter and gets down on his knees again. It doesn't help that he's so tall, and it doesn't help that he's ninety-six. He won't accept my offer of help. And all his pots seem to be kept in low cupboards.

Sue – obviously used to it – ignores him and swishes the suds around the bowl. But I can't help watching. It's funny, troubling, and impressive all at once.

She's well known for her cheery disposition, her optimism, her warmth and gaiety, her level-headedness even. Lucy's always saying that just a minute or two in Bea's company usually reminds her of what's right with the world.

But when Bob breaks it off with her, she loses her balance for once. Not level or optimistic or cheery any more, she goes cold. A rapid chilling, that's what happens. And then, like ice, she dissolves.

She's reduced to a creature Lucy barely recognizes. She lets the letter fall from her hands on to the floor and sinks right down on to her hands and knees, right there on the floor, like a child or an animal, and she weeps. On the blue and yellow tufted rug, which still harbours the crumbs from yesterday's tea, she lies with her head on her arms and she sobs.

Dearest Bea, please forgive me.

He's sorry to break the news this way. He knows she'll think him a coward and maybe she'll be right about that, maybe he is. But the thing is he respects her so deeply and can't bring himself to witness the pain this letter will cause her.

He's had a change of heart. There's someone who ... it was surely a madness, those weeks of theirs in Eastbourne? Of course, he'll never forget them, never forget her. He wants her to know that he'll always hold her in the highest affection and esteem. He wants her to know that he never meant to end things this way and he hopes she doesn't think him a terrible rotter and all that but, well, he's had to look closely at his feelings and he's been quite surprised at what he's discovered there. Sorry, my dear, but there it goes. He's going to marry . . . Florence. He hopes she'll wish him all the best. As he does her. He's ever hers. Ever her friend.

Bea cries. She cries for more than an hour. The rug is damp, her face red and mottled and gritty with crumbs. She never knew a face could hold so much water. She never knew a breast, a heart, a body, could empty this way. She did not know that a single piece of paper could be put into her hands like that and in thirty quick seconds undo the few glowing strands that were her future.

Respect, Affection, Esteem.

At least she knows something now. She knows what she doesn't want. She doesn't want a friend and she doesn't want those other pale and colourless offerings – respect, affection, esteem – either.

No, what she wants is what, for one shimmery August month in Eastbourne, she really thought she had. The swoony warmth of a man's arms around her, his fingers on her face, his lips – dry, rousing, insistent – on hers. The bliss of being wound up tightly with him. The feeling of being desired, explored, touched all over. The sensation of being Engaged.

Beryl Lloyd, niece of Walter Hinkley – I never thought I would ever hear from her – calls and leaves a message on the answerphone. She says she'll call back another time but she doesn't know when. 'Righty ho,' she says quietly, 'over and out.'

I call her back straightaway. I don't know how old she is – all I know is she's the younger sister of Philip who's ninety-three.

Beryl tells me that she is the daughter of Lettie Maddams' twin sister Olivia. Lettie who married Walter Hinkley, son of Isabella and Walter. 'They were very alike in looks, but not in any other way at all!'

Beryl says she knew Wally and Lettie in 1930 when she was sixteen and got a job in the Civil Service and came to live with them at 34 Elmdale Road in Palmer's Green.

'Not the happiest time of my life, being a poor relation and that.' She says she's pretty sure she came with Walter and Lettie to visit the old people in Clapham. She says she doesn't really remember the house but can vaguely recall old Mrs Hinkley –Isabella. 'Rather like Muriel – very dark indeed, glossy black hair, but a mess. Muriel wasn't too fussy about her appearance, you know. Just chucked on a frock and that was that. She was only ten when I first stayed with them, but already there was something about her.'

'How do you mean?'

'Let's just say she was a bit of a disappointment to her parents all round. Her father, you see, had academic aspirations. He was apprenticed at the Chatham Dockyard like his father but somehow he became a Customs and Excise officer. He went to the LSE at night and studied for a B.Sc. – got himself a degree. I think he fancied himself an academic. And he put money away, meanwhile, so that Muriel could go to university. He would've loved her to have done that. But when the time came, she couldn't be bothered. She just went and got married instead.'

I tell Beryl that she herself did well to get into the Civil Service at sixteen.

'Not really,' she says crisply. 'In those days there were only three things you could do if you were a girl – be a nurse, be a teacher, or go into the Civil Service. My older brother Philip didn't even have a job, so someone had to go out and earn some money.'

'Walter Hinkley was OK,' she went on. 'A bit egotistical, I would say. Took himself very seriously. I preferred his brother Charles – he was, I suppose, more easy-going and friendly.'

Charles! I jump on this and ask her if Charles married and, if so, did he have children?

'Oh yes. He married Helen – her name was Helen but everyone in the family always called her Polly. They had a girl called Pat, and I think when they were first married they stayed living with the old folk in Clapham.'

'In Lillieshall Road?'

'I think so. Pat might even have been born there. Charles was a civil servant like Walter. He started as a clerical officer with the Post Office or something and then got evacuated up to Harrogate, but he ended up doing very well because he got on better with people than his brother. He was more approachable and sympathetic. And, you know, I think it always niggled at Walter that Charles had done so well.

'Now I remember, there were two girls, two cousins of Charles and Walter, and they were orphaned and the Hinkleys took them in, I think. Izzy and Nellie – I think their name was Hussey. And the Hinkleys did this good generous deed, but of course their resources had to mainly be concentrated on the boys so, once the girls were old enough, they both went into service – it sounds awful, but it wasn't so bad then.

'And one time – I don't know if it was before or after the war – I met up with Izzy in London when she was working as a parlourmaid in Kensington and we went to see *Aida* at the Opera House! Anyway they both went to work at a house in the country and Izzy married one of the gardeners . . .'

I ask her if they had any children, or if she knows the gardener's name. She says she doesn't but she thinks if they'd ever had children she'd have heard, so maybe they didn't.

I ask Beryl if she has children. She says no.

'My fiancé was killed in the war.'

'Oh, I'm sorry.'

'I did have someone else, but – well, it's all right. Children are sometimes a lot of trouble, aren't they?'

'You know,' she says before we say goodbye, 'I think Walter always fancied himself a writer. He wrote a poem from the point of view of a ginger tom cat once. Quite a good poem it was.'

* * *

The electoral register for 1918 comes in two separate parts: the normal volume and a separate list of absent electors. This tells me that, in 1918, Charles Edwin Hinkley was in France, serving with the 4th Battalion, Bedfordshire Regiment.

Knowing that, I am back at Kew, opening a box of war diaries. Wafer thin paper, each one recording the daily activities of the battalion. No copperplate, just simple pencil-written block letters, the lieutenant colonel's signature in the bottom right-hand corner. I imagine these sheets being written in the trenches, in the reserve lines, in the farmhouse billets. One day's entry might feature 'Battalion Sports Day', the next might record, quite matter-of-factly, '2nd Lieutenant Ruddock killed, 9 Ors killed, 10 gassed'. Medals are awarded, often posthumously.

When I ring the regimental museum in Luton, the man tells me, half-awestruck, half-proud: "They took a pounding, the 4th Battalion: over nineteen thousand casualties."

Charles gets a letter in France to say that, by the way, they've moved – but only round the corner, from Broadhinton to Lillieshall. Renting off a Miss Spawton.

'It's lovely here,' his mother writes. 'We have a room downstairs, which is better for your father's rheumatism. And besides it's got a lovely garden, you should see the garden, Charlie.'

He'd have liked his homecoming to have been a bit quiet and private, but there's no hope of that frankly, none at all. They know so many people in that road already, all those regulars from the Tim Bobbin for a start. He hurries up from North Street, past the cottages, hoping that he might sneak in the white gate of Number 34 without any neighbours snooping on him. But then there's old Granny Potter coming out of Number 27 and waddling off down the road with her ale jug, off to the Tim Bobbin, and he knows it's already too late.

'he hurries up from North Street, past the cottages.'

She spots him and straightaway bobs her head back inside, and before he knows it all the small Potters have been ushered out to wave to him and shout welcome home! He waves back brightly, tries to smile, offers them a salute.

'Do they know you're back? Does your Ma know?'

Granny Potter hurries over and grabs at his arm and he smells her skirts and beer breath. 'C'mon, lad, don't be a slowcoach – she's going to be in heaven, your Ma is – don't keep her waiting. Let's go and tell her together, shall we?'

The front gate of Number 34 is hanging half off its hinges. You'd think Walter would have fixed it for them. But then he's the one who does that sort of thing – practical, handy Charles. Walter's the brainy one – getting out of the war on account of his hearing, turning a convenient deaf ear to anything that doesn't suit him.

The front window's open, drapes grimy with soot from the street. Mrs Potter leans and calls through it.

'Mrs Hinkley? Isabella? Coo-ee. Are you there, my dear? You'll never guess who I got here!'

* * *

Eleanor Bingham's letter arrives as promised. Her writing is solid and determined, not at all Tinkerbellish. Wrapped inside is a tiny black-and-white snap.

'Walter (Mr Hinkley) is standing at the back, the tall one,' writes Eleanor, 'with Lewis (Muriel's husband) next to him. Lottie is seated on the left, my mother in the middle and Muriel to the right in front of Lewis. This is when we first met up with them in the early 50s. You are welcome to keep the photo, also the enclosed letter from Walter. It's addressed to me as "Sheila", the name I used at the time.'

'the sprightly little man with a juvenile wit'

I look at Walter Hinkley. Tall, darkish, with a kindly, angular face. White shirt tucked into high-waisted trousers, shortish dark tie, hands clasped behind his back. He looks genial, as if he had a sense of humour. But nervous too. Shy perhaps. I think I had imagined a thicker set, more solid person.

And then Muriel, his daughter, sitting very calmly, smiling – she's a hefty, plump woman, very dark-haired, almost Latin colouring. Her plump arms clasped in the lap of her floral print dress. Legs slightly apart the way fat people tend to sit. There's something proud and implacable about the set of her face, the way she holds herself. Isabella Hinkley's granddaughter. The girl who let her father down by refusing any further education. 'And what of it?' she seems to be saying.

And then Lewis, her husband. The 'sprightly little man with a juvenile wit', as Eleanor described him. He is small and smiling a little too hard, frizzy hair side-parted and sticky-up. Thick bushy eyebrows, irritating smile.

He sits there in the front room of the new house and tries to get his bearings, tries to get himself steady again; but even here, in peacetime, it's hard to stop his hands shaking and his heart banging.

Charles knew that coming back wouldn't be easy, but he thought at least he'd have a chance to breathe, to think about normal things again. Beer and girls and whatever else he used to fill his head with before he saw men lying face down in the mud in France.

He watches his Ma slowly and calmly laying the table for supper in the kitchen, getting the place settings exactly so, while his father snoozes, safe behind the *South London Press*. He listens to that peculiar Miss Spawton, thumping away on her piano upstairs, or asking Wally – to whom she seems to have taken an unhealthy shine – to lift some books down for her: 'Not that one, the one to the left of it – the brown one, yes, yes, that's it!' and he wonders why he feels so numb, why it all seems to wash over him.

He can't even get himself excited about the Blagrove girl any more. He saw her the other day, walking down Orlando Road, and she even smiled at him but he could hardly be bothered to smile back. They're music people. He saw the great piano being lifted in through the front bay window. He used to love music, before the war. People say there's violins being played there in that house every hour of the day.

Uncle Walter's letter – sent to me by Eleanor Bingham and written on yellowed sheets of A4 pulled out of a ring binder – is sent from St Leonards-on-Sea, dated 15 February 1976.

In February 1976 I am sixteen and we move house – yet again – to 762 Mansfield Road. It's our second move in almost as many years, but my sisters and I don't mind. We like this new house. It has something the last house didn't have. It has boys.

The phrase 'the boy next door' takes on a whole new meaning when we discover that no less than five of them live on the other side of the hedge. Ranging in age from fifteen-ish to twenty-five-ish. We peek over at the evidence: motorbikes outside, bits of cars, grease-stained rags, nuts, bolts. A mother who looks small and tired. A poodle that is always shouted at. Jeans on the washing line – jeans and Y-fronts, endless, glorious pairs of them.

While I was spying on the boys next door in Nottingham in February 1976, many miles away, in a guesthouse called 'Mayfair' in St Leonards-on-Sea, Uncle Wally Hinkley was sitting down with an A4 pad and a biro to write:

Dear Sheila

I see that your last letter is dated 13 Jan. How one's life slips away! We were delighted to learn that you had such an enjoyable Christmas. We had a quite pleasant time here. Quiet but comfortable and as usual we were extremely well looked after. We think ourselves lucky in being at the Mayfair, but we are beginning to wonder how much longer the Taylors can keep the place going. Help in the house is dear and also difficult to get and keep. Without the two mothers who constantly come in to give a hand I am afraid the place would have closed months ago. Things were reasonable before young Robert arrived – his sister is now ten – but two children, plus running the hotel, makes a great deal of work and the house from the point of view of stairs seems to be built on the lighthouse principle, up and up and ever upward. And costs are forever mounting also.

But there, this effusion is becoming a pessimistic moan. And 'why fret about tomorrow if today etc'

345

The great world so far seems to be leaving us alone – and may it long continue. Each passing week seems to make it more and more of a frantic lunatic asylum. 'Those whom the gods wish to destroy' – no need to finish.

Mayfair storms do sometimes occur but compared with events outside they are not storms in a tea cup but rather in a thimble.

And it all began with the pigeons. The advice given to the animals on leaving the ark – go forth and multiply – seems to have been taken very seriously to heart by the tribe and most conscientiously observed over the millennia – judging from the numbers here. People, usually elderly ladies, persistently feed them. In our next room, there is a very small lady, very talkative (she has been a teacher). She has also a very kind heart.

One day a pigeon sat on the balcony rail outside her window. Poor thing he must be hungry – so she put out some biscuit pieces. The next morning two pigeons sat waiting – poor things they must be hungry – so more biscuit pieces etc. But the good news spread rapidly – by pigeon post I presume. Next morning there were four pigeons, the next eight. By the end of the week a dozen or more sat waiting cheek by jowl (if that is correct for pigeons) all along the rail and for most of the day.

So far so good (or not so bad) but the rail is just over the house entrance. And very soon the broad top step, instead of being a shiny red brown became a dirty grey and one came into the house and went out of it at one's peril. All this raised some comment by other residents – and the edict went forth – no more pigeon feeding! The broad top step is now once more a bright shiny brown. And peace reigns again.

Did we tell you before, Muriel and Lewis are coming here for a week March 20–27? Rather early for a seaside holiday – but we are hoping for the best. They are staying at no 11 next door. A little dear perhaps (£25 a week) but we understand the food is good, plentiful and the lounge and bedroom comfortable.

We lost a resident last week, she had been here four years, but joins a friend in a small hotel a little further West, still on the front. We are now only eleven – and this means a considerable financial loss to the Taylors. Somebody may of course come to take her place – but the stairs require someone (especially the last flight) with almost mountaineering ability and a head for heights.

With regard to Auntie Minnie. She was the youngest of three sisters, all clever – she was vivacious and musical. Lettie was about 8 when she died, which means some 87 years ago (1888 or 1889). She bought a house near the Maddams house and let part of it. A Mr Phillips came as a lodger. He seems to have been something of a world traveller (at least abroad). They had only been married, Lettie thinks, about two years when she died of pneumonia. Lettie does not know the church if any. He was very very upset. He married again about a year later but it seems much less happily. He was a skilled cabinet maker and made some beautiful furniture. And now after all this, we do hope you are keeping well and getting better and better and will be kept unharmed in these terrible times. We both send our love to you,

Lettie and Walter

'That's where Alex lived,' I hiss at Jonathan as we walk up the steep, jasmine-scented steps to 762 Mansfield Road. 'Through that hedge there. If we leaned out of our bedroom windows we could wave to each other.'

'He's one of the five boys, right?'

'The one I went out with.'

'I thought you went out with all of them.'

'Don't be silly. Alex was my first real boyfriend.'

'I thought Serge the Smoky Frenchman was your first?'

'That was one kiss. I actually went out with Alex. On the back of his bike.'

'Your mother must have loved that.'

Laura and Nigel, the current owners, have just got back from Brighton with their three kids – and a new baby rabbit.

'She's called Smudge,' says the little girl, as they all crowd and fight to hold her. The rabbit trembles, flattens its ears.

'That rabbit needs to go back in the hutch now,' says their Dad. 'It's going to be traumatized.' He scoops it out of their hands and walks out of the back door.

762 Mansfield Road was unmistakably built in the twenties: mock Tudor, parquet floors, generously proportioned rooms, it has that glamorous Charleston party feel to it. We are in the open hall with French windows onto the lawn, where my sisters and I danced to *Saturday Night Fever* and Abba and *Grease*. The stairs come sweeping down on the left – flapper stairs! – and there used to be a huge fireplace facing the French windows. But now it's been turned into a horrid leather-studded bar. Laura warned me about this on the phone – 'the people before us did it' – in case I thought it was their gruesome taste.

I go upstairs into Laura and Nigel's room – my old bedroom, which faces down on to the lawn. There's now a swanky built-in wardrobe with mirrors all down the side where my bed was. I wept in that bed when I broke up with Alex and wrote in my diary that I would never love anyone again. We only broke up because I demanded that he choose between me and his 'other girlfriend', who was older than me and at Oxford. Asking him to choose was a mistake – he unhesitatingly chose her. I only ever glimpsed Gail once, through the hedge. She had on a long white dress and she seemed to be everything I would never be: beautiful, languid, and terminally aloof.

'Are you all right in there?' Nigel asks me.

'Fine,' I say, realizing I've been standing far too long in silence in their bedroom.

* * *

Three weeks ago, Jonathan sent letters off to half of the Hinkleys in this country. At last one of them pays off.

Our letters feature the one fact we know for sure – that Charles Hinkley had a daughter called Patricia who married a man called Victor Bourne.

> **From:** Pete Hinkley
> **To:** Julie Myerson
> **Subject:** 34 Lillieshall Road
>
> Hi my name is peter I had an uncle eddie and aunty pat who married a vic bourne . . . I look forward to hearing from you.
>
>
> regards
> Peter

'Yesss!' Jonathan punches the air with a fist. 'Our first direct descendant.'

We agree that the reference to Pat and Victor Bourne makes him our man. He has to be some relation – what relation? – to our Isabella and Walter.

'Grandson,' Jonathan says. 'No, great-grandson. If Pat was his aunt and Charles was Pat's father, then Walter and Isabella have to have been Pete's great-grandparents.'

I call the mobile number Peter gave me and he answers and says to call him back on his house number – 'it's cheaper' – then he confesses he can never remember it. After three attempts, he finds it. I call him back.

He says his Dad was from Mitcham and that his Auntie Pat is long dead – twenty years ago now – of a brain tumour. They had a son called Colin who would be a bit younger than him (Pete) now. Pete is fifty-four. But he has no idea whether Victor Bourne or Colin are alive because he lost touch with the family after Auntie Pat died and that was that.

'Do you know what your grandfather was called?' I ask him. 'Was he called Charles?'

'I've no idea. He died before I was born. He was killed at the gas works in an explosion. At least that's what I was told.'

He says his Dad is called Kenneth and he's in a home. 'He doesn't remember anything, I'm afraid. I'm not being funny. He doesn't even remember me.'

I ask if his Dad had any brothers or sisters apart from Pat.

'Oh yeah, about twenty!'

But Beryl Lloyd had told me she thought Charles and Polly only had Pat.

'Let me count . . . there was Wally, who's dead; Bobby, who's dead; Reginald is my Dad, but everyone calls him Kenneth; and there was Uncle . . . Actually my ex was doing some research into the family history, so I'll ask her if you like.'

It's been a flaming hot day but as evening comes, so does the wind. It grows colder, shadows creep over the lawn.

'Why are you getting all dressed up?' Chloë asks me, catching me changing my top and putting on lipstick.

'Pete's coming round. Pete Hinkley.'

'The one who's a plumber?'

'That's right. He's the great-grandson of Isabella and Walter who lived here.'

'Have you had a plumber round for a drink before?'

'I don't think we have, no.'

'Which earrings?' asks Chloë, getting into the spirit now. 'I think the long red sparkly ones!'

'I think that would be a bit much, don't you? On a Sunday evening.'

She flings herself in the chair next to my dressing table. Her feet are black with dirt from the garden.

'So you don't care whether you look attractive?'

'I don't want to make him feel underdressed.'

I get a vodka and curl on the sofa and hope Pete arrives soon. I feel peculiar – raw, unprepared. Isabella and Walter's great-grandson – and we're going to have a drink in the last room they lived in before Reggie threw them out.

'That won't mean much to him,' Jonathan reminds me. 'You've been living with all these stories a long time, remember? And anyway Pete's going to be a lot more nervous than you.'

'How long since a Hinkley was in this house, d'you think?' asks Chloë

'That's a good question,' I tell her. '1948, I suppose.'

On the dot of seven, Pete and his daughter come up the path. The dog goes crazy and I send Jake to tie her up. Pete shakes my hand. He's small, skinny, mid-fifties, ruddy-faced. His daughter is tall, dark, and slender, with glasses.

'I'm Kirsten.'

I sit them on the sofa and we get a beer for Pete. Kirsten just wants a Pepsi. We don't have Pepsi, only Coke. Or lemonade?

'OK, thanks, lemonade is fine.'

Pete sits forward on the sofa and so does Kirsten.

Pete admits he knows nothing of his family – barely more than he's told me on the phone – but that his ex has promised to get in touch. 'She's been doing the family tree.'

'First she did her side,' Kirsten explains, 'then she moved on to his.'

I start by telling Pete all I know. That Walter and Isabella Hinkley lived around the corner at 2 Broadhinton Road and probably had Walter Stephen and Charles Edwin (Pete's grandfather) while living there. Then, at the end of the First World War, they moved in here – Charles, probably came straight back to this house from France – and as far as I know both boys were married from this house. That Walter senior worked as a railwayman and then as a shipwright in Deptford and at the docks in Chatham.

That meanwhile Walter Stephen, the elder son, studied hard and became a Customs and Excise Officer but always begrudged the fact that Charles Edwin got a slightly better job – in the Post Office and then as a civil servant in Harrogate. Walter married Lettie Maddams, who'd lost an eye when struck by the silver knob on a walking stick – 'Oh!' Kirsten laughs 'Horrible!' – and whose twin sister Olivia was the mother of Philip and Beryl, both of whom I've been in contact with.

Pete says he's never heard of any of them.

I then tell him that Walter and Lettie had one child, Muriel, who married Lewis Jones and died at sixty. I show them the photo. Pete says Walter Hinkley's crinkly hair does look a lot like his family.

Meanwhile Charles married Helen, also known as Polly, and they had a daughter called Patricia who married Victor Bourne.

'I knew Vic Bourne,' Pete says. 'He used to drive to the east coast all the time in his dormobile. And Pat had loads of brothers and sisters. About twenty.'

Jonathan looks at him.

'I'm not joking. They lived in Fieldgate Lane in Mitcham and there were hundreds of them.'

'How could anyone manage to have twenty?' says Jonathan.

'Well, three lots of twins – and some died.'

Jonathan looks impressed.

Pete tries to remember the names. 'There was Edward, Wally, Bet – she died – she got a very rare illness where she had to have a special suit made and wear it all the time – '

'An allergy of some sort?' I ask him.

'Think so. Jimmy Saville helped raise money for the suit. It was on the telly. Then Pat – she died of a brain tumour – my Dad, Reginald Kenneth, known as Ken – and then Bobby. That's all I can actually name, but I know there was a lot more.'

Pete says he thinks Bobby could still be alive and may be living in Mitcham.

'Do you know what he did for a living?' I ask him.

Pete looks at us and smiles. 'He was a scoundrel.'

'A what?'

'I'm telling you – that's the only word for it. A con artist.'

'What sort of things did he do?' asks Jonathan.

'Married older women for their money, waited till they died, then married again. He was a right spiv, a charmer.'

'Was he good-looking?' I ask.

'All Hinkleys are,' Pete quips, deadpan.

'Did he have any children?'

'He can't have,' says Jonathan, 'if the wives were all so old.'

'Oh,' says Pete, 'he had a wife, to start with. There was a son called Terry, I know that. He was just as bad though. Another scoundrel.'

Jonathan and I look at each other, both thinking the same thing. We've got to find Bob and Terry.

Kirsten meanwhile has barely touched her lemonade and is still clutching her bag.

'Can I just say, I love the colour you've got on these walls,' she says, and I thank her.

'Yeah, I really love the bright colours.'

I ask Pete if he'd like another beer and he says he would. Jonathan gets it and goes in to start cooking for the kids, who are flumping down the stairs.

Pete tells me about his Dad, who's in a home in Knight's Hill – the one who barely recognizes him any more. 'But his long-term memory might be much better,' he says, and I ask whether he thinks it would be OK for me to go and see him – as long as it didn't upset him. I'd quite understand if he said no, but Pete seems quite happy with this idea.

'Might cheer him up,' suggests Kirsten.

Pete says if the home won't let me see him, then he'll come with me – 'I haven't seen him myself in two years,' he adds cheerily. 'I should've really, but he don't know me so what's the point? I found it a bit depressing actually.'

I ask him what his Dad did and he says he built brick ovens – the kind McVitie's used. 'But he went to pieces when his wife died – attacked my brother with a hatchet and we had to have him arrested. They found seven hundred whisky bottles in his place when they cleared it out. He went in the home soon after that.'

Pete then tells me his mother Eileen was German, from a wealthy family called Weber, and that they had a factory that made prisms in Lancing, used in the Lancaster bomber during the war. But her family never forgave her for marrying beneath her and she cut herself off from them and refused their money when they offered it later. 'She'd put the phone down and say, "I don't want to know."'

I tell Pete and Kirsten about Reggie Povah throwing poor Walter and Isabella out of the house and putting them in an old people's home; and then we realize it happened in the year Pete was born – 1948.

I ask Pete about his work. He's a plumber at St Thomas's Hospital – before that at the Portland.

'You specialize in hospitals, then?'

'I dunno. I've been at Guy's too. One thing I meant to tell you by the way – there's an Australian darts player, name of Peter Hinkley. He's quite well-known down under . . . well, he's related to us. I don't know quite how but my ex found that one out.'

The Archduke's funeral's in all the papers. So much black ink, such worldwide shock. The headlines are stark, almost exciting. They say it's ignited a spark, that something's got to happen now, that Austria-Hungary won't back down, can't back down.

Tom sits in the kitchen at Number 34, knocks the head of his pipe on the table, dabs at the strands of tobacco with his finger and thumb, wonders when he'll get his papers and, if he does, whether he'll be up to frightening the Hun. Matilda dreads him going, dreads being left alone when they've only been married a year or so.

'You think I planned it this way?' he asks her.

For now, there are other things to attend to. He's been summoned by Aunt Lucy because his grandmother is dying. There have been some false alarms recently, but this time they're sure. They think it might even be today. Lucy's been sitting up with her since the middle of the night.

There's only Lucy and him left to mind. She sent John a telegram yesterday, but no one's expecting him to arrive. Tom hasn't seen his father for over a year now.

It's a hot day, record temperatures – it's been a record summer all round. Tom takes out his handkerchief and wipes his head, his neck. All the windows are thrown open on to the garden. He can hear the insects hovering over Lucy's marigolds. And now Lucy's feet on the stairs.

'Poor you, you're worn out.'

She looks terrible, dark shadows under her eyes.

'It won't be long now,' she tells Tom. 'I'm just going to put the kettle on. Do you want to go up, see if she knows you one more time?'

It's eleven in the morning. Tom coughs and climbs the stairs to Lucy's sitting room on the first floor where a makeshift bed has been set up for old Mrs Spawton. The room has all its windows closed and is unbearably fuggy. The smell isn't good either. Tom holds his tobacco fingers under his nose.

Outside in the street, a cart clatters by. But when he glances out of the window to look at it, it's not there. The street's deserted. A ghost of its usual busy self.

And something funny will happen then, on that hot, soaring July morning in Lillieshall Road. Lucy Spawton will be on the point of heating water for tea but will allow herself just one quick moment of sitting down at the kitchen table – just one! – but will immediately be demolished by fatigue and will lay her small dark head down on her arms and, seconds later, will be asleep. Breathing like a baby. She's been attending to her mother since three.

And upstairs, Tom – funny young-old Tom in his waistcoat and slightly effete cravat – will bend to say good morning to his Gran and will take her hot, dry hand in his and, fooled for a moment by the way her head shifts and lolls on the pillow, will believe she is still alive.

But then he'll look more closely, and realize that it was only the head's own weight that made it move, that there's no breath, no pulse, nothing. That her face is strangely clear of expression. He's never seen her look like that, relieved of her burdens – almost hopeful.

> ELIZABETH SPAWTON. FEMALE. 81 YEARS. WIDOW OF THOMAS HARLOCK SPAWTON, MASTER DRAPER. PULMONARY CONGESTION. CARDIAC FAILURE. THOMAS H B SPAWTON, GRANDSON, PRESENT AT THE DEATH. NINTH JULY 1914. 34 LILLIESHALL ROAD.

And he'll have to go downstairs and wake Lucy, who'll be furious with herself for having fallen asleep, and the doctor will be sent for and demand gently to know whether he, Tom – the grandson – was present at the death. And he'll say he doesn't know. He thinks so, but how can he really be sure?

But, almost exactly thirty years on from that day, on another hot July morning, during another World War, in a Battersea hospital, someone will ask him the very same question about his Aunt Lucy and the answer that he will have to give – one that will linger and gnaw at him for the rest of his own life – will be:

'No, I wasn't there, I'm afraid she died alone.'

> LUCY SPAWTON. FEMALE. 77 YEARS. OF 34 LILLIESHALL ROAD. SPINSTER. DRAPER'S BUYER. DAUGHTER OF THOMAS HARLOCK

SPAWTON, DRAPER (DECEASED). TOXAEMIA. LARGE BEDSORES.
PARALYSIS AGITANS. FIFTEENTH JULY 1944.

Thomas Spawton must have finally been reconciled with his father, John.

At the Public Record Office at Kew, I try to find out which regiment Thomas served in. Though his service record is gone, burned in the Blitz, the medal rolls show that he served with the Army Service Corps. Private 022148 Thomas Spawton. And next to him, alphabetically, there in the lists is John H. Spawton, Corporal T2/11651.

There they are, father and son, together at last, serving in what was known as Ally Sloper's Cavalry, providing transport across the entire Western Front.

I like to imagine that Thomas was conscripted – he turned eighteen in 1902 – and that John, by then fifty-something, volunteered so as to be alongside his only son, the only future for the family name of Spawton.

I sit in a brown room at the psychiatric unit of the Maudsley on Knight's Hill and wait to see Kenneth Hinkley, son of Charles Edwin Hinkley, grandson of Walter and Isabella.

The duty nurse – a gently solid, soft-spoken West Indian man – sits me down and explains that Ken's 'lucidity' varies very much from day to day.

'Sometimes he is very hard to wake, sometime he just wants to sleep. He can suddenly become very angry.'

I tell him that I understand all of this, that I don't necessarily expect to get anything from Ken. And I wouldn't want to upset him either. I add for good measure that a long time ago, as a student, I worked in a psycho-geriatric ward.

The nurse smiles. 'You know what I'm talking about then.'

In the 'long-stay' geriatric ward at Sherwood Hospital in Nottingham, I was a nursing auxiliary for a single summer – the same summer that I went out with Alex Next Door. I sluiced out bedpans, spooned mush into toothless mouths. I was attacked twice by a woman called Megan, who gave me three long scratches down one cheek, drawing blood with her thick, yellow nails. In Knight's Hill now, it's actually the smell that takes me straight back to that summer: urine, mashed potatoes, sheets and blankets fresh from the laundry with 'hospital property' stamped on them – and something else much harder to define. The oldness of skin, the closeness of death?

But Knight's Hill is not a depressing place at all. Sitting here in the brown room and waiting for my nurse to fetch Kenneth, I can hear snatches of Radio 2, nurses laughing, trolleys squeaking. The room has pink and blue chairs, a blue filing cabinet, a gently ticking clock and silk flowers – carnations and gladioli – in a vase. Also a table and a blackboard.

I wait for what feels like quite a few minutes, and then the nurse returns looking hassled. He plonks a cup of tea down on the table and looks at me.

'He doesn't want to know. But I'm going to have another try.'

The tea sits there, cooling, half of it slopped in the saucer. Five minutes later, the nurse reappears leading a very tall, slim man by the hand. His thick grey hair is sticking up to one side as if he's slept on it and his ears are tufted with thick black hair, also sticking upwards. He gazes at me with very pale and distant blue eyes. His face is fierce, shattered. His shirt has many stains down the front. He shuffles in and allows himself to be put in a chair. Immediately he picks up the cup of tea and, staring straight ahead of him, starts to slurp.

I've brought him some biscuits, a last-minute present snatched from our kitchen cupboard as I left the house. I ask the nurse if I can offer one to Ken and he nods, so I ask Ken if he'd like a biscuit.

He says nothing, so I tear open the packet – noticing that they're

358

past their sell-by date – and hold it out to him. He does nothing, so I take three of the biscuits out and put them on the table in front of him. He snatches them up immediately and crams all three into his mouth. My heart sinks as I see they've gone completely soft, way past their best.

Ken still stares straight ahead of him and says nothing.

'I'm writing a book,' I tell him, and my clear, friendly voice sounds ridiculous, 'and I want to know if you remember your Dad – Charles Edwin Hinkley?'

He says nothing, doesn't even look at me.

'Or your Gran and Grandad, Walter and Isabella? Do you ever remember coming to their house in Clapham to visit them?'

He turns his head slightly so he can see me, keeps on munching the soft biscuits. I pull a couple more out of the packet and put them near him and he snatches them up. He sucks up his tea and it dribbles down his chin.

'Do you remember your Uncle Wally and Aunt Lettie? Or two girls called Izzie and Nelly Hussey? Did your Dad serve in the First World War? Can you remember anything he told you about that?'

Nothing.

'Can you tell me anything about anyone in your family?' I say at last. The nurse sighs and looks at me. Then he leans over and grabs Ken's shoulder.

'Your Dad, Ken!' he bellows. 'Do you remember what your Dad's name was?'

Ken throws up his hands and looks troubled. 'I can't understand . . .' he mouths, shaking his head. These are the first words he's spoken. I tell him it's OK, that he doesn't have to say anything.

'I'm a total stranger,' I tell him, 'I'm sorry. It's just – so very nice just to meet you. You're very kind to see me at all.'

When I say that, he seems to focus for a moment on my face, as if he's seeing me for the first time. He moves slightly closer, but his eyes are cold. I shiver and have to look away. His face is getting closer and the rest of the room's receding, making me feel dizzy.

'Is there anything you can tell this lady about your family, Ken?' the nurse shouts again.

The shout sounds too loud, too aggressive, but I remember my time on the ward. It's not like the outside world, with its niceties, its polite distances. You have to lose those to do the job. I notice the nurse has a large plaster on one hand. I remember the sudden lashings out, the momentary loss of control.

Ken puts his hands up and mouths 'I don't understand' again.

I can't bear it any longer. 'It's OK,' I tell the nurse, 'I honestly think he's had enough.'

The nurse gets up then and Ken points to himself with a questioning look.

'Yes. Come on, Ken. Let's get you back.'

I ask the nurse if any family members ever visit Ken.

'There's one son comes at Christmas and birthdays and he takes a while to get going but he likes that. No one else, not for years.'

'How many years has he been here?'

'Let me see, he was here before me, so at least five. All he does is sleep,' he says. 'You know? All he wants is bed. Any bed, if he sees it, he just goes right over to it and lies down and closes his eyes.'

I take one more look at Walter and Isabella's grandson as he shuffles slowly out of the door.

'Goodbye,' I say to his tall, erect back. 'It was lovely to meet you.'

He doesn't look back. On the table is half a cup of tea, mostly spilled in the saucer. A cellophane pack of open biscuits, crumbs, my pen, my pad, on which I've written nothing.

I get home to find a message from Jonathan on my machine. 'Call me on my mobile. I've come across something you don't want to hear.'

He's at the Metropolitan Archives. He's supposed to be at the Family

Records Centre, starting the hunt for Edward or Edwin Maslin or Maslen or Maslem. 'Just popped in here. Remember you never finished checking the electoral registers?'

'And ... ?'

'Well, I just got to 1962. Who on earth were Godwin and Mary Akagbu?'

'No idea. Never heard of them.'

'Well, they lived here in 1962.'

'They weren't in Kelly's ...'

'They're on the electoral register, sweetheart. Alvin must have rented them a room. Hey, maybe even married one of them.'

'Oh God.'

'Better start tracing them quick.'

I think about this and feel suddenly exhausted.

'Hmm, it's just ...'

'What?'

'I suppose I just wonder whether ...'

'I know what you're going to say. Don't.'

'No, look, I'm just thinking out loud here. I mean, they were only here for a year, or less from what you're saying, maybe just the month the register was compiled. And we've come across them so late and we never knew about them before and I mean ...'

'Yes?'

'I mean is anyone ever going to know we even found out about them?'

'I thought you had this big thing about honesty?'

'I do!'

'Well, then.'

'Please. Let's at least think about it, OK?'

Later that night, in the hot garden, I tell Jonathan about the visit to Kenneth Hinkley in the Maudsley.

'It wasn't a bad place – really pretty pleasant in some ways. But the idea that you end your days in a building like that, which has nothing whatsoever to do with you or your previous life, surrounded by caring people who you don't know and never did.'

'Same way his grandparents ended theirs,' Jonathan observes. 'Thrown out of here by Reggie and shipped off to Hackney.'

That had crossed my mind too. I'd looked at Kenneth's face and wondered whether that's how Walter had looked at the end – bewildered, displaced, homeless.

I tell Jonathan about the biscuits. 'The awful thing is, I knew they might be past their sell-by date when I took them, but I didn't bother to check. I felt really horrible when he put them in his mouth and I saw they'd gone all soft.'

Jonathan puts his feet on a deckchair. The honeysuckle glows white amid the greenish darkness. It's a hot night, the air barely cooler than it was during the day.

'He won't have noticed,' he says.

'No, I know. But I did. I noticed. My only chance, finally, to meet a grandchild of our Walter and Isabella – Charles's son! – and what do I do? Bring him soggy biscuits.'

Jonathan sips his wine.

'It broke my heart actually,' I tell him.

Chapter Eight

ELECTRIC LIGHT AND A
SEWING MACHINE

The Haywards
1881–1893

The house is perfect. Perfect and entirely, delectably, empty.

She knows this from the first moment that she rocks up on to her toes on the well-kept front lawn and peers in through the dusty bay window. She hopes no one will see her and think she's snooping, but she can't help it: once she's lifted the latch on the wooden gate and crept along the smart tiled path and knocked gingerly and got no answer, then she can't help it. She simply has to peep in.

Helena House, Lillieshall Road, Number 34. There's a new pavement outside and smart black iron railings, and some houses even have the optimistic beginnings of hedges. She's wandered up and down the road once or twice before now, smelling coffee on the wind from the nearby factory, and told herself how promising it looked – though the cottages on what used to be Orchard Street are still as run-down as ever, with their lines of shabby washing blowing outside and old tin cans of pink geraniums, the leaves brown and in need of watering.

Still, Helena House. Sounds imperial, Napoleonic, a bit French. She overheard someone in Stringer & Bird saying it might be for rent, which is odd as there's no sign in the window. But it's just as she thought. An elegant sort of place – high ceilings, well proportioned, pleasing in all its aspects.

She squints to see through a chink in the muslin curtains. The front room is most curiously furnished. Some of the things you'd fully expect are there – such as the large table with a good, heavy cloth on it, the easy chair with its (thankfully) fresh-looking linen antimacassar, even the three separate rugs, quite new-looking, strewn at intervals on the polished pine floor.

But there's no oil lamp – why? – nor even a single brass candlestick on the table. Even more curiously, no coal scuttle. Can anyone manage without a coal scuttle? Well, she'd personally like to see it. And yet there are various fripperies: a great big fern case – empty, yet clean as far as she can see. And a sewing machine – she could do with a sewing machine actually: that would really be a productive thing to have. And yet no books – you'd think there'd be a few books – and not a painting in sight, nor a photograph. No trace of anyone living there in fact.

She's just deciding to herself that this place is most definitely unloved – an empty house, part-furnished and just waiting for her to cherish it – when she spies the most exciting thing of all, and the reason, presumably, for the lack of an oil lamp. Hanging there in the centre of the room is an electric light, complete with electric light bulb and damask shade! Almost as exciting as the sewing machine.

'It's in one of those lovely wide new roads near the Common,' Charlotte Hayward tells her husband Henry that night, 'quite near to the shops but not too near. Lillieshall, with an "ie", not a "y".'

'There's a village in Shropshire called Lilleshall,' offers Frank from his jigsaw on the floor.

'Don't interrupt, Frank. You'd find it just to your taste, Henry, I know you would. Modern and clean and all that. And it's got electricity.'

'Electricity?' Now Henry looks up from his paper.

'Yes, but best of all, do you know, there's a sewing machine!'

'Not a sewing machine!' says Arthur sarcastically. 'Now then, what more could a person want, eh, Frank?'

'There is nothing more truly delightful in all this world,' agrees his brother, 'than a sewing machine. Far more desirable, naturally, than an electric light.'

'Please, boys, please!' Florrie joins in now, rolling her eyes and prostrating herself on the carpet. 'you're getting me into quite a nervous state over this – what did you call it? – a sewing machine!'

At this Molly starts to bark loudly and Henry laughs, but their mother ignores them, chews on a fingernail, twists a light strand of hair back behind her ear.

'Just find out if it's for rent, my dear, please do. It's definitely just standing empty.'

'But how do you know that it's empty?' Henry points out. 'You say yourself that you saw furniture in there, and then also that there's no rental notice.'

'Maybe it's a secret,' quips Frank. 'Maybe it's for rent but they don't want a single soul to know. Don't want them in there, using that sewing machine.'

'My love, the chap in Stringer & Bird said he thought they would be pasting up a notice very soon.' Charlotte turns to Henry, sounding impatient now. 'And anyway, once I'd looked, I was in no doubt. There was dust everywhere, leaves and grit blown up on to the front step. The grass had been recently cut, I think, but the path certainly wasn't swept. It must be available. And if it isn't, we'll persuade them. Please listen to me, my darling. I'm telling you, I just have the strongest feeling about the place.'

Florence glances up from her paper dolls as her mother says this and Henry sighs and puts his head in his hands. They all know what it means when Lottie has one of her 'feelings' about something. It means there'll be no rest till she gets it, whatever the thing happens to be that she's set her heart on.

Last year it was a spaniel. 'Think how good it will be for the children,' she'd implored him, 'and how it will get us out into the fresh air, and such company for me when you go off on one of your trips.'

At first he was firmly set against it but then, after four months' stout resistance, as always, he crumbled. So Lottie got her way as usual. And now look – yes, they all love her, but Molly's also been the bane of their lives. Adored by the children, certainly, but chewing up his papers, knocking over his tea cup with her quick, feathery paws, demanding a walk when London sleet is hitting the window panes. Now Lottie's all but lost patience with the animal and it's him who feeds and grooms it and is glad of its hot little face pressed into his hand.

This year it's this house in Clapham she has suddenly fallen in love with. And next year, when she's had her way and got the house, then what? Actually he knows what it'll be then and he hardly dares think about it. All the warning signs are there, he's just refusing to see them. She's younger than him and strong and healthy, and they always said they'd think about it when Florence was a little older.

'The hall does look a little narrow,' she goes on (Hmm, thinks Henry, too narrow for a perambulator then?). 'But it even looks like it's got a garden at the back, lovely for Molly. Just think, Henry, a garden! To grow things in!'

'Oh my Lord,' says Arthur, 'you don't say? Not a garden to grow things in?' and Florence and Frank fall into giggles all over again.

'That's enough, boys,' Henry says, getting up and folding his paper. 'All right, my dear, I'll see if John Lawrence knows anything.'

'And find out about the sewing machine,' Charlotte adds when he gets up and goes off to write to his friend who works for the *Clapham Gazette*. 'Remember to ask them if it comes with the sewing machine!'

'It's one of those lovely wide new roads near the common.'

The Haywards. Of all the people who have inhabited this space, I like to think they are the most like us.

Same job – well, similar. And the same ages – he's forty-one when he moves in here, she's a little younger. Same number of kids. Henry Hayward, author and journalist. Would we have been their friends if we'd lived next door? Would our children have popped in and out? Would Chloë have sat with Florence and cut and pasted pictures in a scrapbook, just as she does in her curtain-dark, spotlit room now? Would Raph and Frank have tossed a cricket ball or a Frisbee to each other out in the street, while Arthur and Jake sat in an upstairs room and talked about – what? Girls? The Franco-Prussian War? Eminem? Playstation? And would I have exchanged household tips with Charlotte over the hedge? Or maybe I'd have asked her round for a glass of New Zealand Sauvignon Blanc.

Actually, more likely I'd have met up with Henry and talked about writing, about deadlines, about sub-editors. We'd have e-mailed each other in the middle of a long day when bored or stuck. Or, Jonathan and Henry might have played tennis and when we all got together for dinner later, Charlotte, the housewife, might have been miserably left out and I'd have felt bad and tried to include her and failed, and made it worse.

Or maybe it isn't like that at all. Maybe Lottie's a secret, furious writer of poetry – a far more talented author than Henry. Maybe her body of work will be discovered and published and will one day far outlive either of them.

Except if that were the case, we'd know. We'd have heard of her. Hers would be the blue plaque on this house. Charlotte Hayward, poet. *The* Charlotte Hayward.

No, none of it quite works. The easy, seductive parallels stop there. Still, this journey started with them and it almost ends with them. Almost, but not quite.

I used to think they were the first owners, but I know now that they weren't. They never even owned the house in fact – they rented, from the Maslins, who were its real first occupants.

Even so, they're important to me. Henry Hayward – author and journalist – and his wife Charlotte and their two boys and a girl. I still know frustratingly little about them, but we spoke their names in the house on that first autumn day almost a year ago, and those names have lingered tantalizingly in the air ever since.

It was Mr Williams of North Street who saw the drainage going into Orchard Street who heard, over a jar in the Tim Bobbin, that Colonel Bowyer was putting the cricket pitch up for sale.

So he mortgaged himself for a couple of eighteen-foot lots and built Numbers 14 and 15. A few months later he started on 16 and 17. Of course, every few weeks the I'Anson bloke came round and demanded more fees, complained about the quality and strength of the timber, even the colour of the bricks sometimes. Then a little bit of money changed hands and, funnily enough, they began to see eye to eye.

But it's the building that's his thing. Once a house is up and finished, he doesn't really want to know. To this end, he puts his missus in charge of finding tenants. And Edward Maslin is the man that Harriet Williams finds. Edward Maslin, or Maslen, or Maslem.

I'm back in the Family Records Centre trying to find him, however he spells his name. Him and his family – because a single man surely wouldn't rent such a large, family-sized house.

So I decide to start with marriages in 1860. I get an immediate result as the marriage registers show an Edward Maslin getting married to Miss Taylor in March 1861. But then almost immediately they show another Edward Maslin getting married in December 1861 to Miss Dance. Does this mean that Maslin is a commoner name than I have been hoping? Are there going to be far too many Edward Maslins to make my Edward trackable?

But the two marriages so close on each other's heels seem to be coincidence as there are only two more: Edward Maslin marrying Miss Strange in April 1870 and then nothing until Edwin Maslin (could it be Edwin?) marries Miss James in January 1874. I order the certificates, confident that my E. M. must be one of these.

My mother comes for lunch and tells us that my great-aunt Margaret's will is to be read soon. The house in Gainsborough has ten acres of woodland and apparently contains a huge number of valuable violins.

Aunt Margaret – my grandfather's sister – died in February in her late nineties. She never married but kept house for her father after her mother died. Though she had a professional life (playing and teaching the violin), she did what many a young Victorian woman must have done at that time: made herself so indispensable to her ageing father that there was never any question of marriage.

'Your great-grandfather built the house from scratch in the 1920s,' Mum says. 'He refused ever to live in a house where someone had died, you see.'

She says she wants to look around the old house just once before it's sold. She hasn't seen it since she was a child and there were so many stories. The music room where her grandfather, a concert violinist, once saw a ball of fire hurtling towards him. He shut the door and didn't go in for twenty years.

'I sat and ate pigeon pie in the sitting room,' Mum says. 'I remember spitting out the bits of lead shot.'

She adds that she recently discovered that her grandmother had died in suspicious circumstances. 'Alan told me. She's not buried in the family grave. She's in Lea churchyard.'

'In what way suspicious?'

'Just – I don't know – her body was found on the railway line.'

'On the train tracks?'

Mum shrugs. 'Apparently, yes.'

Later, I tell the children the fireball story while they eat their pizza.

'Imagine a big, long, grand, panelled room,' I tell them, remembering my mother's stories, 'and this man goes in and sees this ball of flame rushing through the air towards him. He runs out and shuts the door and doesn't dare go in that room again for many years.'

'How many years?' Chloë asks me.

'Don't know. Lots. Twenty maybe.'

'The room would get so dirty. Who would hoover it?'

But Raphael's still on the fireball. 'Do you think it was real or do you think he was mad?'

I hesitate. 'Well, I don't think I believe there really was a fireball. But, you know, they were a pretty strange family.'

'Your grandfather was the Jesus one, right,' Jake reminds me.

'That's right.'

'The one who had a motorbike accident and hit his head and then said he'd seen Jesus?'

* * *

HAYWARD Henry of Wrencote, 118 Northcourt Road Worthing died 13 November 1917 Probate London 13 December to Florence Hayward spinster and Charlotte Hayward widow. Effects £2569. 5s. 5d.

There he is, dead in Worthing in 1917, with no mention of the boys. What happened? Are they dead? Did they perish in the Great War? I sit down for a moment, not shocked to find him exactly, but just taking in the fact of when he died. I like Henry. I don't want him to die.

Sixteen years later, though, in 1933, there too is Charlotte – she also died at Wrencote in Worthing. Little Florence is named as the executrix.

Henry's will shows that he leaves everything to Charlotte and Florence – including a total of seven houses in Worthing and some Canadian stocks, some War Loan stocks and shares in the Worthing Gas Light and Coke Company. If Charlotte remarries, then the will stipulates that it should all automatically pass to Florence. Is this normal, or is Henry jealously guarding her lonely widowhood? Meanwhile, just a meagre ten pounds each left to Frank and Arthur.

Charlotte's will is in some ways more enlightening – and yet that too bequeaths everything to the girls. By now there's £200 of Canadian Government Inscribed Stock to be divided between her daughter-in-law Lily Matilda Hayward (presumably Arthur or Frank's wife) and her daughter, Ivy Constance, as well as her other daughter-in-law Flora Hayward and her daughter Marjorie Ethel. The rest to Florence. No mention of either of her sons. Has she fallen out with them? Or are they dead? Or is it in fact a rare, enlightened, and resolutely feminist will?

Meanwhile, having discovered that Lily Matilda Hayward, her daughter-in-law, died in 1959, I order her will and find it leaves everything to her son Leslie Bernard, a wholesale confectioner (again, not mentioned in Charlotte's will), and her daughter Ivy Constance, spinster. Wholesale confectioner? A sweet shop owner, then? I can't help smiling at this – the idea that my dashing writer and journalist turns out to have a grandson who makes his living among jars of lemon sherbets and humbugs and rosy apples.

Leslie Bernard died in 1979. He had another brother, Howard Henry Hayward (named after his grandfather?), and he left money to him, to his sister Ivy, as well as to an Alan Hayward and a Winifred Hayward. There's an address for Alan in Glastonbury, Somerset, and 1979 is only twenty years ago. Alan might still be alive.

I'm killing time at the Family Records Centre, waiting until 11 a.m. when my Maslin/Maslen marriage certificates will be ready.

'Do they ever come in early?' I asked on arriving eagerly at 9 a.m.

'Never.'

So I'm checking to see whether Marjorie Ethel Hayward ever married, ever had children. And yes, in 1930, she marries Thomas James Hillier. I march straight over to the birth registers and, almost without trying, find David Hillier born in 1932, mother's maiden name Hayward. I order both certificates and, as it's now 11.30 a.m., head for the collections desk.

I don't know what I hoped for but they're an unpromising crop. My March 1861 Edward gives his profession as 'labourer', as does December 1861 Edward. April 1870 is just a clerk and my January 1874 Edwin is also a labourer. I just don't believe a labourer could have afforded this house.

'You don't want to believe a labourer or a clerk could afford this house,' Jonathan says when I show him later.

'In those days they earned a few shillings a day. A labourer surely couldn't dream of a property like this?'

'They only rented it, didn't they? Maybe the first tenants got it cheap.'

I show him the certificate.

'Look at this one,' he says. 'Amelia Maslin, December 1861, the groom's mother, she couldn't even write – it says "her mark".'

'Maybe Edward made good. It was the Victorian era, age of the entrepreneur.'

It's tempting, but I've learned not to make up excuses when the facts don't fit. I don't think any of these are my Edward. I think I need to look elsewhere.

Later the phone rings and it's the Bank of Scotland.

I'd almost forgotten about the deeds. They've only taken five months to get back to me. The man says that deeds as such do not exist with them – now they tell me – only a single sheet of paper which says we bought the house when we did. He can send me that if I like (how long will that take them?). Meanwhile he gives me our title number and suggests I try the local land registry office.

'But I doubt you'll get much joy,' he adds encouragingly.

Storms all morning. Flower pots fall and break, dustbin lids roll around in the street. I stand on the terrace outside my study and watch as the sky turns the grey-yellow of an ugly bruise and wind rips at the garden. The noise is unearthly and trees are bending right over – I've never seen anything quite like it.

At about eleven, the big old lilac tree outside the kitchen window finally gives a kind of sigh and snaps and falls, on the fence. I run down to the kitchen where the window is suddenly lighter, the quality of the light entirely changed.

Come home later to find a message on my machine from Alan Hayward. Chloë starts telling me something and I tell her to shush.

'That's Henry and Charlotte's great-grandson's voice,' I whisper. She rolls her eyes, kicks off her sandals, and lies melodramatically across the first landing, panting and cross.

I send her away and dial the number. Engaged. But next time I ring, he answers the phone. My heart thumps. I'm finally speaking to an actual Hayward.

'Alan?'

'That's right.'

I explain that it was discovering Henry and Charlotte's names in the 1881 census that started me on this journey. He sounds amused and pleased. Somewhere, he says, he has the family tree – but all that stuff and photos and everything is up in the loft where his wife kept it very neatly. She's dead now.

I ask him what he knows about Henry Hayward and he says he's sorry to disappoint me but he really knows very little. 'I think he was actually a medical journalist, maybe wrote the odd book on medicine too. And Frank, his son – that was my grandfather – was a commercial traveller selling legal stationery or something. And you know, I seem to remember that Henry also did a bit of this.

'My grandfather Frank died before I was born, but I did know Florence, Henry's daughter, as a very old lady. I remember she was a lovely woman, very little and thin and a very kind person. She never married, I don't think.'

'And Arthur?'

'I only recall him vaguely. I think he was good with kids. But my grandfather Frank's wife, Lily Matilda, she was the real character. She was a real terror. A real matriarchal ogre – but she did teach me to play a good game of bridge.'

Alan explains that there was a 'strange situation' in his family. 'Namely that my mother and my father were also stepsister and stepbrother.'

'How on earth . . . ?'

He laughs. 'It's even more complicated, I'm afraid,' he says. 'That's why we need the family tree. But let me try and get it right. You see, after Frank, my grandfather, died, my mother's mother also died and

374

her father married Lily Matilda. So my mother and father grew up in the same house from the age of about twelve or thirteen – and then when they were twenty-four they got married.'

I try to visualize this. 'I still don't get it,' I say.

'I'll send you the family tree,' he says.

Before he retired Alan travelled all over the world working for Clarks Shoes, who were based in Street, Somerset, close to Glastonbury, where he now lives. He gives me the name and phone number of his cousin Julia, who is younger and lives in Solihull and may know more stuff about the Haywards.

I thank him for sparing the time to talk to me and he laughs.

'I've got the time. I'm actually getting undressed right now, would you believe, because I was supposed to be going out to dinner with my son, only it's cancelled apparently and he forgot to tell me.'

He sounds a little disappointed.

I tell him it must be beautiful in Somerset today, much much better than being in London.

'We're lucky,' he says, 'it is. Oh, another thing you may not know. Charlotte and Henry Hayward were first cousins. Their fathers were brothers.'

Later, Jonathan asks me how it was, talking – finally – to Henry's great-grandson?

'It was all right.'

'Only all right?'

'It was – I don't know – it was a bit sad actually.'

'Couldn't he help?'

'He could – and he gave me someone else's number too, but – I don't know. It wasn't him who was sad, it was just the whole situation.'

We sit in the garden among the ruins of the lilac. Hot again, the wind all gone, navy-blue sky, midges biting me all over, twigs strewn on the parched grass.

'It's just, you finally track these people down and when you get them it feels so exciting and you can almost kid yourself that it's a kind of arrival, the end of a journey, but it's not. What can they reveal to you really? Very little. It just underlines what you already know, that Henry's actually gone. He's slipped away. He's unretrievable.'

'Irretrievable,' Jonathan says.

'Even his relatives know almost nothing of him.'

'But you said he did tell you some good things? That Henry was a medical journalist, for instance – we didn't know that. And the thing about them being cousins – I mean it may not have been that unusual then, but it's worth knowing.'

'I suppose it throws some light on them,' I agree.

('I can't think of anything worse,' Raph had said when I told him, 'than marrying India!')

But what else? The conversation with Alan – gentle Somerset Alan, who was supposed to be going out to dinner but had been stood up by his son – only confirmed what I already know. That you live and then you die, and then a few decades zip by and suddenly you're no longer a vivid presence in anyone's life or even memory.

Soon even Auntie Bea's nephew Ted will be gone, and then what will be left? A house sale. Cardboard boxes. Some clearing up, some sorting out, a big, welling grief for Sue. But even that only for a while. And then the space taken up by his long, kind shadow will be just that, a space – unnoticed, never really there.

'I wish we could buy my grandfather's house,' I tell Jonathan. 'Restore it and make it lovely again.'

He looks at me, exasperated. 'You want to live in Gainsborough?'

I smile. 'No.'

He sighs and puts a hand on my knee. 'You've gone all morose, haven't you?'

'The funny thing,' I tell him, 'is that I think a part of me became convinced that if I researched these stories hard enough, I could somehow summon these people back to life, however briefly – and that they'd somehow be here again in this house. It's like I really believed that.'

How could I ever have believed such a stupid thing?

I know from the land tax records that Edward/Edwin Maslin/Maslen went on owning Number 34 until 1898, taking rent from the Haywards and then the Spawtons. So I pay $39.95 to www.ancestry.com to check their indexed 1891 census.

If my Ed was, let's say, at least twenty-one when he moved into the house in 1873, then he was at least forty-one in 1891. There are nine Edward Maslens but none of them over forty. Two of the five Edward Maslins are viable: one a 39-year-old carpenter then living in Maidstone, Kent, and a 59-year-old 'general labourer' living at School Cottage in Barnes. His wife is Eliza and I already have his marriage certificate – it was his mother Amelia who was illiterate. And there's a 44-year-old Edwin Maslin who ran a restaurant in Lancashire and had a wife called Isabel and sons called Alfred and Herbert.

But how can I ever know whether any of these people lived in Lillieshall Road? For the first time, it is proving almost impossible to nail down my man.

'If I never find Edward Maslin,' I tell Jonathan, 'then the whole thing's kind of pointless. He was the first one, the first owner, the first person ever to live here and call it home.'

I wake in the night and stare at the red winking eye of the smoke alarm and wonder if I'm ever going to know any more than I know now.

Here I lie, in the very centre of the house, in the master bedroom on the first floor – most likely the very room that Edward Maslin lay in a hundred and thirty years ago. And yet I'm as far away from him as ever – as far away as I could possibly be. The house won't tell, can't tell . . . but does the house even want to tell?

Sometimes I feel that the house is holding on to its secrets, guarding

377

them jealously. Sometimes I think that, if the house were a person, I'd have lost my temper by now.

Number 34 is full of ghosts. Full! She can't believe it. She thought she would be happy here – in some ways she is, happy, happy, happy, determinedly and joyously so.

Why, then, each night this cold, damp month of February, has she lain awake in the blue darkness, unable to sleep, unable to think, paralysed by – what? – one of her 'feelings'. That everything around her is somehow second-hand, that everything she's thinking and feeling has been felt before and will be felt again. That this means her life is of no account, swallowed up. That sometimes, if she allows herself to dwell on it, she thinks she'll die of the emptiness.

Since Arthur went to be apprenticed at Black's, and Florence moved into the small room upstairs next to Frank, she and Henry are alone on the first floor. Henry likes this – a whole floor to themselves. But she's not so sure. Sometimes she gets up in the night, wanders into the little room that used to be Florence's, and stands there at the window, looking out on to the back garden. Rooftops and chimney stacks of Broadhinton Road. She stares at the bare winter trees, harsh against the pale night sky, and is consumed with sadness. She can't place why – can't decide whether it's her or whether it's just a very sad room.

Sometimes she gets a feeling and snaps around, looks behind her quickly. What is it? Has something happened in there?

'Could this house be haunted?' she whispers to Henry, right back in the summer when they've only been there a few months.

He sighs and draws back the sheet and caresses her shoulder, then presses his lips on it so she feels his whiskers on her skin. She tries to lean into him. She does not want him to sense rejection.

'What is this?' he says. 'Are you unwell? Is that where this morbid mood is coming from?'

'It's not that,' she says hotly. 'That was last week, Henry, you know it was. You can't put everything down to that.'

He sighs again, more deeply this time.

'No,' he says, 'it can't be haunted. How can it be? It's a new house, only one owner before us and we know all about it. What are you trying to say, you funny girl?'

She gets up then and goes over to the window and twitches at the muslins so they let in just a chink of gaslight. An animal nips across the street and disappears behind the hedge opposite. Somewhere, streets away, she can hear two cats locked in battle – a dreadful, eerie caterwauling.

'Is it the children?' he asks her. 'Are you worrying about the children, Lottie?'

She tries to think honestly about this. 'No. The children are all fine and growing bigger every day, and Florence is quite a young lady, isn't she?'

This is true. Florrie, with her blonde's curves, is almost as tall as Charlotte now – edgy and difficult sometimes, but definitely on the cusp of womanhood. And she is the last, the very last. Soon there won't be any little children left, nothing to live for. Quickly, she plucks this thought from her mind – plucks it and releases it, lets it float away.

Henry leans back on the pillow. She can't see him clearly but she knows his eyes are on her in the darkness.

'You're cold. It's freezing out there. Come back to bed, my dear.'

'In a minute,' she says, her eyes still on the dim street, 'in a minute I will.'

'This is a good house,' he tells her. 'We're very happy here. The children love it. It's just as you said – everything, in fact, has worked out as you said. So why are you like this?'

'Why am I like what?'

'Why is it that when everything you want falls into your lap, then you start to look for bad in things?'

He's right. She bites her lip, to stop herself crying.

'I don't know,' she says, 'please believe me, Henry. I don't know what it is, I mean it. It's a good question and one which, for the life of me, I can't answer.'

She has no answer, but she has this. The certainty that she lies there oppressed by a weight she can't justify or fathom. It's a new house, he's right, there can be no ghosts. It can only be the future that she senses, then, the grief and sadness that's stored up to come, the events that will unfurl and happen. It's the weight of the future she feels pressing down on her so hard that some nights she can barely breathe.

Marjorie Ethel Hayward's marriage certificate arrives in the post. She married Thomas James Hillier in February 1932, but her father is George William Hayward, not Arthur, son of Henry. You wouldn't have thought there could be two Marjorie Ethel Haywards, but there were.

To further compound my sense of failure, David Hillier's mother is a completely different Hayward again, Amy Mary. You wouldn't have thought two unrelated Miss Haywards would marry two unrelated Mr Hilliers, but they did.

In 1979, sitting in a baking hot piazza in Florence, I rip open a letter and a photo falls out: my sister Mandy in dungarees, sitting among cardboard boxes and packing cases. My family have moved to a village called Epperstone, ten miles out in the Notts countryside.

'Our new home!' Mum has written on the bottom. 'See you soon.'

I get back from Italy after almost a year away and the bus from Nottingham city centre drops me by the church. Following Mum's directions, I walk up the lane. Twitter of birds, old brick walls, hedges, the putter of a tractor, not a human being in sight. Mum said it's almost the last house, on the left, at the end of Church Lane.

I keep on walking.

*   *   *

Kim, current owner of The Elms, is away but has arranged for a neighbour to let us in. We walk up the lane with Paula, who lives in the Old Doctor's House down opposite the pub. As a student, I often pulled pints at the pub. Bar food and pork scratchings and scampi fries. The lounge bar had peroxide women drinking Bacardi and Coke, but the public bar had a real live poacher, a ferret peeping out of his waistcoat pocket.

Standing in the bright kitchen of The Elms again after more than twenty years, I'm struck by the low door frames. How did my stepfather, at six-foot-something, manage? There were seven of us in this house most of the time – children coming and going from university and college – but sometimes there were so many of us that two had to sleep outside in the converted garage. And if friends came they slept in the caravan at the bottom of the garden.

Twenty years on and the caravan is gone, but there's still the lawn with the shady apple tree that we hung with bunting and beneath which we laid a grand picnic – pork pie and scotch eggs – when Lady Diana Spencer married Prince Charles. And the shed where I wrote my dissertation on 'The Peculiar Vision of Virginia Woolf' (7,000 words), and even the converted garage where Mandy and I slept and where I kept a cold, secret bottle of Chanel No. 5, bought on my overdraft in Duty Free, which I'd dab on before I walked the dog across the fields. Just in case I met someone.

Eventually Mandy and I were moved back into the house and our parents – no doubt craving respite from five child-adults – moved themselves into the converted garage.

Now I stand for a moment in the little front bedroom where Mandy and I had such a bad fight one night that we ended up down in the dark windy lane hitting each other with a chair.

'With a chair?'

'It was an old pine one with a velvet seat, and she broke it.' Or maybe I did. I can't remember.

* * *

I still can't find my Maslins, and I still don't even know for certain how they spelled their name.

I go back to the Probate Room and look up all the Maslin/Maslen wills. If I can find any descendants at all, then I can at least ask them the simple question, 'Did your grandfather/great-grandfather ever live in Clapham?'

I start checking from when Maslin sold the house to Elizabeth Spawton in 1898. But as I pass through 1915, 1916, and 1917 I am mesmerized by the sudden burgeoning of names:

> Maslin William Private 5th East Lancashire Territorial Regiment died on or since 26 May 1915 in the Gallipoli Peninsula Administration (with will) to Henry Maslin Confectioner.

How long did this Henry wait and pray and then, in 1917, give up all hope and seek probate on his son's will?

> Maslen Archibold Victor of HMS Conquest Engine Room Artificier RN died 13 June 1918 at sea. Probate 17 October to William Holloway Maslen gentleman Effects £295. 17. 7.

I find my first Edward in June 1924: Edward Joseph Maslen of Bath. He leaves everything to his son, Edward James Whitefield Maslen. But he disappears, presumably dying intestate.

The next one to emerge from the pages is Edward Charles Maslen of Chesterfield, who dies in 1929 and leaves everything to his 'dear wife Alice', who also seems to die intestate. I do trace a Mary Alice Maslin who dies in December 1934 in Sunderland – maybe Edward always knew her as Alice. She leaves everything to her three daughters, mercifully listed here with their married names: Gladys Nixon, Susanna Emms, and the still unwed Winifred Maslin.

But the Info Disk shows nothing for any of these names and after a few desultory phone calls to Emms families, I give it up. I just don't believe my Edward went up to Derbyshire. Why would he?

Finally in 1943, Edward Maslen of Amberley, Ogbourne St George in Wiltshire, leaves everything to his son Eric. If he was in his nineties, he could just be my man. Eric Maslen dies at the Laurels Residential Home in 1985, and though he leaves Romaine Daw '£500 and my piano accordion for her cheerfulness and willing help' and Aleck Thorne his 'clasp bible and three-legged round table', his surviving nephews assure me that his father Edward never lived in London, never would have.

Edward/Edwin Maslin/Maslen, where are you? Who were you?

Florence Hayward stands sobbing in the kitchen doorway, her eyes on fire, her fingers clutching dramatically at her throat.

Charlotte can't help noticing that she's filling that gown right out, it's far too tight around her ribs – she ought perhaps to buy some material and run her up a good new winter gown on the machine. It's probably even more urgent than the shirts and stockings she's making for Henry.

Except, by the look of her, she'll need a new chemise too – she's surprised she can draw breath in that old child-size slip. Or perhaps it's even time to get her into a boned corset. She's womanly now, new curves all over the place. When she runs, things move. Charlotte pretends not to notice, but it's clear that any time soon she'll be unwell for the first time.

Which is probably what this is all about.

Florrie's weeping but, eyes still wet but dark with anger, she looks her mother slowly up and down and curls her lip, as if she's disgusted by what she sees.

Charlotte laughs. She can't help it. She can't even remember what this tiff was all about.

'How dare you laugh at me! You've no idea, have you, how it feels to be me! All you think about is . . .'

Florrie tails off. She can't really imagine what her mother does think about. And Charlotte stares at her because, for a moment, neither can she. When, last year, she begged and begged poor Henry for the dog, she had no idea why. Couldn't imagine what gap in her life she was trying to fill. And when the puppy came and bounded round the room, then messed on the rug right by the ottoman, she was amazed at herself, distraught. What had she done? Why had she, a fastidious and proud housewife, decided to vex herself like this?

'Come on, Florrie,' she says now, 'maybe you could take Molly out?'

Florence tosses her hair. 'Wonderful. That's exactly what I feel like doing. Walking your idiotic dog!'

She stomps off upstairs, and when she gets up to her room on the second floor hurls the door shut. Charlotte tenses a moment, waiting for the inevitable second slam. Bang! And then she puts on her cape and gloves and makes her way up to the Emporium on the High Street to buy some fine merino wool with a delicate mauve and yellow sprigged pattern. She buys five yards, a little too much, but it'll make a very decent gown for her daughter, generous enough to let out as she grows.

And if there's any material left over, she'll put it aside in her secret drawer. No one knows about this. But if you were to rummage under the layers of stockings and undergarments in Charlotte's top bedroom drawer, you'd find a medium-sized paper box containing two old baby blankets, washed and folded, a bent and bitten silver teething ring of Frank's, a goffered baby bonnet, and a yard of the finest cotton lawn.

Months ago I posted requests on the all-the-family message boards at www.ancestry.com, from Wohl to Maslin to Blaine to Hayward.

Now I suddenly get my first reply. It's only someone telling me that there's a Maslin Family website, www.maslin.org.uk. I log on immediately and the home page looks promising. David Maslin has researched something called I.G.I. Christenings and Marriages for Maslin and

Maslen, the 1851 and 1871 census for Wiltshire, the Address Book from 1813 to date. But then, on the letters page, I find:

> *Hi All*
>
> *I have just found out that this site has been down since December and apologise to those of you who have been trying to contact me. It is just over two years since I created the Maslin web site and the response to it has been tremendous. I would like to thank all of you who have sent information and photographs and hope that we can extend all the family trees back as far as possible. If you are contacting me for the first time please send as much information as possible about the ancestors you are looking for as this will assist in trying to locate further information. Hope to hear from you all in the future and welcome new friends.*
>
> *Regards David M. Maslin*

I send him an e-mail asking for help, but I'm not optimistic.

Henry has a new typewriter. He's very pleased with it. He yacks away at it all day – he has a deadline – and the sound goes straight through her. She tries to go to rooms where she won't hear it, but nowhere in the house is safe. She wanders from room to room feeling bilious. Shudders every time he presses a letter down.

In the kitchen, he comes to her, places his hands on her shoulders. She notices a smear of grease on the range and her stomach turns.

'My love. Please tell me. What is it?'

'Nothing. Please, I'm perfectly all right.'

'You're pale.'

'I don't sleep, that's all. I'm not sleeping very well just now.'

He sighs and walks away to the fireplace, pokes the fire, comes back to her. She knows he cares enough that he can't leave her to suffer, but at the same time dreads being drawn into a conversation that will go nowhere.

'Please,' she says, 'do your work. I'm fine.'

'I wish you'd tell me. About the not sleeping.'

'I do tell you. You don't have time to listen.'

'That's not fair, you know it's not. I could get you a draught for it.'

'It's not just that.'

'What, then?'

'I have – this smell in my nose.'

'What smell? What do you mean?'

'All the time – a smell like burning – burning flesh. It's foul. It makes me nauseous.'

Henry glances back towards the other room where his typewriter awaits him. He's writing about some new tonic derived from willow bark – Saly-something – which, he tells her, will one day be widely available and will change the lives of people with rheumatic pains. She knows he's deep in it and just wants the peace to finish.

'Will you see a doctor?' he says. 'Dr Hitching. He's a good man and he's only round the corner. Would you see him if I arranged for him to call?'

OK, I'm getting desperate now. If I use the reference checking system, I can look for all Maslin and Maslen births registered in Wandsworth from 1872 until they left Lillieshall Road in 1881 and ask them to look for 34 Lillieshall Road under 'Residence of Informant'.

But there are so many. From George Albert in March 1872, past Eveline Sarah and Christiana Edith, through to Florence Maud in 1871, there are fifteen children of that surname born in Wandsworth in those years.

I toss a coin and decide to do the Maslen children first. That's six of them. If this doesn't work, then I really am running out of ideas.

* * *

I phone Alan Hayward's cousin, Julia Cash. She says she runs a lawn-mower business in Solihull and that her father was Howard Hayward, who was one of Frank and Lily Matilda's children, brother of Leslie and Ivy. I ask her if Ivy had any children.

'No. She was in love with a married man all through the Second World War and then, when she was sixty and the divorce laws changed, she married him. And he already had children, so a lot of the money and family photos ended up going to them instead of staying in the Hayward family.'

She asks whether I know about the strange situation of the step-brother and stepsister marrying. I say I do.

'Well, you see, it means that Alan and I are both real cousins and stepcousins!' She laughs. 'I know how it sounds!'

She says she's going to look hard for some photos. 'But you know what I do have here? Henry Hayward's bible. It's in my hands now. Let me put my glasses on and I'll read you what it says inside:

> This book was presented to Henry Hayward on 22nd December 1852 as a reward for diligence, proficiency and general good conduct from W. Tribe Esq. of Worthing and the boys' and girls' national schools established in that town.

'But that's great,' I tell her. 'That bible must have sat here in our house!'

'That's what I thought. I've also got some photos of Frank. There's him in riding gear and a nice one of him and Lily Matilda outside their caravan. They were always going off in their caravan.'

I ask Julia if I can just check – were there definitely no more Hayward grandchildren? Did Arthur only have Marjorie Ethel?

'I'll have to have a look at the family tree – I've got it here but it's such a scrappy bit of paper, we ought to copy it out properly some time. Let me see . . . Yes, I only have Marjorie Ethel down for Arthur.

And we know who Frank's children were. And then Florence, no issue. And – wait a minute – I've got another one here.'

I sit up in my chair and grab a pen.

'Yes, goodness, that's funny, I've never once heard of this one. Elsie Hayward.'

'Elsie?'

'Yes, it says "Elsie born 1883". I didn't even know there was an Elsie.'

I glance up at the date charts on my wall. '1883. But that's when they were living here. That means Elsie was almost certainly born in this house.'

I get the list of Maslen children back from the Family Records Centre. They've looked through all the Maslen births in Wandsworth and against each entry they've written 'No'. None of them were registered by anyone living at Lillieshall Road.

Maybe this line of attack won't work. Who says they had children while they were living here? Maybe they moved here once their children were born.

'Come on, you've got to keep going,' says Jonathan. 'You've got to check the Maslin children as well. You've done the leg work, now it's only a case of filling in the form and paying the money.'

So I write down the names of Edith Mary, and Edith Fanny, and George Seymour, and Emily Jane, and George Albert, and Bernard James, and Eveline Sarah, and pass the form through to the cashier and go back home to wait.

It's still August, but the Holy Trinity churchyard is already thick with leaves. They blow across the white gravel drive where the memorial to the Clapham war dead stands, lonely and stark. The Common is parched and brown from the heat wave, the grass the colour of old sand. But the heat has finally cooled to leave a comfortable wind. Everyone comments on what a relief it is, to be able to breathe again.

Chloë comes back from shopping on the King's Road, cheeks flushed with the joy of spending. Meanwhile, the dog has pissed on the sitting room rug, a great dark stain on the pink and orange kilim. I shout at the children and tell them it's their fault. They say they love this dog and they want her as their pet, but they never hear when she barks asking to be let out.

'I swear she never barked,' says Jake, who swears a lot of things that turn out not to be true these days.

'So, have you found your missing Maslin person yet, Mummy?' Chloë asks me, cheerily changing the subject.

'No,' I tell her as I push the unrepentant dog out of the way and scrub furiously at the dark splodge with odour repellent, 'but if I do finally manage to track him down, and he turns out to be some boring old spinster guy who just lived here alone in this house for all those years and has no interesting story at all, then I'm going to . . .'

'What, Mummy? What are you going to do?'

'I'm going to kill him.'

When Dr Hitching gives Charlotte the good news, she turns crimson. A real, deep flush. She can feel it, the blood rising in her cheeks.

'You don't mean it?'

She sits up on the bed and he smiles and walks quietly over to the pitcher and basin next to the fireplace.

'May I?'

'Of course.'

He rinses his hands.

'You're surprised?'

'Well, I . . .'

'But you said yourself – you've not been unwell since Christmas?'

'Well, no, but . . . Sometimes it's . . .' Charlotte blushes again. 'Uneven.'

He wipes his hands. 'I can't of course be entirely certain. Not for another month at least. But I would say that all the signs are there. You should take exercise as usual, but stay calm and eat well. And certainly I'd leave off the stays for the time being.'

Henry has to sit down. He pushes a pile of papers out of the way and rests his arms on the oilcloth. The front room window is black – it's four o'clock and already dark. Tiny needles of sleet stab the window pane.

'You're shocked?'

'No,' he says, managing a smile, 'no, I'm not, as a matter of fact.'

'I am. I'm shocked.'

'You're not.'

'Henry, I am! How can you doubt it?'

He does doubt it, she knows that, but she is. She is genuinely shocked. She'd thought the all-day nausea and the burnt taste on the roof of her mouth and the uncomfortable heat and prickling in her breasts were all in her mind, a female thing, a fantasy sprung from loneliness. It wouldn't be the first time her body has precisely expressed the sorrow of her mind.

She's been unhappy for a long time, she realizes with a sudden rush of shame.

'You don't mind?' she asks him, and he comes over to her, presses his lips against her hair. Takes her hands, which are hot and faintly sticky.

'My darling Lottie. What a question. How could I ever dream of minding? Arthur's gone and Frank too, all but. It'll be something for you to do. And the infant part doesn't last forever, after all. It won't be a nuisance for long.'

The baby is expected in late October, but in the middle of September, Charlotte wakes in the night to feel water tipping out of her. She cries out and turns in the bed and it happens again, the whole sheet and mattress soaked.

'Heavens above!' Henry throws back the covers. The liquid isn't clear but almost black, half blood, half something else.

'Oh,' says Julia, as she scans down the Hayward family bible, 'hold on a moment. It says here . . . born 1883 and died in 1883. That's why I'd never heard about this baby – I'd never even noticed her here on the family tree. She didn't live. She was born and died in the same year, I'm afraid.'

A hot wind is blowing hard enough to lift the litter along Exmouth Market on the day in late August when I return to the Family Records Centre to look for Elsie Hayward, born 1883.

In the third quarter, among a hundred other small Haywards, I eventually find her. Or at least I think it's her. There's no Christian name given, just 'Female'. No time for a name.

I go over to deaths then and find it straightaway – the same quarter, as I'd suspected. September 1883. How long did Elsie live? A week, a month?

'I eventually find her. Or at least I think it's her.'

The certificates, one red, one black, arrive in the post three days later, both registered on the same day, 17 September 1883. It says that 'Female' Hayward was born on 16 September at 34 Lillieshall Road and that she died a day later of 'Inanition' – general weakness and exhaustion, failure to take nourishment.

She was thirty hours old.

It's a month before Charlotte manages to decide on a name.

Henry would rather leave it, but 'I can't bear for her to remain nameless,' she tells him, 'I want to be able to think of her as someone in her own right.'

It's more than that. When she remembers the quiet, damp, mauve-skinned child she held in her arms for a day and a night, she wants there to be more than a 'she'. She wants there to be a word. 'Daughter' isn't enough and nor is 'infant', she wants . . .

Elsie.

The name comes to her upon waking one morning. It's the first morning she can remember not waking in tears. She knows what an Elsie would look like. She'd have brown curly hair, little Elsie, and a skinny-happy nature. A dreadfully lively and trying child.

So much energy, running her poor mother ragged! Elsie would run off and try and climb trees on the Common and Charlotte, laughing, would have to pull her down. One day she'd get almost to the top of one of the smaller apple trees near Cock Pond and Charlotte would tense up with worry for a moment, afraid to see her crouched up there among the leaves.

She'd want to shout at her to come down, but would be anxious that any sudden loud noise might shock her small daughter and somehow dislodge her. So instead she'd do the sensible thing and, swallowing her shyness, enlist the help of a passing fireman. And he'd laugh to see Elsie's small stockinged legs hanging down and he'd reach up and lift her down, and Charlotte would tell her off gently. But in her heart she wouldn't really be angry, she'd just be so very glad to hold her child and feel her warm and safe and naughty in her arms.

Finally, she brings herself to clear the small room next to theirs that she'd had cleaned and distempered ready to be a nursery. She donates the small rocking crib, the fireguard, and the high chair to the orphanage fund at Holy Trinity. But the little wool blankets and tiny, homemade garments she puts aside. One day, God willing, one of her three will be blessed enough to have their own infants.

Some nights she still gets up out of her bed and goes in there and gazes out at the frozen black garden, sobbing herself wretched, while Henry sleeps on. Other nights, she'll manage not to weep but will instead be so deep in a trance of thought that she'll turn sharply, thinking she feels someone behind her.

One night she dreams there are children in there – big and small children, boys and girls, dark-skinned and light-skinned, all crying out for parents. Their hair is all mussed and their nails unkempt, and their nightgowns are all soiled and they moan and beseech her, telling her they're lost, that they have nothing and no one. She wakes to find herself trembling, her pillow soaked with tears.

Henry tells her she must try to put the loss behind her – it's the only way. 'We have to move forward, Lottie, for the sake of our living children if nothing else.'

But he doesn't understand. 'This isn't about her, it's not about Elsie,' she tells him, 'it's other children. I feel other children in there, in that room.'

He holds her close and shakes his head. What does he think? That she's losing her mind?

When Elsie's room is entirely bare and clear again, Charlotte puts a small writing desk in there with an upright chair and decides she will have the room as her own, to read and write in. She'll write a diary and may even have a try at writing verse. Maybe if she can express her feelings, the room will empty and the ghosts will slip away?

Henry – glad to see her making a plan – says he's all for it. He encourages her. He's not one of these men who thinks women shouldn't use their heads.

But after a month of trying, she gives up. It's not her, it's the room – she knows it is. She can never settle in it. She sits there for an hour at a time and her mind is blank, and then she hears a whispering at her neck, her skin creeps and she has to leave.

One day she walks out and closes the door behind her for the last time. After that, it becomes the lumber room, a place where they store anything they want to hold on to but can't fit in the house. She doesn't go in at all. If someone needs something from there – a box or a chair or whatever – she makes sure Henry's the one to go in and fetch it out.

When the latest and last self-addressed envelope from the Family Records Centre plops through the letter box, I don't even rush to open it. I know it will be another list of 'No, No, No' and that my last best idea for tracing Edward Maslin will be gone.

Jonathan, seeing it still lying there on the bed while I shower, rips it open and then stands riffling through the sheets. I'm half naked and wet when he hands it to me – the sheet with the distinctive green tinge of certificate.

Edith's birth certificate

* * *

394

'Not only the right Edward Maslin,' Jonathan says, 'but the first baby to be born here in this house.'

'Probably born right here where we're standing now, in our bedroom. And it's Maslin, after all. After all that.'

I gaze at the paper and sigh, suddenly deflated.

'What's the matter?'

'Nothing. I suppose I just didn't think we were ever going to get there.'

'Funny though,' Jonathan says, 'it says here on the birth certificate that it was already called Helena House.'

'Why's that funny?'

'Well, I'd kind of assumed that whoever called this house Helena House was naming it after someone. But the wife's called Mary and the baby's called Edith.'

Late spring: out in the garden, Charlotte and Henry plant a rose for Elsie.

A pink climbing rose. They plant it on a crisp day a whole half year later, down the bottom of the garden, near the old wooden seat where Charlotte often sits.

Even though Henry digs it in well, adding plenty of bone meal, it struggles for the first year, not putting on much growth at all. Charlotte can't help but think Inanition. Charlotte wonders whether they should dig it up and plant another one, but Henry tells her to be patient. 'Roses often don't get going for a bit.'

He's right of course. Henry's always right. Come spring 1885, she's astonished to see how vigorously it climbs, its optimistic buds unfurling as fast as they possibly can to blink up at the bright dazzle of the sun.

In the post, a stiff brown envelope postmarked Bath& Taunton and addressed to me in large biro capitals. It's from Alan Hayward, great grandson of Henry and Charlotte. He says in his note that he hopes the enclosed 'may prove useful.'

Out fall some photocopied sheets, family trees, some printed, some hand drawn. But I hardly look at them, because in my hand is a fading Victorian postcard of a portly yet dashing man in riding clothes – buttoned breeches, crop, bowler hat, handlebar moustache. He half stands, half leans against a strange gnarled wooden table, as if afraid it might not quite take his weight. His face is immaculate, inscrutable, absolutely of its time. He's got himself dressed up for this photograph and it's going to be a good one – one which will last and be handed down the generations.

'My grandfather Frank,' Alan's written on the back. This is Henry and Charlotte's youngest son – the travelling salesman who sold legal stationary and enjoyed riding and fishing in his spare time. But he's also the ten year-old child who lived in this house, as my children have, as my children do. He's the Frank whose name Chloë and I called on that winter evening that itself now feels like a hundred years ago. Arthur! Florence! Frank!

For the very first time, I'm looking into the eyes of a Hayward.

Chapter Nine

RIDING HORSES IN BED

The Maslins
1873–1880

Hear that dear old Maslin died this morning. Too sad! Such a loss!
He knew me from my 9th year, having come into Mama's service
in January 1828!!

QUEEN VICTORIA'S JOURNAL, 14 November 1891

'It's my house, I'm telling you – mine.'

'No, it isn't.'

''Tis.'

''Tisn't.'

'I'm telling you, you troublesome little Ediebug, it jolly well is!'

'How do you know?'

'Because it has my name written on it, that's why. Go and look. You just go outside into the street this very minute and you look up at the glass and you'll see it.'

Edith does nothing, stares at her big sister.

'Go on, are you especially hard of hearing? I'm telling you, just do it.'

But Edith doesn't make a move to go outside – she's not allowed anyway. Instead she just shuffles further up the stairs on her bottom. She folds her small fat arms and lays them on her knees.

'I can see the writing from here very well actually and it doesn't even say a single thing. It's all loops and squiggles and whatnot.'

'First of all, Edie, you can't read. And second of all, you're looking at it inside out, you little goose. You have to go outside and then you'll see. Helena's House is what's written there, bold as anything.'

Edith juts out her lip and starts to cry. 'You weren't even born here,' she says. 'I was born here in this house and that makes it mine.'

Helena laughs and kicks the hall wall hard with her boot. There's a scuff mark but she doesn't care. Her Ma won't notice, and if she does she'll tell her Edie did it.

'You think that makes all the difference? People are born in all sorts of houses but they don't get named after them. The house where Grandpa works isn't called Queen House, is it? This is my house, it was named after me, and it will be mine forever and ever and that's that.'

Helena considers the beauty of this and laughs again. Edith loops a strand of hair around her fist, sticks her thumb in her mouth, and gloomily sucks on it.

Helena's house, Helena's house, Helena's house!

A frozen January day in 1873. Silence, cold, brightness.

The house is empty, but it's a different kind of emptiness – the bald and certain emptiness of a space that's never been filled. No echoes of anything or anyone. No one but the builder and his men have ever stepped on these bare boards, or climbed these steep, clean stairs – which still lack runner and rods. There are no curtains at the icy windows, no swags or pelmets, no rugs on the floor, not a single stick of furniture – no voices, nothing.

Light spills in from a white freezing sky. The silence itself has a par-ticular quality – thick and shocked – maybe because these solid red bricks inhabit a space that was until so very recently open field, fresh air, green grass.

'Cricket pitch,' says Raph quickly, 'I thought you said it used to be a cricket pitch?'

'It bloody well still is,' remarks Jonathan, glancing out of the window where the central part of the lawn is worn to a scrubby run of hard-baked mud.

But the open green spaces of 1870s Clapham are shrinking, sucked up by the urban sprawl that has now begun in earnest. Streets and streets and more streets. Each one knows exactly why it's there. Each one can give you a precise, minuted reason, heads nodding at the Metropolitan Board. Every street leads somewhere, joins something to something, has its own particular, ongoing logic. The process continues – unstoppable, relentless, exhilarating, some would say. In committee rooms up and down the land, men in suits are signing papers which, a few months on, will lead to a brickie somewhere trowelling cement, waiting for his hod-carrier.

Not this one, though. This street's almost done. The first few houses, including this one, went up in six months, begun over the summer and done by Christmas. Now all it wants is a tenant.

But will anyone who can afford it even walk this far?

Because out in the street, it's a different story. The going's still rough, the ground dirty and uneven. There's no paving yet, no railings or walls, no front paths or baby hedges or front gardens. The mud and dung – kept at bay only by the young crossing-sweeper who starts at dawn and finishes at dusk – comes right up to the doorstep.

When the coal is poured down into the cellar, you drop the hatch back into place fast or half the street will be tipped in there too. Women coming inside from the road brush the bottoms of their gowns for a good hour if they want to keep the mud off their rugs and floors.

Not only that, but it's dark, too. There's no lamp lighter yet, no elderly man shambling along with his ladder, because there are no lamps yet. At night the street is washed with moonlight and pricked with stars, tinted by the faint gas and electric glow that is the faraway city. A milkman still drives his two cows down Lillieshall Road, back from the Common, on his way home for milking. Sometimes he stops off for a jar at the Tim Bobbin and leaves the poor beasts tied up outside, bellowing with discomfort and fury. He may get complaints from the folks in the cottages. Or they may just take things into their own hands, literally, and come and help themselves – passing their pennies through the window in return for a jugful of milk.

It's not uncommon, either, to see a lone sheep nibbling the scrubby patch of grass on the corner, where thin-faced watercress girls stop at the end of the day for a smoke and a chat. Sometimes they'll wave and joke with the Italian ice cream sellers who traipse back from the Common, their feet sore and their barrels empty. Or call out to the man who hurries past with his hurdy-gurdy and his monkey.

'What, a real, live monkey?'

'Yes, a real one. Victorian entertainers had them in the streets. Sometimes they'd dress them up in little jackets and hats.'

'That's so cruel,' says Raph with feeling.

'They didn't think or care so much about animals then.'

'It'd be illegal now though, wouldn't it?' says Jake.

'I wish I had a little monkey,' Raph sighs, 'just a little one. I'd keep it in my room and . . .'

'You don't need a little monkey, because you are one,' his sister reminds him.

'And it'd be illegal,' his brother insists again.

'And there's no way we're having any more animals in this house,' I add, as if another reason was required.

But these voices come from another place – they wait a hundred and thirty years in the future, in a house that will by then boast a Sexy Pink hall and halogen lighting. Right now, the house is young and new and stands empty. It fervently hopes that the young couple making their way up past the cottages might in fact be coming to look at it.

But it's cold this morning, the ground frozen so iron-hard that there's precious little filth or muck to stick to a woman's skirts. Except that it creates other problems. The woman, fair and soft-featured, holds on to her husband, careful not to slip. He walks equally slowly, because he's carrying a child – a little girl, about two years old, clutching a rag monkey.

'Not a real one?'

'No, this one's a toy.'

'How do you know the little girl had one?'

'Well, OK, I don't.'

But I do know she's not making life very easy for her father. She won't stay still, she's a mad little thing and all she wants is to get down and stand on her own two feet, only he's worried she'll slip over, so he's not allowing it. And she's getting crosser and crosser and she knows how to play him, she knows how to get her way. Every so often she makes her whole body go completely rigid, then throws her head back and squeals with frustration and rage.

I decide to look the Maslins up on the 1881 census. I know that by the time Henry and Charlotte Hayward move into this house, in April 1881, it's been standing empty for several months. The land tax collector noted it as empty in February 1881. So where have the Maslins gone?

I type in Edith Maslin's name and she pops up at 5 Glebe Place, Chelsea. I think that's just off the King's Road, somewhere near the fire station. A wealthy upper-middle-class area, surely, even then?

But the list of occupants makes startling reading. No sign of Edward or Mary. Instead:

Stephen Maslin (widower) 70 years old, born Melksham, Wilts.
Amelia Mary Maslin (unwed) 37 years old, born London.
Ann King (widow) 80 years old, born Melksham.
Edith Mary Maslin, 7 years old, born Clapham.

I stare at the printout. Why on earth is seven-year-old Edith – our Edith! – living over in Chelsea with someone I presume is her grandfather? Where are Edward and Mary? Is it possible that both her parents have died?

'Suicide pact,' Chloë mutters immediately, but I shush her. We don't want to start that one all over again.

'It's possible of course that he was sent abroad for his job,' suggests Jonathan, 'as an army agent's clerk, I mean – posted somewhere like India. It happened all the time.'

'And took his wife but not his daughter? Would you do that?'

'He decided she was too frail?'

'Or Mary and Edward were dead by then.'

The young couple stand in the frozen mud and gaze up at the house. Red brick, white-washed window sills, blue-grey Welsh slate roof.

'The outside's dreadfully bare-looking,' says the woman. 'It badly wants a creeper round the door. You could plant an ivy, couldn't you, my dear?'

The front door's painted but it hasn't even got a number on it yet. But next door, also empty, has a wooden sign leaning in the window with '14' chalked on it.

'Must be number 15, then,' guesses the man, 'if they're counting from the old part, down there by the cottages.'

The child twists and he gives in and lets her squirm down.

'There you go,' he says and straightens and rubs his shoulders.

She stays still a quick moment, swaying, surprised, rejoicing in her sudden freedom. She's a strong girl. She took her first tentative steps a month ago and already she's unstoppable, rushing forwards whenever she gets the chance.

'Whether it's 15 or not, we can always name it ourselves,' says his wife. 'I'd like that. To have a new house and name it from scratch. We'd always be the people who named it.'

He smiles affectionately at his wife. 'Funny Mary,' he says, 'to be thinking about something like that.'

She shoots him an amused look. 'You like the idea too, you know you do. You can decide what to call it if you like.'

He looks surprised. 'You want to rent it, then? We haven't even seen inside . . .'

She lays a gloved finger on her cheek.

'I love it, Eddie. Even from here I can tell. There's something about it. I just like the look of it.'

So, apparently, does their daughter. Because it's at that very moment that she decides to take off, tottering straight across the frozen ground to the black-painted front door. Using her hands to steady herself, she gets on the step.

'My,' she shouts, looking back at them, 'my, my, my!'

They smile at each other. It's her first word. She said it at breakfast about a week ago and she's been saying it ever since. Now she says it about almost everything.

My, my, mine!

It doesn't take long at the Family Records Centre to pin it all down. Believing Edith was an orphan by the time of the 1881 census, I start in the death registers.

And, yes, our Edward died in August 1885 – of alcoholism and meningitis. Only thirty-six. Edith would have been eleven. He and Mary had left Lillieshall Road by then and were living at Eccles Road off Battersea Rise, not far away, but not remotely as smart a house. If Edward was drinking himself into an early grave, was Edith sent off to live with her grandfather for her own good?

But Edward wasn't the only loss to the family that year. Three months later, Stephen Maslin's only daughter Amelia dictated a hasty will on 10 October, 1885 leaving everything to 'my dear father', and then died only two days later of phthisis. That lung thing again. She's forty-two.

403

But by now I'm barely taking these deaths in. The truth is, I can't take my eyes off Amelia Maslin's will, which has suddenly revealed, in curling inky letters, Stephen Maslin's profession: Page of the Back Stairs to Her Majesty the Queen.

'The father of the first person ever to live in this house worked as a servant for Queen Victoria!' I tell the children.

They go on forking pasta and peas into their mouths, unmoved. Just another Wednesday night, their mother raving about another dead person.

'Great,' says Chloë, in a tone that lacks either sarcasm or interest.

'Can we take our tea in the sitting room and have it in front of the cricket highlights?' asks Raph.

Next day I phone the Royal Archives at Windsor. I'm not hoping for much, but is there any chance that they still hold any staff records that mention Stephen Maslin's name? Or even – actually I hardly dare hope for this – a staff photograph, taken at Windsor with him somewhere on it?

The crisp-voiced lady says they may well be able to help, but they only deal in faxes. The Curse of the Bank of Scotland. She says I should fax my request through and they'll search the archives for me.

I ask her how long it will take.

'Mark it urgent and we'll see what we can do.'

But it changes things a bit, doesn't it, knowing about Edward's alcoholism and early death? I don't really want him to have a drink problem, and I don't really want him to have died so young. His poor wife. Was it a slightly different scene, then, that cold January morning in 1873?

Was it Mary who had to carry the child down the street, half-slipping on the icy clods of earth, because her husband was unreliable – already half-cut by that time in the morning? Walking with a wobble? Tripping over his words? Had Edward already eagerly noted that there was a public drinking house, the Tim Bobbin, conveniently situated at the end of the street? And had Mary seen it too and said nothing?

And did Mary stand there in the freezing cold, gazing up at the red brickwork and white paintwork and listening to the din of the workmen still building the other, larger houses further down the street? And did she bite her lip and try to calculate whether they could really afford to rent such a decent-looking place when any minute her husband might lose his job?

'You're forgetting,' Jonathan says, 'Stephen Maslin lived in Chelsea and worked at the palace. I imagine Edward would have been bankrolled very nicely by his dad. Look, his death certificate describes him as "Fundholder".'

And the child?

I trawl carefully backwards through Maslin births – I've now got Mary Goodall Strange's maiden name, which makes it even easier – to see if there was another child before Edith.

I don't have to go back very far. They had a girl, born just two years earlier, in 1871. She'd have been about twenty months old when Edward and Mary moved into Lillieshall Road.

Her name?

Helena, of course.

Jonathan and I sit in the Calf, a newish gastro-pub with squishy sofas which opened recently down the road. This summer, high on the fact that we no longer need babysitters, we've started coming here whenever we need to escape from the children.

'So anyway,' I say, 'all the babies and toddlers in Number 34. Do we know the final tally?'

'You mean children under five who've lived in the house, or all children?'

'I don't know. Little ones. Maybe children under five.'

We make a list, working backwards: Jacob, Chloë, and Raphael, obviously. Collette and Barney – the Pidgeons' youngest children. Yvette Duncan and Michael and Marcia and Sheryl Reynolds. Quiet, good Winnie Bartolo. Abandoned Rodney Wohl. Thirty-hours Elsie Hayward. And now eponymous Helena and baby Edith.

'But what about babies who were actually delivered in the house?' says Jonathan.

'Well, only Michael Reynolds and Elsie Hayward and Edith Maslin. Michael was born downstairs in the sitting room, we know that. But the other two must have been in our bedroom, don't you think?'

'Impossible to know,' he says.

But I would so love to know! Except he's right, of course. I never will. Those are the forgotten moments that I simply can't pull out of the house. Did Edith first draw breath in our bedroom? Did little Elsie die there? The house shrugs. The house isn't telling. Some secrets it's hanging on to, some stories it's never giving up.

'Actually, you know, it's not that many,' I point out. 'Only thirteen. I actually thought it would be many more. In a hundred and thirty years, I mean.'

'Well, Lucy the childless spinster took up a lot of years, remember. I think thirteen is enough.'

The house agrees. The house thinks thirteen is comfortably enough. Thirteen sticky pairs of hands on its banisters, twenty-six little knees shuffling over its floors. Thirteen tantruming toddlers carried howling down its front path. Twenty-six screaming lungs piercing the silence at night, while anxious, exhausted parents wonder how long to leave it before going to them.

We give up on the baby conversation and instead watch a good-looking man who's been leaning against the bar and talking on his mobile phone for the past half hour. He's right next to the speaker.

'Why's he staying there? How can he possibly hear?'

'You'd think he'd move away at least to the other end of the bar.'

We move on to debating who he might be talking to – it seems difficult, strained, yet not angry, just sad, regretful.

'He's giving her the push.'

'It's the other way round.'

We must have stared too hard, because when he finally rings off he comes over and sits with us.

'I saw yous both looking at me,' he says, half shyly. He tells us his name's Steve.

'We were just wondering whether you didn't find the music too loud, that's all,' Jonathan says politely.

The man sighs. 'I was on the phone to my ex, trying to get back together with her. But she won't have it. Not an easy conversation, you see.'

I don't ask him why he undertook such a difficult conversation against a background of deafening acid-techno. Instead I ask if he has any kids.

'Yeah, three boys actually. They're all with her. I hate it. I miss them like crazy.'

We tell him we're sorry and he brightens. 'The older one's a real character. He's fourteen and he keeps bunking off school, going fishing.'

He says this as if he's proud of it. I can feel Jonathan at my side, struggling to control himself.

The man tells us he's a fireman. He lives in the flats in Grafton Square. 'It's a good place. Brigade accommodation or I could never afford it. But I don't work at this station, I work at the one in Shaftesbury Avenue, Soho. If you's ever down there, pop in and I'll show the kids round.'

I tell him that thirteen years ago I would have jumped at this offer. When Jake was a toddler I couldn't get him past Clapham Fire Station without a tantrum. A firefighter had once made the mistake of inviting us in and letting him sit up in a fire engine and now he wanted to do it again and again and again. 'It got so bad I used to have to avoid the fire station altogether,' I tell him, 'go home the long way round.'

He laughs and asks what we do for a living and we tell him. He tells us he did an A level in English when he was in the army.

'I really enjoyed it. I never knew *King Lear* was actually about anything – you know? I couldn't believe it had a story and all that. And who was that poet – married to another poet, I think?'

'Robert Browning?' I guess.

He shakes his head and shuts his eyes.

'No, no – Tod something.'

'Ted Hughes?'

'That's right! I liked his stuff so much.'

He says by the way, did we know that the Calf used to be called the Bull? We say we did. And that the Firkin and Forget-Me-Not up the road was the Cock?

'No,' I admit, 'I didn't know that. I knew it was Cock Pond opposite.'

'Well, and that's where the phrase Cock and Bull comes from. Carriages used to stop at one pub and then at the other and stories would get passed on. And by the time they'd told them over and over, they'd be a load of old cock and bull, you see.'

'That's really true?'

'No, it's a load of cock and bull.'

I laugh but he nods solemnly. 'God's truth actually, it's true. I love this part of London,' he adds. 'Clapham, it's so old. It's full of stories.'

We get up to go and he says maybe he'll see us in here again.

'Maybe,' I say.

'Get your boy to go back to school,' Jonathan says, 'please, it's so important.'

The fireman shrugs. 'Not much you can do though, is there?'

'I knew you wouldn't be able to resist saying that,' I tell Jonathan as we walk away down the hot, dark street.

'But it's ridiculous. He admits he was moved by poetry and by Shakespeare but doesn't think it's important that his son should stay in school!'

I can't argue with this.

'You know, I'd quite like to rename it Helena House.' I realize I'm still excited about the Helena thing. 'It ought to have its old name back, don't you think?'

He makes a face.

'But why not?'

'Just because it's the original name, why's it such a good thing to put it back? You'll want to restore all the original features next. And we know nothing about Helena Maslin anyway. She might have grown up to be quite poisonous. You might as well call it Chloë House.'

He hesitates and then we both burst out laughing as we realize what he's just said.

But the only way I'm going to trace any living Maslin descendants is by finding out who Edith and Helena married. Assuming, that is, that Edward and Mary had no sons – and they don't appear to have had any more children before Edward died.

'Well, you won't believe this,' I announce to Jonathan after yet another hot afternoon at the Family Records Centre. 'You know I was hoping and praying that Edith wouldn't have married a Smith or a Jones?'

'Let me guess. She married . . . a Spawton, a Hinkley?'

'Nearly as good. Wettlauffer.'

'Sorry?'

'Wettlauffer. W-E-T-T-L-A-U-F-F-E-R. George Albert Charles Wettlauffer. Little baby Edith married him in 1903. She was twenty-nine and he was twenty-five and was a journalist.'

'Another journalist. Maybe he knew Henry Hayward?'

'Doubt it, this is long after she left our house.'

Edith marries George Wettlauffer in Hammersmith, where her

address is given as King Street. George's parents Dora and Albert seem to have been present, but, with Edward long dead, someone called Joseph Bass appears to have been Edith's witness.

'Funny,' says Johnathan studying the certificate, 'who the hell's this Joseph Bass? And I wonder why Mary's name isn't on it?'

Never mind that, there's more. I tell him I also found Edith's children – three of them – Eric Maslin Wettlauffer, born 1904; Frank I. Wettlauffer, born 1911; and Sybil M. Wettlauffer, born 1913.

'Sybil Wettlauffer, I love it. Well, it's a godsend anyway, a surname like that,' says Jonathan. 'Why don't you just look and see if there are any in the phone book.'

I do. There's only one, in Balham. I call them, but they're Canadian and no relation of our Maslins.

'But hold on, those three Wettlauffers must have had children,' Jonathan says.

'No,' I tell him. 'Two sons, so I thought it was worth immediately checking for Wettlauffer births, from when Eric was eighteen right up until 1956, which you think would be far enough; but there was nothing.'

'They can't have both been childless?'

'Gay?'

'Or,' says Jonathan, 'with a name like that, so German . . .'

'And such a mouthful.'

'And then there's the First World War . . .'

In all the excitement about Wettlauffers, I'd almost forgotten about my fax to Windsor. A letter plops on to the mat in a thick white envelope with the royal coat of arms.

I pluck it from the dog's jaws and wave it at Raphael.

'From Her Majesty, look!'

'From Queen Victoria?'

'No, silly. From this Majesty, the alive one. Queen Elizabeth the Second – remember her?'

He gawps, suddenly genuinely impressed. 'The real Queen's written you a letter?'

'Not exactly. But this is what I've been waiting for – a letter from the Royal Archives at Windsor.'

'Oh.' He puts his feet up on the sofa and turns back to the cricket. 'I wish we could go to Legoland again sometime.'

Our records show that Stephen Maslin was born on 4 June 1810 and entered the service of the Duchess of Kent (mother of the future Queen Victoria) on 1 February 1828, commencing as a Steward's Room Boy with a salary of £18 per annum, but being promoted to Footman, with a salary of £24 on 1st August 1829. He became a Page in 1840 and at the time of the Duchess' death in 1861, he was one of her two Grooms of Chambers, with a salary of £100, £64 board wages and free apartments.

The Duchess' affection for Maslin is reflected in her accounts, where there are frequent references to presents (unfortunately not specified) given to him, his sister, and his children. She also paid for the education of Maslin's son, Victor. Under the Duchess' will, all her servants received legacies, the sum concerned being based on their wages and their length of service and Maslin received £538. 2s. 7d.

Maslin was then taken into Queen Victoria's Household as a Page of the Back Stairs and his salary was £290 pa plus £73. 16s. 0d board wages. In 1872, the Queen presented him with the Victoria Faithful Medal for his long years of service.

On 26th November 1887 Queen Victoria noted in her journal, 'My good faithful old Maslin who was with Mama and me for 60 years, has been unwell & very failing, to my great regret. He was unable to come to Balmoral, but it was hoped he would be here (Windsor) on our return, which he alas! Has been unable to do. He has had a slight stroke.' At his own request, Maslin then retired.

On 14 November 1891, Victor Maslin telegraphed from the Fulham Road, London, to Mrs Macdonald the Queen's dresser at Balmoral, to report that 'my Father passed quietly away this evening'. The Queen wrote in her Journal, 'Hear that dear old Maslin died this morning. Too sad! Such a loss! He knew me from my 9th year having come into Mama's service in January 1828!! & remembered dearest Feodora's wedding [the Queen's half-sister], which I do, as yesterday. He was a most devoted & faithful servant to Mama & me. On my Jubilee morning, he wished me so kindly joy. But 4 years ago he had a sort of little seizure & had to retire, to my great regret. I missed him so much, as I felt he was a link with the past & dearest Mama, with whom he remained till her death, then coming to me. I could ask him about many things connected with her & my early years, & now that is gone! He came to see us every time we went to London, & also stayed at Windsor for a day or two, the last time being in July. He was so active, & tripped about, going up & down the stairs like a young man.

I hold this letter – carefully typed on cream paper with the red lion and unicorn at the top – in my hand and read it several times over.

Every single thing about it – from the royal names, the emotions she expresses, the link to our house, the fact that it exists at all – is hard to take in. It feels almost like a joke letter – a parody of the sort of golden moment amateur historians dream of.

Helena has been waiting at the front room window for more than an hour. Every few minutes she lifts the muslin drapes then lets them fall again. In between she tears at her fingernails or taps her boots on the polished wooden floor.

'I do wish you'd stop twitching those drapes,' her mother says yet again. 'He'll come when he comes. No amount of twitching and fiddling is going to make him come any sooner, young lady.'

'When's he expected?'

'I don't know.' Mary checks herself in the glass, wishes she didn't look so pale, wishes her hair would not fluff up so much. 'Not yet.'

Helena spins on her heel and tuts. She takes a strand of her long fair hair and puts it in her mouth.

'But when exactly? You must know! When did you invite him for? When, when, when?'

Mary plumps up the cushions on the best sofa, flicks on the electric light. It's so dark outside, an oppressive and heavy day. It feels like it must rain.

'Within the hour, all right? Don't chew your hair, please Helena.'

She sighs. Her eldest is such an impatient child, quick-tempered, slow to settle. Full of questions, furious when the answers don't suit her, and yet somehow sorely lacking in concentration – abandoning each task almost as soon as it's started. Quite different from Edie, who's already reading and writing, who has a good understanding of arithmetic and has the patience to spend an hour on a single drawing. Everyone says Edie will go far.

Helena frowns and tries to think. She doesn't know whether to leave her post or not. She desperately wants to be the first to spy her Grandpa when his carriage draws up. But she's bored and would also like to go upstairs and make life difficult for Edie. Upstairs – the idea of upstairs prompts a sudden wave of pain, a thought.

'Why's Father still in bed?' she demands to know.

'He's unwell,' her mother replies without looking at her.

'He's always unwell.'

'He's had a bad time of it lately, that's all. You know that, my darling.'

Mary sighs again. She sighs all the time these days and she knows it. She sighs because she's bored, frankly – bored and tired. She loves Eddie dearly; he's a good, sweet man despite his problems, but he provides no companionship any more. Yes, she's bored and lonely. Feels her whole life is slipping away and what's there to show for it? A

413

husband who is always sleeping it off. A great big house – oh, she had such plans for this house, but she's fast losing heart – and two furiously alert and difficult little girls. Well, not difficult perhaps, but active, constant, persistent.

Suddenly there's a shriek and a clatter from upstairs and Edith comes rushing down, slipping down the final length of banister and making the front door just before Helena, who's close on her tail.

'I was first! I saw him first! I saw him coming from upstairs!' Edith bellows joyously.

A whole hour Helena's been standing waiting by the front room window. In the hall, she stands back in the shadows round the corner and folds her arms, her face dark with anger. And when her Grandpa, closely followed by her Aunt Amelia, comes in, she will refuse to kiss his cheek or look at him, she'll refuse to do anything in fact. Whereas little Edith, six years old and quicker off the mark (this once), will climb into his great, tobacco-scented lap and gaze up into his old face and stroke his pure white whiskers.

'Here you are,' he'll say, holding something up in the air. 'A present from Windsor.'

And Edith will slip down off his lap and undo the package and it will be one of those wonderful little barrel organs – where you slot in the punched cards and turn the handle to play each different tune. And for Helena there'll be a tin puppy on a string, a puppy that really goes along, but she'll be furious because she's wanted one of those organs for so long. The puppy's a baby's toy anyway, it hardly even does anything, can't they see that?

And even when Amelia tries to cheer her up, tries to cajole her and begs her to tell them all why the house is called Helena House – as though she doesn't know! – still she'll stamp her feet and turn away.

Is that what happens? Could it be why, a year later, with Edward and Mary in a crisis and forced out of Lillieshall Road, it's Edith that Stephen offers to have come and live with him?

Does he tell Mary, 'I can only manage one, my dear, and I really don't like to pick and choose, but how about Ediebug? She's such a dear, really such a good girl, such a lamb.'

If the Wettlauffers did change their name sometime during the First World War, then I have to hope that they did it officially.

On a hot and cloudy day in late August, I head off to the Public Record Office yet again, to look at deed polls. I'm not really that hopeful – the whole name change thing is really just a hunch. But I think I have to be able to say I tried.

Somewhere here in this building, my own deed poll name change must be lodged, too. More than a decade ago, in 1991, I changed my name from Pike to Myerson, when I suddenly realized that, though I wasn't married to Jonathan – we'd agreed that we didn't feel the need – my feelings about my own name had changed forever.

By then, I had two babies called Myerson. My father had recently committed suicide, and in the years before that he hadn't wanted to know me. Why, I wondered, was I hanging on to his name? Not only that, but there was something pleasing and somehow organic about making ourselves into a family, all sharing a common name. I liked the idea that every letter that came through the letter box would have the same name on it.

Secretly, I think I quite enjoyed the sheer perversity of it, too. Most of my friends were married but had doggedly kept their maiden names – whether for professional or personal reasons – many of them therefore ending up with a whole different surname from their children. Where was the romance in that?

I asked Jonathan's permission to appropriate his name.

'Sure. Because you'll never do it,' he teased me, and at first I believed him. I thought it would be complicated, a big red tape process. But in the end it was surprisingly easy. Our solicitor on Clapham High Street – a man who had grown up with Jonathan's late father and probably knew more Myersons than I ever will – helped me fill in some forms. I informed the bank, got a new passport and driving licence – and threw a party to celebrate.

Anyway, Myerson was definitely a cosmetic improvement on Pike – which had always made me think of a large, ugly fish with sharp teeth. But if you were going to ditch Wettlauffer, what would you go for instead? Westlove? Less Germanic perhaps, but not exactly a name that would stop you being teased in the playground. Whitelaw? Whitlaver?

The PRO archivist isn't encouraging. She says that, quite honestly, I'm unlikely to find what I want – 'Most people in those days didn't bother with legalities. They just called themselves something different and that was that.'

'And if it's not here then there's nowhere else I can look?'

''Fraid not, no.'

But she leads me over to the huge books of High Court indentures. They're better than I thought they'd be – wonderfully dramatic – and glamorous-looking things, enormous and bound in snowy white leather, a huge flapping volume for each year, every thick page hand-written in semi-gothic script.

I begin in 1913 and start wading through the 'W's. It turns out that it's not just deed polls listed here but any indenture at all made before the High Court. So there's the Duke of Westminster making some order – I can barely read it – or the Waifs and Strays Society appointing some new trustee. I begin in 1913 and by 1915 there is, unsurprisingly, a huge tidal wave of people with German-sounding names seeking to change them. Weissmuller, Wegner, Wednacht. But no Wettlauffers. I close the book and pick up another. It'll be here.

By the end of 1918, though, there's still nothing and I wonder whether it's really worth going on. Would anyone bother to change their name once the war was over? I didn't really expect to find anything and I haven't. I decide I'll go as far as 1925 and then call it a day.

But only two volumes on, in 1920, there it is:

Wettlauffer, Eric Maslin (late) Eric Maslin Ingrey (now).

'here's the written proof.'

Edith's son Eric changed his name to Ingrey! And he did it officially by deed poll, and here's the written proof.

I look up, glance around me. In the room, research goes on as usual. People are flicking, clicking, staring, writing, unfurling. I look back at the page. Wettlauffer's still there – definitely there.

From Wettlauffer to Ingrey.

But Ingrey? Such a funny name, not unattractive, but not especially English either – and not even close to Wettlauffer. I'm so overwhelmed at simply finding the entry that I've forgotten to wonder where I've seen that name before. Then it comes to me.

The week before I had checked the indexed 1901 census – Jonathan wanted to know if (like his ancestors) the Wettlauffers were Jewish. But with first names like George and Albert and Florence and Amy, we decided they weren't. But also living in the family house in Stoke Newington was George's maternal aunt, Emily Ingrey. Eric took his father's mother's maiden name.

I heave the book off the table and carry it over to the photocopying counter. The man looks left and right like a burglar going to work: 'These handwritten volumes are supposed to be scanned not photo-copied – but I'll do it for you.'

Back home, Jonathan and I spread the huge photocopied document on the kitchen table:

> I, Eric Maslin Ingrey of 7 Coleridge Road, Crouch End, London N
> – a natural born British subject send greeting . . . I have heretofore
> been known and described by the name of Wettlauffer . . . and
> whereas I have determined to change my said surname of
> Wettlauffer and to adopt and take in lieu thereof the surname of
> Ingrey . . .

The document is witnessed by Eric's father George (who definitely won't be changing from Wettlauffer), his great-aunt Emily Ingrey, and Joseph Bass.

'Joseph Bass again?' says Jonathan. 'Who is this Joseph Bass? Sounds like a Jewish comedian. Is he related to them? He keeps on cropping up everywhere.'

We sit and stare at the document for some time.

'Why don't I feel more excited at finding this?' I ask Jonathan, because I realize that's what it is: I don't, I just feel I've sunk still deeper into a puzzle I can't solve.

'Because we thought you'd find nothing and you found something. But it's not what we expected and we don't know quite what to do with it.'

I realize he's right. The name change discovery has actually thrown up as many questions as it's answered. Why would Edith and George's sixteen-year-old son Eric suddenly, in 1920, take his great-aunt's name? Why just him, and why so long after the end of the war, and why that name?

'I suppose we can at least now start searching for Ingreys,' I say.

'But you know something else I thought of? You checked for Wettlauffer births but not marriages. Didn't it occur to you that the daughter, Sybil, may well have used marriage to change her name. You can easily find her offspring – with a mother's maiden name like Wettlauffer.'

The hunt for Maslins seems to have acquired a stop-start rhythm all of its own. It's almost as if it's out of my hands now – as if this final, odd, sad, exotic chapter in the life of the house is unfurling at its own pace and in its own way.

Again and again it happens. I stumble on something amazing, then I get stuck, hugely stuck. Then, just when I've almost given up and I'm expecting nothing, I get a break and it all comes clear.

Ever since we had the three maddening possible spellings of the name – Maslin, Maslen, or Maslem – we've joked about it. It's almost as if the Maslins are playing with us – letting the information trickle out as and when they feel like it. And the house? It's in on the game. It's enjoying the fun.

But the dog days of summer have filled me with a strange kind of energy.

'I'll have them before the month's out,' I tell Jonathan. And as if to prove me right, the following day, a Saturday, two things happen.

First, in the post, a stiff brown envelope with the royal coat of arms: 'Look, she's written to you again!' says Raphael, rushing to pick it up off the mat.

I rip it open and pull out a Windsor Archives comp slip and a large black-and-white photo wrapped in a translucent tissue sleeve. I remove the sleeve and feel my heart race. It's way more than I'd expected. But then again, this is Maslinland.

'Do you know who that is?' I ask Raph, pointing to a seated figure in the picture.

He shrugs.

'The old fat one? Nope.'

'Come on, have a guess.'

'Lucy Spawton?'

'No, she was little and thin, remember.'

'Someone else who lived here?' He rolls a tennis ball backwards and forwards under his foot, fast losing interest.

'No, it's someone extremely famous who at your age you really ought to recognize.'

He peers again at the picture. 'Margaret Thatcher?'

'No, silly, it's Queen Victoria. Don't you know what she looked like? It's Queen Victoria as quite an old lady, having tea on the Isle of Wight.'

It is 1887. Queen Victoria is taking tea at Osborne. A rug is spread on the lawn, with a tea table and chairs. Above, a tasselled, fringed canopy. On either side, an Indian servant in turban and long jacket. Two little girls are standing on her left and next to them a man in a bowler hat, seated, is about to pour tea from the heavy silver tea pot. Four young women in straw boaters sit around the table. Some of their faces are visible, some have their backs to us.

The caption reads:

> (left to right) Abdul Karim, Princess Marie and Princess Victoria Melita of Edinburgh, Duke of Connaught, Queen Victoria, Beatrice, Princess Henry of Battenburg, Princess Alix of Hesse, Princess Alexandra of Edinburgh, Princess Irene of Hesse, Mohamed Bulchsh.

But behind them all stands the most important person – an elderly, placid-looking gentleman with white whiskers and black frock coat, straight-backed, carefully holding a tray. He waits dutifully, soberly, neutral-faced. An invisible man, eager to anticipate the needs of the tea table.

I don't even have to check the caption to see who he is. I know already. He's Edward's father – 'good faithful old Maslin'.

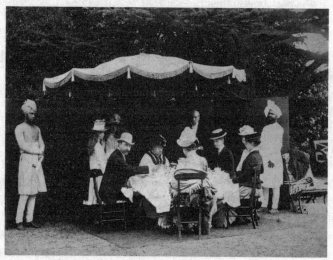

'He peers again at the picture. "Margaret Thatcher?"'

That afternoon, Chloë and I pop up to the Family Records Centre together. Actually, pop is the wrong word. It's a boiling day and the front windows on the car are stuck. The streets are empty of traffic but by the time we get there we're both hot and cross, clothes and hair sticking to us.

'Am I looking in births or deaths?' Chloë sighs, throwing herself into a chair and taking great gulps of cold, air-conditioned air. 'I do find the death area a bit creepy.'

'Marriages, then births.'

'No deaths?'

'No deaths.'

'OK.'

It takes us precisely twenty minutes to discover something I should probably have arrived at a week ago. That in December 1940, Sybil M. Wettlauffer married Francis Leo Towers. We quickly find that in 1943 and 1948, they had two children Patrick L. and Bridget A.

'It was me! I found them! I found the Towers babies!' Chloë shrieks to an empty hall as soon as we get home.

There's no one to hear her. The boys are both out and the house is cool, all the curtains drawn against the heat. Three cats lie on the landing, eyes half-closed, tails curled under their chins.

I slip up to my study and load the Info Disk. There's one Bridget A. Towers and she lives down the road in Richmond.

In a trail that seems to have flushed alternately hot and cold, it makes an eerie kind of sense to discover that Bridget Towers is a historian – 'Well, medical history really – I write books on medicine and I also lecture in criminology.'

But I barely manage to take in these words. All I can think of is, I'm finally talking to Edward Maslin's great-granddaughter and she lives only a few miles away and she sounds incredibly friendly; and though she's never heard of our house – 'Gosh, what a fascinating project!' – she says I've come to the right person: she knows everything there is to know about the Maslins.

'Oh dear,' she says, 'there's so much to tell. It's hard to know where to start. What you need to understand is that both my grandmother Edith and her mother Mary were amazing women, quite amazing – both of them career women in a time when that was completely unusual, unheard of.'

I ask her what they did, but she tells me I have to wait. The story has to be unravelled in the right order.

'And Helena?'

'Hmm, yes, well, we'll come to her.'

Late August 2003. The story's almost told and the house is glad. It's getting tired now, bone tired. We've come a long way from that frozen day in January 1873 when it was new and young and startled – waiting anxiously for its first tenants.

Now, at the age of 130, its white wood window frames are blistered and splintering – whole wedges of wood missing in places: they'll need to be redone sooner rather than later. And its bricks too, those old mauve bricks, blackened with age and soot, they badly need repointing.

And if you look at it from the street, it's always been a bit lopsided – most of us are – but it's been such a long, hot summer that some of its doors have warped a little, the wood shifting and stretching on its hinges. The front door sticks if you don't open it in a certain way – giving it a little shove to the left as you turn the key – though that'll return to normal once the cold weather's back.

The house is tired. The house wants to sleep. It actually quite likes it when the Myersons, the latest family, go out. When that happens, it takes a breath, sighs, settles a little deeper in its old foundations, shifts its weight a touch so the mud and rubble don't press on its sore old haunches, and it dozes – snatching a few moments' respite until they all come crashing back in.

10.40 p.m., later that Saturday night. The whole family is crammed on to the little terrace outside my study.

From here, if you sit back against the low, white-painted wall, you can imagine you're not in a house at all but in the treetops – that's all you can see: sky and trees. The children love it out here. It's so hot that we've let them stay up and drag out cushions and a rug. A plate of yellow-mauve plums donated from the house over the road. Some lemon squash. A bottle of wine.

Chloë's wearing rosebud pyjamas, but Raph's wearing nothing but a pair of boxer shorts with dogs all over them. Jake, despite the heat, wears jeans.

Raph wins the toss to light the candles, eight of them – tea-lights in saucers and a thick yellow citronella one to keep the insects away. As he bends with the matches, striking a new one for each wick, you can see every single knob on the astonishingly skinny, translucent arc of his spine. But he still looks like a little boy, while Jake has grown with such furtive speed this summer that I glanced in the mirror the other day and saw with an ache of surprise that he's done it. He's taller than me.

I lean back against the cushions in the blue darkness and breathe in the scent of honeysuckle. Even this late at night, the air still crackles with heat.

Jonathan looks at me. 'Come on then. We're waiting.'

Once upon a time there was a man called Edward Maslin.

'And he lived in this house!'

Yes, he lived here in this house but, please, darling, if you all keep on interrupting I won't be able to tell the story.

'Shh. Shut up. Let Mummy tell the story.'

Edward was born at Windsor, where his mother Amelia and father Stephen both worked for the Duchess of Kent, who was the future Queen Victoria's mother.

Stephen was in fact the godson of the Duchess of Kent and he started working for her when he was just eighteen and it was while he was working there at Windsor that he met his future wife, Amelia Harrison.

'Edward's mother?'

That's right. In fact she was pretty important because she was one of the ladies-in-waiting looking after the young Victoria on the morning when the ministers came in early to say, 'Le Roi est mort, vive la Reine . . .'

'Reine is queen and mort is dead,' says Chloë quickly.

'Shh, Chloë.'

Well, on that morning it was Edward's mother Amelia who got the young Queen Victoria up and helped her get dressed so they could tell her the King had died and she was now Queen.

'She couldn't do it on her own?'

'This is royalty, remember.'

'Plus they had a lot of buttons in those days.'

Quite. Anyway, this just gives you an idea of the kind of life Edward would have had as a child. I think his growing up would have been quite glamorous – parties and visits to amazing places. As children, for instance, he and his brother Victor accompanied their parents on all sorts of trips with the Queen.

'What about Amelia?' demands Chloë.

'She probably stayed home because she was a girl.'

They went to all the stately homes of England – Blenheim, Chatsworth, Belvoir Castle, Warwick Castle, Knole, Alton Towers . . .

'Alton Towers?'

I knew you'd say that, Raph. Well, yes, it says it here on Stephen Maslin's obituary from the *Windsor and Eton Gazette*. It wasn't an amusement park then – it was obviously a stately home in those days. The Maslins also went abroad with the Queen on long tours to the continent – to Switzerland, Paris, the Rhine, all sorts of faraway places.

But when Edward grew up he went to work as a clerk for Cox's, which was an army bank, and his poor old father worried that it was then that he fell in with what he called 'a fast set'. They encouraged him to drink and gamble and spend every penny he had. His father used to say those men, they weren't the right kind for Edward, he was nothing like them. Everyone thought of Edward as a really gentle, good man. He liked to paint watercolours of flowers and he kept a diary where he wrote about weather and wildlife.

'He sounds a bit camp, if you ask me,' says Jake.

'Do they still have the diary?' Jonathan asks.

Yes, Bridget thinks her brother Patrick might have it in Ireland. Look, does anyone want to hear this story or not?

'Yesss! Get on with it!'

Then, in 1870 – two years before this house of ours was even built – Edward got married at Windsor to a grocer's daughter called Mary Goodall Strange. And they went to live in Pimlico and, just over a year later, they had a little girl –

'Called Helena!' says Chloë.

'a grocer's daughter called Mary Goodall Strange'

Yes, she was christened Helena. And when they moved in here, the very first people ever to live in this house, they decided to name the house after her and it became Helena House. The name was painted on the glass over the front door.

Two years later, another daughter, Edith, was born here in this house and around that time they actually bought the house, so they weren't just renting it any more. The first real owners. But Edward had started drinking by then and had lost his job with Cox's and was working for the railways instead, as a clerk. The family moved to Eccles Road in Battersea – a much smaller house – though they still owned Lillieshall Road and presumably they must have looked around for a tenant.

'Funny though,' says Jonathan, 'they obviously didn't find one very quickly. The Haywards didn't get here till almost a year later.'

'he fell in with a fast set'

426

Well, in August 1885, Edward died – 'riding horses in bed', Mary always told people, which means he had the DTs.

'The what?'

'Delirium tremens, Latin for shaking and hallucinating. It's what you have if you're an alcoholic.'

And Mary was very sad, but she had to pull herself together quickly because she had these two little girls to look after and she knew they'd been getting poorer and poorer as Edward poured all their funds down his throat.

So she set up a business of her own. She started by taking over her father's grocerery business in Windsor, but quickly turned it into something a little grander. By the time Maslin's moved to King Street in Hammersmith, it had a By Appointment thingy.

'Royal Warrant,' says Jonathan.

Yes, Royal Warrant and it had turned itself into a high-class importer of fine wines, sherries, coffees, teas, spices and provisions. They were doing well.

And the store became successful and it needed a manager, and so Mary, who was in her mid-forties by now, appointed a young man, in his early twenties, with some experience as a grocer. He was called Joe Bass.

'Joe Bass! The name on all those documents!'

But wait, it gets better. Joe Bass was about Edith's age – I'll tell you in a minute what Edith and Helena had been doing all this time, by the way – and Joe had great business acumen and the business did better and better and Mary made money and in 1890 – only five years after Edward's death – guess what she did.

'I know,' says Chloë. 'She made Edith marry Joe Bass.'

No! She married him herself!

There's a collective gasp on the terrace. Jonathan smiles and pours more wine.

'But he was twenty-three and she was . . . way too old!'

She was about my age actually, Jake. But yes, it was pretty amazing.

She loved him, though – it was a marriage of pure love – and they were very happy together until he suddenly dropped dead without having made a will but leaving the business in trust to Mary. The problem was it only went to her in trust and when Mary finally died it passed straight to the Bass family and not to Edith or Helena. They thought about going to court – 'the Bass family are still in smocks!' was the cry in the Maslin family – but they didn't remotely have a case. All Edward and Mary's money was finally gone.

'But what about Edith and Helena? What happened to them?'

Well, Edith, the little baby who was born right here in our house, she went off to Paris to finish her education – that's what posh girls did in those days – and then when she returned to London she was apprenticed to a costumier on Bond Street where she learned to design clothes. She turned out to be so good at it she became a royal costumier and went to work at Windsor, designing clothes for the Court.

'Wow,' says Chloë. 'Was she rich?'

She would certainly have earned a decent living. And on a trip to Paris, she met George Wettlauffer – she was on holiday there and he was singing in a choir – and soon after they came back he proposed. In 1903, they were married. In time he became Deputy Head of the Press Association, but not an establishment figure at all – radical, politically liberal, anti-monarchy.

'Anti-monarchy?' says Jonathan. 'So the big Maslin royal connection wouldn't have cut much ice with him?'

Well, apparently if Edith and George were at the theatre or some-

'he was singing in a choir'

428

thing and the national anthem was played, she stood up and he stayed firmly sitting. But certainly Edith's Uncle Victor remained a staunch monarchist – the Duchess of Kent had actually paid for his education in fact – so yes, George's views must have led to a few arguments round the lunch table.

And there's a photo of Edith in her wedding dress – Bridget's going to send it to me – and she kept the dress all her life, and when she died she was cremated in it.

'when she died she was cremated in it.'

'Yuk, that's horrible,' says Raph. He shudders. 'I never want to get married, or to die.'

'Get on with the story,' says Jake.

Well, Edith and George had three children – Eric, Frank, and Sybil.

'George's views must have led to a few arguments around the lunch table'

'And why the name change?' asks Jonathan.

That one's a bit weird actually. George and Edith were apparently increasingly uncomfortable with the name but didn't bother to change it. Instead they encouraged Eric and Frank to do so – which they did – but never Sybil.

'I suppose she was always likely to marry.'

But she was apparently quite bloody-minded too and would never do anything because someone told her to.

George died at his desk of a heart attack in 1942. Not long before, Lord Beaverbrook had offered him the editorship of the *Express*. He'd turned it down because he knew he was ill. Edith died in 1967.

'And Helena?' says Chloë. 'You haven't said what happened to Helena!'

Ah, Helena. Well, for many years the family never spoke about her at all. She was a huge source of embarrassment. She disgraced them all, you see. She got married much earlier than Edith, when she was only twenty-one, to a boilermaker called Jim Mayer.

'But that's not so bad.'

430

No, but after a few years and a few children, she just took off to America and never came back. But while there, she married again. And she hadn't ever divorced Mr Mayer.

'A bigamist,' says Jonathan. 'I like her.'

'What's a bigamist?' Raph asks eagerly.

'Someone who marries more than once without getting divorced first.'

'I thought it might be to do with sex.'

Well, there might have been a sex thing too. Her mother apparently used to say that Helena only had to look at a man's trousers to have a baby. And later in her life, though it's not clear quite when, she spent some time being looked after by nuns in a convent in Paris.

'Why? To stop her having sex?'

I don't know. No one really knows. But certainly she had a lot of children too, apparently, from both marriages. But the family was so shocked they cut her off and never spoke of her again. Except that's not quite true because Edith continued to send her money all her life. On the quiet, never telling George what she was up to.

I don't know how long she lived or where she died or anything else, I'm afraid.

'But that's awful,' says Chloë, clearly disappointed. 'I mean that no one knows.'

Well, someone does, obviously. There must be children or grand-children around somewhere. But how can we even begin to find them?

'Mayer children?' Jonathan says.

I tried looking. There are literally millions.

Chloë looks at me.

'More researching? I'll do it!'

I sigh.

Haven't we almost got to the end of the story of our house?

'There is no end,' says Jake suddenly from his place in the shadows. 'There isn't, not really, is there? You could go on forever.'

I look at him. All I can see is his white T-shirt, pale in the darkness.

'You could spend the rest of your life on it,' he says.

'Or you could tunnel down,' adds Raph, 'go down under the earth and find Roman remains.'

Jonathan laughs. 'You probably could, boy. The thing is, you could go as far down as possible and do an archaeological dig. And you could also spread out sideways, go further and deeper into the lives of these people. But Jake's right, Mummy's right. There has to be a place where you say: enough. I know enough, I won't ask any more questions. There has to be a place where you just decide to stop.'

'But,' says Chloë impatiently, 'the whole house was named after Helena Maslin. Helena's so important!'

I think about this. And I peer at the faces of my family in the hot summer darkness and I see that it's almost midnight and here we all still are, perched on a terrace that didn't even exist a hundred years ago, listening to all the extraordinary lives of the house. On the outside of Number 34, looking in.

I push open the door back into my study and reach in and turn on a light. Everyone blinks.

'Everyone's important,' I say, 'every single one of these people who lived here is equally important. That's the whole point.'

'Even us?' says Raph.

In winter the light disappears in a snap at about four o'clock, sucked up while you're not even looking. Helena's glad. Soon the lamplighter will come and she'll wave to him from an upstairs window and if it's a lucky day, he'll see her and wave back.

It's been glorious since they put lamps in the street – not because she cares about the light one jot, but because she really likes waving at the man. She thinks that when she grows up she may be a lamplighter herself, then she can always carry a ladder and a handful of fire, which would annoy Ediebug no end, she knows it would.

The hall wall still shows the mark where her boot kicked it this morning – a bruise of dirt over the chalky paintwork. She licks her finger and rubs at it, immediately making it worse. She decides she doesn't know she did that and instead stomps upstairs and into her father's little study on the first landing – the room where he keeps his books and paints and sketchbooks. He has a wooden box of paints in here, with his name engraved on it, a present from Queen Victoria when he was young. He's never used them, they're too special. Sometimes, if she's careful, she's allowed to take them all out one by one and then put them back in again, in the same order.

She's actually thinking of doing this now, when something catches her and she stiffens. It's a sound but she can't tell where it's coming from – inside or outside? – or inside her head perhaps?

She's not scared. She's heard things before in this house. Small creaks and shuffles and sobs and funny little laughs that shouldn't really be there. All houses have it – a layer of life that keeps on going when you're not in its rooms. It tries to trick you, the life of the house. You have to be pretty quick and silent if you want to creep in and see who's making the sounds.

This time the voices are coming from the space outside the window. Hmm. Very clever. A space beyond the room, above the garden only higher up. A space that isn't anything but blackness and air – a space where no voices should be.

She stands for a moment in the room and listens.

She thinks she hears children. And she's sure one of them says her name – why would they say her name? But then again, why not?

'Hello?' she says, as loudly as she dares.

Nothing.

If she decides to pull a stool over and stand up on it and look out right now, what will she see? The light of eight or nine small candles? The glow of a white T-shirt? A bottle, the brief shine of a glass? Several hands moving, a knee, a foot in a navy-blue espadrille, a rosebud pyjama sleeve, a mouth talking, an open eye? The faces of three children who ought to be in bed?

She's about to do it, she's about to pull the stool over, when she suddenly remembers something – the whole reason she was going upstairs in the first place. The lamplighter!

She turns on her heel, runs from the room, and dashes as fast as she can to the top of the house. She's just in time. She bangs on the window, waves hard. The old man turns slowly, lifts his hand, waves back.

She can relax now.

Chapter Ten

GRASS AND SILENCE

Before 1871

Number 34, it's time to finally undo you.

You're coming apart pretty fast now – bricks, slate, cement, mortar, nails, joists flying away as hurriedly as they appeared. London gravel and clay are pouring back into your deepest foundations – shovelled and levelled, a layer of turf and gorse flung quick as a blanket over the top.

'Not gorse, remember? Not for a cricket ground.'

All right, not gorse but green turf, then – smooth and even and lovingly maintained, stretching as far as The Chase on one side and almost to Broadhinton Road on the other. And turn your head southwards and there's still green and trees and flowers rolling on just about as far as the eye can see – chestnut, ash, beech, oak and rowan, buttercups and milkwort and bird's-foot trefoil. Not to mention the birds that sing here. Skylark and fieldfare and missel thrush.

'Never mind about that, is there a match being played?'

Actually, there is. The London and South-Western Railway are up against H. Doulton & Co. and it's not looking good for the latter.

'Why? What's the score?'

Not sure, but . . . oh look! Spicer runs in harder and the ball moves off the seam and just nips the top of the batsman's off-stump. There's a wooden click that bounces off the trees followed by a fluttery whisper of applause from the few passing spectators.

'You just made that up, didn't you?'

'Did I? How can you tell?'

'Because you don't understand anything about cricket and it just doesn't sound right when you say it.'

Well, yes, it's true I might have made some of it up. But I based it on a real match, actually. Here's the score card, look – there's Spicer, whoever he was. It might have been the last match ever played on this piece of ground.

'Hmm. It might, but you don't know, do you?'

I don't, it's true. But shall we, for the sake of an ending, just say it was?

London and South-Western Railway v. H. Doulton and Co.'s. C. C.

This match was played at Clapham on Saturday, and owing to the fine bowling of Bishop and Brown, resulted in an easy win for the London and South-Western Railway. Score:

LONDON AND SOUTH-WESTERN RAILWAY.

Brown, c Spicer, b Bolton	6
Milner, b Cook	4
Rawnsley, b Bolton	8
Phillips, c Cook, b Bolton	1
Bishop, run out	9
A. Taylor, c Cook, b Bolton	8
Chadwick, c Bryon, b Spicer	9
Nelson, b Barrel	5
W. Taylor, c Bryon, b Spicer	1
Hogg, not out	0
Gilroy, c Bolton, b Barrel	2
Extras	6
Total	59

H. DOULTON AND CO.'S.

Cosham, run out	0
Spicer, b Bishop	19
E. Bryon, b Bishop	2
Bolton, c W. Taylor, b Bishop	0
H. Carr, b Bishop	0
Barrel, c Hogg, b Brown	0
Cook, l b w, b Bishop	0
H. Bryon, b W. Taylor	6
A. Bolton, b Brown	1
Potter, b Bishop	14
Pierce, not out	0
Extras	2

'It might have been the last match ever played at this piece of ground.'

The game's over now, the people have all trailed off home. Everyone gone – the ginger beer seller with his handcart and the hatless children squinting in the sunshine. Even the women in aprons who bothered to come out of the cottages on Orchard Street and stand, arms folded, watching, because they knew it might be the last game here.

Bazalgette's men break soil at first light on Monday.

'That's it? It's all over? But I've been waiting and waiting for the cricket match bit!'

Shh. The sun's almost gone, sliding away, the horizon's a lit-up blur of gold that in less than a minute will dissolve to dusk. The air smells almost perfect – the perfect end of a perfect summer's day. One solitary shiny black beetle is clambering over a single blade of grass, purposeful and oblivious, while beneath him the earth hums and shivers.

'So, no more cricket then?'

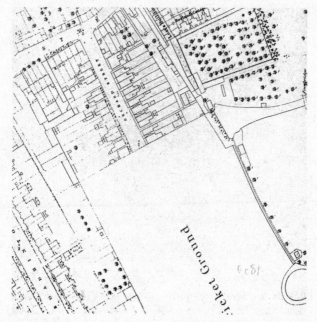

No. No one will hear the thwack of leather on willow on this ground again, but a whole, shuddering future is waiting to happen right here in this spot.

ACKNOWLEDGEMENTS

Writing novels is easy. You just pull stuff out of the dark, cobwebby places in your head and if it doesn't sound so good, or if it embarrasses you, you shove it straight back. No One Ever Need Know. But writing about real life demands much more responsibility. In the long, strange journey of this book, I came across the kind of material most writers can only dream of: a clutch of human stories so touching, pungent, and outlandish that, had I invented them, I might have worried they were too far-fetched and flung them speedily back.

But I didn't have to. These stories were all true. Not only did I never have to invent anything, but these intimacies were handed over to me with a warmth and generosity that always took me by surprise. As I cold-called and visited so many strangers, enticed them back here into my home, and questioned them about their lives in the most intensely personal way possible, I grew more and more touched and amazed. Not once did anyone put the phone down on me, shut the door in my face, or tell me to mind my own business. But then real people aren't like authors – they're not in it to spin tales or fake it. They already believe in the story – because it's true. In writing about and around these lives, I've tried to preserve this truth and dignity. I've tried hard not to invent or judge – and if at times I've fleshed out the truth, I can only say I did it with the best of intentions, in an honest attempt to recreate a real episode from this or that person's real life. But my imagination is, at the end of the day, no more than that – a subjective place of flimsy imaginings, so if I've misrepresented or disappointed anyone, I can only apologise with all my heart.

Making this book has been the biggest, strangest, most heart-shaking adventure. The people I came to know along the way not only crowded and coloured my text but touched my life too. I am indebted to all of them – the living and the dead, the one-time residents of 34 Lillieshall Road, and the relatives and friends who knew and loved them.

My special thanks to:

Diane Askew (for fixing things with Auntie Joan); Bob Askew (for ringing me back); Tony Bell and Valerie Johnson-Bell across the road (for lending me a cool quiet space to write in during the heat and noise of August . . . and their nimble-footed if hissy tortoise Marmalade for keeping me company there); the Bank of Scotland (for taking five months to tell me they didn't have the Deeds – well, hey, at least they got back to me); Mr John Brown (for being kind enough to share his local history knowledge with me); Dorothy Bartolo and her daughter Winnie King (for being so willing to step back over the threshold after more than fifty years); Eleanor Bingham (for an hour of torrid telephone tales); Mrs Gwen Bennie (for her fantastically long memory); Julia Cash (for looking out the family bible); Mr and Mrs Creed (for describing the vicarage toilet with such passion); Gloria and Yvette Duncan (for entrusting me with the most beautiful photograph in the world); Jean Denham (for talking to me about her Battersea snipe-shooting ancestors) and her daughter Jo Bowyer (for fixing my back while telling me ghost stories); Vincent and Shirley Dias (for remembering where he bought his hat and exactly what he paid for it); Richard Goddin (for being kind enough to call me on what must have been a sad and difficult day); Alan Hayward (for telling me family anecdotes as he undressed); Pete Hinkley (for encouraging me to go and see his Dad), his father Kenneth Hinkley (I'm so sorry the biscuits were soggy), and the staff at the Maudsley at Knight's Hill for making the visit to Kenneth possible; Her Majesty Queen Elizabeth II (for use of material from the Royal Archives at Windsor) and Pamela Clark and Frances Dimond (for producing such magical Maslin material); Louisa Heron (for not hanging up on me on a stifling morning in Queens, New York, though she certainly did not want to be in a book); Pat Cumper (for putting us on to the Jamaican High Commission); Rachel Hosker at Glasgow University Archives (for so swiftly unearthing Lucy Spawton's employment records); Ted Huddart (for talking to me even though the Test Match was at a crucial stage) and his daughter Sue Sumner (for a perfectly inspiring day out); the London Metropolitan Archives, the Public Record Office at Kew, the Minet Library and Clapham Library (for their patience as I fumbled around and asked embarrassingly obvious questions); the Revd David Isherwood (for help with parish and burial records – and because he made me promise to mention him); Patrick Loobey and Ron Elam for use of local photos; Beryl Lloyd (for the poem about the ginger tom cat); Philip Lloyd (for writing back to me twice); Colin and Gwen Murhall (for sharing lemon squash and their auntie with me on a hot day); all the kind people of Nottinghamshire who let me into their homes purely because I once happened to live in them; Alexa Povah and her family (for the biographer's ultimate fantasy – a fifty-year-old box of letters – and for huge generosity in trusting me with them); Barbara Queensbarrow (for sharing her childhood memories); John and Julia Pidgeon (for sharing so much and for the zebra loo); Leon Pidgeon (for having the good sense to support Tottenham Hotspur); Lucy Pidgeon (for trying hard to meet up – it was my fault, Lucy!); Gemma Rain at the Law Society (for trying to find the elusive and clearly unqualified Thomas Kyle); Alvin Reynolds (for dreaming of the house and telling me so); Surrey County

Cricket Club (for the view over the Oval from their library); Bridget Towers and the Revd Patrick Towers (for providing the perfect finale); Doreen Webley (for coming to tea and looking around with such a frank eye); Alison Wylson at the Clapham Society (for valuable information at an early stage); Rodney Wohl (for being so gracious when I barged into a past he thought he'd put behind him – and for his amazing generosity in letting me put it in a book); Rita Wraight and her husband Don Sherman (for letting me include their letters). I also have to thank all the extremely kind people who bothered to write and phone to tell me they *weren't* the ones I was looking for. In some ways, actually, they *were* the right ones. I hope they'll see that if they read the book.

My thanks also to Gill Coleridge, Lucy Luck, Philip Gwyn Jones, and Caroline Michel for never doubting for one moment that this was something worth writing about. And to Clare Reihill at 4th Estate for jumping on board so late, but with huge warmth and such a zest for checking and double-checking that this author was able to sleep soundly at night. And a special mention to Aga, without whose constant care this house – with its menagerie of humans and animals – sould be a far dirtier place.

To my children – Jacob, Chloë and Raphael – for constantly reminding me that they're the Important Ones. They live in the house now and have asked me to make sure you realize this! And to my mother and sisters (for enduring yet another journey into my biased memory of our shared past).

And, most of all, to Jonathan. I thought, when I started, that I could manage this book alone. I was wrong. I was never any good at history, I don't understand computers, I certainly can't do archives, and microfiches drive me mad. More times than I care to admit, I gave up on finding a Maslin or Schloss, only to have Jonathan spend the day in a library and return home triumphant. Not only researcher, he was also Project Manager, Master of Structure, and, as if that weren't enough, he also let me give myself all the best lines and snatch all the wittiest gags while usually sending him up. Come to think of it, wasn't the whole thing sort of his idea? Any of the people who met him during the course of our research will know what I owe him and Thank You doesn't begin to cover it.

And, finally, to the late Mrs Joan Clayton who once, in the middle of yet another intensely fascinating phone conversation, suddenly stopped and asked me rather beadily, 'Are you really finding all this interesting, dear?' She died on 16 September 2003, just days after I finished the book. My first and most prolific witness, she had a memory made in researcher's heaven – disk upon disk of crunchy anecdote and descriptive detail saved and stored. I was so looking forward, finally, to pressing a copy of this book into her hand, as proof that, Yes, I Did Find It All So Very Interesting – and I'm sadder than I can say that I never got to do it.

Julie Myerson
34 Lillieshall Road, London
October 2003

CHRONOLOGICAL LIST OF RESIDENTS

To 1872
The Cricket Ground, Clapham Common

1873–80
Edward and Mary Maslin, with Helena and Edith

1881–93
Charlotte and Henry Hayward, with Florence, Arthur, and Frank

1893–1944
Elizabeth, Catherine, and Lucy Spawton

1918–48
Walter and Isabella Hinkley, with Walter Allen and Charles

1926–44
Beatrice Haig

1939
Vera Palmer

1946–7
Peter and Phyllis Askew

1948–58
Annie and Theodore Blaine

1948
Wilfred and Dorothy Bartolo, with Winnie
Mavis Jones-Wohl, with Rodney
Olive Russell

1949
Rita Wraight
Patrick J. Costello

1952–8
Amy and John T. Costello
Patricia C. Reynolds

1959–79
Alvin and Merciline Reynolds, with Sheryl, Marcia, and Michael

1959–68
Melda McNish

1959–61
Gloria Duncan, with Yvette
Aston McNish
Clarence Hibbert
Florence and Trevor Schloss, with Ivo
Salome Bennet
Louisa and Stanley Heron
Godwin and Mary Akagbu

1976–80
Veronica Ricketts, with Doreen

1976–8
Gerald Sherrif

1979–80
Thomas H. Kyle

1981–7
John and Julia Pidgeon, with Lucy, Leon, Barney, and Collette

1988 onwards
Julie and Jonathan Myerson, with Jacob, Chloë, and Raphael

'Julie?'

'What?'

'Well, I hate to break it to you now but you know that woman who lived here in 1939, Vera Palmer?'

'Yes . . . ?'

'You never did anything about her. Never even tried.'

'Oh God.'

'But it's OK. I have an idea.'

'Tell me.'

'It was only when I reread it all that I noticed that Walter Hinkley's mother's maiden name was Palmer.'

'And?'

'Vera lived in the house at the same time as the Hinkleys. 1939. It's not impossible that she was a relation.'

'It's a very common name, Palmer.'

'But still.'

'I suppose it might be worth a shot. What would you have to do?'

'I don't know. How would you ever trace Walter's mother's descendants on that side?'

'Well, you could, actually . . . If you know she was his mother and you know what date he was born, then you make a guess that she was maybe twenty-one when she had him and then you work back from there . . .'

'But then what?'

'Once you've found her birth date, you've nailed down her parents' names.'

'And? I know it was my idea, but I'm not sure this is going anywhere.'

'Yes, it is. Listen. Once you have her parents and their marriage date, then I suppose you have to hope she had brothers and sisters.'

'Yeah . . . and then?'

'If she had brothers, then you trace them and hope one of them had a daughter called Vera.'

'But hold on a moment. Even if you do find one called Vera, and even if you can somehow prove she's the right Vera Palmer, well, what then?'

'How do you mean?'

'What will it tell you about her?'

'Oh. I hadn't thought of that.'

'It won't tell you anything at all, will it?'

'It'll tell you when she was born.'

'Great.'

'And that won't really help, will it?'

'Sorry, but it won't.'

'Mmm. You know what?'

'What?'

'I think you're right. It's not worth it.'

'No.'

'But it was your idea in the first place, for God's sake – you started this whole Palmer thing.'

'I just mentioned it!'

'But you know what? If I get a bit of spare time towards the end of next week . . .'

'When you've arranged for the man to come and look at the washing machine and got the dog some worming tablets and got Jake's new shoes?'

'Yes, when I've done that, I might just go down the Family Records Centre and just see how easy it is to find Walter's mother's birth. OK?'

P.S.

Ideas &
features . . .

About the author

DEAR MS MYERSON …

Many books are launched with a party but the one for *Home* was special. It was held on the evening of 5 May 2004 here at 34 Lillieshall Road. We expected about sixty people – we invited everyone who had lived here, or whose ancestors had lived here, and their families. In the end about a hundred and fifty people turned up. Far more than Number 34 was ever designed to hold.

A marquee extended our kitchen into the garden, and the children and I went around the house sticking blown-up photos of the people who had lived in the various rooms on the relevant doors. Auntie Bea, Dorothy and Winnie Bartolo and Leon Pidgeon on the top bedroom door, Vinnie Dias and Lucy Spawton and Edith Maslin on ours, and so on for every room. Though we had no red ropes and we were the only guides and curators, Number 34 had to feel like a stately home for the night: we wanted people to walk around and gape and sense the terraced grandeur of its history.

It rained all day – the first hard, black rain of a sodden summer. I worried – that no one would come, that everyone would come, that there would be no room for umbrellas and raincoats, that no one would talk to anyone else, that it would all be a wet and chaotic disaster. The dog was on edge, the cats ran away, the children told me to stop screeching.

But then at six o'clock, the clouds dissolved and the sun came bursting to the rescue. And half an hour later, the house rocked with laughter because there they all were. Not only ex-residents of the house and their descendants, but sisters and uncles and daughters and sons, grandmothers, aunts and toddlers. Haywards rubbed shoulders with Duncans and Pidgeons, Maslins met Povahs and Askews, Beatrice Haig's great and great-great nieces ate canapés with Winnie Bartolo. A handsome Jamaican lady with a wonderfully funky hat told me proudly: 'I dressed her when she got married,' pointing to her cousin Shirley whose dreamy wedding picture graced the cover of the first edition.

Unexpected moments gave me indescribable pleasure. When Dorothy Bartolo set eyes on 'little' Rodney Wohl for the first time in fifty years and said, as if she half expected him to be wearing one, 'I knitted you two sweaters, one red, one yellow!'

Or the moment when Henry Hayward's great-great-granddaughter Julia Cash put a small gold locket into my hand. 'Open it.' Nestling inside it were five gingery locks of hair. 'Henry, Charlotte, Frank, Arthur and Florence. You see,' she said, 'you guessed right about the colour of the hair!'

From Ted Huddart, Steyning, W. Sussex, 30 April 2004

Dear Julie

Just writing to say that my thoughts will be with you on May 5th and I'll drink at least one drink – perhaps two if I seat myself in a low chair, difficult to fall off! It was such a pleasure in meeting you last year and telling you of memories of my dear old Auntie B. A funny thing is that telling you of such memories made me feel younger ...

❝Haywoods rubbed shoulders with Duncans and Pidgeons, Maslins met Povahs and Askews, Beatrice Haig's great and great-great nieces ate canapés with Winnie Bartolo.❞

LIFE
at a Glance

BORN

2 June 1960, Nottingham.

EDUCATED

1967–78 Nottingham
Girls High School.
1979–82 Bristol
University.

FAMILY

Lives with Jonathan
Myerson (since 1986).
Children: Jacob (born
1989), Chloë (born 1991),
Raphael (born 1992).

CAREER

1983–87 National Theatre
Press Office; 1987–93
publicist, Walker Books.
Books: *Sleepwalking*
(1994); *The Touch* (1996);
Me and the Fat Man
(1998); *Laura Blundy*
(2000); *Something Might
Happen* (2003); *Home*
(2004); *Not a Games
Person* (2005). ▶

From Julia Cash, Solihull, 8 May 2004

Dear Julie and Jonathan
    … We arrived home about midnight. I had
to read the chapter about the Haywards
before going to bed. Then I was compelled to
start reading the book from the beginning. I
went to bed at 3 a.m.! Alan and another
cousin Elaine from Australia stayed for a long
weekend and we were able to place a few more
pieces from the family jigsaw. I think Henry
Hayward was the great grandfather who
spoke many languages – I was told 9 but the
source was prone to exaggeration! I
understand he earned a considerable amount
of money translating. I guess that is why he
moved from Worthing into no. 34 to be
nearer the City. I note your reference to Flora
(daughter-in-law). According to the family
tree Arthur was married to Maud Cook – I
wonder if this is one and the same person? As
you can tell you have started me wondering
about my family …

From Vincent and Shirley Dias, Catford, 13 May 2004

Dear Julie and Jonathan
    Just a few lines to thank you for inviting
Vincent and I along to the book launch. I and
our family had a very nice evening. I have
enclosed a couple of photos along with the
negatives, I am sorry they are so dark but at
least everyone is clearly visible. I do hope that
Home will be made into a film or serial on
television at least. All the best to you and your
family, bye for now.

From Winnie King (née Bartolo), Guildford, 19 May 2004

Dear Julie

I cannot begin to put into words what tremendous pleasure it has given to be part of your investigations and your work. You have really made a distant and shelved part of our lives come flooding back into our consciousness – and for me happy memories of my father … You may well feel that we are all part of your life by being in your house in the past, but you yourself are now inhabiting our present with this book …

From Rodney Wohl, via email, 8 May 2004

Thank you for allowing Bev and me to come to your book launch, your family made us feel welcome. Being inside a book is a strange experience and takes some getting used to. Having met you I can understand why people do as you ask them to.

From Mrs Joy Kenward, Somerset, 6 May 2004

Dear Julie

Late last night Alan and Robert dropped me and Peggy off in Weston and went on to Glastonbury. This morning I gobbled up the Hayward chapter prior to starting properly from the beginning. Thank you again for writing the book that is making me think about those people who touch the places where we live and how, however well we try to know them, we never really do …

LIFE *at a Glance*
(continued)

AWARDS

Sleepwalking shortlisted for the John Llewelyn Rhys Prize; *Something Might Happen* longlisted for the Man Booker Prize 2003.

But those letters were in fact just the beginning. No author allows their home address to be known without some trepidation. But to research and write *Home* and then keep its address secret would have been both ludicrous and impossible – like writing the biography of an anonymous person.

So I suppose I knew from the start that not only was I going to strip this poor elderly lady who is our home down to her flimsiest underclothes, but I was also then going to shout out her name to the whole world. Has she minded? I don't think so. In fact I'd like to think that she's been rather thrilled by the outpouring of warmth, curiosity and affection – not to mention the touching sense of ownership – that has come her way.

Anyway, her foundations are still subsiding, her front hedge badly needs a trim and she just reminded me that I promised her exterior woodwork a lick of paint this autumn. But if she could speak I think she'd ask me to say a big thank you to all those kind people who have so far responded with so much heart to her story. I really wish I could include every single one here but that would probably require another whole book and, as our Jake pithily observed, someone has to call a halt …

From Pamela Simpkins (née Dickson), 13 May 2004

Dear Ms Myerson

I do hope you won't mind me writing to you … I was born in the first-floor front room of No. 36 on 8th October 1934 … I just remember Miss Spawton as a very frail old lady sitting in the garden on warm days. One

> 'No author allows their home address to be known without some trepidation. But to research and write *Home* and then keep its address secret would have been both ludicrous and impossible – like writing the biography of an anonymous person. '

day she was shouting to her housekeeper that there was an alligator in the garden, but it turned out to be a tortoise. My Mum said it could come and live with us and as mine had recently died I was very pleased. It was a fast mover and soon escaped again.

Miss Spawton's housekeeper was a lovely kind lady, but I can't remember her name. She was delighted that she heard my first cry through the wall, I must have had a good pair of lungs. My Dad was on a strict gastric diet and she would bring a couple of eggs when she could. I don't know where she got them from. She was still living locally when I married and gave me some money for a wedding present. We still have the bone china tea set we bought with it.

Mr and Mrs Hinkley were a lovely old couple. There was another drama there. My beautiful, but very wicked, cat stole their Sunday joint from their kitchen and took it to the bottom of your garden under the apple tree. My poor Mum was so angry with him, but all they said was 'Bless him, let him have it.' I don't remember them being turned out of the house but maybe Mum and Dad did. I would only have been 14 so maybe I wasn't told.

I left school in 1953 and went into nursing so I didn't see much of Mr and Mrs Blaine. I married Brian in 1959 and moved here to Hitchin. We visited no. 36 about every six weeks and all I can remember about the McNishes is that they had numerous cats that sat on Mum's shed outside the back door hoping for food. They also had their kittens in Mum's tall flowers ...

**From Barbara, Bury St Edmunds,
28 June 2004**

Dear Julie Myerson

I lived in Lillieshall Road in 1954 when I was first married. It was just 2 rooms which we had to pay a very high rent for in those days – my first daughter (now 47) was conceived there.

I can't remember the number but it was on the corner going towards Clapham South – I worked on Lavender Hill at the time – so walking from there our house was on the right. I do wish I could remember the number. The house had a bay window on the left as you went up the steps – our bedroom window was on the wall leading around the corner on the next road – Polish people lived below, a Jamaican in the front room and others above us … This was the house where we had our first row (Ron and myself) and – once – when I came home from work the downstairs lady's cat had got shut in our bedroom all day and had 5 kittens on our bed. A little Polish boy downstairs was backward, bless him – he would push our door open, make funny noises and then run away!

**From Mrs Edith Holding, Clacton-on-Sea,
23 June 2004**

Dear Mrs Myerson

In 1916 we as a family moved into No. 26 Lillieshall Road, we were a four-generation family and my grandmother continued to live there until after the 2nd World War was ended. Why I am writing is because we must

6 This was the house where we had our first row (Ron and myself) and – once – when I came home from work the downstairs lady's cat had got shut in our bedroom all day and had 5 kittens on our bed. 9

have known some of the people who lived in your house. I am now 95 and can't remember names but I remember an old lady, this must have been Miss Spawton. I wish I could remember so I could give you a clearer picture of her. The picture of the old Tim Bobbin pub reminded me of when my granddad used to go there with his jug to get my great-grandmother a half pint of stout and bring us kids a big biscuit back called a Brighton biscuit. There was only gas lighting then and I can remember the gas lighter coming round with a pole to light the lamps …

From Sue Sumner, Putney, 8 May 2004

Julie

I am mortified!!! Why didn't you tell me you were vegetarian!! Well at least the meat balls had a mention! But I am sorry about that, had no idea!

Hope all OK with you. Dad was asking after you today – he is in good form (for 98!).

From Mrs J. Ovenden (née Maslin), Deal, Kent, 20 April 2004

Dear Mrs Myerson

Our family name is Maslin and we know that our great grandparents were employed by the Royal Family – I am 78 by the way so the dates would put us in the mid to late 1800s, Victoria's era. My paternal grandfather was Frederick but I don't know what his father's Christian name was, but grandfather named two of his sons Victor and Edward, names which you mention in your story. You

> ❛I am mortified!!! Why didn't you tell me you were vegetarian!! Well at least the meat balls had a mention! ❜

also say that the family moved to Battersea, that is where my grandparents lived, in fact I still have an aunt living in Battersea …

From Eileen Murray, Norbury, 13 July 2004

Dear Julie

I lived at 13 Broadhinton Road from October 1931. My memories, especially the early ones, I share with Mrs Creed who I think was Joyce Potter – yes, I remember seeing Granny Potter with her jug!

From Mrs Joyce Creed, Mitcham, 13 May 2004

Dear Julie

Seeing Lillieshall Road and the house I was born in brought tears to my eyes. I wanted to knock on the door but was not bold enough to do so, many memories of my childhood floating around in my head … I just walked away. I have finished reading the book … lots of people you wrote about were familiar by name, still I could not put a face to them. Keep on writing, Julie.

From Pat Reevey (née Hinkley), Harrogate, 10 June 2004

Dear Julie

I have been on cloud nine ever since I read your book, especially the chapter about the Hinkleys. I am Patricia Helen Reevey née Hinkley, the only child of Charles and Amelia Helen (Polly), therefore the last of the Hinkleys. I was born on the 27th January 1930 and my home was 29 Queensville Road, Balham SW12. From that day until WW2, I

> **Seeing Lillieshall Road and the house I was born in brought tears to my eyes. I wanted to knock on the door but was not bold enough to do so.**

with my parents visited 34 Lillieshall Road about 3 times a week and as well as my grandparents I also remember Lucy Spawton and Tom.

The start of WW2 caused a big change in our lives, my father Charles was sent to Harrogate with the Post Office Savings Bank, my mother Helen also went to work there for the duration of the war. At that time I was at boarding school in Hampshire but joined my parents in about 1940–41 where I finished my schooling. On leaving school I trained as a dancer and toured with various revues before marrying Derek Laurence Reevey on 14 June 1952. I can assure you I did not marry Victor Bourne, I have never heard of him, but I have taken a great deal of ribbing from our family i.e. Michael our son, Mary our daughter-in-law and Alexandra our granddaughter.

Now I turn to Helen Hussey (Nellie) my godmother and the older of the 'two girls' and Jane Isabelle (Issie) who I know married Albert Smith in the mid 30s. The photograph of Uncle Wally and family was taken at the back of their house at Arnos Grove which backed onto Arnos Grove Park. I have a letter from the army to my grandfather Walter stating that my father Charles had been gassed while serving in France during WW1 and was in hospital in Rouen.

I have a photograph of Walter and Isabella. The tragedy in their lives was that just over a year after my Uncle Wally was born they had a daughter who only lived for 3–4 years and died on the 22nd August 1893, her name was Isabella Sarah Ann – this all happened some years before my father was born. My parents both lived into their

‘Being inside a book is a strange experience and takes some getting used to.’

nineties as did Nellie and Issie. I am enclosing some copies of a few documents and a photograph of Walter and Isabella. I expect it is rather late in the day now but I am sure I can find some photographs of the family if you would be interested. Many thanks for a most enjoyable book

Regards
Pat

PS I have never heard of Pete Hinkley and cannot work out how he can be a grandson of Walter and Isabella.

From Pearl Oag, Brixton, 2 August 2004

Dear Julie

… I have spent every spare minute of the past few days reading [*Home*] and I absolutely loved it. I also found it quite frustrating that … I can't remember anyone who lived in the house prior to 1959 when my grandmother started looking after Yvette. I remember the Murhalls at 32 and the Dicksons at 36 but 34 is a blank.

Much as I enjoyed the book I must take you to task over one thing you said. When you were describing the mixture of houses in the road you stated the cottages had been 'short life squatted since the fifties'. That simply isn't true. Up until the early seventies those houses were much loved and cared-for homes, where some families had lived for generations. The people who lived in them were the heart of the community. From (in my memory) VE night onwards, whenever there was cause for a celebration, 'Auntie' Mary Horsley from number 13 (a five-foot-nothing human dynamo) would rally the troops, form a committee and organise a street party or coach trip to Margate at the drop of a hat.

At one point in your book you mention serendipitous coincidences. Well, here's another one for you. When you were a child, long before you had ever heard of Lillieshall Road, you had a link to it. A very, very tenuous one but a link nonetheless. Your suicidal goldfish (why do fish jump out of their tanks?) were called Tish and Tosh. Tish and Tosh were characters in a very popular radio comedy show called *Stand Easy*. They were a couple of cockney spurs and their sketch always started the same way with

'Allo Tish.'

'Wotcher Tosh.'

The star and chief writer of the show was comedian 'Cheerful' Charlie Chester. Charlie's real name was Cecil Manser and he lived in Wandsworth Road, in the terraced houses just past the junction with North Street. Early in his career, while he was waiting for his 'big break', he worked for the gas company and was great friends with my uncle, Don White, who also worked there. Charlie used to rehearse his comedy routines with uncle Don in the front room of my Nan's house at 23 Lillieshall Road. Like I said, a tenuous link, but there you are …

> ❛I knew from the start that not only was I going to strip this poor elderly lady who is our home down to her flimsiest underclothes, but I was also then going to shout her name to the whole world.❜

> **There was another feeling too, of ghosts stirred up, of time pleating and folding in on itself. How often, after all, do so many different people revisit the same old home in the space of a single evening?**

From Richard Goddin, Cambs, 12 July 2004

Dear Julie

… What has truly amazed me about your book is the way you have captured the essence of my Mum in your description of that meeting with her and Diane in Cambridge. For me this is a real treasure and I have read and re-read that section quite a few times. You can I hope understand that I now see the book from a perspective which would have been different if my Mum had still been alive. As it is, though, I can think of no better way of augmenting my own personal memories and I am astonished that you, a stranger, were able in such a short time to come to conclusions which are evident in that description. Even down to the word 'beady'. I have never used this word in the whole of my life but I cannot think of a better word to apply to her!

My Mum made the remark that I did not care so much for family history and would discard all the papers when she died. She never understood that as families grow, their patterns change as other families join the stem. So for her the major focal point of the Scotts was only a small part of my own interest – I had a great interest in exploring my father's side, a subject which never interested her. You will have gathered from meeting her that she had a very definite view of what she thought was important and little real time for anyone else's views. It was very easy to have a one-sided conversation with her. I am told I am just the same by the way, so this is not a criticism!

I loved your description of Uncle Tom (Spawton) being 'camp' in that photo of him in uniform. We have that picture now and some time I must put together a proper family archive although I fear that my own two sons, for whom this is a very minor and distant part of the family, will not be terribly interested. I shall feel though that duty has been done. We do have hanging in our hall here a marvellous and very large sepia photograph of Aunt Matilda taken we think in about 1910. One of the photos in the book intrigued me – the one on Eastbourne beach with my grandfather (yes, he was a chain smoker so it would have been a cigarette), Aunt Tills and Lucy, my mother and late aunt, her twin sister. Who did take the shot? I wondered. I can't remember my grandmother ever using a camera and where was Uncle Tom? We shall never know.

We do have two occasional chairs here, in the Chippendale style but Edwardian, which belonged to Aunt Lucy and it is amazing to think they once stood in the house in Clapham which subsequently became your home. I shall now always see them in that light.

My mother would have loved your book and would have been very proud to feel that you found her contributions to your research so helpful. Your very kind acknowledgement is a memorial which she did not expect.

The party which launched *Home* was a very special event, full of humour and warmth and goodwill. Everyone seemed to feel it and I certainly felt it and I like to think the house also felt it as its rooms slowly filled up with all those people in whose lives it had played a part.

‘I woke up with a jump in the small hours. Someone had called my name. Neither spoken nor shouted, but loud and urgent enough to make me sit up quickly in bed and stiffen and answer, "Yes?"’

But there was another feeling too, of ghosts stirred up, of time pleating and folding in on itself. How often, after all, do so many different people revisit the same old home in the space of a single evening?

The strangest moment of all came much later, long after the party had ended and everyone had gone home. I woke up with a jump in the small hours. Someone had called my name. Neither spoken nor shouted, but loud and urgent enough to make me sit up quickly in bed and stiffen and answer, 'Yes?'

'A dream,' says Jonathan (of course).

But was it? I can't prove it wasn't, but it didn't feel like one, not at all. I felt awake, clear-headed, unafraid (and, before you ask, sober). I also felt somehow unsurprised. Was it so odd, after all, that on that night of all nights, things should somehow come full circle? That the thing which had begun with Chloë and me standing on the landing on a chilly autumn evening and calling: 'Florence! Arthur! Frank!' should end with someone else waking me up in the middle of the night a couple of years later and calling, 'Julie!'

Find out more at
www.homethestory.com

Julie Myerson, Clapham Town,
September 2004